PARS IN CHARGE
RESOURCES AND STRATEGIES FOR ONLINE WRITING PROGRAM LEADERS

Practices & Possibilities
Series Editors: Aimee McClure, Mike Palmquist, and Aleashia Walton
Series Associate Editor: Jagadish Paudel

The Practices & Possibilities Series addresses the full range of practices within the field of Writing Studies, including teaching, learning, research, and theory. From Richard E. Young's taxonomy of "small genres" to Patricia Freitag Ericsson's edited collection on sexual harassment in the academy to Jessie Borgman and Casey McArdle's considerations of teaching online, the books in this series explore issues and ideas of interest to writers, teachers, researchers, and theorists who share an interest in improving existing practices and exploring new possibilities. The series includes both original and republished books. Works in the series are organized topically.

The WAC Clearinghouse and University Press of Colorado are collaborating so that these books will be widely available through free digital distribution and low-cost print editions. The publishers and the series editors are committed to the principle that knowledge should freely circulate and have embraced the use of technology to support open access to scholarly work.

Other Books in the Series

Douglas Hesse and Laura Julier (Eds.), *Nonfiction, the Teaching of Writing, and the Influence of Richard Lloyd-Jones* (2023)

Linda Adler-Kassner and Elizabeth Wardle, *Writing Expertise: A Research-Based Approach to Writing and Learning Across Disciplines* (2022)

Michael J. Faris, Courtney S. Danforth, and Kyle D. Stedman (Eds.), *Amplifying Soundwriting Pedagogies: Integrating Sound into Rhetoric and Writing* (2022)

Crystal VanKooten and Victor Del Hierro (Eds.), *Methods and Methodologies for Research in Digital Writing and Rhetoric: Centering Positionality in Computers and Writing Scholarship, Volumes 1 and 2* (2022)

Heather M. Falconer, *Masking Inequality with Good Intentions: Systemic Bias, Counterspaces, and Discourse Acquisition in STEM Education* (2022)

Jessica Nastal, Mya Poe, and Christie Toth (Eds.), *Writing Placement in Two Year Colleges: The Pursuit of Equity in Postsecondary Education* (2022)

Natalie M. Dorfeld (Ed.), *The Invisible Professor: The Precarious Lives of the New Faculty Majority* (2022)

Aimée Knight, *Community is the Way: Engaged Writing and Designing for Transformative Change* (2022)

Jennifer Clary-Lemon, Derek Mueller, and Kate Pantelides, *Try This: Research Methods for Writers* (2022)

PARS IN CHARGE
RESOURCES AND STRATEGIES FOR ONLINE WRITING PROGRAM LEADERS

Edited by Jessie Borgman and Casey McArdle

The WAC Clearinghouse
wac.colostate.edu
Fort Collins, Colorado

University Press of Colorado
upcolorado.com
Louisville, Colorado

The WAC Clearinghouse, Fort Collins, Colorado 80523

University Press of Colorado, Denver, Colorado 80202

© 2023 by Jessie Borgman and Casey McArdle. This work is released under a Creative Commons Attribution-NonCommercial-NoDerivatives 4.0 International license.

ISBN 978-1-64215-198-5 (PDF) | 978-1-64215-199-2 (ePub) | 978-1-64642-570-9 (pbk.)

DOI 10.37514/PRA-B.2023.1985

Library of Congress Cataloging-in-Publication Data

Names: Borgman, Jessie, 1980– editor. | McArdle, Casey, 1974– editor.
Title: PARS in charge : resources and strategies for online writing program leaders / edited by Jessie Borgman and Casey McArdle.
Description: Fort Collins, Colorado : The WAC Clearinghouse ; Louisville, Colorado : University of Colorado Press, [2023] | Series: Practices & possibilities | Includes bibliographical references. | Summary: "This edited collection, the third in a series of books by editors Jessie Borgman and Casey McArdle, explores the complexity of administrative positions within writing programs and how online courses make administration even more complex. Drawing on the PARS framework (Personal, Accessible, Responsive, Strategic) used in the first two books, PARS in Charge provides insights and examples from administrators across the country focusing on how they have implemented the PARS framework to be successful online writing program leaders in their specific leadership positions"— Provided by publisher.
Identifiers: LCCN 2023028993 (print) | LCCN 2023028994 (ebook) | ISBN 9781646425709 (paperback) | ISBN 9781642151985 (adobe pdf) | ISBN 9781642151992 (epub)
Subjects: LCSH: English language—Rhetoric—Web-based instruction. | English language—Composition and exercises—Web-based instruction.
Classification: LCC PE1404 .P373 2023 (print) | LCC PE1404 (ebook) | DDC 808/.0420785—dc23/eng/20230807
LC record available at https://lccn.loc.gov/2023028993
LC ebook record available at https://lccn.loc.gov/2023028994

Copyeditor: Meg Vezzu
Designer: Mike Palmquist
Cover Image: "PARS in Charge," by Jessie Borgman. Used with permission.
Series Editors: Aimee McClure, Mike Palmquist, and Aleashia Walton
Series Associate Editor: Jagadish Paudel

The WAC Clearinghouse supports teachers of writing across the disciplines. Hosted by Colorado State University, it brings together scholarly journals and book series as well as resources for teachers who use writing in their courses. This book is available in digital formats for free download at wac.colostate.edu.

Founded in 1965, the University Press of Colorado is a nonprofit cooperative publishing enterprise supported, in part, by Adams State University, Colorado State University, Fort Lewis College, Metropolitan State University of Denver, University of Alaska Fairbanks, University of Colorado, University of Denver, University of Northern Colorado, University of Wyoming, Utah State University, and Western Colorado University. For more information, visit upcolorado.com.

Land Acknowledgment. The Colorado State University Land Acknowledgment can be found at https://landacknowledgment.colostate.edu.

Contents

Foreword. Keep Playing, Friends vii
    Tiffany Bourelle

Glossary xi

Introduction. And Three Makes a Trilogy . . . or a Par 3! 3
    Jessie Borgman and Casey McArdle

Chapter 1. PARS for Writing Program Administration 10
    Jessie Borgman and Casey McArdle

Chapter 2. So, you want to be an OWPA? 20
    Shelley Rodrigo

Chapter 3. Championships Are Won at Practice: How Our OWI Initiative Inadvertently Prepared Us to Navigate a Pandemic 36
    Jennifer Stewart and Tiffany N. Mitchell

Chapter 4. Designing Anchor Points 54
    Andrew Hollinger

Chapter 5. Institutionalizing Online Writing Instruction 70
    Stuart A. Selber, Daniel Tripp, and Leslie Robertson Mateer

Chapter 6. Agile Writing Programs 86
    Marisa Yerace

Chapter 7. Research is a Team Sport: A Collaborative PARS Approach to Sustainable Hybrid and Online Writing Instruction Development 102
    Lourdes Fernandez, Ariel M. Goldenthal, Kerry Folan,
    Jessica Matthews, and Courtney Adams Wooten

Chapter 8. Transitioning Online Writing Instruction from Crisis to Sustainability 116
    Bethany Mannon

Chapter 9. Sustaining Empathy and Community in a Large First-Year Writing Program 128
    Rachael Groner and Tania Islam

Chapter 10. Personal, Accessible, Responsive, and Strategic Assessment: Creating a Faculty Community of Practice 142
    Jennifer Trainor and John Holland

Chapter 11. Professionalizing from the Fringe: Informally Supporting Teaching Assistants via (and Welcoming Them Into) the OWI Community 154
    Miranda L. Egger

Chapter 12. Professional Development for Online Writing Instruction: The Place of Instructional Design 172
    Joseph Bartolotta, Anthony Yarbrough, and Tiffany Bourelle

Chapter 13. Strategic Administration for Online Courses in Communication and Writing Programs 186
    Abram Anders, Jenny Aune, Katharine Fulton,
    Anne Kretsinger-Harries, Amy Walton, and Casey White

Chapter 14. Promoting Instructor Agency and Autonomy with Pre-Designed Courses 208
    Catrina Mitchum

Chapter 15. Third Personal, U Variable: Complicating PARS and UX in Pre-Designed OWI Courses 224
    Dylan Retzinger and Kellie Sharp-Hoskins

Chapter 16. Pre-Designed Courses and Instructor Autonomy: Emphasizing the Personal in Course Design 242
    Mariya Tseptsura

Chapter 17. Fairway Finder: Implementing an Online Student Orientation 256
    Julie Watts

Chapter 18. Literacy Loads, Readiness, and Accessibility: Addressing Students' Perceptions of OWI through Pre-Course Modules 268
    Lynn Reid

Chapter 19. Inclusive, Equitable, and Responsive Strategies for Redesigning Open-Access Online Literacy Courses 284
    Joanne Baird Giordano and Cassandra Phillips

Chapter 20. Wayfinding in Distance Learning: Finding Our Way Through Times of Stress in Online Writing Graduate Programs 300
    Heidi Skurat Harris and Rhonda Thomas

Afterword. Before, During, and (Hopefully) After COVID 317
    Steven Krause

Contributors 325

Foreword. Keep Playing, Friends

Tiffany Bourelle
UNIVERSITY OF NEW MEXICO

Years ago, when I was first entering the world of online teaching, I attended the Computers and Writing Conference alone. I didn't know many people and was nervous, like it was the first day of school, and I was the new kid. As I walked into lunch the first day, I wondered if I would have to take my tray (literally, as the lunch was cafeteria-style) and sit by myself. To my relief, a group of friendly faces called me over to sit with them. I sat down and chatted easily with many of them and left with business cards and new scholarship to read. This simple twist of fate would change my research and teaching trajectory in ways I hadn't imagined. I had found my people: the online writing instruction (OWI) community.

    I paint this introductory picture for my readers because this is what it means to be part of the OWI community. Its members are accepting, loving, warm, and helpful—all the traits you want in friends and colleagues. The editors of this collection, Jessie Borgman and Casey McArdle, as members and leaders of this community, are no exception. And here's the thing: The OWI community isn't exclusive. As evidenced by my first encounter with the OWI community at Computers and Writing, it is a community that welcomes and embraces everyone who is eager to learn more about the world of online instruction, including new and veteran instructors, teaching assistants, lecturers, adjuncts, and professors. This edited collection embodies that spirit. Born out of the need to further guide online instructors, this collection picks up where the first two PARS collections left off, adding much-needed advice about leading/administering online writing programs and ensuring student success, accessibility, and inclusion. Many of the chapters provide personal accounts—the first tenet of PARs—letting readers know what skills an online administrator needs or providing "how-to" recommendations based on the authors' experiences.

Although this is not a book about teaching in light of the COVID-19 pandemic, the seismic shift to education caused by the transition to emergency remote instruction during the pandemic makes this collection an important contribution for those teaching writing online and leading online programs. Back in 2015, in their final chapter of *Foundational Practices of Online Education*, Beth Hewett and Scott Warnock (2015) argued that all instruction was online in some capacity. Dear readers, if you didn't believe it then, certainly you do now as we continue to navigate an educational world with new teaching environments such as fully online, fully remote, spatio-hybrid, and chrono-hybrid. Where in spatio-hybrid classrooms students spend part of their time in the onsite classroom and part of their time online, chrono-hybrid may replace the onsite time with video conferencing (Warnock, 2020). These new hybrids differ from traditional onsite classes, fully online classes that are mostly asynchronous, and fully remote classes which are offered via video-conferencing software in an effort to mimic onsite learning. Whew! It's enough to make anyone's head spin. While the 2021 *PARS in Practice: More Resources and Strategies for Online Writing Instructors* collection addressed pandemic challenges to teaching online, this newest collection offers pedagogical and administrative strategies as we continue to make our way through the myriad of teaching environments.

Instructors and administrators alike recognize that students were struggling during the pandemic, with lockdowns and social distancing making it harder for students to physically go to campus. And while emergency remote instruction was in response to the pandemic and is arguably not the same as teaching fully online courses in a "normal" semester, we know that students struggled because instructional quality wasn't at its best. This was not anyone's fault; it was a biproduct of the sudden switch to online education for all students (hence the name *emergency* remote instruction). Many instructors and students alike were simply unprepared for online education. Instructors who had no experience teaching online—and, in some cases, no desire to teach online—were thrust into a new teaching environment with little to no training. Administrators scrambled to get their instructors up to speed in a short timeframe. In addition, the pandemic exacerbated pre-pandemic challenges of online education, with many students unable to access course materials. Arguably, the pandemic simply illustrated problems that were already there—only this time, they are now at the forefront for everyone to see. *These challenges will remain if we don't address them.* Again, this is what I like about this newest PARS collection; it offers real, practical solutions for addressing challenges both now and in the future.

What these challenges reiterate is the continued need to train instructors to teach online. Previous scholarship has clearly outlined this need and ways to address it; however, as Jessie and Casey mention in the introduction to this collection, there is little scholarship regarding the overall administration of online writing programs that encompasses much more than just training. There are those like me who administer an online program as an arm of a larger writing program, and there are even more who administer large writing programs and oversee online classes or programs as part of their charge. All of us need this collection to guide us as we tread unfamiliar territory or to reassess what we did previously to better understand what is working and what is not.

We can use the tips in this collection to reconsider or revise current practices, including assessment as a big aspect to tackle as an administrator or even as an instructor doing a small-scale assessment of individual classes. Many institutions have expanded their online writing course offerings, and administrators can use this collection to better understand how to offer consistent, quality education that runs through all of their courses. Online education will only continue to grow, as administrators, instructors, and students are now enjoying the freedom, flexibility, and overall learning experience that online education affords. Indeed, there are lessons offered in this collection that will help readers deal with this growth and expansion of online classes.

I have long been friends with Jessie and Casey, keeping up regular communication with them despite our busy lives, and they both know that I experienced extreme burnout during the pandemic. I'm not alone in feeling this way. As a group of instructors and administrators, I think it's safe to say that we are all exhausted from the last few years (as much of society is as well). In addition to offering solid theoretical and practical advice, this collection offers hope. It offers a real sense of how to effectively do the job of administration while still maintaining our sanity and not sacrificing student or instructor success. With many tips, such as creating pre-designed template courses or offering training sessions and faculty support, this collection can guide us in a post-pandemic world. As Jessie and Casey note in their introduction, much of what this collection offers is in response to *The 2021 State of the Art of OWI Report*, a direct response to what instructors and administrators have suggested they want and need.

I am honored to write the foreword to this collection, as I feel like I am in the same situation as its readers—I may be a seasoned administrator, but I am also a lifelong learner who wants to continually shape my practices based on my colleagues' tried-and-true advice. In her book *Make It Happen: A Healthy, Competitive Approach to Achieving Personal Success*, Lorii Myers (2012) suggests that golfers need to understand the value of routine in order to trust their swing. This quote applies to online writing instruction and administration: we just have to keep at it. We have to rethink what we do and try new things, constantly improving our practice. By doing so, we can trust that we are providing sound mentorship to instructors and quality education for our students. I can think of no better group than the OWI scholars in this book to guide us in those endeavors.

References

CCCC Online Writing Instruction Standing Group. (2021). *The 2021 state of the art of OWI report*. Conference on College Composition and Communication. https://sites.google.com/view/owistandinggroup/state-of-the-art-of-owi-2021.

Hewett, B. & Warnock, S. (2015) The future of OWI. In B. Hewett & K. DePew (Eds.), *Foundational practices of online writing instruction* (pp. 553–569). The WAC Clearinghouse; Parlor Press. https://doi.org/10.37514/PER-B.2015.0650.2.18.

Hodges, C., Moore, S., Lockee, B., Trust, T. & Bond, A. (2020). The difference between emergency remote teaching and online learning. *EDUCAUSE Review*. https://er.educause.edu/articles/2020/3/the-difference-between-emergency-remote-teaching-and-online-learning.

Myers, L. (2012). *3 off the tee, make it happen: A healthy, competitive approach to achieving personal success*. Leda Publishing.

Warnock, S. (2020, July 30). New teaching modality terms: Chrono-hybrids and spatio-hybrids? *Online Writing Teacher*. http://onlinewritingteacher.blogspot.com/2020/07/new-teaching-modality-terms-chrono.html.

Glossary

Golf Terms

Ace: A hole-in-one. Hitting the ball into the hole in one stroke.

Birdie: 1 stroke under par

Bogey: 1 stroke over par

Bunker: (a hazard) usually a hole of sand

Caddie: the person who carries a golfer's clubs

Double Bogey: 2 strokes over par

Drive: a golfer's first stroke from the tee box on every hole

Eagle: 2 strokes under par

Fore!: A warning shouted when the ball is heading toward a person or object

Fairway: A long stretch involving a neatly maintained grass which runs between the green and the tee box

Green: The smooth grassy area at the end of a fairway prepared for putting

Handicap: A system used to rate the average number of strokes above par a player scores in one round of golf.

Hazard: Anything on a golf course that is designed to be hazardous to one's score

Mulligan: A second chance (do-over) to perform an action, usually after the first chance went wrong through bad luck or a blunder

Par: The number of strokes a golfer is expected to need to complete the play of one hole on a golf course

Rough: The taller grass that borders the fairway

Other Terms

PARS: personal, accessible, responsive, strategic (Borgman & McArdle, 2015; 2019)

OWI: online writing instruction or instructor

OWC: online writing course

OL: online learning or online learner

LMS: learning management system

CMS: content management system

GTA: graduate teaching assistant

WPA: writing program administrator

OWPA: online writing program administrator

AWPA: associate or assistant writing program administrator

F2F: face-to-face

UX: user experience

FYW: first-year writing

PARS IN CHARGE
RESOURCES AND STRATEGIES FOR ONLINE WRITING PROGRAM LEADERS

Introduction. And Three Makes a Trilogy . . . or a Par 3!

Jessie Borgman
ARIZONA STATE UNIVERSITY

Casey McArdle
MICHIGAN STATE UNIVERSITY

Here we go again! What started out as a funny observation from one of our academic friends—"Hey, you guys should do another edited collection and call it *PARS in Charge!*"—ended up a reality. So, yes, here we go again, offering you more resources and strategies centered on our PARS (personal, accessible, responsive, strategic) framework for online writing instruction. For readers who may not know, our PARS framework is inspired by the game of golf. We see a lot of similarities between the game of golf (a sport you play and practice for life) and online writing instruction/administration (a career you do and get better at). In golf, the term "par" stands for the number of strokes a golfer is expected to take on a given hole. Shooting a par is a goal for both inexperienced and experienced golfers, which is why we thought "PARS" was a great term for our holistic approach for online writing instruction. As instructors and administrators of online writing courses, we want you to be "par for the course," and we encourage you to continually hone your "game" as you progress in your career.

We have always included administration as part of the discussion, for example, in our discussion of the PARS layers (design, instruction, and administration). Additionally, our focus on leadership was expanded in 2020 when we were asked by the Council of Writing Program Administrators to host a series of workshops

DOI: https://doi.org/10.37514/PRA-B.2023.1985.1.3

to help struggling leaders across the country as they faced a shift in moving their programs and courses online due to the impact of the COVID-19 pandemic. We've outlined our previous work on PARS and administration in the chapter following this introduction. In this section, we explore how PARS applies to administration of online writing programs and courses and how you can utilize a PARS framework to your advantage when creating/running your online writing program.

The more we thought about it, the more we realized we (as a writing studies field) really did need a book on administration of online writing courses and programs, which is something that doesn't exist. There are several articles on administration in the current and past online writing instruction (OWI) scholarship, but we aim to bring you an entire collection here to help you with your own writing programs. In the spring of 2022, we sent out a call for chapters, and we were overwhelmed by the response. There were so many great ideas that spanned leadership styles, issues, and university demographics.

When putting together our call, we wanted to acknowledge that there are a multitude of types of leaders in writing programs across the country. Leadership itself comes in many forms, and sometimes leadership is done by a small team. We also wanted to recognize the reality that not all leaders are writing program administrators, that many leaders hold contingent positions, and some leaders are graduate students acting as assistant director to the first-year writing or program director (Calhoon-Dillahunt, 2011; Hollinger & Borgman, 2020; Leverenz, 2008; Malenczyk, 2016). In short, we wanted to bring readers a book that was diverse, a book that leaders across the world in all types of leadership positions could use.

Based on our own personal experience being leaders and working for leaders, we know that there is so much work being done behind the scenes as it were. That is, leaders do a lot of other work beyond their job descriptions. We wanted to acknowledge this as well with our collection, and we feel that the chapters within the collection really point to this "invisible work," the work that is untitled and uncompensated, that so many leaders take on and deal with daily (Kynard, 2019; McLeod, 2007; Penrose, 2012; Perryman-Clark & Craig, 2019; Rodrigo & Romberger, 2017). So, while the chapters in this collection give readers an idea of what an online writing program administrator, or OWPA, is, they also illustrate that the term OWPA is hard to fully capture (Borgman, 2016). To make things more complex, we are in the midst of experiencing the impact of the COVID-19 pandemic, and because this impact will continue to manifest, many in leadership will continue to face challenges they've never dealt with before. We also know that because of the challenges of the past few years, many leaders in all types of roles might have some great insights to share with others.

Collection Overview

For this collection, we decided not to group the chapters into sections like we did in our 2021 edited collection. Instead, we decided to offer the chapters openly

Introduction   5

in an effort to give you a chance to read them based on topics and themes. Each chapter is its own narrative that guides you through the authors' processes and experiences. You will see repeating themes as you read through the collection (pre-designed courses, instructor preparation and training, reactions to the challenges of the COVID-19 pandemic, program identity and movement, and many others). These themes align with a lot of what was found in *The 2021 State of the Art of OWI Report*—areas of OWI that still need attention and work from universities, administrators, instructors, and scholars. As we've done in past books, we've incorporated a golf theme, and each chapter represents a hole on a traditional 18-hole golf course. We've also identified some of the themes and chapters below to aid you in understanding our organizational structure.

Being an OWPA/Building and Running a Writing Program

- Rodrigo
- Stewart & Mitchell
- Hollinger
- Selber et al.
- Yerace
- Fernandez et al.

Faculty Training & Support

- Mannon
- Groner & Islam
- Holland & Trainor
- Egger

Course Design & Pre-Designed Courses

- Bartolotta et al.
- Anders et al.
- Mitchum
- Retzinger & Sharp-Hoskins
- Tseptsura

Inclusion/Student Preparation & Support

- Watts
- Reid
- Giordano & Phillips
- Skurat Harris & Thomas

Below, we've also included an overview of PARS for administration, where we go through each element (personal, accessible, responsive, strategic) of our PARS approach and set up the various ways administrators can use PARS in their work as they direct writing programs, or any program really. This PARS for administration overview also will aid you in understanding how authors in the collection applied our PARS framework, from administration style (Be personal, be a human!) to outlining how one will respond (Make a plan!) to faculty, staff, and students in their leadership role. This overview of PARS for administration will also illustrate that as administrators, you are crafting user experiences for your faculty and students, so the more that you can keep these individuals in mind as you create your program and courses, the better.

As with our 2021 collection, we asked authors to use a conversational academic tone and speak to the audience in their chapters. We want the chapters in this collection and all of our work to be accessible. We also encouraged authors to include visuals and key takeaways so that readers could apply the chapter concepts in their own programs/university situations. Like our first two books, our focus with this collection is application. We hope that you read these chapters and are inspired to refine your practice, try something new, or adopt a new approach to managing your program and courses. As we noted previously, we tend to use golf as a metaphor to talk about online writing course design, instruction, and administration. You will notice that some of the authors in this collection extended our golf metaphor in their chapters; therefore, we have provided a short glossary of some common golf terms at the end of this introduction.

Key Takeaways

Brené Brown (2018) defines a leader as "anyone who takes responsibility for finding the potential in people and processes, and who has the courage to develop that potential" (p. 4). We hope that you will read these chapters and utilize PARS as a way to develop and support the potential of your faculty, staff, and students. We hope that you will also understand the complexity and challenges of leading writing programs and the processes associated that can help, or hinder, potential for change. And we hope that you will gain a better understanding of the diverse leadership roles people hold throughout the field of writing studies. In addition to these hopes, we also envision these key takeaways for you as our readers:

- Leading others is challenging work! It's work that takes a lot of time and effort, and while rewarding, it is also, at times, defeating.
- Leadership comes in various forms, and often, the most effective leadership is team leadership, or having a leader that listens to their team.
- Leadership is listening to and working with faculty and students to support the mission of a program.
- Leadership is advocacy. Leaders advocate for the values and goals of their program, which always comes first because it is made up of students and faculty who care about the work.

We are excited to bring you this collection that illustrates the various ways that the PARS approach can be applied to leading entirely online writing programs or hybrid programs with both face-to-face and online courses.

As we close our introduction, we want to acknowledge all the leaders who have inspired and led us along the way in our lives and careers. Leadership is a challenging but rewarding position, and acknowledgment and thank you(s) can sometimes get missed. Beronda Montgomery (2021) notes, "If we want more equitable outcomes, we would do well to recognize that everyone benefits when we cultivate people's diverse talents and promote synergies and collaborations among them" (p. 144). We are grateful to all of those who have mentored us and given us the courage to explore synergies and collaborations across the discipline, in our classrooms, and in our scholarship. Without you, we wouldn't be where we are. It is now our responsibility to support others who move toward equitable outcomes and to cultivate diverse talents and promote synergies and collaborations with new and exciting voices, many of whom we think you will find in this collection. So, dear readers, as you make your way through these chapters, we encourage you to reflect on your own experiences with the leaders in your lives and to reflect on your experiences of being mentored and mentoring. We encourage you to explore and be empowered by these chapters and hopefully find support for the challenges you have faced, and continue to face, as a leader.

We hope that this collection inspires you to use the PARS approach in your own leadership position. As we've said before, the PARS framework "offers a holistic approach to online instruction that acknowledges the complexity of course design and its facilitation in digital spaces" (Borgman & McArdle, 2021, p. 4). We also assert here that the PARS approach to online program/course administration offers a holistic way to approach the everyday realities of leading a group of faculty and staff in educating the students at your university effectively.

If you have not already done so, we invite you to please join our community!
Website: www.owicommunity.org
Facebook Group: www.facebook.com/groups/owicommunity
Twitter: @theowicommunity

References

Borgman, J. C. (2016). The online writing program administrator (OWPA): Maintaining a brand in the age of MOOCs. In E. A. Monske & K. L. Blair (Eds.), *Handbook of research on writing and composing in the age of MOOCs* (pp. 188–201). Information Science Reference.

Borgman, J. & McArdle, C. (2021). *PARS in practice: More resources and strategies for online writing instruction*. WAC Clearinghouse. https://doi.org/10.37514/PRA-B.2021.1145.

Brown, B. (2018). *Dare to lead*. Vermilion.

Calhoon-Dillahunt, C. (2011). Writing programs without administrators: Frameworks for successful writing programs in the two-year college. *Writing Program Administration, 35*(1), 118–134.

Hollinger, A. & Borgman, J. (2020). (Dis)similarity and identity: On becoming quasi-WPA. *WPA: Writing Program Administration, 44*(1), 129–147. https://wpacouncil.org/aws/CWPA/asset_manager/get_file/555791?ver=3.

Kynard, C. (2019). Administering while Black: Black women's labor in the academy and the "position of the unthought." In S. M. Perryman-Clark & C. L. Craig (Eds.), *Black perspectives in writing program administration: From the margins to the center* (pp. 28–50). National Council of Teachers of English.

Leverenz, C. (2008). Remediating writing program administration. *Writing Program Administration, 32*(1), 37–56.

Malenczyk, R. (2016). *A rhetoric for writing program administrators* (2nd ed.). Parlor Press.

McLeod, S. (2007). *Writing program administration*. Parlor Press.

Montgomery, B. (2021). *Lessons from plants*. Harvard University Press.

Penrose, A. M. (2012). Professional identity in a contingent-labor profession: Expertise, autonomy, community in composition teaching. *WPA: Writing Program Administration, 35*(2), 108–126. http://wpacouncil.org/archives/35n2/35n2penrose.pdf.

Perryman-Clark, S. M. & Craig, C. L. (Eds.). (2019). *Black perspectives in writing program administration: From the margins to the center*. National Council of Teachers of English.

Rodrigo, R. & Romberger, J. (2017). Managing digital technologies in writing programs: Writing program technologists & invisible service. *Computers and Composition, 44*, 67–82. https://doi.org/10.1016/j.compcom.2017.03.003.

Fundamentals Before Course Play

You can't play a game of golf without knowing some of the basic rules. Golf like all sports has a set of rules that are clear and specific. However, like all sports golf also has unwritten rules that you learn by experience and playing with other people. So, to set you up, we wanted to provide you with some fundamentals of the game. Well not really... because our book isn't a game... but you get the picture. We wanted to aid you in understanding what PARS is and how it might be applied within the chapters of this text.

Therefore, this first chapter, authored by us, your editors, provides a foundational base for the PARS framework and its application to writing program leadership. We provide a brief overview of the PARS framework in case you are not familiar with it and then we explore each of the PARS elements (personal, accessible, responsive, strategic) as they apply to running a writing program with online courses. We hope you will enjoy the list like format for some quick tips and tricks on how you can be a better leader, support your faculty with purpose, and create and maintain the online courses in your program so that students enjoy them and are successful taking them.

Chapter 1. PARS for Writing Program Administration

Jessie Borgman
ARIZONA STATE UNIVERSITY

Casey McArdle
MICHIGAN STATE UNIVERSITY

Abstract: This first chapter provides a brief overview of the PARS framework and how that framework can be used in a writing program that has online courses as part of the program offerings. In this chapter we cover each PARS element and explore the layers of design, instruction, and administration for program leaders. Each section highlights ways that program leaders can use specific techniques that align with the PARS framework to better support their faculty, to craft a stronger more effective writing program, and to create better user experiences for the students taking their classes.

Keywords: online writing instruction (OWI), personal, accessible, responsive, strategic (PARS), program leaders, design, instruction, administration

As you get started with this collection, we thought it would be useful to provide an overview of the functionality of PARS for administrators, that is, how each letter works to ensure you have a program that is focused on being personal, accessible, responsive, and strategic. In our first book, we provided an overview of PARS for administration in each lettered chapter because administration is one of the PARS layers (design, instruction, administration). However, the layers of PARS are obviously interconnected (you have to design a course for it to be instructed and administered), and this interconnectedness is what makes up the entire user experience.

So, for each of the PARS letters, we will quickly highlight how you can consider the layers (design, instruction, administration) in your own program. Use the PARS approach to guide your course (design and administration) and your interaction with students (instruction). Keep it simple (online teaching doesn't have to be elaborate). Remember, you are creating and participating in an experience alongside your faculty (if you're an administrator) and students, so keep notes and think about what did and did not work, and be ready to iterate.

Personal

For us, personal is self-explanatory. Don't act like a computer/machine; be a human instead. Writing is personal and teaching is personal, so make it that way in your online writing programs/courses. Focus your efforts as an administrator on making a connection beyond content delivery, and help your instructors make a connection beyond teaching the content and assigning course grades. As an administrator, build a community in your department, and help foster positive interactions between you and your instructors. Encourage your instructors to do the same with their courses and students.

Personal Design

When designing online writing courses for or with your faculty team, consider the following to make the design more personal:

- Use colors and images on the content pages in the learning management system.
- Ensure the tone of your course content (e.g., announcements, assignments, and discussion prompts) is upbeat/friendly/inviting.
- Make your instructors create an introduction video or bio post in the discussion forum and share research interests with students.
- Have your instructors put their picture on the syllabus.

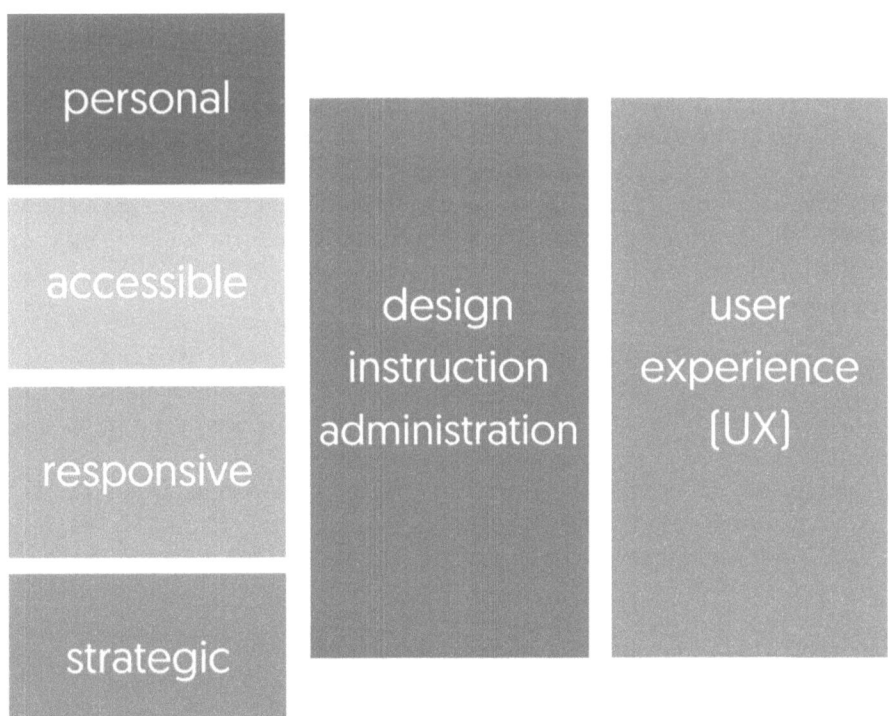

Figure 1.1. PARS+UX=OWI. Created by Kate Fedewa, Michigan State University, 2022.

Personal Instruction

As you work with your instructors and coach them in their instruction of the online writing courses in your program, encourage them to be caring and compassionate in their communication with students, to show they are human. Model this by example in the way you communicate with your instructors. Additionally, as you train them in some of the differences in teaching online versus other modalities, encourage instructors to do the following:

- Create an information office card with their contact information on it and share personal information (hobbies/interests) with students
- Add a picture to their email account and learning management system (LMS) profile
- Have students complete an ice breaker activity early in the course
- Hold virtual office hours, send weekly "check-in" emails to students, or contact students by phone or via Zoom

Personal Administration

In your day-to-day work as an administrator, try to be as personal as you can with faculty and staff. Focus on supporting your staff in whatever way you can! Hold virtual administrator office hours, and/or work in weekly check-ins (meetings or emails) with your staff. Remind them you are there for them. Consider hosting weekly or monthly "lunch and learns" to share online teaching/LMS tips and tricks and talk about what they're doing in their courses. Remind your faculty that you've been there, you've had challenges and successes as an instructor yourself. Remember, your faculty and their students might come to you with problems, and it's your job to advocate for them both. Here are some other ways to make your administration style more personal:

- Provide online training sessions on specific topics, such as workload management, discussion participation, and grading expectations.
- Send reminders of the academic and personal school/program resources so your faculty know about them.
- Ensure your staff have access to internet speeds and technology that can support the work they will be doing.
- Work with faculty to create a backup plan for personal emergencies.

Accessible

When we talk about creating accessible programs and courses, we're talking about removing barriers to learning and leveling the playing field for learners. We're not just talking about compliance with the Americans with Disabilities

Act (ADA), though that is very important! When we talk about accessibility, we're focused on things like making accessible content, having an accessible navigation in your LMS, and being accessible to your faculty and, if you're an instructor, your students.

Accessible Design

As you design your courses alone or with a team of instructors, make sure you're thinking about the affordances of the modality. That is, don't just put content built for face-to-face courses into an online space. Instead, take advantage of the affordances of a digital learning environment and design for it. Make sure that if you use something built for a face-to-face course you adapt it to work in a synchronous or asynchronous online setting and you ensure it's accessible. Re-imagine and test assignments for digital spaces before deploying them to your students. Also consider how students will access the content, and ensure you use file formats that they can open (e.g., Word, PDF, Google Docs, static LMS content pages). Most importantly, make sure your courses meet ADA compliance standards for online courses. We encourage you, as the administrator, to do the following things as you and your team design your online writing courses (OWCs):

- Provide faculty with exemplary OWC examples. Teach them some basic accessible course design best practices related to
  - LMS tools/navigation
  - modules or chunking
  - file formats and file naming
- Simplify the navigation in the LMS.
  - Limit the choices that students have to pick from on the left navigation.
  - Consider how many times students have to click to open something (the fewer clicks the better).
- Use videos! But when you use videos, keep them short (five minutes or less), and make sure you caption them or provide a written script.
- Ensure you create (or adapt) assignments that allow for flexible submission formats as some students may be working only from their cell phones.

Accessible Instruction

As you work with your instructors on coaching and training them to teach online, help them understand how to be accessible in a myriad of ways. Help them understand what ADA compliance is and how to incorporate some best practices of accessibility into their classes. Explain to your instructors how ADA accommodations work and what kinds of accommodations students might expect. Ensure that your instructors know how to provide various accommodations and how to get in touch with your accessibility office. Aid your instructors in planning and creating points of contact where they are able to connect and engage with their students. Lastly, encourage your instructors to:

- Provide content for different learning styles (audio, text, video, interactive readings)
- Explain LMS access to their students in a video or live session and post LMS resources
- Make a video that walks students through where things are in the course; finding content shouldn't be a barrier to learning it!
- Advertise their availability (how to contact them and when) and how students can contact their peers if they want to create study groups

Accessible Administration

Consider how you can be a more accessible administrator and what habits or routines you can adopt to model best practices of accessibility for your instructors. We encourage you to note your availability and how/when your faculty can get in touch with you. Considering some of the basic "rules/expectations" of your program is also part of accessible administration. Just as students want to know the expectations, faculty deserve to know them too. Before the semester and faculty training begin, make a decision on some of the very basic day-to-day items, such as whether or not your instructors should hold office hours, or whether or not you want to have grading turnaround time frames. Not making a decision on these things *is making a decision*. As you work with your faculty, also consider doing the following:

- Make sure faculty know how to get in touch with tech support if they have issues with technology.
- Create and convey clear expectations for
  - grading turnaround for assignments, including longer written ones and shorter ones like discussions or quizzes
  - response times for emails and questions
- Ensure faculty have access to the things they will need to do their jobs, such as
  - hardware
  - software
  - orientation to the LMS
  - support documents
- Aid faculty in understanding grading issues and processes for
  - plagiarism

- complaints
- incompletes

Responsive

For administrators, responsive OWI is about establishing guidelines for *how* you're going to respond to your instructors/students and *when* you're going to respond. It's about setting real expectations and turnaround times so that you're responding to solve student problems early. The responsive part of OWI for us is about establishing a pattern or routine for how you administer and/or teach your online writing courses. So, as you read through this section, consider the how and when.

Responsive Design

When designing your online writing courses, either as the administrator or along with your instructional team, ensure you have designed places in the course where instructors can post their availability, including days off and office hours, as well as response times for grading and email. Encourage a course design that provides students with the following information:

- How/when/where the class meets
  - Is it all asynchronous or synchronous?
  - Is there a synchronous meeting time?
  - Are you using the college LMS or another platform?
- A calendar for planning ahead that includes
  - major writing assignments
  - smaller assignments (e.g., Eli Review; discussion posts; shorter writing assignments, such as journals)
  - peer reviews
  - group work
  - synchronous meeting times (if applicable)
- Program(s) you'll use beyond the LMS, such as
  - Eli Review
  - Google Docs
  - social media (e.g., Instagram, Twitter, Facebook)
- How they will be graded (contract grading; portfolio grading; standard grading using points, percentages, or scales)

Responsive Instruction

As you think about training your instructors to teach online, you'll want to encourage them to develop their own routines and identify their own hows and whens. Some instructors, especially those new to online instruction, will need help creating their own patterns and routines, and sometimes that takes time, trial, and error. Encourage your instructors to think about the following.

How **they are going to respond to their students?**

- What course platform they will use (e.g., LMS, Zoom, Google Meet)
- How they will respond to their students' writing
  - end comments
  - in-text comments
  - LMS commenting feature
  - Microsoft Suite commenting
  - Google Docs commenting
- What kind of responses they will make in the discussions
  - general ones to the whole class
  - individual ones to each student

When **they are going to respond to their students?**

- When they will participate in the class and what days of the week they will take off
- When they will hold office hours and when they'll be available for asynchronous emailing or chatting via the LMS
- When they will give feedback on student work
  - discussions (24–48 hours)
  - shorter assignments and quizzes (48–72 hours)
  - longer assignments (3–5 days)
  - email responses (24–48 hours)

Responsive Administration

As you think about your own administration style, make sure you also think about your hows and whens. Responsive administration is much like responsive instruction except that you're being responsive for your faculty and staff instead of your students. Responsive administration is about identifying various responsive strategies and then figuring out how and when you'll participate in them. For example, consider

- Aiming to respond quickly to email when you can and notifying your faculty and staff of your email response timeframe (24 hours? 48 hours? 72 hours? Weekend availability?)
- Holding WPA office hours and making sure you convey your availability to your staff, including when (e.g., weekly, biweekly, monthly) and where (e.g., Zoom, F2F, Google Meet)

- Facilitating a department space in your college's LMS, Slack, or MSTeams where you can post resources
- Developing workflow systems for things like course observations and annual/biannual faculty evaluations

Strategic

When we talk about our PARS approach, we note that everything comes together with strategy! Strategy is the biggest part of being an online administrator and instructor. Strategy gels the PARS layers (design, instruction, administration), and it aids you in creating and facilitating a superior student user experience.

Strategic Design

The grounding point in all course design is strategy. You have to have a plan, and you have to be able to carry out that plan in the content and design of your course. As you work to create your online writing courses, either with your team or by yourself as the administrator, make sure you

- Plan your personal course design by
    - considering where you can put images and videos
    - considering where you can incorporate color
    - including instructor information
- Plan your accessible course design by
    - simplifying the course navigation
    - creating assignments that can be submitted in multiple formats
    - ensuring content caters to different learning styles
- Plan your responsive course design by
    - providing information about when/where/how the course meets
    - providing a course calendar
    - conveying grading policies, email response times, and office hours times and locations

Strategic Instruction

As you work with your instructors on creating their strategic plan for instructing their online writing courses, make sure you help them

- Plan their personal instruction strategy, making their presence known and connecting with the students so that they see their instructor as a real live person and not just a computer
- Plan their accessible instruction strategy, including planning their audios and videos so that they can aid students in accessing the material of their courses

- Plan their responsive instruction strategy so they know how and when they will give feedback
- Plan out their teaching to determine where in the course they can best insert themselves as a teacher and make the most impact. Encourage them to think about their participation in the course.
  - Will they be present in the discussions or have a student be the discussion moderator each week?
  - How many days will they be "present" in the course?
  - How will they respond to students (as a group? individually?)
  - What kind of posts will they make?

Strategic Administration

Just as you must help your instructors think about their strategic plan for teaching, you should also think about your strategic plan for administering your program. All managers must be strategic in their decisions and have a plan for how they get the work done. All managers must be prepared to handle things they didn't plan for, and they must be agile in their approach. As you think about your own strategic management plan, you should also consider

- Planning your **personal** administrative strategy; how will you show your faculty you are someone they can trust?
- Planning your **accessible** administrative strategy and making a plan for how you'll help your faculty with things they will need to do their jobs
- Planning your **responsive** administrative strategy, including how and when you'll communicate with faculty and staff
- Strategizing how you'll prepare your online instructors for teaching different student demographics, such as
  - underprepared students
  - ESL students
  - students with learning disabilities
  - working students with families
  - first-generation college students
  - returning students

Before the Game Practice Swings!

When playing in a tournament, professional golfers don't just go out and begin play on an 18-hole course without any pre-game practice. Many professional golfers spend time at the driving range and/or putting green, collecting themselves mentally and getting warmed up physically.

We decided to start off the collection with Shelley Rodrigo's text about being an online writing program administrator (OWPA) because some readers may want to practice or get warmed up before jumping into the ideas/concepts in the other chapters. We felt that it would be a good start for readers to get a feel for the course, that is, to understand the role of the online writing program administrator (OWPA).

We felt Rodrigo's chapter was a great place to start because it offers a glimpse of the day-to-day challenges and successes one may face when they administer a program with online writing courses. Rodrigo's chapter provides experienced and novice administrators with solid advice based on her lengthy experience as an OWPA.

Chapter 2. So, you want to be an OWPA?

Shelley Rodrigo
University of Arizona

Abstract: Individuals can be both unofficial or official online writing program administrators (OWPAs) throughout their career. Becoming and being an OWPA requires developing expertise in writing studies, online pedagogy and technologies, as well as leadership and managerial skills. More importantly, being a successful OWPA requires being a leader with integrity, vision, and values; a person who is inclusive, transparent, and has a strong work ethic; plus, of course, an administrator who is personal, accessible, responsive, and strategic (PARS; Borgman & McArdle, 2019). The OWPA's day is long and the work hard; however, there is a large community of people to help with both developing and using administrative skills for good as well as learning to draw boundaries, rest, and be human.

Keywords: vision, values, professional growth, community, boundaries, rest

Although the term *writing program administrator* (WPA) historically emphasized the individual who oversees the program offering the required first-year writing courses, it has grown to encompass all individuals who oversee different types of writing programs (Malenczyk, 2016), whether or not the program or the position is institutionally recognized (Rodrigo & Romberger, 2017). If someone is making decisions about writing instruction or the support of writing instruction, they are a WPA. Jessie Borgman's (2016) experience as an adjunct OWPA is an example that demonstrates *online WPA* can be defined and described similarly to WPAs. Therefore, an OWPA is an individual who officially, or unofficially, oversees digitally mediated writing programs (defined broadly). With this broad definition of OWPA, I claim I have been an OWPA most of my 20+ year career. I started in unofficial programs and roles and have more recently been the lead administrator of an online writing program (OWP) as well, shifting to *the* WPA of a first-year (and beyond!) writing program just before the COVID-19 pandemic starting in March 2020. I can say with confidence, being a successful OWPA requires being

- a leader with integrity, vision, and values;
- a person who is inclusive, transparent, and has a strong work ethic;
- plus, of course, an administrator who is personal, accessible, responsive, and strategic (PARS; Borgman & McArdle, 2019).

Theory and Practice

In this chapter, I use Borgman and McArdle's (2019) PARS approach to frame a reflective narrative of my professional career, connecting to other scholarly research and theory, to provide suggestions, take-aways, and applications for the readers who are either running an OWP (again, defined broadly) or want to do so in the future. In the original *PARS* text, Borgman and McArdle (2019) provide descriptions and definitions for *personal, accessible, responsive,* and *strategic*; before reflecting, I want to map how I'll be adapting the PARS framework in this chapter.

Personal—Borgman and McArdle (2019) emphasize "serving faculty and students" (p. 26). I emphasize having a theory of interactions. My theory specifically includes being accessible, willing to share, and transparent about my experiences and expectations.

Accessible—Borgman and McArdle remind us of the obvious interpretations of administrative accessibility: being accessible to stakeholders and providing support to make digital learning environments accessible. I especially appreciate their emphasis on being an inclusive leader, ensuring programmatic decision-making and resource development are accessible to faculty in the program.

Responsive—As administrators, Borgman and McArdle suggest that responsiveness emphasizes preparing and continuing to support online faculty. I want to expand this to think about responsiveness as a type of interaction or engagement that emphasizes listening and paying attention to what somebody (or something, sometimes it's the technologies we need to engage with) wants and needs and then responding accordingly. Similar to a responsive instructor, I'd argue responsive administrators are transparent about their philosophy of engagement so that all stakeholders know when and where they can communicate and are aware of when and where administrators respond.

Strategic—Especially as online administrators, Borgman and McArdle stress having a plan. I appreciate their emphasis on making the plan user-centered and add that it also needs to remain flexible. Being strategic means also having specific goals and values that guide the plan and any decisions that need to be made (for example, like in March 2020 when you must support an entire unit transitioning from in-person to online instruction).

My mapping of PARS suggests that an OWPA needs to have vision and values that then frame being personal, accessible, responsive, and strategic. Whereas visions change, they must adapt to new contexts; identifying core values is one of the most important strategic moves an OWPA can make. While reading my adaptation and framing of PARS, hopefully you identified my repeated emphasis on inclusivity and transparency; those are the values that I'll continue to emphasize below.

So, You Want to Be an OWPA? (Preparation & Education)

Let's be honest. Just as an experienced writing instructor does not a WPA make, having a lot of experience teaching online writing courses does not necessarily prepare someone to administer an online writing program. Before discussing how to prepare to be an OWPA, let's talk about what *skills* an OWPA needs. Some of the earliest OWPA positions were in writing centers (or, to claim the catchy name, online writing labs [OWLS]). There is scholarship about writing centers needing to support online students as early as the mid–1990s (e.g., Blythe, 1997; Harris & Pemberton, 1995; Healy, 1995). Even where an institution's first-year writing program was not offering online courses, the point at which an institution starts to offer online courses in other disciplines requiring writing-intensive courses prompted administrators to call upon writing centers to support that new online student population. These writing center (O)WPAs were initially concerned about the ability to share materials with online students (thus we have the robust Purdue OWL resource, among others) and how to work with students in different locations. Lots of early discussion about OWLs focused on what technologies to use (e.g., Coogan, 1995; Harris & Pemberton, 1995; Simons et al., 1995) and maintaining the ethical philosophy of not being a drop-off editorial service, especially when so many could only work with students through asynchronous means (e.g., Healy, 1995; Johanek & Rickly, 1995; Jordan-Henley & Maid, 1995).

This particular history of OWPAs emphasizes that OWPAs must have the technical knowledge of computers and networks as well as the theoretical and philosophical frameworks to pedagogically and ethically implement them. When, mostly unofficial (Rodrigo & Romberger, 2017), OWPA positions emerged, those folks had to understand the technologies as well as how the technologies played out with writing-specific pedagogies and institutionally contextualized students. Many initial OWPA positions were offering training to support faculty teaching in computer labs and/or online environments like learning management systems (LMSs). The subfield of computers and writing is filled with calls for faculty to be technologically trained in a disciplinary and contextually grounded manner (e.g., Hewett & Ehmann, 2004; Mirtz & Leverenz, 2000; Palmquist et al., 1998). For example, the "average" computer and Wi-Fi access of my community college students in the first decade of the 21st century was different from university students during the second decade. I had to understand the pedagogy, the technology, and the context in which I worked and how the context may have been different than the ones many scholars wrote about. Other (un)official OWPA positions include website or lab managers, department technological liaisons (Rodrigo & Romberger, 2017), and managers of makerspaces (Selber, 2020). Stuart Selber (2020) describes how these types of positions can "run the spectrum from modest university engagements . . . to ambitious interventions that aim to achieve large-scale change in how digital technologies are institutionalized" (pp. 1–2).

I'll pull from my own history as an example of early OWPAs balancing technical knowledge with theoretical frameworks and contextual realities. As a graduate student in the late 1990s, I taught the second online writing course offered at the university. I was offered that course because I had already demonstrated my commitment to and skills with digitally facilitated pedagogies. Without having phrases like OWPA or writing program technologist (WPT; Rodrigo & Romberger, 2017), I already knew I wanted to be someone who specialized in digitally mediated teaching. I requested teaching in computer-mediated classrooms and volunteered to facilitate workshops where I shared with others what, how, and why to teach writing with computers. When I served as the writing program's graduate assistant WPA, I helped develop digital newsletters and training materials. Very quickly, my interest in and experience with teaching in digitally mediated spaces expanded to OWPA type work supporting other instructors.

My interest in digitally mediated pedagogies transferred over to my scholarly projects as well. As I started to study digitally mediated writing instruction, I immersed myself in the computers and writing community (in which I initially participated as a graduate student in the Computers and Writing Conference's Graduate Research Network (GRN) and continue to contribute to as a mentor in the GRN). More importantly, however, I also found a whole world of online and digitally mediated pedagogical research and theories by education scholars. As an online teacher-scholar, I looked to all these places for inspiration and camaraderie. Later as an OWPA, I found that just as there is a robust field of online and distance learning scholarship outside of what is produced within writing studies, there is also scholarship about administering online programs, which includes the *Online Journal of Distance Learning Administration (OJDLA)*. OJDLA has published two articles about online writing programs (i.e., Stella & Corry, 2013; Tucker, 2012). Finding and reading this scholarship helped grow my knowledge of technologies and expanded the frameworks I used to implement them.

Having the experience of teaching online as well as the knowledge to talk about digital technologies and how they applied to teaching writing allowed me to land a full-time job before I had completed my doctorate. (I'm not suggesting this path is for everyone; it's just what I did.) I gained a lot of online teaching experience (my position was a 5/5 teaching load at a community college); I also started to find the unofficial OWPA positions that parallel unofficial or quasi-WPA positions (Hollinger & Borgman, 2020). For example, depending on the year and the institution's commitment, I both unofficially and officially (aka, a title, maybe a stipend) supported online instructor colleagues in English and across the college. I would also (un)officially liaise on behalf of my online students and colleagues in various decision-making processes like revised student learning outcomes, textbook selection, and teacher evaluation processes.

Preparing and educating yourself to be an OWPA means strategically deciding what you want to do and being transparent with yourself and others about your goals. Based on my experience, one of the best ways to prepare and educate yourself is to start acting the role before you have it. Be personal, accessible, and responsive to your students and colleagues by listening, learning, and, most importantly, sharing what you've learned. Use the opportunities to help others to grow your own knowledge base; for example, I always offer to facilitate sessions about ed tech policies and legal issues as an excuse to grow and update my own knowledge on the topic. Almost every OWPA and WPT I know was facilitating workshops and digital pedagogy sharing sessions before they were ever in either an official or unofficial position.

Balancing What? Do What I Say, Not What I Do.

Before I go any further, I must insert a warning. If this were an old-school set of instructional documents, it would have a triangle in red or yellow with an exclamation point or the word *warning* in all caps. If it were multimodal, it would be beeping.

The single most important thing I have learned as an administrator in higher education is the need to take time off—this warning is for WPAs and OWPAs alike. Our profession rewards people who have terrible work-life balance (and I'm one of them!). Not only is this an equity problem for faculty and administrators in the profession who have legitimate competing responsibilities, it is ultimately unhealthy for the individual as well. Especially as administrators who are savvy about using technology, we not only have but usually embrace the ability to be *on* all the time:

- responding to email in the line at the grocery store (or Disneyland),
- writing up an observation while sitting at our kid's swim practice (or at conferences), and/or
- checking Slack/Microsoft Teams while on vacation (anywhere with a signal!).

The most important suggestion I can give, as repeatedly mentioned by both Borgman and McArdle (2019), counselors (e.g., Tawwab, 2021), and scholars discussing how to teach online courses (e.g., Boettcher & Conrad, 2016; Riggs, 2019; Stachowiak, 2020), is that we have to be strategic about how we balance the thrill and satisfaction that comes from being personal, accessible, and responsive to our students, faculty, staff, IT colleagues, and other extended professional network members with the strategic decisions to draw boundaries and disconnect from work (and technologies!).

For example, although I would have loved to submit a proposal for Borgman and McArdle's 2021 *PARS in Practice* collection, I knew I didn't have the bandwidth to do justice to a chapter at that time. Besides trying to say "no" more often, I have also committed myself to taking at least two weeks off each year (usually separately) to make sure I rest. Although I wish I could say I completely disconnect every time, I have challenged myself the next time I vacay to both leave my laptop at home and take the email app off my phone. Health and wellness, whatever that is and means for you, is just as critical as disciplinary and technological knowledge. Maintaining your health and wellness is one of the philosophical frameworks to embrace as an OWPA. If you aren't healthy, you can't support the students, faculty, staff, and others in your program.

Stop reading, stand up, stretch, grab a drink of water (I just did!).

Back to our regularly scheduled chapter.

You Are an OWPA, Now What? (Strategies & Growth)

I wouldn't be surprised if many of the readers of this chapter are already OWPAs, official or not. If you are helping your writing program support digital pedagogies and your program either offers or supports online classes . . . you're an OWPA. A TED talk by Simon Sinek (2014) about inspirational leadership includes this quote:

> Leadership is a choice. It is not a rank . . . I know many people who are at the bottoms of organizations who have no authority and they are absolutely leaders, and this is because they have chosen to look after the person to the left of them, and they have chosen to look after the person to the right of them. This is what a leader is. (09:47)

You're a leader! So now what? One of the biggest problems with being an OWPA or WPT is staying up to date with information in the discipline, with technologies, and a sometimes-shifting student population. It's not enough to know when the institution will update the LMS and what technology-related policies (e.g., accessibility, privacy, copyright) might change; you need to carefully look at and listen to the updated LMS to see, feel, and learn how the changes will impact the pedagogical framework you use and support. And, to top it off, whether or not your leadership role is official, you'll want to continue to grow those leadership, administrative, and/or managerial skills as well. You'll need to balance becoming overwhelmed with too much work, as well as too much continuous professional growth; remember, you are not alone!

There are the stories and scholarship that talk about the lone WPA in a department; however, those people were never alone. They always had a group of colleagues in similar roles at other institutions. The lone WPA just needed to build their network (or, from 1993 to 2019, join the WPA-Listserv). You need to build your OWPA network as well. I drafted parts of this chapter while sitting at Computers and Writing in spring 2022. For many of us in attendance, we got to see our professional family for the first time in two years. The Online Writing Instruction (OWI) Community—an online community developed and maintained by Borgman and McArdle, the authors of the PARS framework—greatly expanded as a professional network during the pandemic. If you live in a region with many educational institutions, you might build your own network of people who meet regularly to talk tech like I did when creating CyberSalon in the metropolitan Phoenix area. We had regular meeting attendees from across the disciplines who worked in community colleges, universities, and even high schools. I have called upon many of these individuals from Computers and Writing, The OWI Community, and CyberSalon, these disciplinary and academic family members—many fellow OWPAs, WPTs, and WPAs—over the years with questions, concerns, and occasionally the need to complain.

Your scholarly and/or disciplinary colleagues are not the only folks who might fill the role as a professional family member. My high school yearbook advisor reminded me that the office staff were the folks who kept the school running and got things done: "Treat them well." I continue to live by that philosophy and have found it is just as relevant to working with IT staff (again, defined broadly, this might include instructional design and instructional technologist staff working in a center for teaching and learning). Since you are likely to be the one pestering them more than normal anyhow, be sure to make friends. One year when my institution's IT department decided to lock down instructors' ability to do updates on their machines, I was teaching with podcasts, and the iTunes app updated five times in two weeks. The IT staff hated my phone calls by the end of those weeks! But I was already friends with them, and they continued to quickly respond to my requests. This experience also got them rethinking their policy.

If possible, attend professional development activities with students, IT staff, and leadership. I've asked both students and IT staff to attend and/or present with me at teaching and learning conferences. I've attended EDUCAUSE. My current institution holds a yearly IT conference event that includes a teaching and learning strand. I'm most lucky to be the sole faculty member at the University of Arizona who was accepted into and attended the university's IT Leadership Academy, where I met with other IT leaders across campus once a month over an academic year. Not only did I learn from them, but occasionally they benefited from my perspective as a faculty member as well as a leader from a unit that managed the first-year writing requirement. I still occasionally receive emails from some of my cohort members who want to ask questions of someone with a teaching perspective.

Increasingly, there are online pedagogy-focused disciplinary specialists in other departments parallel to OWPAs that you might add to your network of professional family. Also, don't forget the specialists that exist, or that you are continuing to grow, in your own unit. As instructors continue to teach online, they'll want to step up and help guide decisions and do the work of running and maintaining the program. Ann Penrose (2012) reminds us to foster the expertise, autonomy, and community in our programs, especially with our contingent faculty. As painful as it is to lose some of your better instructors, knowing that folks have moved on to better jobs (I'm proud to say six individuals from my unit have been made offers to become instructional designers) means you've not only grown your family, but continue to expand your network.

The point is that if you are open and inclusive when it comes to expanding your professional network, you'll be pleasantly surprised with who you find and what you learn from and with them. Being transparent about why you want to become friends, even family, lays the groundwork for developing robust cross-directional mentoring and support networks. Being transparent is also about being ethical, especially when building professional relationships with students. Scott Wible (2019) reminds us that a "critical part of building" mentoring and collaborating relationships, especially across color lines, "is being open to criticism and critique" (p. 87). One of Wible's (2019) anonymous Black WPA interviewees emphasized the need for both mentors and mentees to be "very direct . . . but doing it not in patronizing ways and instead just leaving things open" to whom you want to work and learn with and from. Planning to build your professional network is strategic; it's being personal, accessible, and responsive that will strengthen the connections between you and your colleagues.

Pause; Take or Schedule a Break

The point of building a network of colleagues (as well as treating staff well; don't forget that!) is not only to have a group of people you can go to for guidance and help, but to develop a web of relationships that can help steer the ship when you step out for a moment, hour, day, or vacation. If you are sick, continuing to work will not allow you to recover. I'm speaking from experience; in January 2021 I needed to recover from a December 2020 holiday hospital stay with COVID. It didn't matter that I technically and technologically could work; my body and brain were not up to the task.

As much as it feels like no one can replace you, the job and the institution can and will move on without you. Strategically scheduling breaks (use that alarm in your phone, do a few stretches or yoga positions in your office), and occasionally just taking a day because you really need to, benefits you, your program, and your colleagues. Planning breaks means you can use your network to keep the ship afloat, even providing professional growth opportunities for others while you are out. And, barring freaky pandemics and other crazy accidents, scheduling breaks should also keep you from having unexpected absences that might disrupt your program or unit.

How Do You Apply OWPA Skillz in Other #AdminLife Positions? (Survival & Beyond)

Some of the most exciting work as a WPA or OWPA is also the most challenging. Both must work closely with a variety of individuals, including other faculty, staff, and administrators, in a variety of units across the institution. All these people, and the individuals they work with, impact the ability to support teachers, teaching, students, and learning; however, neither the WPA nor the OWPA usually has direct managerial control over these people. Skeffington, Borrowman, and Enos (2008) open their chapter about WPA work by describing the "paradoxical" and "mutually exclusive" work of WPAs. On the one hand, WPAs must perform the job of *the good faculty member* who excels at teaching, participating on committees, and making friends within the home department and across the university (Skeffington et al., 2008, p. 5). However, WPAs, the work they do, and the decisions they make can greatly impact the teachers, staff, and students in their unit (and sometimes beyond). Skeffington et al. (2008) continue describing how WPAs must also fight battles in the unit and department and across the camps:

> fighting to protect the budget for the composition program, fighting to maintain or improve working conditions for composition instructors, fighting the fights that must be fought—and making enemies (at least some of whom are virtually guaranteed to serve on either reappointment committees, tenure and promotion committees, or both). (p. 5)

OWPAs usually have similar fights, or rhetorical work, in relation to slowing down, historicizing, theorizing, and pedagogically framing technology adoption and use (Day, 2006; DePew et al., 2006; Selber, 2020). Developing the ability to successfully navigate and negotiate institutional politics prepares many WPAs for administrative positions at the dean level or above, or, as Carmen Kynard (2019) calls some of them, "Super-WPAs." And, of course, these rhetorical skillz (yes, z!) align with being personal, accessible, responsive, and strategic.

If you think the rhetorical skillz of WPAs are well sought after, obviously the additional technologically savvy skillz make an OWPA even more desirable. As we move into an era when academic administrative leaders are increasingly held accountable for digitally managing their programs, including using data analytics to inform decision-making, understanding how technologies work (as well as their biases and weaknesses) makes you an effective leader. The writing program and I have benefited from my ability to design new formulas and sling around data in a spreadsheet handed to me from administration on high.

I've also been able to slow down discussions about what, how, and why we can use data being generated from LMSs and other learning environments. My favorite example of incorporating my technological savvy was during a meeting with a company demoing an adaptive learning application for our institution. I started to ask questions they did not like, especially this one:

> "As an instructor, how am I supposed to adapt what and how I'm teaching if I don't understand what data points you are pulling from and what formula you are using to tell me who is doing well and who needs more support?"

The company representative then said these presentations are not for faculty and that they couldn't tell us this information because it was the "secret sauce" of their software. Needless to say, "secret sauce" is the term I use to refer to black box elements of any given data analytics process. I know that by asking these questions I prompted the other administrators to slow down and think about what our institution needed from an adaptive learning application—we ended up not making any institutional contracts for an adaptive learning application. It's the OWPAs' skills as a technorhetorician (Day, 2006) that will make us even more desirable for advanced administrative positions.

With great technorhetorical powers comes great responsibilities. The research that Julia Romberger and I did on WPTs repeatedly found that much of the tech support labor was invisible labor not adequately recognized or compensated by the institution (Rodrigo & Romberger, 2017, 2021). Staci Perryman-Clark and Craig (2019), along with Kynard (2019), remind us that the work of any WPAs, especially a WPA of color, can be devalued and made institutionally invisible. More than once I have been in a room full of colleagues who did not blink an eye when I was the one willing and able (including carrying the correct dongle) to get the presentation equipment set up. Sometimes I get frustrated that I am a woman with the last name "Rodrigo" and wonder if those details impacted what sometimes felt like a lack of appreciation for my time, labor, and expertise. It's critical that official, unofficial, and former OWPAs use their technorhetorical skillz to be transparent about their own labor and identify other OWPA labor. We need to be allies, be willing to "put something on the line" (an anonymous Black WPA as quoted by Wible, 2019) to make visible OWPA positions, especially if our disabled, neurodiverse, and queer colleagues and colleagues of color are doing the work.

I'm Not a Superhero; Avoid Burnout!

Many in academia refer to official scholarly mentors (usually dissertation advisors) using parental terms and discuss researchers' scholarly lineage. If this is the case, Duane Roen is both my scholarly and administrative dad. A few of my graduate school colleagues and I made baseball hats that adapted the *Wayne's World* title and logo to say *Duane's World* (mine sits in my office to this day). When having a professional crisis, that same group of friends would also reference *WWDD?* (What would Duane do?). We were always amazed by all that Duane accomplished in any given day, week, or year. More than once I have reached out to Duane to ask him for guidance. I'll never forget the time he told me how many hours a week he worked. I didn't want to work that much; I cried when I got home.

Not surprisingly, I now easily work over fifty hours a week. One of my problems is I like what I do, and most *opportunities* usually fall under "the good fight" or "this is fascinating, and I want to do it!" I laugh as I realize I've become increasingly like Duane. As a graduate student and early career faculty member, I never understood how he could respond and reply to emails and draft submissions so quickly and how he could cram in work, especially writing, into 10–30-minute chunks throughout the day. I get it now. I think many would say that it's about having too much to do (it is!); however, it's also a sign about breaking larger projects (teaching, research and writing, service to the profession and community) into smaller chunks to which you continuously make progress. I can get writing projects done with only 15–30-minute chunks a day because I'm continuously working on them. Since I work on writing projects regularly, I don't need to waste time figuring out where I was and what I need to do next. (I don't know about you, but if I go more than two weeks without working on a project, I lose a lot of time getting my head back into the game. It's a miracle I ever finished my dissertation while teaching a 5/5 load—that's a story for another time or article, or chase me down at a conference.)

Reading Daniel Pink's (2018) book *When: The Scientific Secrets of Perfect Timing* helped me own that I'm early to bed and early to rise. I work best in the morning, and if I want to make sure writing and exercise happen, they must happen before #AdminLife begins each day. I also appreciated Pink's emphasis on beginnings, starting again, and starting together. He acknowledges that we all fall off the wagon and that it's OK to begin again and starting over with a group is powerful. Although I was on sabbatical this past term, and I did complete a lot of scholarly work, I did not write every day until my colleague Chris Tardy kicked off her *Write Every Day in May* Facebook group. You, reading this chapter, are benefiting from that new beginning.

Saying "no" and scheduling breaks are strategically critical to avoiding burnout. Accepting your rhymes and rhythms (and that they might change over time) and acknowledging your humanity helps as well. Although we may be tech savvy as OWPAs, we are not androids or AIs; we need to engage personally with both our bodies and our brains, listening and responding to their wants and needs. As best we can, we need to design our professional lives to work with our physical and mental needs.

Conclusion and Takeaways

Why Do You Want to Be an OWPA?

The same reason I liked sharing how I used computers to better facilitate learning with other faculty is why I like being an O/WPA. I want students to learn the course objectives and to be successful in their classes (these are not necessarily the same!). I want faculty members to be good at *and* enjoy their jobs, not be overwhelmed by either the technologies or the work. I enjoy the technological and technorhetorical challenges of being a WPT and an OWPA. And although these challenges are what keep me up at night (or in my case, don't allow me to go back to sleep early in the morning), they are also what give me the thrill of the win when I figure them out.

You read the warnings on hours and life-work balance above, right? So why do you want to do this? Wanting to be an administrator because it's the next step in the career ladder or because you want a bit of extra money is not reason enough. If these are your reasons, you'll burn out. Honesty with yourself is a critical form of transparency. You need to be personal, accessible, and responsive to yourself before any strategic professional planning to become an OWPA. But if you still decide you want to do it, here's a recap of my advice (see Table 2.1):

Table 2.1 Advice for O/WPAs to Maintain Success

Preparation & Education	Strategies & Growth	Survival & Beyond
Develop your vision and values.	Commit to continuous professional growth.	Do good with your knowledge and authority.
Take care of yourself; draw boundaries!		
Even if unofficial, be the OWPA and support others.	Listen and learn from others; build community.	Break up and scaffold work.

References

Blythe, S. (1997). Networked computers + writing centers = ? Thinking about networked computers in writing center practice. *The Writing Center Journal, 17*(2), 89–110. https://www.jstor.org/stable/43442023.

Boettcher, J. V. & Conrad, R. (2016). *The online teaching survival guide: Simple and practical pedagogical tips* (2nd ed.). Jossey-Bass.

Borgman, J. C. (2016). The online writing program administrator (OWPA): Maintaining a brand in the age of MOOCs. In E. A. Monske & K. L. Blair (Eds.), *Handbook of research on writing and composing in the age of MOOCs* (pp. 188–201). IGI Global.

Borgman, J. & McArdle, C. (2019). *Personal, accessible, responsive, strategic: Resources and strategies for online writing instructors*. The WAC Clearinghouse; University Press of Colorado. https://doi.org/10.37514/PRA-B.2019.0322.

Borgman, J. & McArdle, C. (Eds.). (2021). *PARS in practice: More resources and strategies for online writing instructors*. The WAC Clearinghouse; University Press of Colorado. https://doi.org/10.37514/PRA-B.2021.1145.

Coogan, D. (1995). E-mail tutoring, a new way to do new work. *Computers and Composition, 1 2*(2), 171–181. https://doi.org/10.1016/8755-4615(95)90005-5.

Day, M. (2006). The administrator as technorhetorician: Sustainable technological ecologies in academic programs. In D. N. DeVoss, H. A. McKee & R. Selfe (Eds.), *Technological ecologies & sustainability*. https://ccdigitalpress.org/book/tes/.

DePew, K. E., Fishman, T. A., Romberger, J. E. & Ruetenik, B. F. (2006). Designing efficiency: The parallel narratives of distance education and composition studies. *Computers and Composition, 23*(1), 49–67. https://doi.org/10.1016/j.compcom.2005.12.005.

Glover Tawwab, N. (2021). *Set boundaries, find peace: A guide to reclaiming yourself.* TarcherPerigee.

Harris, M. & Pemberton, M. (1995). Online writing labs (OWLs): A taxonomy of options and issues. *Computers and Composition, 12*(2), 145–159. https://doi.org/10.1016/8755-4615(95)90003-9.

Healy, D. (1995). From place to space: Perceptual and administrative issues in the online writing center. *Computers and Composition, 12*(2), 183–193. https://doi.org/10.1016/8755-4615(95)90006-3.

Hewett, B. L. & Ehmann, C. (2004). *Preparing educators for online writing instruction: Principles and processes.* National Council of Teachers of English.

Hollinger, A. & Borgman, J. (2020). (Dis)similarity and identity: On becoming quasi-WPA. *WPA: Writing Program Administration, 44*(1), 129–147. https://wpacouncil.org/aws/CWPA/asset_manager/get_file/555791?ver=3.

Johanek, C. & Rickly, R. (1995). Online tutor training: Synchronous conferencing in a professional community. *Computers and Composition, 12*(2), 237–246. https://doi.org/10.1016/8755-4615(95)90012-8.

Jordan-Henley, J. & Maid, B. M. Tutoring in cyberspace: Student impact and college/university collaboration. *Computers and Composition, 12*(2), 211–218. https://doi.org/10.1016/8755-4615(95)90009-8.

Kynard, C. (2019). Administering while Black: Black women's labor in the academy and the "position of the unthought. In S. M. Perryman-Clark & C. L. Craig (Eds.), *Black perspectives in writing program administration: From the margins to the center* (pp. 28–50). Conference on College Composition and Communication; National Council of Teachers of English.

Malenczyk, R. (2016). *A rhetoric for writing program administrators* (2nd ed.). Parlor Press.

Mirtz, R. & Leverenz, C. S. (2000). A mediated coexistence: The case for integrating traditional and online classroom training for new and experienced college teachers. In S. Harrington, R. Rickly & M. Day (Eds.), *The online writing classroom* (pp. 319–338). Hampton Press.

Palmquist, M., Kiefer, K., Hartvigsen, J. & Goodlew, B. (1998). *Transitions: Teaching writing in computer-supported and traditional classrooms.* Ablex.

Penrose, A. M. (2012). Professional identity in a contingent-labor profession: Expertise, autonomy, community in composition teaching. *WPA: Writing Program Administration, 35*(2), 108–126. http://associationdatabase.co/archives/35n2/35n2penrose.pdf.

Perryman-Clark, S. M. & Craig, C. L. (2019). Introduction: Black Matters: Writing program administration in twenty-first-century higher education. In S. M. Perryman-Clark & C. L. Craig (Eds.), *Black perspectives in writing program administration: From the margins to the center* (pp. 1–27). Conference on College Composition and Communication; National Council of Teachers of English.

Pink, D. H. (2018). *When: The scientific secrets of perfect timing.* Riverhead Books.

Riggs, S. (2019). *Thrive online: A new approach to building expertise and confidence as an online instructor.* Stylus.

Rodrigo, R. & Romberger, J. (2017). Managing digital technologies in writing programs: Writing program technologists & invisible service. *Computers and Composition, 44,* 67–82. https://doi.org/10.1016/j.compcom.2017.03.003.

Rodrigo, R. & Romberger, J. (2021). Actors and allies: Faculty, IT work, and writing program support. In K. Cole & H. Hassel (Eds.), *Transformations: Change work across writing programs, pedagogies, and practices* (pp. 146–164). Utah State University Press.

Selber, S. A. (2020). Historicizing infrastructural contexts for teaching and learning: A heuristic for institutional engagement. *Computers and Composition, 58.* https://doi.org/10.1016/j.compcom.2020.102602.

Selfe, R. (2005). *Sustainable computer environments: Cultures of support in English studies and language arts.* Hampton Press.

Simons, S., Bryant, J. & Stroh, J. (1995). Recreating the writing center: A chance collaboration. *Computers and Composition, 12*(2), 161–170. https://doi.org/10.1016/8755-4615(95)90004-7.

Sinek, S. (2014). *Why good leaders make you feel safe.* TED: Ideas worth spreading. https://www.ted.com/talks/simon_sinek_why_good_leaders_make_you_feel_safe.

Stachowiak, B. (2020). *The productive online and offline professor: A practical guide.* Stylus.

Stella, J. & Corry, M. (2013). Teaching writing in online distance education: Supporting student success. *Online Journal of Distance Learning Administration, 16*(2). https://ojdla.com/archive/summer162/stella_corry162.pdf.

Tucker, V. M. (2012). Listening for the squeaky wheel: Designing distance writing program assessment. *Online Journal of Distance Learning Administration, 15*(5). https://ojdla.com/archive/winter154/tucker154.pdf.

Wible, S. (2019). Forfeiting privilege for the cause of social justice: Listening to the Black WPAs and WPAs of color define the work of white allyship. In S. M. Perryman-Clark & C. L. Craig (Eds.), *Black perspectives in writing program administration: From the margins to the center* (pp. 74–100). Conference on College Composition and Communication; National Council of Teachers of English.

You're on the Tee!

Professional golfers always tend to plan out their play on a given course. Pending how many times they've previously played the course, the terrain, their mindset, etc., all golfers spend time anticipating challenges prior to play, and they know that this exercise of planning is key to a good round and can help prepare them physically and mentally for play on the rest of the holes. Just like golfers, administrators need to plan their strategies and their semester initiatives. All administrators know that planning is an important part of the job and that all things must be done for a reason.

We really like the concept of planning and preparing for the worst. Jennifer Stewart and Tiffany N. Mitchell's chapter offers a good way to think about how pre-planning allows for rapid adaptation when it's needed. This chapter provides readers with an overview of how experimenting with a programmatic change can yield good results and inadvertently lead to preparation for other collegewide or nationwide changes.

Chapter 3. Championships Are Won at Practice: How Our OWI Initiative Inadvertently Prepared Us to Navigate a Pandemic

Jennifer Stewart and Tiffany N. Mitchell
UNIVERSITY OF TENNESSEE AT CHATTANOOGA

Abstract: This chapter details the use of affinity groups within a mid-sized writing program to generate faculty buy-in for an online writing instruction (OWI) hybrid initiative. Using community of practice (CoP) scholarship, we identified practice leaders and community elders to engage faculty in OWI. Over three years of using the CoP practice leaders and affinity group modeling, OWI hybrid and online instruction grew from one percent of the program to 26 percent of the program. This chapter also describes how this initiative and PARS principles supported emergency remote teaching (ERT) during the COVID-19 pandemic. This programmatic framework to increase hybrid and online sections established a model that ultimately helped the program navigate the beginning stages of the COVID-19 pandemic and manage the new normal of OWI in a pandemic-impacted world. The OWI hybrid initiative created new practice leaders who helped their peers through ERT. This growth resulted in pedagogically flexible faculty and "post"-pandemic first-year composition (FYC) offerings that now stand at 46 percent hybrid and online.

Keywords: online learning, online writing instruction, writing program administration, teacher preparation, hybrid instruction, communities of practice, affinity groups, emergency remote teaching, COVID-19 pandemic

Instituting programmatic change in a writing program with an established, diverse faculty can be daunting, particularly for a new writing program administrator (WPA). As universities push for more modalities in their course offerings, WPAs are often tasked with offering more hybrid or online courses, and also with training and mentoring for their faculty. When Stewart was hired as the University of Tennessee Chattanooga (UTC) English Composition Program[1] WPA in 2016, only two percent of first-year composition (FYC) courses offered were online, and none were hybrid. In spring 2017, Stewart began an online writing instruction

---

1. The English composition program consists of three rhetoric and writing courses. The program is taught by one or two tenured or tenure-track faculty (varies by term); 25 full-time, non-tenure track faculty; and an average of 15–20 adjunct faculty. Each fall term, the program offers approximately 90 sections of FYC; it offers 65 sections in the spring.

(OWI) cohort initiative to increase hybrid and online sections; some faculty had indicated an interest in learning about OWI, and our program values multiple modalities. This initiative ultimately helped us navigate the beginning stages of the COVID-19 pandemic and has since helped us manage the ever-challenging new normal of OWI in a pandemic-impacted world: Our "post"-pandemic[2] FYC offerings now stand at 37 percent hybrid and nine percent online.

We met when Mitchell attended Stewart's candidate visit events. Mitchell asked Stewart how long she intended to stay at UTC, and Stewart replied that when she is somewhere that fits, she "digs in like a tick." This interaction told Stewart that the non-tenure track faculty were seeking consistency and showed Mitchell that Stewart was intentional in her pursuit of UTC's WPA position and, if hired, that she would offer needed long-term stability. Because we discovered our pedagogical and administrative approaches both aligned and complemented each other early in our interactions, we have been close pedagogical allies and friends since Stewart arrived. Mitchell's institutional history input and technological savvy have been key in helping Stewart shape the writing program. Mitchell's service as associate writing program administrator (AWPA) for two semesters and her ongoing service as departmental technology coordinator and composition committee member have made her a key contributor to program initiatives, particularly in OWI. While Stewart is the WPA of the UTC writing program and ultimately responsible for any major decisions, she rarely moves forward with any initiative unilaterally, consulting the composition committee and UTC faculty regularly.

Although we hadn't come across Borgman and McArdle's PARS framework during the creation of the initial OWI cohorts, it aligns with the steps we took in preparing faculty for OWI. Specifically, we highlighted the importance of having a personal presence in the OWI course; organizing accessible materials in a strategic, conscientious manner; and, most importantly, remaining responsive to student engagement and needs. Like Lyra Hilliard (2021), we see our OWI leadership aligning with PARS in that we use our cohorts to develop a strong group identity and we encourage their agency by letting them develop their own OWI courses. We are also continually responsive to both faculty and student feedback as the OWI portion of our program grows. Further, PARS has informed how we navigated the initial Spring 2020 pandemic semester and the 2020–2021 pandemic transition year, as well as the "post"- pandemic landscape of OWI. In this chapter, we will describe the recruitment and development of OWI cohorts using

---

2. We struggled with what to call this point in our teaching, when COVID-19 outbreaks are still happening, when its death toll has surpassed one million citizens, and when our institutions are stressing "getting back to normal." We considered using *endemic*, as that's where the world is moving with this virus, but because it's not yet defined that way by the CDC, we resisted that term. We have opted for *"post" pandemic* because we feel it best represents this space in which we are still in a global pandemic, but many of our peers, students, and citizens have decided that the pandemic is a thing of the past.

community of practice scholarship, how PARS informed the emergency remote teaching (ERT) instruction of spring 2020, and the use of PARS to cultivate an OWI mindset in our writing program. Finally, we will offer WPAs suggestions for OWI recruitment and growth in their own programs.

Theory and Practice

Like many online writing program administrators (OWPAs), we both were mostly self-taught in OWI as non-tenure-track faculty members. Mitchell began OWI in 2012 after a professional development course in online teaching. Stewart began OWI in 2009 and used her doctoral studies to further develop her theoretical and practical understanding. Stewart knew that, as Borgman (2016) argues, a WPA cannot always wait for faculty to find new technologies and pedagogical approaches; she must bring these opportunities to her faculty. Most importantly, as Stewart began to develop OWI in the program, she adhered to Borgman's call that an OWPA have "an ability to create and maintain a support system for OWI faculty" (p. 195).

We believe that successful changes in a program result from consultation with the affected writing faculty; this belief is influenced by Jean Lave and Etienne Wenger's (1991) discussion of communities of practice (CoP), as a writing program is a diverse community of engaged practitioners. Additionally, most FYC courses at UTC are taught by contingent faculty, so Mahli Mechenbier's (2015) concerns about funding and time dedicated to professional development, the availability of OWI courses, and equity issues had to be considered. These practitioners are both full- and part-time faculty, and we were hesitant to ask part-time faculty to engage in this initiative for fear of exploiting them (see Babb, 2016). While teaching online may appeal to part-time faculty, departmental policy privileges assigning OWI courses to full-time faculty; the work a part-time faculty member may dedicate to developing their OWI may not translate to teaching OWI courses regularly. Selecting faculty to participate in the OWI cohorts required more consideration than just asking for interested faculty; we needed an OWI CoP with targeted recruitment. Lisa Melonçon and Lora Arduser (2013) argue that an intentionally developed CoP can encourage professional development and course enhancement while also "validating teaching as an intellectual endeavor" (p. 84). For the CoP to develop organically after the targeted recruitment of the initial cohort, the first faculty involved—who eventually become mentors and leaders in the CoP—have to see that OWI is valued and supported in the program.

Within a CoP, practitioners can function in different roles; as a WPA develops various initiatives within their program, identifying which roles are needed per initiative is key. To generate buy-in for an OWI cohort, Stewart worked to identify faculty who fulfilled Amy Jo Kim's (2000) elder role and Fred Nickols' (2000) practice leader role. For Kim, the elder is familiar with the theme–in this case OWI–and the community, while also agreeing to be consulted by other community members; Stewart's relative newness to the community required an elder participant to bring ethos to the initiative. Additionally, Nickols identifies the practice leader as someone whose leadership is defined by skill competence. In terms of OWI, Mitchell already fulfilled both the role of elder and practice leader, having been a faculty member for over ten years and having taught OWI the longest of any contingent faculty member in the department.

As we planned the first OWI cohort, our work was situated in established scholarly approaches to OWI pedagogy (see CCCC, 2011, 2013; Hewett, 2010; Warnock, 2009) that informs the PARS framework. We asked our faculty to consider the tenets of Beth Hewett and Christa Ehmann Powers (2004) and Lee-Ann Breuch (2015): investigation, immersion, individualization, association, and reflection, as well as migration, model, modality and media, and morale. We also asked them to remember that failures in early OWI endeavors happen and are an opportunity for reflection (Grover et al., 2017). Additionally, our university required all general education online courses to be Quality Matters (QM) certified through our teaching and learning center (TLC), which required faculty to take a course in online instruction using the learning management system (LMS) of the institution. While QM certification does not necessarily align well with composition's pedagogical approaches, this requirement allowed our faculty to be students in the online environment (see Cargile Cook, 2007).

In later cohorts, we used Michael Greer and Heidi Skurat Harris' (2018) emphasis on terminology; we asked faculty to consider their students as both students and users, just as we were engaging with them as both mentees and users. Stewart's interest in human-computer interaction (HCI), particularly activity theory, helped give faculty a vocabulary to discuss their OWI environments, specifically considering how the subject, tools, community, and rules influence how instructors and students engage in the OWI environment (Stewart, 2017). This perspective also connects to Jessie Borgman and Jason Dockter's (2018) call for faculty and administrators to look at OWI design from a user-centered design (UCD) perspective. As WPAs engage faculty in OWI, these connections to HCI, UCD, and PARS should be foundational in training and professional development and inform the design of the actual courses.

Pre-Pandemic OWI Cohorts

Some of the goals for the OWI initiative were to create more online and hybrid classes, encourage the use of more online writing technology, and increase faculty knowledge and use of accessibility and universal design. One of the first steps in establishing the OWI cohorts was for Stewart to get to know the faculty personally. In 2017, approximately 41 full- and part-time faculty were teaching in the composition program. This step required assessing the ability and initiative of faculty members in terms of leadership roles. Stewart accomplished this by mapping out the existing full-time faculty to identify their affinity groups (Gee, 2004) and peer groups, as well as their interconnectedness.

Stewart observed the faculty and connections, specifically focusing on professional *and* personal interactions. She attended to the following questions:

- Who sits together at workshops?
- Who subs for whom?
- Who hangs out in whose offices when walking through the hallways?
- Who socializes before and after department meetings?
- Who shares assignments/projects with whom?
- How do they treat each other in committee? At department social functions? In department meetings?
- Who has coffee, lunch, parties with whom?

Figure 3.1 represents Stewart's initial analysis of the 2017 faculty. Ultimately, she identified three major groups among the full-time faculty in her notes as

- the full-time tech strong
- those with institutional memory
- the gents, a group of male colleagues who were collegial and grouped together often with varying institutional history and technology savvy

A fourth category of technology strong part-time faculty was added to the list so that Stewart could encourage OWI among those faculty who had taught at UTC for several years or expressed an interest in OWI. As Figure 3.1 shows, there were many connections among the faculty; some had written textbooks together, some played Dungeons and Dragons together, some served as graduate tutors in others' classes, some bonded from regular attendance at the summer AP readings. Understanding the existing connections among the faculty allowed for the strategic selection of the initial cohort. With her extensive OWI experience and mentoring, Mitchell was a natural choice to serve as the practice leader and elder in the 2017 OWI cohort.

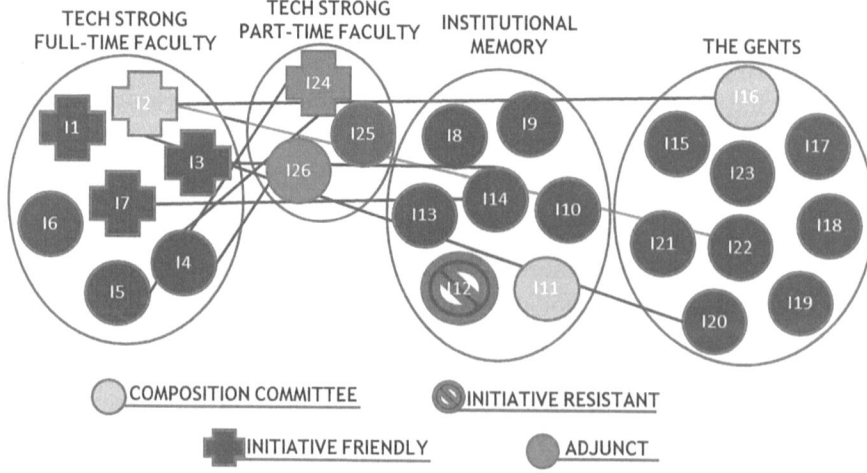

Figure 3.1. Faculty affinity groups and connections.

Championships Are Won at Practice 41

OWI training consisted of two group meetings and one-on-one mentorship. In the initial group meeting, we presented guides for faculty to rethink their classroom, emphasizing the importance of a personal presence, of being responsive, of being strategic. Because of the QM training requirements, we did not have to offer significant LMS or course organization training. QM's focus on universal design, accessibility, and usability trained faculty in these areas. After the initial group meeting, we met with cohort members to provide feedback on their course designs. A second group meeting was called, allowing faculty to share their course plans and ideas. We continued to mentor these cohort members through their first year of OWI.

Figure 3.2 shows that Stewart selected initial cohort members to represent all four peer groups among the faculty; she used the affinity and peer group mapping to strategically select these members, as they had the potential to influence the next cohort. She believed that developing smaller cohorts in consecutive years would generate more buy-in among faculty than instituting a wholesale programmatic change. Creating an OWI CoP allows OWI to grow organically among affinity/peer groups and by word-of-mouth. Figure 3.3 shows that three of the four peer groups had 2017 cohort members encourage and engage 2018 cohort members.

This gradual approach to faculty buy-in for the cohorts informed both the training sessions Stewart offered during the semesters as well as the annual workshops held before the start of each fall semester. With established cohorts, the OWI initiative was functioning and gradually increasing OWI participation and OWI technology use among faculty. By fall 2019, Stewart, an untenured WPA, let the OWI CoP naturally recruit and train two new faculty while she focused her attention on publications for tenure. AY 2019–2020 was intended to be the pause year with the intention of resuming active OWI cohort participation in fall 2020; however, when the COVID-19 pandemic began in spring 2020, all plans, goals, and intentions shifted from long-term OWI cohort planning to mental, physical, and pedagogical survival.

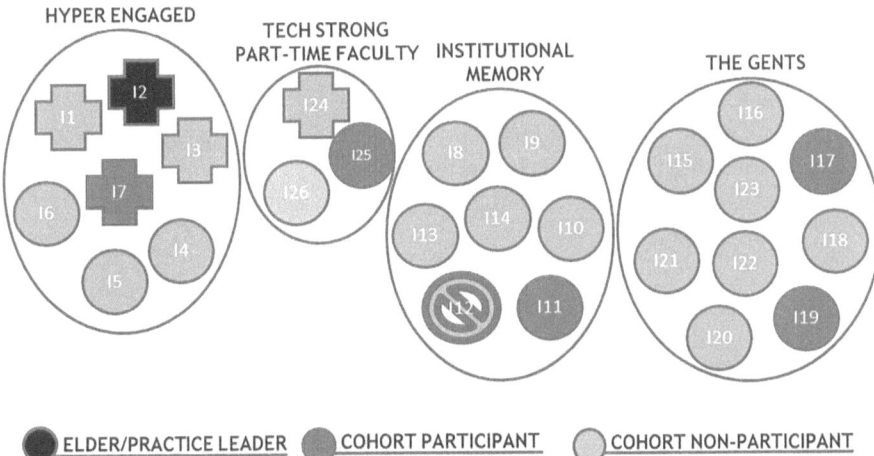

Figure 3.2. The mapped 2017 OWI cohort.

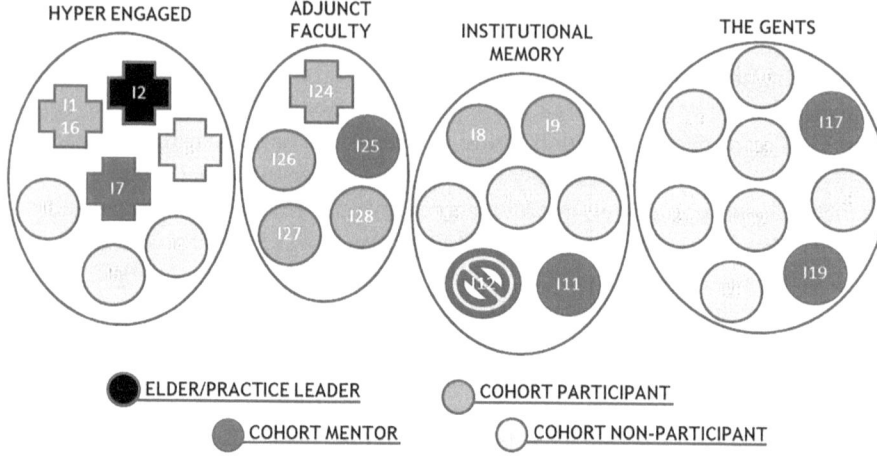

Figure 3.3. The mapped 2018 OWI cohort.

Pre-Pandemic Phase Strategies

These strategies were key to developing faculty with OWI skills who could mentor and guide their peers during the pandemic.

- Strategic recruitment of initial cohort
- Pre-instruction cohort meeting I (semester prior to OWI)
- Review of similarities and differences between OWI and F2F instruction
- Discussion of OWI course model: organization, planning, language, repetition
- One-on-one Q & A/reflection session
- Individual meetings with cohort members to review/discuss OWI plans (prior to OWI)
- Pre-instruction cohort meeting II (semester prior to OWI)
- Discussion of OWI ideas/plans
- Peer review of OWI materials/sandbox courses
- One-on-one Q & A/reflection session
- Individual meetings with cohort members to review/discuss OWI (during OWI)

Pandemic ERT

As the pandemic hit in March 2020 and UTC moved all courses online, we knew that our non-OWI faculty could not be expected to become instant OWI instructors. We were engaging in what Charles Hodges et al. (2020) term *emergency remote teaching* (ERT), and the Expectations for Online Courses Canvas announcement Stewart sent on March 12, 2020, was clear about that (see Figure 3.4).

Mitchell was serving as Stewart's AWPA that semester, and together, we met and established an action plan to help faculty navigate the increasing uncertainty, while still trying to remain professional and provide instruction to students.

During the later weeks of March 2020, WPA communication focused on simplicity and kindness. Having a well-established CoP as well as personal connections to the faculty meant that Stewart understood how best to emphasize and explain that we were shifting to ERT rather than OWI for the remainder of the Spring 2020 semester. Stewart's Canvas announcements preparing faculty for the move online asked faculty to consider students' needs and accessibility: "Take into account that some of your students may be returning to homes/situations with limited technology (they didn't sign up for online instruction either), so adjust expectations accordingly." Similarly, we asked faculty to not get overwhelmed by Canvas tools and technology but to instead consider what outcomes still needed to be met: "Before you think about tools or templates or anything technical, ask yourself some really basic questions about how the rest of your class will function. What is left to be done? How do you want to accomplish those goals?" Stewart's announcements provided practical tips for managing online instruction and, because of her presence in the CoP and knowing the faculty to be dedicated and diligent instructors, she frequently reminded them that everyone's goal was to make it through unscathed (see Figure 3.5).

> I would like to reiterate Andrew's point that we remember that this move online is a response to a pandemic, and that the situation and conditions are not ideal. As an online writing instructor and scholar, I can say with certainty that it takes many years to develop an innovative, effective online pedagogy; we do not expect this from you by March 23. But I want you to take next week to think about how your students can best achieve our course outcomes using the resources we have available with the training you do have.

Figure 3.4. Canvas announcement emphasizing the difference between ERT and OWI.

> Final Thoughts
>
> A few of you will feel compelled to do more, to build an amazing and exciting online experience for your students, to learn several new tools on Canvas. Now is not the time for this. Less is more. Simple is better. We need to help the students get to the end of term, to meet their course outcomes. Joe mentioned in his email to CAS that we need to remember that some of these students will be moving all their courses into an online environment and may struggle. Let our classes be the ones to cause them the least amount of stress and trauma during this already trying time.
>
> Please do not hesitate to reach out to me if you have questions.

Figure 3.5. Canvas announcement encouraging faculty to embrace ERT.

By reiterating the messages from the department head and dean, Stewart was both ensuring that faculty had received the messages from other administrators and reinforcing that these administrators functioned within the CoP as well. These messages from dean to department head to WPA created consistency and comfort during a time in which those traits were greatly needed.

Creating this transitional content tested the bounds of the personal connections and the OWI CoP Stewart had been cultivating. Knowing which faculty would be the most comfortable *or* the least comfortable with the sudden change was informed by the established OWI cohorts and our personal connections. Because the cohorts had increased the program's OWI sections, as well as the overall number of faculty who were more versed in OWI and OWI technologies, developing tailored resources for less than half of the faculty was more manageable than doing so for most or nearly all of the faculty.

In our initial meetings, we discussed two main approaches: (1) leveled content and (2) mentoring. These approaches were informed by the existing OWI cohorts, knowledge gained via the cohort initiatives, and resources the faculty would need based on how they aligned in the cohorts. We first took steps to develop and organize an online move page within the program's LMS (see Figure 3.6).

Knowing that faculty would need different types of help depending on their skills and comfort with ERT, we established three levels of experience with which to organize the information we offered: Level 1: Novice, Level 2: Intermediate, and Level 3: Experienced. These levels were defined to help faculty better self-identify (see Figure 3.7).

Because we had spent time deliberating which tools and resources faculty would need in preparation for the OWI cohorts, we were able to more quickly identify which LMS tools users needed. We felt confident in our assessment of which faculty needed which level of engagement; however, it was important to allow self-selection based on the descriptions to offer agency in a time in which many of us felt we had little to no agency.

Although we had the levels set up, we made all content for the different levels accessible to all, so that if a Level 1 felt they needed more advanced knowledge or if a Level 3 needed a refresher, they could access the content that met their needs at any point.

Regardless of faculty comfort level with OWI, we understood that everyone was feeling varied degrees of stress given the challenges of an abrupt move to ERT. Acknowledging these stressors, we knew it was important to rely on OWI practice leaders as mentors for the OWI nervous/averse faculty and to make these practice leaders known to all the faculty. One way we established this mentoring was via frequent communications. When she began as WPA, Stewart sent weekly "Notes from Jenn" Canvas announcements to the composition faculty. As our campus shifted to ERT, Notes from Jenn helped to assuage fears, keep focus, share tips and tools, reaffirm the practice leaders, and encourage realistic expectations.

> Online Move Page
>
> This is the main page that will guide you through our move to online instruction. It will be divided into two sections:
>
> 1. Online Writing Instruction Tips
> 2. Tools and Resources
> 3. Screencasts
>
> Introduction to Online:
>
> We've set up help pages based on your current level of comfort with using Canvas. On each of the pages, you will find links labeled with levels to help you adjust to moving your course online. To better guide you through simple online instruction, we think it's best for you to consider what level user you identify as and material will be organized that way.

Figure 3.6. Main online move page content in Canvas.

> Level 1: You have little or no experience with Canvas beyond the shell that was created and the required syllabus submission. You manage most of your course outside of Canvas or in your own manner (a hard copy grade book, your own personal Excel file, etc.)
>
> Level 2: You have limited experience with Canvas. Perhaps you have posted assignments, you have created a discussion board, you can enter grades in Grade book.
>
> Level 3: You have some experience with Canvas. You have many/most assignments of different varieties on Canvas, but you need help making this process easier, more simplified since everything is now on Canvas.

Figure 3.7. Description of experience levels to help faculty self-select.

Reconciling what was possible during ERT meant that attention to accessibility was sometimes less diligent. We frequently reminded faculty to ensure students could engage with course material and provide alternatives for students who had accessibility issues. We also emphasized that ERT was triage teaching that acknowledged and adhered to accessibility as much as possible while recognizing that in many ways accessibility was being redefined. By focusing on surviving and meeting basic course outcomes, triaging the rest of the Spring 2020 semester helped adjust faculty and student expectations.

For many, accessibility during ERT, when students were abruptly sent back home and displaced from the campus, meant considering the material constraints students may have with technology and internet access. These concerns were further exacerbated in April 2020 when an EF3 tornado hit our community. Students who had been sent home were then doubly impacted by loss of power or much worse; both accessibility and the focus on what "barriers to learning" meant were redefined. At that point, the hierarchy of needs became more prominent during the last weeks of the Spring term.

By using our OWI CoP knowledge and reviewing our OWI cohort maps, we were able to provide appropriate, comfortable paths for the faculty to navigate the impending upheaval to the Spring 2020 semester. We considered the fundamental elements of remote teaching: organizing course material, communicating with students, generating student activities, and assigning and grading material. Each of the three levels was broken down into these four elements to allow faculty to find the help they were seeking quickly and efficiently. We selected Canvas resources based on what we expected faculty who were new to online teaching would need to understand. We included content on the most basic organizational structure in Canvas to the more technologically complex, such as Canvas grading and conferencing.

On our Tools and Resources page, we provided links to resources according to these levels so faculty could more quickly find their materials. Level 1 had the least amount of content and mostly presented overviews of Canvas' basic tools, such as modules, announcements, discussions, assignments, and gradebook. Level 2 offered content on intermediate Canvas navigation, such as adding an announcement; creating and assigning peer review assignments; creating, editing, and deleting discussions; entering and editing grades; and copying assignments to another section. Level 3, which was the most extensive, offered content on more complex Canvas operations, such as managing and customizing the course home page; organizing, locking, and adding items directly to modules; scheduling announcements; creating rubrics; setting up conferences; and accessing and using Speedgrader. The levels, and tools/resources offered within, were designed to be gradual steps suited to faculty's skills. We knew that this would be a crash course for many, so we frequently considered our early OWI instruction and asked ourselves, "What do they need to know how to do immediately to get through this semester?" We felt confident these levels and elements would get them through.

Beyond collecting and posting resources for LMS navigation, we sought other resources for the faculty. Stewart contacted our textbook provider to request temporary online access to the textbook and disseminated that information to faculty. We encouraged faculty members to send OWI tips, tools, and resources to us, which Stewart then shared via Notes from Jenn. Also, we shared links and content about our campus' resources, such as technology requests for students and faculty and online access and consultation requests for our writing and communication center and library studio.

Throughout this time, we were using OWI to model OWI practices, as faculty in the Canvas Composition Faculty organizational page function as students in the environment. For instance, on the cusp of moving fully online, Mitchell was setting up common reader book clubs to prepare faculty for the next academic year (see Stewart & Andrews, 2020). The book clubs shifted to recorded sessions with open discussion boards. Also, Stewart created and shared a screencast video about how to screencast, using a Canvas tool to offer training on a Canvas tool. She incorporated online teaching tips into nearly every Notes from Jenn for the rest of the semester. As the Spring 2020 semester slowly ended and the pandemic showed no signs of waning, Stewart's notes also began to include looking ahead content to prepare us for what the next academic year might look like.

ERT Phase

The ERT Phase of this initiative used several PARS principles. We of course hope that there isn't another need for ERT in our future, but these ERT strategies could be useful for programs that have a need for rapid OWI growth.

Personal
Provide one-on-one mentorship.
Pair faculty in similar affinity groups.

Accessible
Take advantage of TLC or LMS accessibility features, if available.
Ensure faculty know that sometimes maintaining overrules accessibility.

Responsive
Articulate clearly mentorship availability and modality.
Provide a variety of tools and levels to help faculty respond to most emergent situations.

Strategic
Send pre-instruction directions via email.
Highlight triage/focus on outcomes.
Have faculty self-identify levels.

"Post" Pandemic

Knowing that the pandemic would still affect AY 2020–2021 and that multiple OWI modalities existed for Fall 2020, Stewart began to encourage faculty to consider moving from an ERT mindset to developing their OWI skills as they returned for the fall semester. Once again, the training and development that occurred in the initial OWI cohorts prepared us to face these changes. The university offered faculty the option of teaching F2F rotating, in which students attended classes in pods to maintain social distancing, and online synchronous and asynchronous modalities. Within the composition program, approximately 48 percent of FYC classes were offered on a F2F rotating schedule, 18 percent synchronously online, and 37 percent asynchronously online. To prepare the faculty for this non-ERT term, Stewart continued the mentoring and customized guidance she'd employed since the start of the pandemic. Mitchell remained a practice leader and elder and often served as a sounding board for Stewart to talk through plans for those new to non-ERT OWI in Fall 2020. Together, we continued offering expanded guidance and modeling OWI best practices for the faculty.

While it was important to give faculty time to rest and recover from the Spring 2020 term, resituating their mindset for OWI meant asking faculty to think about their classes before their nine-month contracts began on August 1. In July of 2020, Stewart sent some of her earliest Notes from Jenn, which included resources for teaching OWI, such as a link to Borgman and McArdle's (2019) *Personal, Accessible, Responsive, Strategic: Resources and Strategies for Online Writing Instructors*, and other resources that both faculty and students might need to navigate the OWI-heavy semester ahead. Stewart reminded faculty of the electronic access to the textbook and continued suggesting best practices and tips for the start of a new semester of OWI, such as sending welcome emails and remaining responsive. Stewart included tips for F2F instruction since its rotating schedule modality and greatly reduced classroom capacities affected instruction.

In the pre-Fall 2020 professional development workshops, we used a combination of asynchronous content and synchronous videoconferencing sessions. Modeling OWI best practices, Stewart asynchronously posted a fall introduction video, new information, library content, and tutorial content so people could consume it at their own pace but made all group interaction synchronous so content could be discussed and questions could be addressed in real time. Several breakout sessions addressed further adjustment to OWI. We, along with two other practice leaders, co-led the synchronous OWI sessions. Practice leaders also offered their availability for questions and meetings beyond the workshops. We held synchronous sessions in Kaltura Classroom, a videoconferencing tool our TLC encouraged as an alternative to the bogged down Zoom. The 40-faculty Kaltura sessions were buggy and problematic, at best. These Kaltura problems afforded us the opportunity to discuss managing technical bugs when teaching synchronously. After the workshops, Stewart sent an announcement recapping content and tips shared during the workshops to ensure everyone was as prepared as possible to face OWI and rotating F2F instruction.

In that semester, Mitchell set up OWI coaching sessions for the faculty on using various technology tools to conduct peer review online. These coaching sessions, as well as the common reader book clubs, were all held synchronously via Zoom. Within just one year, we were learning what worked best and adjusting our methods, continuously being responsive to the needs of faculty and program; in Spring 2020 ERT, it was more practical to provide links and asynchronous, recorded information. By the Spring 2021 term, despite its challenges, faculty engaged with and responded better to synchronously distributed information. Just as we had shifted from ERT to increased comfort with OWI, we are now shifting from mostly fundamental OWI training to more in-depth and tailored OWI training.

Conclusion and Takeaways

From 2017 to 2022, our program has gone from nine percent OWI instruction in second-semester FYC only to almost half of the entire program of FYC1, FYC1 with tutorial, and FYC2 engaged in OWI. More pointedly, instruction in AY 2021–2022 increased OWI ten percent in FYC1, 47 percent in FYC1 with tutorial, and three percent in FYC2, compared to AY 2019–2020. Our faculty are now comfortable keeping some OWI features in their F2F classrooms and requesting more hybrid/online sections. Since the pandemic, upper administrators required that we move our fully online sections course caps from 15 to 20 so that they match the existing hybrid and F2F modality course caps. Though Stewart and the English department head tried to argue for the online classes to remain lower, citing the Conference on College Composition and Communication's OWI Position Statement (2013), upper administration demanded that FYC courses have the same class size. This change in course caps also moved several fully online faculty into hybrid instruction. As we move further into "post"-pandemic instruction, Stewart will encourage faculty who've not taken QM training to do so to pay greater attention to their accessibility and course organization. Future fall workshops will include more attention to OWI pedagogical approaches, and a PARS book club is planned for fall 2022 to help faculty be more conscientious about the OWI methods they've kept from their ERT and pandemic OWI semesters.

What began as a programmatic initiative to develop more instructional modalities inadvertently prepared a portion of our faculty for ERT and slightly lessened the mental and emotional load they carried in spring 2020. We believe this moment of kismet for our program can provide some takeaways for WPAs as they maneuver their own OWI programmatic growth or change. If WPAs accept the premise that a writing program is an ever-evolving community of practice, initiatives of any sort require that the WPA know the members of their community, their skills, their interests, and their interconnectedness. As we reflect on the OWI cohort initiative, we have identified a few suggestions for WPAs as they enter and/or observe their own CoPs.

While the suggestions here are specific to our OWI initiative, some of these suggestions can apply to *any* initiative. Stewart uses models similar to those in Figures 3.1 to 3.3 to generate faculty buy-in in the various concurrent initiatives existing within the composition program. This mapping method supported six major initiatives in Stewart's first six years as WPA: the OWI initiative, a peer review feedback and revision initiative, a program revision and assessment initiative, a textbook initiative, an information cycle research initiative, and a diversity-themed common reader initiative. There is no way Stewart could manage so many simultaneous initiatives on her own; the diverse skills and interests of the composition program CoP allowed her to engage elders and practice leaders in the various initiatives, so no one faculty member was carrying the load for any initiative.

Learn your faculty. Personally knowing who the faculty were, who the practice leaders and elders were, who would be receptive to OWI and new teaching tech tools, who would be resistant to change, and how to respond to their needs was probably the most beneficial information that helped us navigate both the initial OWI cohorts and especially the ERT management of guidance and resources.

As other initiatives were developed within the composition program, Stewart could enlist different members of the CoP to facilitate cohorts with different foci. It should be noted that because the UTC composition program has over 20 full-time non-tenure-track faculty in its CoP, Stewart can manage multiple initiatives concurrently with different elders and practice leaders.

Always ask "What's next?" As a *West Wing* fan, Stewart keeps the words of President Bartlett in her mind always: "What's next?" Stewart's CoP-informed approach helps leverage the knowledge of the faculty to move toward programmatic change.

Identifying key players to participate in initiatives and to foster interest among new faculty in the initiatives is key to a long game strategy. In this chapter, we discussed how the faculty who participated in the 2017 OWI cohort created the 2018 cohort. These same 2017 OWI faculty served as the 2018 peer review cohort; the success of their interest in that initiative generated peer participation in the 2019 peer review cohort. As the seeds of one initiative begin to grow and bloom, Stewart is moving on to planting the seeds of the next initiative. A WPA who is continually reviewing and supporting their faculty's pedagogies and developing those faculty's skills and engagement in trends and shifts in the field of rhetoric and composition is one whose program is in a constant state of development and growth. That said, a "what's next" mindset doesn't mean continual, rapid growth, as that's unsustainable and can lead to burnout; reflecting on initiatives and assessing their effectiveness maintains long-term growth at a reasonable pace.

As we begin to ask what's next for our program, we see our OWI developing in both quality and size. We would like to help those faculty who have come to OWI via ERT review and assess their OWI practices via the PARS framework. ERT and "post"-pandemic instruction have been attentive to the personal, responsive, and strategic elements, but we can see a need for growth and revision in accessibility. Additionally, as we consider the findings of *The 2021 State of the Art of OWI Report* (CCCC, 2021), we also are considering offering more OWI pedagogical training sessions not connected with our LMS and offering compensation for these sessions, as OWI training is often unfunded.

Within a year of being hired and assessing the CoP that was the UTC composition program, Stewart said she would like to see the program offer 50 percent of its courses F2F, 25 percent hybrid, and 25 percent fully online. This statement was mostly grounded in the hesitance some faculty had toward OWI and technology specifically. However, the spring 2020 ERT threw many faculty into the OWI deep end and forced them to learn to stay afloat; the AY 2020–2021 OWI helped them transition from survival floating to developing a rudimentary stroke and direction by the end of the Spring 2022 semester. After continuing to talk to faculty about their ERT and "post"-pandemic OWI experiences, Stewart feels it's more fitting to aim for 40 percent F2F, 40 percent hybrid, and 20 percent fully online, as many faculty appreciate the balance that hybrid instruction affords over both F2F and fully online instruction. Regardless of how quickly we reach these modality percentage goals, our experiences with the OWI cohorts, ERT, and "post"-pandemic OWI have prepared us to face virtually any challenge and not only survive but grow into wiser, more skilled instructors and program administrators.

References

Babb, J. (2016). Reshaping institutional mission: OWI and writing program administration. In E. A. Monske & K. L. Blair (Eds.), *Handbook of research on writing and composing in the age of MOOCs* (pp. 202–215). IGI Global.

Borgman, J. (2016). The online writing program administrator (OWPA): Maintaining a brand in the age of MOOCS. In E. A. Monske & K. L. Blair (Eds.), *Writing and composing in the age of MOOCS* (pp. 188–201). IGI Global.

Borgman, J. & Dockter, J. (2018). Considerations of access and design in the online writing classroom. *Computers & Composition, 49*, 94–105.

Borgman, J. & McArdle, C. (2019). *Personal, accessible, responsive, strategic: Resources and strategies for online writing instructors.* The WAC Clearinghouse; University Press of Colorado. https://doi.org/10.37514/PRA-B.2019.0322.

Borgman, J. & McArdle, C. (Eds.). (2021). *PARS in practice: More resources and strategies for online writing instructors.* The WAC Clearinghouse; University Press of Colorado. https://doi.org/10.37514/PRA-B.2021.1145.

Breuch, L. K. (2015). Faculty preparation for OWI. In B. L. Hewett & K. E. DePew (Eds.), *Foundational practices of online writing instruction* (pp. 349–388). The WAC Clearinghouse; Parlor Press. https://doi.org/10.37514/PER-B.2015.0650.2.11.

Cargile Cook, K. (2007). Immersion in a digital pool: Training prospective online instructors in online environments. *Technical Communication Quarterly, 16*(1), 55–82.

CCCC Online Writing Instruction Standing Group. (2021). *The 2021 state of the art of OWI report.* Conference on College Composition and Communication. https://cccc.ncte.org/cccc/2021-state-of-the-art-of-online-writing-instruction/.

Conference on College Composition and Communication Committee for Best Practices in Online Writing Instruction. (2011). *Report of the state of the art of OWI.* https://www.owicommunity.org/owi--distance-education-resources.html.

Conference on College Composition and Communication Committee for Best Practices in Online Writing Instruction. (2013). *A position statement of principles and example effective practices for online writing instruction (OWI).* National Council of Teachers of English. http://www.ncte.org/cccc/resources/positions/owi principles.

Gee, J. P. (2004). *Situated language and learning: A critique of traditional schooling.* Routledge.

Greer, M. & Skurat Harris, H. (2018). User-centered design as a foundation for effective online writing instruction. *Computers and Composition, 49*, 14–24.

Grover, S. D., Cargile Cook, K., Skurat Harris, H. & DePew, K. E. (2017). Immersion, reflection, failure: Teaching graduate students to teach writing online. *Technical Communication Quarterly, 26*(3), 242–255. https://doi.org/10.1080/10572252.2017.1339524.

Hewett, B. (2010). *The online writing conference: A guide for teachers and tutors.* Heinemann.

Hewett, B. L. & Ehmann Powers, C. (2004). *Preparing educators for online writing instruction.* National Council of Teachers of English.

Hilliard, L. (2021). Using PARS to build a community of practice for hybrid writing instructors. In J. Borgman & C. McArdle (Eds.), *PARS in practice: More resources and strategies for online writing instructors.* The WAC Clearinghouse; University Press of Colorado. https://doi.org/10.37514/PRA-B.2021.1145.

Hodges, C., Moore, S., Lockee, B., Trust, T. & Bond, A. (2020, March 27). The difference between emergency remote teaching and online learning. *Educause Review.* https://er.educause.edu/articles/2020/3/the-difference-between-emergency-remote-teaching-and-online-learning.

Kim, A. (2000). *Community building on the web.* Peachpit Press.

Lave, J. & Wenger, E. (1991). *Situated learning: Legitimate peripheral participation.* Cambridge University.

Mechenbier, M. (2015). Contingent faculty and OWI. In B. L. Hewett & K. E. DePew (Eds.), *Foundational practices of online writing instruction* (pp. 227–249). The WAC Clearinghouse; Parlor Press. https://doi.org/10.37514/PER-B.2015.0650.

Melonçon, L. & Arduser, L. (2013). Communities of practice approach: A new model for online course development and sustainability. In K. Cargile Cook & K. Grant-Davie (Eds.), *Online education 2.0: Evolving, adapting and reinventing online technical communication* (pp. 73–90). Baywood Publishing Company.

Nickols, F. (2000). *Community of practice start up kit.* The Distance Consulting Company. https://www.nickols.us/CoPs.htm.

Stewart, J. (2017). Introduction discussion forums in online writing courses are essential. No, really. They are. In E. A. Monske & K. L. Blair (Eds.), *Writing and composing in the age of MOOCs.* (pp.294–316). IGI Global.

Stewart, J. & Andrews, H. (2020). Reading and writing diversity: Scaffolding and assessing a common reader initiative at University of Tennessee at Chattanooga's writing program. *Composition Forum, 43.* http://compositionforum.com/issue/43/utc.php.

Warnock, S. (2009). *Teaching writing online: How & why.* National Council of Teachers of English.

Set Your Stance!

All golfers have an identity and specific traits, movements, and idiosyncrasies that make them unique. Every golfer approaches the course and each hole on the course differently. These characteristics shape a golfer's identity. They are always present, and they often show up in a golfer's stance and approach to the tee box.

Just as golfers have identities, writing leaders also have their own identities that have been shaped by their prior experiences. Additionally, every writing program crafts its own identity through the leadership of the program administrator.

We really like that Andrew Hollinger's chapter asks readers to think about crafting their identity and to think about "anchoring" their practice in specific ideas, moves, and practices that make them unique. We love this concept of anchoring one's program. Given the complexities of the last few years and the myriad of possibilities for modalities, we see the value in thinking about how to cultivate and keep a programmatic cohesion.

Chapter 4. Designing Anchor Points

Andrew Hollinger
University of Texas Rio Grande Valley

Abstract: Writing programs that offer a range of instructional modalities (such as online synchronous, online asynchronous, face-to-face [F2F], and hybrid) can find it difficult to maintain programmatic identity and instructional or course comparability across modalities. Part of the difficulty is that each delivery modality has specific material and pedagogical requirements for success. That is, an online asynchronous course must look, feel, and act differently than the F2F iteration of the course—which also means the online version cannot be simply the digital version of the F2F course. How, then, does a writing program develop and maintain itself as a "program" amidst so many material entanglements? In this chapter, I present anchor points as a pedagogical and administrative PARS-based approach to developing cohesion between instructional modalities.

Keywords: anchor points, writing program administration, curriculum design, first-year writing, equity, instructional modalities, programmatic cohesion

"We're all online writing instructors," say Jessie Borgman and Casey McArdle (2019, p. 3).

Pre-2020: OK, sure. It makes sense. Between the various technologies students use to write and read, the hardware and software we incorporate into our teaching, acknowledging the hybrid ways face-to-face (F2F) instruction uses learning management systems (LMSs) or OneDrive/Google Drive/the cloud, yes, we're all online writing instructors. Maybe I don't *exactly* do my lecturing and instruction online, but I get it, yes.

Post-2020: Ain't that the truth.

This chapter is not about the COVID-19 pandemic. It's about developing curricular and programmatic cohesion between face-to-face (F2F) and online instructional modalities. But it's also uncritical (at least) or disingenuous (at worst) to pretend that online instruction in 2023 and beyond is not informed by the sudden and nearly ubiquitous shift to online learning in 2020. Moving forward, however, we are no longer subject to "emergency remote instruction" and need to ensure that the lessons from the last three years *and* the previous decades of online writing instruction (OWI) research are applied. This chapter is about using anchor points—designed instances of commonality across program elements such as content, assignments, texts, and experiences to develop programmatic cohesion between instructional modalities. To establish our own parity across our writing program, we developed the following:

- *anchor concepts*, the philosophical and pedagogical foundations we build curriculum from;
- *anchor practices*, the skills and habits students should engage with throughout the course sequence; and
- *anchor texts*, common texts that all sections of a course will include as part of instruction.

These anchor points (concepts, practices, texts) are part of a larger practice of our developing courses that are personal, accessible, responsive, and strategic (PARS). Throughout this chapter, I will discuss the anchor concepts, practices, and texts that our writing program developed; the process for creating and shaping anchor points; and the connections between anchor points and PARS. I will also argue that the use of anchor points is a progressive and equitable pedagogical practice that is particularly effective at attuning large writing programs (or, really, any program, department, or unit) to the needs of their students, faculty, and discipline.

Institutional Context

For example, at my institution (where we have a two-course first-year writing [FYW] sequence), pre–2020 we generally offered two fully online asynchronous sections of 1301 (course one) and two to four fully online asynchronous sections of 1302 (course two). These courses were taught by instructors who had robust training in online instruction, including (but not limited to) the writing program's professional development for online instructors, our institution's learning management system (LMS) training, and Quality Matters (QM) certification. So, that's four to six online sections (out of 165!) each semester taught by instructors who had participated in significant professional development for online instruction.

Our pre–2020 goal was to deliberately and methodically develop a path toward online instruction for faculty while also determining the threshold at which adding online sections increased overall 1301/1302 enrollment. That is, we learned that adding online sections increases overall enrollment for the writing program, but only up to a point. There is a threshold at which adding online courses decreases F2F, and thus overall, enrollment. Slow progress was perfectly acceptable. We didn't have a large demand for online courses during the regular semesters. Students showed more interest in online instructional options during the summer (perhaps because it allowed them more possibility to work or travel), and we provided both asynchronous and synchronous online instruction during the two summer sessions.

The COVID-19 pandemic dramatically altered the course of our designed and programmatic approach to developing online writing instruction. We went from four to six online sections per semester to 165 online sections (about 40% asynchronous and 60% synchronous) per semester through Spring/Summer 2021. In the Fall 2021 semester, we began reintroducing hybrid courses (courses that are 15%–85% online, F2F for the remaining portion). We had a few fully F2F courses but were still largely online. In the Spring 2022 term, our institution began returning to pre-pandemic scheduling and modality. But it really didn't. The writing program offered in Spring 2022 more online sections and more hybrid sections than we ever had before. And the scheduling for Fall 2022 showed that our online offerings, instead of creeping toward our enrollment threshold, are right at the point where we maximize overall enrollment.

More than that, to revise Borgman and McArdle (2019), we're *all* online writing instructors *now*. Pre-pandemic, we had a few instructors with online teaching experience. Today, everyone has 18–24 months of online teaching experience. Not everyone has completed our online training professional development, of course. But we've all got experience with LMS environments, online feedback, virtual lessons, technical difficulties, and the strangeness of student retention that is somehow different online than in person. Instead of the delicate piloting of new ideas or strategies, most of our instructors had to learn by doing, which is equal parts thrilling and terrifying. On one hand, having/not having professional development in online writing instruction might be the difference between having *experience* with online writing instruction and *being* an online writing instructor. On the other hand, the experience of teaching online is incredibly valuable to honing one's skills as an online writing instructor. For example, we also have much more data, post-emergency remote instruction, than we otherwise would have. At our institution, for instance, online synchronous courses have a better pass rate and better student retention than online asynchronous courses; and the second course in our FYW course sequence has better passing and retention numbers than the first course. The result is that we have an entire faculty increasingly equipped to teach online, and we have more opportunities for online instruction than we would have had following our original plan. Following the data, we schedule more synchronous online sections than we do asynchronous sections, though we continue to work on increasing our asynchronous pass/retention rates. Online writing instruction is here to stay (at our institution, but also, just generally as a desired and increasingly less stigmatized instructional modality).

I don't think it's an unfair observation, however, that *even though* we had, from our previous piloting, several developed course shells, examples of activities and tasks, guidance on creating rapport, and suggestions for framing the content and projects for online learning, the primary objective for most instructors during the last three years was to survive physically, mentally, and emotionally. How do we take the experiences of the last three years and the growth and development plan from before the pandemic and re-establish a programmatic approach toward online instruction? And, also, why bother?

Theory and Practice
Arguing for Anchor Points

I'm the quasi-writing program administrator (qWPA; Hollinger & Borgman, 2020) for a large writing program, serving 3,500–4,000 students each semester in 155–170 sections. Our goal is to be a writing *program*, identifiable by a shared mission and vision, pedagogical philosophy, and curricular foundation (as opposed to a collection of classes that all just happen to be called "ENGL 1301" and "ENGL 1302"). I'm not interested in deploying identical courses across 155–170 sections. That doesn't make use of the individual skills, talents, and interests of our more than 30 full-time lecturers or the handful of part-time lecturers and teaching assistants (TAs) we hire each year. However, I think it's important for a writing program, in order to be a cohesive program, to provide comparable experiences for students across a designed and purposeful curriculum. Comparable experiences might also be framed as "accessible" curriculum. Of course, online and F2F learning spaces need to be accessible in terms of usability, support, and the Americans with Disabilities Act (ADA). But, all 165 sections of ENGL 1301 should also provide equitable and comparable access to the content, knowledge, and skills of the class being taught. We could call this programmatic accessibility. When a program offers both F2F and online versions of the same courses, ensuring curricular cohesion and programmatic accessibility simultaneously becomes more important and more difficult.

Borgman and McArdle (2019) point out that "it is difficult to shift F2F instruction to a digital space" (p. 11), a commonplace now well established as part of the lived experiences of all those who taught through the pandemic. More to the point, however, is that different modalities have different affordances and capacities, and entangle students, instructors, and content in differing and particular ways. In "(Re)turning to Hypertext: Mattering Digital Learning Spaces," Manuel Piña (2023) argues that material conditions of online (or any, really) learning spaces *matter*, both metaphorically and literally. Everything from the chair the student is using to their computer or device to whether they're using wireless headphones changes how a student engages with the course material. We can't necessarily design the student's space, but we can design *for* the student's space. Heidi Skurat Harris and Michael Greer (2016) affirm that "to teach writing online is to design an environment" (p. 46). I'd argue that to teach at all is to design an environment, but their point obtains: What's important is that each environment is responsive to the material conditions in which it exists. F2F classes exist in different ways than online classes. And online asynchronous classes exist in different ways than online synchronous classes. Curriculum design, then, is not a one-size-fits-all endeavor; courses must be intentionally designed for F2F, online, or hybrid entangled encounters. Each modality needs instructional approaches and support specific to its material conditions. At a programmatic scale, maintaining alignment between modalities can become tricky.

The solution for designing curriculum and courses flexible enough to adapt to varying modalities while also providing programmatic accessibility and cohesion is *anchor points, designed points of commonality shared between diverse iterations of comparable courses.* Anchor points can be any combination of texts, concepts, experiences, tasks, activities, and assignments that exist across all sections of a course. For example, an anchor experience might be attending a special lecture sponsored by the university or participating in service learning. Although our courses do have anchor experiences, we primarily design around anchor concepts, anchor practices, and anchor texts. Anchor concepts are the large/umbrella ideas that inform our course content and pedagogy. These are ideas that every student who comes through the writing program should engage and grapple with by the end of our FYW course sequence—that is, things we want our students to know. Anchor practices and skills are those things we want our students to be able to do at the end of our course sequence. Anchor texts are common and foundational texts that all sections of ENGL 1301 or ENGL 1302 must include (instructors can add texts to their courses; the anchor texts are simply designed moments of parity).

Anchor points allow instructors to remain personal/personable (the *P* in PARS) in their instruction and approach while also allowing the writing program to be accessible and strategic (the *A* and *S* in PARS) about curriculum and institutional positionality. Whatever instructive path an instructor might take—whether service learning, project-based, thematic, cooperative learning focus, small tasks, large tasks, writing in the disciplines, writing for your life, writing about writing (and so on)—there are a few first-year writing common *places* (it's not a golf pun but the wordplay between *common place* and *commonplace* is nice, no?) all students will pause and consider. In addition to developing programmatic identity and cohesion, designing anchor points allows us to identify sites of equity, sites of practice, and sites of engagement that all students and instructors will encounter—which has also been an important element of our developing pedagogy that focuses on languaging and antiracist practices.

What does this mean for designing online instruction?

There is curricular parity between F2F and online instruction. Even if the course narrative or instructor's path is different, students across 150+ sections have moments of similarity.

Following backward design/understanding by design, anchor points make developing assignments and projects easier and better scaffolded.

Students are engaging with designed experiences.

Instructors can move between F2F and online courses more easily.

An important consequence of this process is that, as a program (which includes full-time three-year and one-year lecturers, tenure/track rhet-comp profs, TAs, the writing center, even the library), we are constantly talking about what our first-year writing program should be about. What do we want to teach? What do we want our students to walk away with? Designing anchor points results in a highly reflective cohort of instructors learning from each other, challenging each other, and collaborating about the direction and future of the writing program. Rhonda Thomas et al. (2021) argue that "the department chair and the WPA need to regularly talk with instructors about important values, such as student success, not just talk at faculty about the basic requirements for their online classes" (p. 200), and that's what designing anchor points does for a writing program. To be clear, anchor points (whether concepts, texts, practices, or experiences) are not merely "basic requirements." It's more productive to think about anchor points as the pedagogical philosophy and foundation of the program, the stuff from which we design and develop assignments, lessons, and assessments.

Mid-chapter takeaways and anchor points' connections to PARS are shown in the following Table 4.1.

Table 4.1 **PARS and Anchor Points**

Personal	Accessible	Responsive	Strategic
Instructors retain creative autonomy. Identical courses and materials are not required.	Sections are comparable in content and scope.	Programmatic mission, curriculum, etc. is reflective and progressive	Program positionality is designed and articulable.

Developing Anchor Points

Because anchor points are so specific to a writing program's context and goals, a universal step-by-step guide is impractical (perhaps impossible). But throughout this section, you'll find practices and a heuristic that will be helpful for any program or faculty group interested in developing a set of anchor points. Looking at examples of anchor points should also be helpful. The following anchor concepts, practices, and texts are iterations of our own anchor point development (see Table 4.2).

There are a few important things to notice here. These concepts and skills begin in 1301 and continue through 1302 (our two-course FYW sequence), and that's why we note "by the end of ENGL 1302, students should . . ." It's possible to articulate specific knowledge and skills as anchor points for individual courses in a sequence, but we've opted not to do that. For us, these concepts and practices are additive, and we want them to be part of all our writing courses.[1]

---

1. For what it's worth, our first course, 1301, could be called "Writing Studies," where students confront assumptions about what writing and composition *is*, and what "good" writing is, how composition works, the creative/writing process, and writing inquiry. Our second course, 1302, could be called "Research Studies," and, building from 1301, asks

Table 4.2 Anchor Points and Anchor Concepts

Anchor Concepts	Anchor Practices
By the end of ENGL 1302, students should (at least) know . . .	By the end of ENGL 1302, students should be able (at least) to . . .
Writing/reading/literacy are activities and subjects of study	Revise a project through several drafts + incorporate feedback into a revision plan
Writing/literacy are social and rhetorical activities	Give effective feedback
Writing speaks to situations through recognizable forms	Develop inquiry from experiences, texts, etc. (primarily 1301)
Writing/literacy enacts and creates identities and ideologies	Develop research question(s) (primarily 1302)
All writers have more to learn	Synthesize multiple sources/perspectives
Writing/reading/learning are processes	Evaluate sources and evidence
"Good" writing depends on the expectations of the discourse community/audience	Incorporate and appropriately attribute source material and evidence
Writing involves making choices about language	Articulate the purpose, form, and audience of their own texts and the texts of others
Rhetorical ecologies are robust, entangled networks of human and nonhuman rhetorical agents	Make sophisticated languaging choices
	Articulate their rhetorical composing choices
All writing is multimodal	Discuss their learning and how their emerging knowledge and skills transfer to other contexts, areas, ecologies, and communities

Also, these concepts and practices are (or are very close to) writing studies threshold concepts, many of which were described in Linda Adler-Kassner and Elizabeth Wardle's (2016) *Naming What We Know: Threshold Concepts of Writing Studies*. We didn't set out to develop our anchor concepts alongside threshold concepts, but it makes sense that we ended up there. Threshold concepts comprise the difficult-to-understand but critical-to-know knowledge in a discipline. If we treat composition and rhetoric as an introduction to the discipline, then the concepts and practices we articulate as foundational are likely to sound like threshold concepts. Finally, anchor points, framed as concepts and practices, might look a bit like student (or course) learning objectives (SLOs), but they're not. Take, for example, our SLOs at the time we developed our anchor points (this is directly from the university-required syllabus language; see Table 4.3).

---

students to engage with research practices, developing lines of inquiry, informational literacy, and so on.

Table 4.3 WP Student Learning Outcomes

WP Student Learning Outcomes
The following statements describe what we want our students to know, think, value, and do when they finish the First-Year Writing Program and successfully complete 1302 with a C or better. • Students use the writing process to compose with purpose, creating multimodal texts for various audiences. • Students productively interact with their peers, often in small groups, in the reiterative processes of feedback, revision, and editing. • Students think critically about their position in the context of a larger ongoing conversation about the issues they are investigating. • Students find, evaluate, meaningfully integrate, and correctly document appropriate sources for research. • Students are aware of the choices writers make and gain confidence in their ability to employ that awareness for a variety of future writing tasks.

These were our SLOs when we first developed our anchor points (in spring 2022, we began the process of revising and updating our SLOs, and at the time of this writing, that work was still in progress). These objectives are similar to the course/learning objectives of programs around the country. The anchor concepts and practices are more granular points of focus than even SLOs are. For example, "writing/literacy enacts and creates identities and ideologies" is a more precise articulation of SLO 3, "students think critically about their position in the context of a larger ongoing conversation." So, students don't just think about their positionality, which is a sophisticated task already, but also work to understand the ways in which composing practices, conventions, genres, opportunities, and constraints contribute to their positionality and also to the positionalities of the rhetorical agents in the "larger ongoing conversation." What's the point of this? The SLO describes a direction of learning (critical positioning in ongoing conversations), but the anchor concept describes a disciplinary and pedagogical philosophy that a critical element of positionality is the way those ongoing conversations actually interpolate our own identities and ideologies. The disciplinary and pedagogical philosophy leads to discussions/lessons/assignments about genre, conventions, hegemony, power structures, languaging, and so on—which is one of the ways our antiracist pedagogy and languaging-focused philosophy and mission moves from mission statement to pedagogical foundation to classroom lesson.[2] The takeaway is that SLOs accomplish a certain kind of work, and

---

2. Smith et al. (2021) present a 3x3 grid for developing online writing curriculum using the PARS framework. Their grid is an example of how anchor points can lead to curriculum decisions. The theory, foundations, and philosophies that their grids are based on are anchor concepts and practices. The grid shows one way anchor concepts/practices can be translated into curriculum, projects and assignments, and instructor choice. Their grid is also similar to our anchor texts list, using potential projects instead of potential reading.

anchor points another. The anchor points help facilitate the "walk the talk" of our pedagogies, SLOs, and equity and language statements. Anchor points represent an important waypoint between values and doing.

Along with anchor concepts and practices, we also developed a list of anchor texts (see the appendix for examples of our current list). Notice that the texts are not all required. Instead, instructors choose a few texts from the lists to add to their courses. And, as long as instructors choose three texts from the lists, they can add as many other texts or excerpts as makes sense for their course. The anchor texts are the most concrete element of our anchor points because although we are all teaching toward the anchor concepts and practices, the way that happens is designed by the instructor. The texts, however, are a commitment we make to each other and the program to design for and around. These are discrete instances of commonality across all sections. But these aren't just texts. These texts support the anchor concepts and practices, and so support our pedagogical goals.

Freewrite, Part I: Brainstorming Anchor Points

What do you want your students to know and do by the end of your program's course(s)? Brainstorm your ideas in Table 4.4.

Table 4.4 Anchor Concepts and Practices

Anchor Concepts	Anchor Practices
This column represents the content and disciplinary knowledge you want students to walk away with.	This column represents the skills, practices, and habits you want students to walk away with.

As you work through this process, here are some things to consider:

- Sometimes it's helpful for faculty or a committee group to do this activity separately and then build collaborative lists. This allows all voices to be heard, not just the loudest ones (who might benefit from doing more listening . . .). But it's also an important reflective practice. We should regularly engage with this question: What do we want students to know and do?
- Lists shouldn't be too long. Both anchor concepts and practices should have pedagogical space that leads to several different lessons, activities, and potential projects. For example, our anchor concept that "writing/literacy are social and rhetorical activities" leads to lessons about giving and receiving feedback, doing revision, and making decisions about writing, but also discussions about how and where writing and literacy norms are established.
- Concepts and practices are not static and should be revisited at regular intervals (more on this later).
- Concepts and practices should have connections to the program (or institutional) value statements (these could be mission, vision, or objective statements). For example, if a program's philosophy statement includes a bullet point like "students have a right to their own language and a responsibility to engage with their own languaging practices" *but* an anchor practice is "students must be proficient at APA formatting," there's been a disconnect. A better anchor practice would be something like "students make citational choices" because that leads to lessons about what citation accomplishes and asks students to become rhetorical agents of when and how and where to give credit to their sources.

Designing Anchor Points, Process

All combined, consider how the anchor concepts, practices, and texts reinforce our program's commitment to languaging and antiracist pedagogy (and how anchor concepts/practices/texts can demonstrate and describe the philosophical and pedagogical goals of your writing program). These texts ask students to confront their assumptions about language and the ways certain languaging practices become labeled "good" or "smart" or "academic" or "professional."[3] Additionally, in 2020, our writing program began an audit of our practices and texts to ensure

---

3. This is particularly important for our institution. We are a Hispanic-Serving Institution (HSI) with over 92 percent of students identifying as Hispanic. Additionally, the institution made a commitment to be bilingual, bicultural, and biliterate, though in the writing program we prefer to frame it as multilingual, multicultural, and multiliterate. Our SLOs ask students to "be aware of their choices," but our anchor practices ask students to "make sophisticated languaging choices." For our program, understanding how students can and should employ language is critical to the mission of the university and of our writing program.

our pedagogy was equitable and antiracist. We realized that our texts were overwhelmingly written by older, White scholars. We also came to understand the financial burden requiring a specific textbook had on our students. So, when we designed our anchor texts, we worked to ensure that the texts were available as PDFs and that we were integrating the work of Black, Indigenous, people of color (BIPOC) and multiply marginalized scholars into the concrete, common moments across all 1301 and 1302 sections. The point isn't that any writing program should use these particular texts but that the combination of anchor concepts, practices, and texts can be used by writing programs to describe and demonstrate the values, objectives, and work that their curriculum and pedagogy are doing.[4] This is part of the strategic work we can do programmatically to ensure that our courses are doing what we say we're doing in our mission statements and SLOs.

The process for developing anchor points is not complex, but it might be difficult.

We began by interrogating our perceptions of ourselves as a program: Who are we as a program? What do we value? What do we stand for? What are we teaching?[5]

Then, we mapped those values and reflections onto our SLOs. This helped us determine if any of our current SLOs did not appear in our values or if any of our values did not appear in our SLOs.

We continued the discussion and mapping by very seriously grappling with two more questions: What do we want students to know? (these became anchor concepts) and What do we want students to be able to do? (these became anchor practices). Of course, because we're teachers, we implicitly address these questions all the time. But it's not as common to have these discussions as a program and to make decisions about that knowledge and those practices that will then be somewhat codified into program documents. The results of these discussions were again mapped onto our SLOs and to our values. (The document gets messy, heavily annotated, and difficult to read by anyone who isn't part of the group. But that means it's working.)

---

4. However, for anyone interested in using texts from BIPOC and multiply marginalized scholars for first-year writing or technical communication courses, we developed this crowdsourced list to help get the process started: alternative texts and critical citations for antiracist pedagogies.

5. Because we are a large writing program, I asked for volunteers to be on a committee to evaluate and design program documents and curriculum. As the WPA, I made the decision to develop this system of anchor points, though I was open to this failing and needing to develop some other idea. The committee and I did the initial design work for the anchor points, sent our work to writing program faculty for comments, revised, and then as a writing program we sort of ratified the plan (though that's not exactly the right word). We worked from committee because it would have been impractical to have the entire program design together. However, we accepted the work and established the system as a program.

After we had determined the values, concepts, and practices, we looked for texts that would support the teaching and doing of those anchor points. We wanted to provide more texts than necessary so instructors could choose the texts that were most meaningful and productive.

Finally, you have to determine the revision cycle. Every three years? Every five? Any administrative initiative or practice will become entrenched and part of a new hegemony if there aren't deliberately designed opportunities to revise the system. Revising every three or five years seems to make sense because it's enough time to implement, tweak, assess efficacy, and determine what works and how to improve.

Freewrite, Part II: Designing Anchor Points

Let the process of developing anchor points be rough, sketched out, annotated doodles. This process is messy and a continual work-in-progress. Your process should look a little like Figure 4.1 though you should also add or remove elements to make the process meaningful for your program. For example, we worked our process on dry erase boards in F2F meetings. This could also be done on a Miro board to great effect (miro.com is a digital collaborative space that is free and has a ton of helpful elements). The example is abridged for space and readability. The mapping and annotation process is generally more developed.

Take a moment to begin developing your own anchor points (see Table 4.5). Using the concepts and practices you sketched out in Freewrite Part I, Brainstorming Anchor Points, add annotations, map connections, and begin suggesting anchor texts. Annotations might include shared assignments or experiences, course sequence planning, ideas for collaborative lesson planning, and so on.

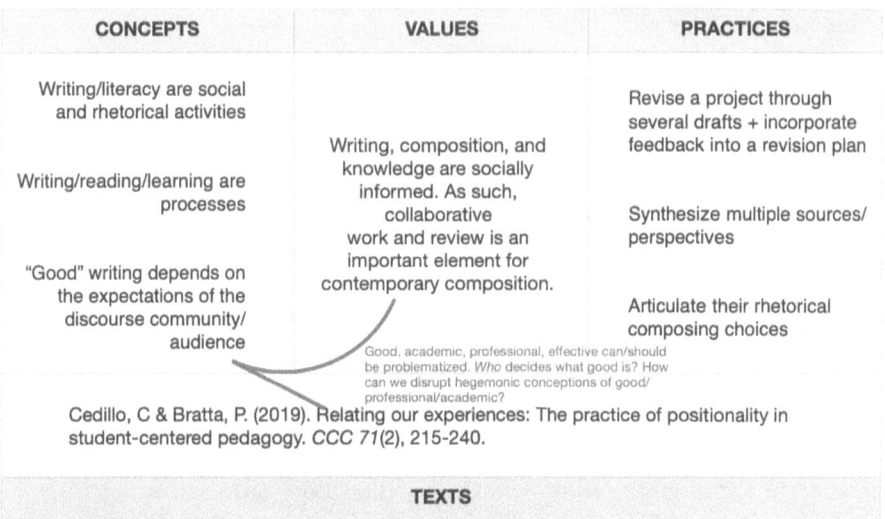

Figure 4.1 Concepts, Values and Practices

Table 4.5 Anchor Points Mapping

Concepts	Values	Practices
Import from Part I	What philosophy, mission, vision guides your programmatic decisions?	Import from Part I
Texts What texts connect the concepts, practices, and program values? List and annotate those texts above.		

Conclusion and Takeaways

There are two main takeaways for this chapter:

1. Instructional modalities (online synchronous, online asynchronous, hybrid, F2F, traditional, flex path, etc.) cannot use a one-size-fits-all curriculum or delivery method. Each modality has its own material boundaries in which success can be articulated.
2. Anchor points are a valuable programmatic tool that, when developed strategically, can facilitate cohesion between instructional modalities, maintain program identity, and describe and articulate pedagogical foundations.

Historically, writing programs have had difficulty articulating their value to the institution. Anchor points are a codification of programmatic value in institutional terms rather than (only) rhetoric and composition terms. That is, instead of saying "FYW is important because it teaches students to write and to think critically," we can say "by the end of FYW, students will know [these things], be able to do [these things], and all this aligns with our program and institutional vision statements in [these ways], and these documents articulate the disciplinary foundations that connect our philosophy to our pedagogy to our institutional mission." Anchor points make tangible the work that writing programs are already doing.

Anchor points also highlight opportunities for personal, accessible, responsive, and strategic (PARS) connections between program and faculty. One of my fears as the WPA for a large writing program is that some mandate will come down from a non-writing administrator that all sections need to use identical syllabuses, projects, tasks, assignments, lessons, everything so that all our students are having the same experience. Although I've seen successful writing programs under this model, my concern is that (in this hypothetical scenario) the decision was made for administrative and austerity reasons and not because it is good teaching. How, then, can I ensure that all sections are providing comparable learning experiences for all students, especially in light of our new online course offerings, while also allowing instructors creative autonomy and room to develop their own ideas, assignments, and activities?

For us, the answer has been anchor points, particularly because anchor points fit within Borgman and McArdle's (2019) PARS framework so well. That is, anchor points provide personal-accessible-responsive-strategic common *places* within a semester and course sequence. Faculty continue to design and develop course materials that are interesting and meaningful to them and their students (*personal*). The anchor concepts, practices, and texts ensure that all sections have moments of curricular and pedagogical commonality (*accessible*). And the anchor points are regularly examined and revised to ensure the writing program is reflective, responding to changes in the discipline and the institution and the students' needs (*responsive*). All this is particularly important (and good news) for programs that offer a range of modalities. For example, we offer F2F, hybrid, online synchronous, and (some) online asynchronous. Even though instructors in online and hybrid spaces need to design environments and classroom practices that are specific to the material affordances of those spaces, and even though F2F instruction has different material realities than those online spaces, the curricular and pedagogical experiences of students in both those spaces are designed to be both relevant and comparable. At the same time, the writing program is able to articulate how all sections of ENGL 1301 and ENGL 1302 are doing analogous work that is pedagogically rigorous and aligned with institutional goals (*strategic*).

References

Adler-Kassner, L. & Wardle, E. (Eds.). (2016). *Naming what we know: Threshold concepts of writing studies*. Utah State University Press.

Borgman, J. & McArdle, C. (2019). *Personal, accessible, responsive, strategic: Resources and strategies for online writing instructors*. The WAC Clearinghouse; University Press of Colorado. https://doi.org/10.37514/PRA-B.2019.0322.

Hollinger, A. & Borgman, J. (2020). (Dis)similarity and identity: On becoming quasi-WPA (qWPA). *WPA: Writing Program Administration, 44*(1), 130–149. https://wpacouncil.org/aws/CWPA/pt/sp/journal-archives.

Phillips, T., Shovlin, P. & Titus, M. (2018). An exercise in cognitive dissonance: Liminal WPAs in transition. In C. A. Wooten, J. Babb & B. Ray (Eds.), *WPAs in transition: Navigating educational leadership positions* (pp. 70–86). University of Colorado; Utah State University Press.

Piña, M. (2023). (Re)turning to hypertext: Mattering digital learning spaces. *Rhetoric Society Quarterly, 53*(2), 153–171. https://doi.org/10.1080/02773945.2022.2095424.

Skurat Harris, H. & Greer, M. (2016). Over, under, or through: Design strategies to supplement the LMS and enhance interaction in online writing courses. *Communication Design Quarterly* 4(4), 46–54. https://dl.acm.org/doi/10.1145/3071088.3071093.

Smith, A., Chernouski, L., Batti, B., Karabinus, A. & Dilger, B. (2021). People, programs, and practices: A grid-based approach to designing and supporting online writing curriculum. In J. Borgman & C. McArdle (Eds.), *PARS in practice: More resources and strategies for online writing instructors* (pp. 83–96). The WAC Clearinghouse; University Press of Colorado. https://doi.org/10.37514/PRA-B.2021.1145.2.05.

Thomas, R., Kuralt, K., Skurat Harris, H. & Jensen, G. (2021). Create, support, and facilitate personal online writing courses in online writing programs. In J. Borgman & C. McArdle (Eds.), *PARS in practice: More resources and strategies for online writing instructors*. The WAC Clearinghouse; University Press of Colorado. 185–207. https://doi.org/10.37514/PRA-B.2021.1145.

Appendix

Anchor Texts (2020 Fall–present)

ENGL 1301 (please include 3 of the following texts in your ENGL 1301 course)

Brandt, "Sponsors of Literacy" (recommend excerpt instead of full text) AND Medina, "Decolonial Potential in a Multilingual FYC."

Vasudevan, "Literacies in a Participatory, Multimodal World: The Arts and Aesthetics of Web 2.0."

Villanueva, "Writing Provides a Representation of Ideologies and Identities" [short text from *Naming What We Know*] (pp. 57–58).

Villanueva, "Bootstraps" [excerpt from *WAW* 4th Ed.] (pp. 272–285)

Cedillo, "What Does it Mean to Move?: Race, Disability, and Critical Embodiment Pedagogy" (recommend excerpt instead of full text).

Alvarez, "Official American English is Best" [short text from *Bad Ideas About Writing*, the title is meant to be tongue in cheek] (pp. 93–98).

Pattanayak, "There is Only One Correct Way of Writing and Speaking" [short text from *Bad Ideas About Writing*] (pp. 82–87).

ENGL 1302 (please include 3 of the following texts in your ENGL 1302 course).

Cedillo & Bratta, "Relating Our Experiences: The Practice of Positionality in Student-Centered Pedagogy."

Olivas, "Cupping the Spark in Our Hands: Developing a Better Understanding of the Research Question in Inquiry-Based Writing."

Wilson, "On the Research Journey" (from *Research is Ceremony: Indigenous Research Methods*).

Gonzales, "Multimodality, Translingualism, and Rhetorical Genre Studies."

Young, "Should Writers Use They Own English."

Remember Your Training!

Golf courses are redesigned all the time, but you can still see parts of the old course that remind you that no matter what, the fourth green still breaks towards the road or the wind still comes into play even if the trees have grown. Understanding a course's history can inform how you play the current course and provide greater context for your overall mental approach.

Writing programs have histories. They have been designed, built, redesigned, rebuilt, and redesigned again—some on the same learning outcomes or some on the same labor of faculty and institutional relationships. Writing program leaders of all experience levels should recognize their history, their training, and their expertise when administering their program. And using this identity to sometimes resist higher level initiatives in favor of a student-focused program can be a good thing.

What we like about Stuart A. Selber and colleagues' chapter is that it focuses on stabilizing online writing instruction (OWI) process and practices at an institutional level in order for them to be productive and effective. What Selber et al. argue about aligning online and face-to-face courses and offering some level of institutional standardization has real value because it places the student user above the institutional, teacher, or programmatic agendas. It factors in history and builds for a more stable future.

Chapter 5. Institutionalizing Online Writing Instruction

Stuart A. Selber, Daniel Tripp, and Leslie Robertson Mateer
PENN STATE UNIVERSITY

Abstract: An ongoing tension in online writing instruction (OWI) is balancing the interests of writing programs and individual teachers. On the one hand, centralizing certain practices and elements of OWI enables a program to achieve its goals. On the other hand, decentralizing certain practices and elements of OWI enables individuals to teach to their own strengths. Successfully institutionalizing OWI involves finding a useful balance between teacher and program needs, an objective that can be difficult to achieve in the complex contexts of higher education. We found a useful balance by distinguishing between standardized and personalized course content, articulating approaches to instructional design, and aligning residential and online courses to a certain extent. But these areas of emphasis are not particular to our writing program. They're relevant to nearly any program that has evolved to include OWI.

Keywords: online writing instruction, institutions, centralization, decentralization, instructional design

Discussions of institutions in professional journals, on listserv lists, and on social media platforms often focus on what's wrong with academic workplaces and who's to blame for problems that undermine the efforts of writing program administrators (WPAs). There are plenty of problems to contend with that are a function of larger contexts and forces—budgetary decisions of upper administrators (Welch & Scott, 2016), gray areas of copyright laws (Galin, 2009), and labor crises in universities, including the emotional labor involved in running a writing program (Wooten et al., 2020), to name a few. But writing programs must still institutionalize online writing instruction (OWI) if they're to realize the purposes of having a program in the first place and achieve the desired outcomes. By institutionalize, we mean stabilizing the practices of OWI in ways that are productive for both teachers and universities as organized sites of higher education (Selber, 2020).

Historically, various versions of distance education (DE) were considered to be innovations. Penn State offered its first version of DE in 1892. It consisted of correspondence courses provided via Rural Free Delivery, which extended the home delivery of print mail to rural locations (Smutz & Weidemann, 2012). These correspondence courses enabled a new population of workers to access college-level instruction for the first time. A little over a century later, Penn State expanded its scope by offering instruction online to students living anywhere in the world. Quite naturally and quietly, early versions of online instruction reflected the approaches to DE that had become institutionalized over many decades, but not all of these approaches have been fruitful for OWI. As the people responsible for the current online courses in Penn State's English department, we've spent many years destabilizing and restabilizing institutional dimensions to make things work for a large writing program with our own priorities.

This chapter discusses how we assumed ownership over the English portfolio of online courses, which historically has been controlled by a centralized delivery unit (the World Campus), and what this development has meant for teachers, students, and writing program administrators. Although our story is a positive one, it has required us, among other things, to

1. distinguish between personalized and standardized course content,
2. articulate our approaches to instructional design, and
3. align residential and online courses to some extent.

Our efforts in these three areas have created new programmatic practices, but we've tried to implement our approaches in ways that make sense for everyone and not just OWI enthusiasts. These areas of emphasis—the chapter takeaways—are not particular to our writing program. In fact, we imagine them to be relevant to nearly any program that has evolved to include OWI. Our hope is that others can benefit from how we've thought about the need to accommodate, and sometimes resist, both teachers and institutions.

The thinking we share has been informed by PARS, a method for approaching OWI that encourages teachers, and their courses and programs, to be personal, accessible, responsive, and strategic (Borgman & McArdle, 2019). These guiding concepts have multiple meanings and applications in the institutional contexts for design, instruction, and administration. For our purposes, *personal* refers to how we encourage individuals to teach to their own strengths and embrace their own pedagogical styles: Any approach to OWI must emphasize teacher buy-in and support. *Accessible* refers to how we have integrated OWI into our larger writing program, making it inclusive of everyone who teaches in our department. *Responsive* refers to how our instructional designs for OWI model a writing workflow, which requires teachers to be fully present and active in their courses. And *strategic* refers to how we balance programmatic and individual needs to make OWI work as a productive institutional operation. For us, the PARS framework functions heuristically to help us give disciplinary meaning and pragmatic shape to OWI.

Theory and Practice

Stuart directed the Program in Writing and Rhetoric (PWR) at Penn State from 2006–2012. PWR is responsible for two general education writing requirements. English 15 is our first-year writing course, focusing on argumentation. In a typical calendar year, about 10,000 students are enrolled in English 15. English 202, our upper-division writing course, divides students according to majors for workplace-facing instruction. The four versions of English 202 cover social science, humanities, technical, and business writing. In a typical calendar year, another 10,000 students or so are enrolled in English 202. During the COVID-19 pandemic, all of the sections of these courses were delivered in a modified online format, but normally we see around 4,000 students in the online versions of English 15 and 202. This considerable number will only grow as we continue to wrestle with space and scheduling constraints and accommodate new populations of students.

Each director of PWR has put their stamp on the program. Stuart especially focused on digital dimensions of writing, teaching, and administering a large-scale program. Some of his projects included growing the portfolio of online courses, refocusing teacher-training courses to address OWI, and spearheading the hiring of technology specialists (Daniel and then Leslie) to assist the department with OWI. Stuart also convinced the department head to increase the number of course releases for program assistants from two and a half, which is a full-time load for one person for an academic year, to three course releases. Stuart then distributed the course releases, giving one each to three different graduate students. The result was that three people now work eight hours per week versus one person working twenty hours per week. Although the increase in support was modest, this more all-hands-on-deck approach has allowed us to leverage a wider and more specific range of pedagogical expertise: PWR assistants can now be hired for their ability to support OWI.

As Stuart was finishing his directorship, he was worried about what would happen to the progress the program had made on OWI, for, in our experience, the advancement of institutional agendas can hinge on the energy of a few individuals or even a single individual. Stuart speculated that the best way to proceed was to persuade the department to create a new position: director of digital education. This position would assign responsibility for making progress to a tenure-line faculty member whose institutional status would indicate the importance of OWI. Importantly, it would not splinter off OWI from PWR but would create a support system in the department. The system would support the program, as in centralization practices, as well as individual teachers, as in decentralization practices, helping both to succeed and accomplish their goals: Centralization and decentralization are not binary oppositions but rather interdependent modes of institutionalization (Simon, 1980).

There are two reasons why our portfolio of online courses has become a marquee project in the English department: The portfolio generates two-thirds of the operating budget for the department; and the portfolio has an annual impact on dozens of teachers and thousands of students. So, there are institutional incentives for making our online courses as effective as possible for everyone involved. The problem was that we inherited an institutional process for online course development that was meant to be a solution for an entire campus rather than a specific program. Although certain instructional-design concepts can transcend fields, a one-size-fits-all approach can never accommodate the pedagogical differences that exist within, between, and among fields. Let us clarify the situation by working through some of the backstory.

In 1998, Stuart received a grant to create the online version of our technical writing service course, the first English department DE course. The funding for the grant came from the then university president, who was rolling out the World Campus—the centralized unit that supports online courses. The World Campus was considered to be the twenty-fifth Penn State campus, but this designation has always puzzled us because it does not hire faculty or do many of the other things a college campus does. In reality, the World Campus is a delivery unit, and this fact helps to explain its processes and relationships.

As opposed to hiring faculty, the World Campus collaborates with departments to develop online courses. Although our delivery platforms have evolved since 1998, the process for online course development has remained constant over the years. Assuming that a department, its dean, and the World Campus have all agreed to develop an online course, the World Campus assigns an instructional designer and the department assigns a faculty member, establishing the basic project team. The faculty member is responsible for authoring the content, and the instructional designer is responsible for structuring that content into a course. This construct creates a form/content binary that drives the entire development process. The main upside is that faculty members who know little to nothing about teaching online are paired with instructional designers who can apply their trained skills to solve certain types of institutional problems—among them, staffing academic departments with faculty members who can design online courses, leveraging knowledge across siloed departments, creating and managing shareable content, and complying with accessibility standards. But for OWI, the downsides far outweighed the positives.

We will sort a few of the main downsides into two categories: design and implementation. By design, we mean how the World Campus asked us to approach the look, feel, and function of OWI. By implementation, we mean how we were able to put designed courses into action in our writing program. The specialists at the World Campus face a daunting task: designing online courses for any and all fields. Because it is impossible to have the requisite domain knowledge needed in every situation, the World Campus separates form and content and focuses just on form, or design, leaving content decisions to faculty members. This is an understandable strategy for a centralized approach to the process of online course development, especially in a large institution, and it can be successful when the instructional-design process is compatible with how faculty think about the nature of their courses. Form and content, however, are not so easily separated or contained. As two sides of the same coin, form and content are dependent upon each other in a mutually constitutive relationship. The point of the project team is to help instructional designers and faculty members negotiate this relationship, but, in reality, faculty members have little influence over the instructional-design process. For us, there was simply too much of a mismatch between the standard process and our goals for OWI.

From our perspective, the standard process overly prioritizes student-teacher interactions. As we noted above, DE at Penn State began with correspondence courses. But, in certain contexts and cases, including writing and writing instruction, a correspondence model has proven rather difficult to overcome. For example, the content development workflow for the World Campus stresses the elements of a syllabus. Institutionally speaking, a syllabus is understood as something of a contract between students and teachers, but in the context of instructional design, it was rearticulated as a guide for mapping interactions. First and foremost, we were encouraged to think of the role of teacher presence in online courses. However, this important concept was interpreted as being about the aspects of teacher presence that are discernible in a syllabus, such as information about satisfying course expectations, completing and turning in assignments, and grading practices. The result was a series of instructional-design patterns that centered more on the teacher and content than on student interaction and learning. Online courses, for instance, begin with an overview of requirements and deadlines. Although the overviews are useful, they don't warrant a central location in the template grid. We wanted to redesign our courses to foreground student interaction and learning. In a subsequent section, we'll elaborate on how our instructional-design approach now models a writing workflow.

In terms of implementation, we were highly constrained by how we were able to put our designed courses into action. A key constraint was an inability to change the content once a course had been finalized by an instructional designer. Online courses are revised on a three- to five-year cycle, depending on need and justification, and in between revisions, changes can be submitted to the World Campus. But the expectation is that such changes will simply correct typos or other small mistakes. Although we had academic oversight over the content, it was locked in and locked down until it was time to revise. Once revised, a course was locked down once again for another three to five years. The product of this approach was a canned course teachers could not personalize to suit their own strengths and styles. Not surprisingly, the pedagogical experiences of teachers produced low morale and negatively affected how they thought about OWI. We had created a two-tiered program in which online courses were considered to be inferior to face-to-face courses rather than different types of courses with other possibilities.

These design and implementation problems were so significant that we were able to destabilize the status quo and make a successful institutional proposal to assume control over both form and content. As far as we know, we're the only disciplinary unit at Penn State that has complete responsibility for this otherwise centrally governed enterprise. Our proposal to control our portfolio was successful because we already had experience with key instructional-design tasks, such as establishing learning objectives, designing courses around them, and assessing the extent to which students are able to achieve those objectives. In addition, we already knew about employing educational technologies, complying with accessibility standards, and interpreting copyright laws. At the time of our proposal, then, we were functioning in fundamental ways as instructional designers, defying institutional job classifications that segregate the overlapping work of instructional designers and teachers in fields with a productive and rich history of studying and practicing online learning.

Conclusions and Takeaways
Restabilizing OWI

By destabilizing the institutional status quo, we were able to realize significant improvements for teachers and students. Teachers can now create customized versions of online courses, for example, and students experience a product of instructional design that makes much more sense for OWI. But teachers and students don't exist in a vacuum or operate independently. To help teachers function successfully in our program, and to help our program achieve its goals, such as assigning an equal amount of work to all students and building consensus around grading expectations, we needed to restabilize our operation in certain respects. Focusing only on how we broke down hierarchies fails to account for the nature of work in institutions or what can be useful about hierarchies. The trick is to balance the impulse to decentralize decision-making with centralization practices that help to produce the right overall effect: Any approach to OWI must work for both programs and individual teachers. Three takeaways that can help programs find a useful balance include distinguishing between standardized and personalized course content, articulating approaches to instructional design, and aligning residential and online courses to a certain extent. For analytic purposes, we align these takeaway points with phases in a conceptual model for institutional innovation and change.

B.K. Curry (1991) advanced a generative model with three recursive phases: mobilization, in which institutions are readied for change; implementation, in which innovations are introduced into institutions; and—more to our point—institutionalization, in which innovations are stabilized by institutions. According to Curry, innovations achieve an appreciable level of stability once they have become integrated into the structures, procedures, and cultures of institutions. Structural integration involves developing formalized support systems for innovations and realizing significant moments in which innovations are merged with established institutional formations. Procedural integration involves routinizing the activities associated with innovations, developing workflows, and adapting innovations to existing ways of working. And cultural integration involves accepting or tolerating the norms and values associated with innovations and attempting to use them for principal job activities. The conditions associated with these phases can domesticate innovations but also engender alternatives and new possibilities.

Three Takeaway Points

To restabilize OWI at these three levels, we

1. articulated boundaries between the different types of online course content, specifying what instructors are allowed to personalize in order to leverage their instructional strengths and what needs to remain standardized for programmatic purposes (structural integration);
2. prepared a design statement for online courses that articulates our educational philosophy and guides our instructional-design workflow (procedural integration); and
3. aligned our face-to-face and online courses to a point where all teachers can be assigned any version of a writing course (cultural integration).

Per the PARS approach, our strategy was to implement the elements that help us institutionalize OWI in concrete ways, making them legible to teachers in our program and to broader communities.

Structural Integration: Distinguishing Between Personalized and Standardized Course Content

Keri Dutkiewicz et al. (2013) explored the problem we've noted of managing a multiple-section course in ways that are useful to all stakeholders. They conclude that "a balance of faculty autonomy in customizing courses with the inclusion of required pre-designed elements best serves to meet instructor expectations in meeting the unique needs of online learners" (p. 46). But what, exactly, might it mean to distinguish between personalized and standardized course content, especially when striving for a maximum amount of teacher autonomy? Answers to this question will likely vary somewhat across institutions, but we offer our approach as something of a heuristic for thinking about distinctions. After all, conventional thinking in the field has produced a fair amount of consensus around writing program development. In our program, teachers can personalize

- non-standardized elements of the syllabus, such as expectations for the number of posts and their word counts in discussions, weighting scales for final grades, and late policies;
- weekly overviews and commentaries;
- prompts for discussions, workshops, and exercises;
- evaluation criteria;
- assignments, their order, and assignment instructions; and
- supplemental materials.

Let us note two things. First, this list is roughly ordered from less to more complex. It is one thing to change late policies or rewrite discussion prompts and quite another to swap out entire assignments, which would have more of a ripple effect throughout the course. Second, any changes must comply with copyright laws and accessibility standards. Stuart reviews copyright considerations for any new materials, but teachers must provide alternative texts (alt texts) for image files, transcripts for audio files, and transcripts and closed-captioning for video files. To help with decision-making, teachers need to know how much work it will be to personalize aspects of a course.

To help our program achieve its goals, the following must remain standardized:

- course descriptions and learning outcomes;
- textbooks, required materials, and required software programs;
- grading scales;
- descriptions of World Campus or university policies and services, including those pertaining to deferred grades, academic integrity, the TEACH Act, disabilities, nondiscrimination, IT support, libraries, veterans and service members, counseling and psychological services, and university emergency procedures; and
- instructional-design frameworks, including the design of the role of teacher presence in discussions, workshops, and exercises.

One of our frustrations is not being able to allow teachers to select their own textbooks. The issue is that the World Campus abides by a federal law stating that students should know their true costs at least six months in advance. Because the English department doesn't assign courses until closer to the start of the term, well after textbook orders have been submitted, teachers can't personalize textbook choices. From our perspective, the problem is with the scheduling process and not the law, which provides much-needed transparency in an age of rising educational expenses. Also, the irony is not lost on us that we have restabilized the instructional-design frameworks for OWI. Although we restrict teachers in the same ways the World Campus restricted us, there are two key differences: We now have instructional designs that are appropriate for OWI, and we can allow teachers to personalize if they have a sound justification and the ability to implement the changes. One of the reasons we restrict personalization in this area by default is to establish an effective level of teacher presence. As we discuss in the next subsection, our online writing courses are discussion-based courses that model a writing workflow and involve regular and routine interactions among everyone involved.

Procedural Integration: Articulating Instructional-Design Approaches

To destabilize the institutional status quo, we needed to make the case that we had a better approach to instructional design than the World Campus and that we could operationalize our vision in an academic department. We made that case successfully with slide decks in a variety of meetings with stakeholders, but since then we have turned our talking points into a student-centered design statement that articulates our approach. Design statements are used to externalize and make explicit fundamental assumptions, concepts, and processes employed in a creative project. The surface structure of the genre varies according to the specific circumstances of rhetorical situations. For example, design statements that serve invention purposes tend to focus on the concepts behind a project, driving forces, and pathways of development. Like certain types of deliberative proposals about the future, they tend to be more speculative in that the project under consideration does not yet exist for users. Our design statement is more epideictic in nature, praising the present and what students can now expect in online courses. The exigence for our student-centered design statement was the COVID-19 pandemic. Literally over a weekend, all students in English 15 and 202 shifted to OWI, leaving more than a few of them—and some teachers—with understandable questions about how our online courses work. It was an unforeseen opportunity to re-institutionalize our discourse for a new audience and remind ourselves of the reasoning that guides our instructional designs.

To provide a model for OWI, the appendix contains our full design statement. We identify a few elements here that we consider to be particularly pertinent to administrators. Any design statement should discuss the contexts for the task at hand, for OWI will be enabled, constrained, and otherwise shaped by a panoply of institutional circumstances. In our case, we review background information on the role of the World Campus and our history with OWI. The point is to inform students about our considerable experience, which is invisible to them, and to persuade students that our courses will deliver a meaningful education. We recognize that students can be skeptical about online learning—and often rightly so. A design statement for OWI should also discuss pedagogical assumptions or knowledge claims. In our case, we assume, among other things, that

- writing is a skill that can be trained through ongoing practice;
- successful writers follow a deliberate and deliberative process;
- a key component of this process is receiving feedback on plans and drafts; and
- although grammar is important, writing often fails in the first place because of higher-order considerations.

Being explicit about assumptions or knowledge claims increases the likelihood that everyone will better understand where our approach is coming from and what form it will take.

Importantly, the form of instructional designs should be described concretely and in detail. Instructional designers reference any number of learning theorists and frameworks—Benjamin Bloom (1956) and his taxonomy are popular choices in our setting—but for OWI, the form should primarily support how people learn a skill versus, say, understand or recall information. As Ron Berger (2018) put it in his critique of Bloom, to learn a skill like writing, "we have to apply and create in order to understand. The creation process is where we construct deep understanding" (n.p.). The implication is that instructional designs for OWI should model a writing workflow.

In a typical assignment in our courses, students learn how to

- diagnose a writing situation;
- determine the best option for responding to the situation;
- plan a response;
- draft the response systematically, strategically, and ethically;
- incorporate feedback to improve the draft;
- design the documents—print and digital—in ways that aid reader comprehension;
- polish their prose; and
- reflect on their own processes and products.

In the regular way of thinking, the items in this list constitute learning outcomes, but in the context of instructional design, they provide a specification for mapping teacher-student, student-student, student-content, and content-platform interactions. We scaffold these interactions in ways that guide students through increasingly more complex writing problems and rhetorical processes for understanding and solving them. The design statement makes this approach explicit for students, for us, and for any other interested stakeholders or parties.

Cultural Integration: Aligning Residential and Online Courses

A thorny challenge for WPAs is preparing a teaching staff for both face-to-face and online courses. Recall that at one point we had unwittingly created a two-tiered program in which online courses were considered to be inferior to face-to-face courses. We straightened out that problem by enabling teachers to personalize their online courses. Now, we have more and more teachers who want to teach online. In addition, the COVID-19 pandemic has driven up demand for a few different reasons, including an ongoing interest in social distancing and an interest from teachers who were intrigued by OWI and want to improve upon their pandemic experiences. Increased demand is a good problem to have, but it can be a problem nonetheless, particularly of coordination.

Our writing program has always taken teacher training seriously. Everyone who teaches English 15 must take a two-semester practicum, and there are one-semester practica for each version of English 202. Before OWI played a significant role in our program, and while our courses were locked down by the World Campus, we covered some basic issues in our regular teacher-training courses, which were primarily focused on residential instruction. We have expanded our coverage in these courses, but we also created a new course that focuses specifically on OWI. People who want to teach online must now take this new course as well as the regular practicum. It's not unusual for graduate students to complete four or five semesters of teacher training, depending on their pedagogical interests.

The coordination issue is a function of media specificities, for the most part. Many of our residential courses actually meet in computer classrooms and have a strong technology component, so much so that we also added a practicum for integrating technology into residential courses. They also use the same learning management system as online courses. There's a certain amount of planned overlap, then, between all of the courses in our program. The issue has been that people teaching multiple sections of the same course in both residential and online versions have had a workload closer to two course preparations than one, a situation that was all the more problematic for those who teach different types of courses in the same term. Our solution has been to align the standard versions of residential and online courses, which originated at very different times and under very different conditions, to some extent to help minimize labor and time requirements. We want every teacher in our program to be able to teach any type of course and coordinate their pedagogical efforts in effective ways.

Although teachers can now personalize all of their courses, we still ask new teachers and experienced teachers new to a teaching field to start with the standard syllabi introduced in our practica. A standard syllabus presents a basic or "vanilla" approach to a course, one that is manageable for teachers and conventional enough to be recognizable in a job interview: Our practica aim to prepare people for the academic job market and not just our program. The technical writing service course, our example here, was originally organized around a major analytical report—a recommendation report, to be more precise. Students began with a literature review to identify and explore a problem of professional interest, wrote a proposal, conducted primary and additional secondary research, drafted the recommendation report, wrote a progress report, shared their findings in an oral presentation, and completed the final version of the recommendation report. The pedagogical scaffolding was obvious to even a casual observer, and the assignment genres required students to pay attention to a range of rhetorical issues, including text and page design, even if instructors accepted electronic files for final submissions. The analytical report has long played an organizing role in many technical writing courses.

When Stuart created the online version of this course, he did not use the residential syllabus as a starting point. Instead, he saw an opportunity to consider what might be involved in creating a course from the ground up that is more born-digital in nature and more sensitive to the media specificities of OWI. After all, the course would take an asynchronous approach, mediate all discussion and communication via a learning management system, use an online textbook, use resources from anywhere on the internet, and provide students with access to cloud-based software for creating websites, ePortfolios, and a variety of other online documents. The new syllabus scaffolds assignments not so much by interrelating report genres and elements but by unfolding the complexities of technical writing in a digital age. The course still employs certain conventional genres, as in resumes, technical descriptions, and instruction sets, but spends time exploring what happens to those genres when they move online. Online instruction sets, for instance, can be self-contained, leveraging the features of fixed instructional content; embedded, leveraging the features of user-generated metadata; or open, leveraging the features of mutable instructional content (Selber, 2010). The dynamics of genre migration across media platforms provide a potent site for rhetorical education.

Not aligning a new online course with an old residential course was a good decision, but it did destabilize our approach to technical writing and create new labor problems, as discussed previously. To solve these problems and restabilize things, we adopted a shared set of genres for both versions of the course. The key is that the genres have more interpretive flexibility than the analytical report, which is a rather more conservative genre in structural and sociocultural terms. We already mentioned the instruction set. Teachers can approach final products as print-based or born-digital documents, and online instructions can take radically different forms, depending on assumptions about audiences, tasks, and knowledge production. Another shared genre is the resume, which can be designed and delivered in traditional and non-traditional ways. The non-traditional ways include visually enhanced resumes, infographic resumes, video-based resumes, and portfolio-style resumes. Teachers can and do approach the same genre differently in residential and online versions of the course: Stuart teaches portfolio-style resumes in a campus computer lab and not online, for example. But aligning residential and online courses to some extent delimits and focuses the pedagogical terrain for teacher training and helps teachers coordinate and dovetail their daily efforts.

OWI is enabled, constrained, and otherwise shaped by an array of institutional forces and circumstances. WPAs must contend with this reality in an ongoing fashion if they hope to run a productive operation. A productive operation manages the tensions between the institutional needs of writing programs and the talents and strengths of individual teachers. To help achieve the right balance, WPAs can work to destabilize aspects of the status quo that are incongruent with OWI and work to restabilize OWI practices in ways that better benefit students, teachers, and programs. We restabilized our practices by distinguishing between standardized and personalized course content, articulating our approaches to instructional design, and aligning residential and online courses to a certain extent. These areas of emphasis are relevant to nearly any program that has evolved to include OWI.

References

Berger, R. (2018, March 14). Here's what's wrong with Bloom's taxonomy: A deeper learning perspective. *Education Week*. https://www.edweek.org/education

/opinion-heres-whats-wrong-with-blooms-taxonomy-a-deeper-learning
-perspective/2018/03 .
Bloom, B. S. (1956). *Taxonomy of educational objectives, handbook 1: Cognitive domain*. David McKay.
Borgman, J. & McArdle, C. (2019). *Personal, accessible, responsive, strategic: Resources and strategies for online writing instructors*. The WAC Clearinghouse; University Press of Colorado. https://doi.org/10.37514/PRA-B.2019.0322.
Curry, B. K. (1991). Institutionalization: The final phase of the organizational change process. *Administrator's Notebook, 35*(1), 1–5.
Dutkiewicz, K., Holder, L. & Sneath, W. D. (2013). Creativity and consistency in online courses: Finding the appropriate balance. In K. Cargile Cook & K. G. Davie (Eds.), *Online education 2.0: Evolving, adapting, and reinventing online technical communication* (pp. 45–72). Routledge.
Galin, J. R. (2009). Own your rights: Know when your university can claim ownership of your work. In S. Westbrook (Ed.), *Composition and copyright: Perspectives on teaching, text-making, and fair use* (pp. 190–216). State University of New York Press.
Selber, S. A. (2010). A rhetoric of electronic instruction sets. *Technical Communication Quarterly, 19*(2), 95–117. https://doi.org/10.1080/10572250903559340.
Selber, S. A. (2020). *Institutional literacies: Engaging academic IT contexts for writing and communication*. University of Chicago Press.
Simon, H. A. (1980). The consequences of computers for centralization and decentralization. In M. L. Dertouzos & J. Moses (Eds.), *The computer age: A twenty-year view* (pp. 212–228). MIT Press.
Smutz, W. & Weidemann, C. D. (2012). Penn State World Campus: Ensuring success, not just access. In D. G. Oblinger (Ed.), *Game changers: Education and information technologies* (pp. 343–347). EDUCAUSE.
Welch, N. & Scott, T. (Eds.). (2016). *Composition in the age of austerity*. Utah State University Press.
Wooten, C. A., Babb, J., Costello, K. M., Navickas, K. & Micciche, L. (Eds.). (2020). *The things we carry: Strategies for recognizing and negotiating emotional labor in writing program administration*. Utah State University Press.

Appendix: Design Statement for OWI

If you are enrolled in one of our two general education requirements, English 15 or English 202, you might be wondering what it is like to take an online version. Let us share our approach with you, but we want to start with a bit of history.

In the English department, we have been offering online courses for over two decades. In fact, our portfolio now includes 17 online courses, and students in World Campus programs can earn an online English minor. You may have heard of the World Campus. It is not actually a campus in the usual sense of the term: They do not hire instructors, for example, or develop courses or programs on their own. In collaboration with academic departments, the World Campus offers more than 150 accredited graduate degrees, undergraduate degrees, certificates, and minors. There are over 20,000 World Campus students, and at times, some of them are our residential students.

Nowadays, distinguishing between online and residential students is less important than leveraging all that we have learned about distance education in order to help everyone manage and succeed. Although the online versions of our general education courses were designed to be taken by students living in any time zone—that is, the courses take an asynchronous approach, for the most part—thousands of residential students have succeeded in these courses, and students have reported positive experiences.

When designing an online course, we begin by specifying goals, asking what we want students to know and be able to do by the end of the term. We then fashion interactions and activities to support these goals. We have the same goals for all of the sections of a general education course, whether that course runs online or in a campus building.

The goals for our courses are informed by what we know from research about the nature of literacy. We know, for example, that writing is a skill that can be trained through ongoing practice. We know that successful writers follow a deliberate and deliberative process. We know that a key component of this process is receiving feedback on plans and drafts. And we know that although grammar is important, writing often fails in the first place because of higher-order considerations, such as understanding how to appeal to readers or organize ideas logically and compellingly.

These evidence-based findings guide how we design and run our online courses. More specifically, we show students how to apply a durable approach to writing that will serve them both here at Penn State and on the job. In a typical assignment, students learn how to diagnose a writing situation; determine the best option for responding to the situation; plan a response; draft the response systematically, strategically, and ethically; incorporate feedback to improve the draft; design the documents—print and digital—in ways that aid reader comprehension; polish their prose; and more. But we do not stop there. Importantly, we also teach students how to reflect on their own processes and products, for we know that an ability to mobilize meta-awareness distinguishes expert from novice writers.

In the interest of time, we have glossed over much of the richness and nuance of the learning experience in our online courses, but we hope our thumbnail description is informative. As you can see, our writing courses are not lecture courses, and we do not ask students to read for the sake of reading. To put it differently, content is not the course. If it was, we would simply give everyone an Amazon gift card and tell them to go read. Content is important, but online learning spaces are created one interaction at a time, over and over again, as students engage with systems and materials, work with one another and their teachers, and participate in meaningful activities. The role of teachers in online environments is as crucial as in any other environment. Our teachers, therefore, are present, active, and involved.

Finally, we want to emphasize that writing in the twenty-first century is always already a digital enterprise, and that writers often work remotely anyway. Taking a writing class online is actually a natural way to learn to become literate in our technological world.

We look forward to seeing you in one of our online courses. If you have any questions, please do not hesitate to contact Stuart Selber, Director of Digital Education. You can find his contact information on the English department website. Thank you.

Woah, Water, Bunkers, the Rough! Yikes!

When golfing anytime or anywhere, whether you're a professional golfer, an amateur golfer, or it's your first time out on a course ever, you will need to anticipate obstacles. There will be things you don't plan for and you'll need to decide how to react. Fast greens, sudden bad weather, annoying playing partners, lots and lots of hidden bunkers, and so on!

This can also be true of administering a writing program. There will always be things that occur that you don't anticipate or don't plan for, and because you're in charge, you'll have to decide how to handle it.

What we like about Marisa Yerace's chapter is that she raises this idea of preparing for the worst through the use of the word and the concept of *agile*. To be agile means you're able to move quickly and easily. Yerace draws from her previous research to argue that putting together a plan based on PARS can aid administrators in responding effectively to problems that arise, such as an unexpected pandemic.

Chapter 6. Agile Writing Programs

Marisa Yerace
Purdue University

Abstract: This chapter presents findings from my ongoing study involving conversations with writing program administrators (WPAs) about how they navigated their programs' emergency switch to remote instruction in spring 2020. I use these reflections and recommendations to give readers a starting point for making their own writing programs more agile in the face of crisis and change—so that instructors and administrators can think on their feet without falling over. In doing so, I draw upon ideas from personal, accessible, responsive, strategic (PARS) principles for online writing instruction (Borgman & McArdle, 2019) and Agile software development (Beck et al., 2001). Agile development's values align easily with PARS in some ways, so this chapter uses these values to reinforce a main takeaway from conversations with study participants: Identify your program values, then build sustainable, agile structures that will last future challenges.

Keywords: agile, crisis, learning management systems, program flexibility, responding to change, program strategy, values

In March 2020, most everyone in writing programs got a crash course in teaching writing online.[1] What happened in spring 2020 wasn't typical online writing instruction (OWI)—there wasn't always a clear plan for how lessons would be translated online or how assignments might have to change in a new modality, plus many instructors and programs adjusted their expectations because of the difficulty of the move and the beginning of a global health crisis. The oft-used "emergency remote instruction" acknowledges that hastily moving face-to-face classes and content online isn't the same as carefully planning fully online courses. Still, this shift revealed to writing program administrators (WPAs) how flexible their curricula, programs, and instructors were.

This chapter uses the PARS framework and data from my ongoing dissertation study to examine ways writing programs can adjust their best OWI practices to be more agile in the face of change. Almost two years after the emergency shift to remote teaching, I began my study by asking WPAs to share their reflections from the Spring 2020 semester. In our discussions, participants reflected on "good enough" results, successes, lessons learned, and unexpected opportunities to focus on OWI.

---

1. This study has been approved by Purdue University's Institutional Review Board: IRB–2021–779.

These conversations have led me to think about what I'll call the *agile writing program:* a team of instructors and administrators with consistent practices and principles that make changing curricula or shifting modalities in crisis situations smoother for everyone involved. Some of the WPAs I spoke with were already preparing for these kinds of pivots because March 2020 wasn't their first emergency switch to remote teaching. Others were seeking greater flexibility and agility because the pandemic remained in flux. I ask, *Can writing programs create sufficient infrastructure and cultures of OWI among instructors strong enough to reduce labor, worry, and revision in future pivots?* Alongside these ideas of agility, I began thinking of how Jessie Borgman and Casey McArdle's (2019) PARS (personal, accessible, responsive, strategic) framework could inform this type of writing program development. As more and more parts of the writing process and higher education are digitally mediated, even courses labeled as traditional face-to-face become more entangled with OWI strategies. I realized agility was not only useful during crises but as a key to articulating approaches to improving program sustainability.

The term *Agile* has also gained popularity as a software development strategy that strives to be both flexible and clear about its values. As Susan Lang (2016) describes it, Agile would be useful for rapid and chaotic situations like the ones faced in March 2020 (pp. 82–83). Rebecca Pope-Ruark (2014) has proposed that faculty should engage Agile, finding that "Agile encourages flexibility of mind, responsiveness to change, collaboration with cross-functional team members, and attention to smaller project tasks rather than only end products" (p. 324). For our purposes, I find that the principles of capital-A Agile development can organize thinking about agility in WPA work.

In this chapter, I use Agile software development's four main values to develop practical applications for WPAs based on my discussions with participants. I align Agile with the PARS framework and illustrate how PARS can help shape and direct an agile writing program, in particular because PARS makes similar moves away from procedures to people based on local contexts. Rather than suggesting all programs should implement Agile as a strategy for administration, I want to advocate instead that, like the developers who came up with Agile, *each program clearly articulates their own values* to encourage thinking on our feet without falling over.

Theory and Practice
Agile's Values and Our Values

The need for flexible and values-focused writing program administration became clear in March 2020, but for some programs, this wasn't the first pivot. For example, when asked what advice she would give new WPAs, one participant (see participant descriptions in the appendix) responded to encourage having support for our instructors in a variety of forms, having professional development so that our instructors know how to work technology and how to teach an array of delivery modes, having a flexible enough curriculum, spending the time to invest in curriculum for different delivery modes like online, hybrid, face-to-face—*trying to really create an agile writing program that can respond to changes.* As universities change, as student demographics change, as situations change, trying to do that sets you up for these crisis situations. ("Imelda")

Another similarly experienced WPA suggested looking at program outcomes *before* making these large decisions for change, calling those outcomes the "North Star" for faculty and administrators as they change courses, programs, and curricula ("Fernand").

Defining those guiding values to make other processes more flexible was exactly what the Agile developers did when writing their manifesto: As Miriam Posner (2022) describes it, Agile allowed software developers to do the job they were best at while leaving room for quick thinking. Agile, like PARS, provides a stable framework that allows individuals to call on their own expertise.

Posner (2022) acknowledges that Agile has become "corporatized," noting, "Agile has veered from the original manifesto's vision, becoming something more restrictive, taxing, and stressful than it was meant to be" (n.p.). Still, Rebecca Pope-Ruark (2022) suggests her idea of Agile Faculty can promote productivity, vitality, well-being, and connection. That is, Agile can still be helpful when thinking about writing programs' flexibility, as it is "an intentional shift away from the manufacturing mindset of project work to one that is more open to incremental but intentional progress and to a view of humans as the most valuable resource in an organization" (Pope-Ruark, 2017, p. 11). Here, I think through similar processes and ways of prioritizing humans in programs. The original Agile Manifesto succinctly articulates the following priorities:

- **Individuals and interactions** over processes and tools
- **Working software** over comprehensive documentation
- **Customer collaboration** over contract negotiation
- **Responding to change** over following a plan

That is, while there is value in the items on the right, we value the items on the left more (Beck et al., 2001).

It might seem weird to bring Agile into a WPA context, especially when the WPA is often seen as a middle manager (Strickland, 2011) and Agile's roots are anti-bureaucratic. However, we can see how Borgman and McArdle's PARS framework for OWI also maps onto Agile's values: *Individuals and interactions* are personal; *working software* is accessible; *customer collaboration* is responsive; and *responding to change* is strategic. For our purposes, "customers" can serve as both the instructors that WPAs are trying to support through their administrative work and their students, who are directly affected by many of these decisions. Through examining our post-pandemic lessons on WPA work through Agile, I hope to illustrate how accepting uncertainty and instead centering our own values can make writing programs more (lowercase A) *agile* for changing situations.

Getting Ready for the Course!

My dissertation study began with a survey sent in fall 2021 to people who were working in writing program administration in March 2020 ($n=55$). This survey was also used to recruit for Phase 2 of my study, a two-part interview series ($n=13$). In the first interview, participants answered general questions about supporting instructors during the emergency switch to remote teaching, with questions partially tailored to survey responses. Later, participants and I examined texts produced by their writing programs during that critical time. Interviews were recorded, transcribed, and de-identified before analysis, and I assigned each participant a pseudonym. Though about half of my Phase 2 participants were tenure-track faculty at larger public institutions, I also had participants who were graduate WPAs and who held non-tenure-track appointments, and participants who worked at smaller public universities, community colleges, and small liberal arts colleges. This study is ongoing, but this chapter uses data from Phase 2, ending in spring 2022.

Creating Agile Writing Programs

My research has suggested that writing program leaders can make their programs more agile by utilizing the PARS framework as mapped onto the four main values of Agile (see Table 6.1).

Table 6.1 PARS and Agile

Personal (P)	Individuals and interactions over processes and tools
Accessible (A)	Working software over comprehensive documentation
Responsive (R)	Customer collaboration over contract negotiation
Strategic (S)	Responding to change over following a plan

Personal: Individuals and Interactions Over Processes and Tools

Agile's first value centers people—developers, collaborators, users, customers—over bureaucracy. As we know, the PARS approach also advocates for OWI where instructors and students feel like *real* people having personal interactions. What are some more ways we can apply this to writing program administration?

For many WPAs, an emergency shift to remote teaching meant changing the *processes* of curriculum design to prioritize the *personal* well-being of their instructors. Designing online courses was already difficult, but designing them with the added exigencies of a pandemic, of student accessibility concerns, of the emotions involved in an uncertain condition, of the isolation brought on by quarantining, of the stress of designing courses in a modality that *many had not taught in before* was, to put it mildly, a lot to handle.

My participants emphasized they believe in academic choice for their instructors and want instructors to design courses in their own personalized ways. However, the *personal* in many cases took precedence over the *personalization*: The labor involved in making big changes on short timelines was, many WPAs felt, unfair. In some cases, union contracts explicitly saw it as a problem. WPAs, then, made curricular revisions themselves or created fully pre-designed courses for instructors to adopt ("Melissa;" "Karen").

Some programs already had pre-designed courses from previous online summer session offerings. Before their Fall 2020 terms, some prepared shells because of the uncertainty surrounding the pandemic and modalities. In many cases, these pre-designed courses were meant to be adapted for whatever modalities their institutions deemed appropriate during the pandemic—traditional face-to-face, hybrid, remote synchronous, asynchronous.

Being so prescriptive often goes against local departmental cultures. One participant described the reaction to pre-designed courses by saying, "I had a lot of my lecturers angry . . . because, in their mind, it completely trampled on their autonomy and agency as instructors," but she insisted on that approach given their inexperience teaching online. Notably, many of those instructors came to appreciate pre-designed courses because 1) they realized they were still allowed to adapt them to their teaching, and 2) she likened learning a new course delivery mode to learning a new genre of writing: You usually start by looking at examples ("Melissa"). Another participant noted that a degree of choice—like asking instructors to personalize their own email policies, for example—created conditions for them to set boundaries for self-care ("Rebekah").

So, what could this mean for OWI going forward?

Borgman and McArdle (2019) explain that the "personal" of PARS in OWI applies to personal design as well as personal instruction in online writing courses. Some of the initial design can still be labor-intensive, so agile WPAs should consider developing strong starting points for instructors to teach online, with resources like repositories and course shells. These can be framed as examples to adapt and learn from, as well as tools that can help instructors save time and energy. At the same time, integrating choice in certain areas such as assignments or communications will be helpful for instructors who need to set boundaries to manage their workload, especially in difficult times.

One approach is the grid described by Allegra Smith et al. (2021), which begins with learning outcomes before offering choices for project ideas suited to those outcomes. Making this kind of backwards design explicit for instructors helps them find options that fit both their priorities as instructors and program values. Asking instructors to choose between a range of assignment types isn't feasible for every program, however. In these cases, customization options in course shells, for example, can be used by instructors to personalize their virtual offices or upload their own videos and materials.

Douglas Hesse (2012) lists documents that WPAs should keep in their "digital cupboard" (pp. 155–156)—staple materials, like staple ingredients, that should be ready to go for any sudden changes or reporting. I'd like to expand that concept for OWI based on my interviews. WPAs could consider having the following ready:

- At least one course shell in the institution's learning management system (LMS) with modules already created for weeks or units, as makes sense for the course. Programs should have separate shells for separate term lengths (such as 8-week summer courses versus 16-week semester-long courses).
- At least one sample syllabus with areas marked for customization by the instructor. This syllabus can be pre-designed with all necessary language and outcomes included and accessibility already in mind.
- A repository for course materials, which can be borrowed from other instructors, including
  - assignment sheets and rubrics (if instructors design their own, it still helps to build upon examples);
  - sample online activities, such as discussion board prompts or peer review activities;
  - sample course calendars; and
  - course readings external to the textbook that instructors may find useful.

Programs should also seek to make this kind of sharing part of program culture by regularly pointing new instructors to the repository of resources and asking continuing instructors to donate their materials.

Accessible: Working Software Over Comprehensive Documentation

The necessity of *working software* for accessibility became very apparent during the early days of the pandemic. One participant created guides for instructors based on their comfort levels with teaching online but said that she knew the "novice" level was necessary "Not just for faculty, but for students who didn't have access to high-tech stuff" ("Karen"). In this analogy, *comprehensive documentation*, referring to *recordkeeping of processes that might become unsustainable busywork*, can be translated into providing *multiple, advanced digital tools* for OWI. Comprehensive documentation can lead to better software *and* can hinder the development of better software, and using digital tools in an online course can make the course richer *or* can add too many new skills for students to learn. Online courses open up a number of opportunities for smarter learning software that we can use with our students for writing, peer review, and interacting in class—but there is also the question of whether all those new tools are *usable* for students and instructors. Hardware and software issues abounded in terms of accessing courses early on in the pandemic—some students joined Zoom sessions from their cars outside coffee shops to access free Wi-Fi. WPAs also realized the ways accessibility needs to be personalized at times. One WPA described an instructor who couldn't look at screens for as long as needed to grade and keep up with students, so the program had to find a printer ("Olga"). At the same time, other accessibility concerns fell by the wayside, as one participant noted:

> I honestly think that so many people were just struggling so much that thinking about accessibility, beyond what it took for them to move their courses online, was just above and beyond what they had the bandwidth to do at that point. ("Erin")

Still, we should take note when software opens up new opportunities for accessibility. One participant was pleasantly surprised that their school's LMS would perform quick accessibility checks on a course site ("Fernand"); another found that their Zoom class sessions were, in some ways, *more* accessible to multilingual students, who could send private messages to clarify what was being said ("Erin").

So, what could this mean for OWI going forward?

Basic accessibility principles need to be standardized across programs: Instructors need to understand how to make the learning software *work*. According to my survey data (Yerace, 2022), 75 percent of WPAs reported paying special attention to accessibility concerns as they supported instructors in spring 2020, and 89 percent reported providing additional technology support, even though many campuses have some form of IT department already. Borgman and McArdle (2019) discuss having plans in place for when technology fails, but in spring 2020, many IT departments were overwhelmed and not working at full functionality. Having resources already created for instructors to adapt can both alleviate the workload for instructors *and* ensure accessibility concerns are met.

It helps to have a broader understanding of what tools for online courses instructors and students already know. This is part of why technology access surveys became so widely recommended at the start of the pandemic. While we can make assumptions about tech access for students who sign up for online courses, keep in mind that even courses at the same institution may use different tools in addition to the course site.

A culture of accessibility—that is, incorporating accessibility concerns into a program's conversations—is important, but other tools, like quick accessibility checklists for LMS courses and syllabi, will be handy when setting up online courses and when courses suddenly need to pivot.

There's an important nuance here, however. One participant told me she couldn't fault her contingent faculty for not being experts with the school's LMS, as it had recently changed and many of them worked at multiple schools with different learning management systems ("Chantal"). It may be that WPAs in similar situations should find ways to *incentivize* LMS training, particularly for building online writing courses.

Responsive: Customer Collaboration Over Contract Negotiation

In Agile, customer collaboration is in line with the move to focus on people over processes. Here, the "customers" make sense as instructors in the program—the people WPAs are trying to support. Any "product" is the resources and tools WPAs make and share among the program, so instructors are important collaborators to make sure that the support they receive is the support they need. Further, considering students as additional "customers" in this analogy (whether we like that language or not) means considering them as potential additional collaborators.

We can see some helpful tools from WPAs who were thinking about this. One, as I said previously, wrote a guide that can be navigated based on the instructor's comfort level with technology ("Karen"). Another had a green/yellow/red email check-in system with their instructors before the initial migration online, using the codes to keep the check-ins brief; then, when it became clear that emergency remote teaching was going to last longer than their institution first thought, they made sure everyone had a one-on-one chat with someone from the writing program team to see if there were any needs that could be met. For instructors in the program who hadn't taught online before or indicated they needed extra help, the writing program team made a "mentoring matrix" to determine who would focus help to whom ("Humberto").

Building OWI infrastructure for a program can be collaborative, too. At least a couple WPAs asked their instructors for modules or course videos to share with the whole program when the emergency shift began, and at least one was able to compensate those instructors for their effort ("Karen"; "Barry").

So, what could this mean for OWI going forward?

Leverage the strengths of the instructors in your programs, as equitably as you can. Some of this can be done through the repository recommended above, which highlights what instructors do well and alleviates the workload for others. Programs can also highlight the strengths of their staff members: For example, a graduate assistant WPA can be more hands-on with less experienced graduate teaching assistant (GTAs) as a type of strategic mentoring. Borgman and McArdle (2019) write that *personal* administration in writing programs starts with "treating your faculty with respect and acknowledging that they are contributors to the larger field of writing studies," and *responsive* administration includes explicitly involving non-tenure-track faculty (pp. 27, 63–64); collaborating with faculty to determine the program's way forward, or to build something like the repository mentioned earlier, means highlighting the contributions that instructors can make to their programs simply with the good work they are already doing.

Writing programs should have continuous modes of assessment—however brief—for thinking about how your program can continue to support your instructors. Programs can also support instructors in assessment of their own courses, opening up collaboration in course design to students.

Strategic: Responding to Change Over Following a Plan

While you would think the value with the word "responding" would pair with the "responsive" of PARS, I've paired it with "strategic" because of the pandemic context. Spring 2020 was a quick change for a lot of instructors, but what came after was at least a year or more of changing or unclear policies for health guidance, educational delivery, and instruction. Although they had to respond to each situation, WPAs quickly realized they needed to *strategize*.

For some, this meant coming up with multiple plans for instruction after spring 2020 based on whether their schools decided on remote synchronous, remote asynchronous, hybrid, or fully face-to-face instruction. As mentioned previously, some of the infrastructure to help instructors start their courses was designed strategically for adaptation to these different situations.

Effective WPAs already think strategically: They leverage the strengths of their instructors and find ways to improve curriculum and support people more equitably. WPAs with teams can think strategically with those different team members. One WPA described getting a grant from the institution to design their online course shell and giving the task to a graduate assistant on the team, paying the student with the grant money to do the work ("Barry"). Another asked their graduate assistant WPA to have one-on-one meetings with other graduate assistants, encouraging peer-to-peer mentoring ("Humberto").

Not all writing programs have large, dedicated teams, but WPAs still found collaborators for what they needed to do. One described working with a college dean to advocate for different Fall 2020 course modes with the provost ("Chantal"); another collaborated with GTAs in the practicum she led on resources instructors could use ("Karen").

Other WPAs were able to make lasting changes from the pandemic. At least a few took the opportunity to revise old procedures like assessment measures. One WPA took the opportunity to make an old portfolio system less penalizing and was able to keep the lower-stakes portfolio for future terms ("Olga"). Another was able to move a self-directed placement pilot into a program-wide rule because it was easier to do online ("Fernand").

Not all lasting changes are tangible: Many WPAs discuss how program cultures have shifted because of the pandemic. One said, "I'm so proud of my faculty that emerged [from the pandemic] with a much more nuanced understanding of their students as people who have lives and responsibilities—and even other classes!—outside of their class" ("Melissa"). These types of lessons are learned in the classroom, but WPAs can take the next step to codify them into values going forward.

So, what could this mean for OWI going forward?

Borgman and McArdle (2019) frame administrative strategy in terms of thinking of student populations: Demographics for online courses are often very different than those for more traditional face-to-face courses (p. 77). Likewise, instructors may be more dispersed, making a communications strategy even more important. This means responding to changes in expectations as we encounter differences in teaching modalities *and* responding to changes in the populations we serve.

The recommendations I make in this chapter are not just small acts but are products of a larger attitude that asks, constantly, *why* we do what we do, in order to make sure we are still achieving our goals. This is why WPAs made progress on getting their instructors more comfortable with teaching online as well as other changes they had wanted to see in their program: Such a crisis prompted them to ask these kinds of questions. Writing programs need to be on the lookout for opportunities to move towards their goals. This falls in line with scholarship we have about strategic WPA thinking: Mike Ristich et al. (2021) describe "archi-strategic decisions" made in the pandemic to determine ways of supporting faculty, with decisions that also outlast the current crisis and work toward a fairer, more sustainable future; Melvin Beavers (2021) uses "administrative rhetorical mindfulness" as a means of faculty development, particularly for part-time faculty.

Continuous assessment of instructors' strengths and areas for development, especially in terms of online teaching, means that programs can strategize professional development activities that help prepare instructors for sudden changes. As described above, this assessment can be incorporated into existing structures in the writing program. Borgman and McArdle (2019) describe user experience (UX) as part of the "strategic" arm of OWI, and continuous assessment with users (teachers) in mind follows their recommendations on strategy. In the same way, conversations about the direction of the program can become regular ways for staff and instructors to collaborate on development that creates a more agile writing program.

Conclusion and Takeaways

Implementing Agile Writing Programs

A discussion of strategy and looking for opportunities to make progress towards our goals leads naturally into, perhaps, the main takeaway of this chapter. Many of these recommendations—talk more about accessibility, have course shells ready, look for opportunities to make good and lasting changes—may seem obvious but become more effective once we first *articulate what, exactly, our values are*. From there, we can begin to think about the *agility* of our writing programs, including their flexibility in the face of large changes and preparation of instructors for different course modalities, more meaningfully. Many of the questions I am using for this study come from trying to determine how WPAs suggested cuts and changes to curriculum in the face of crisis: How do you decide where you're lowering the stakes, and how do you balance that with a program's goals and outcomes?

However, through these conversations in my study, I realized that this question becomes less complicated *when we know our real priorities*, as one participant articulated for me: "I care about our standards, I care about our outcomes, I care about our pedagogy, but *the reason why I care about all those things is because I care about the faculty and the students* [emphasis added]" ("Olga"). Writing programs, before they involve technology and assignments and learning outcomes, don't work without *people*, and that was illustrated clearly in the early stages of the pandemic. This is, perhaps, why the organization of this chapter falls in line with the Agile Manifesto easily, when the Manifesto was created to reposition software developers as an equally important part of the development process.

Questions of how you redesign a course or a program, or how you design infrastructure that withstands crisis, fall in line with other calls to consider design thinking in composition studies. For example, Jim Purdy (2014) considers design thinking to be oriented forward and recursive (pp. 620, 627). These agile recommendations are not just meant to think about sustainability but are meant to be revisited, strategically, to make sure they are still responsive, accessible, and personalized.

In many programs, the pandemic naturally spurred conversations around how that priority of *people* can be articulated into revised policy. After all, choices made by WPAs during the pandemic often made this priority more explicit: Some WPAs described how their practicum courses for new GTAs became less about teaching and more about checking in with each other ("Dexter"; "Karen"). One participant notes that, among her instructors, "I'm thrilled that right now we're having really hard discussions about attendance. And I think it has everything to do with [the pandemic]. What's important? And what do we value?" ("Melissa"). Many of those who used that moment to make lasting changes had already articulated their eventual goal in some way: Some had been trying to change their assessment procedures and simply saw the opportunity to do so, for example. Others had already considered what the strengths of their team members were and made a commitment to use them.

There are many nuances to pick out of the lessons and successes I've collected here. I've mapped agile concepts with PARS in Table 6.1. And here are a few final points. Design a course shell, but leave room for your instructors' personalization.

Use a pre-designed course to teach the new genre of course delivery, but leave it flexible enough to be adapted for other modalities. Highlight the strengths of your team or collaborators, but be conscious of adding to their labor, especially during difficult times. Keep technology simple, but take advantage of its new allowances. Continually assess what your instructors need, but don't create too much more work for them. I can sum this up with my final point: Be *strategic*. Borgman and McArdle (2019) remind us that strategy is the most fundamental part of OWI: "The most important thing a (novice or experienced) instructor or administrator can do is be strategic about their process" (p. 71). I will reiterate that in order for your program to become more agile, you need to be strategic, responding to change as it comes (Agile), but also, *be strategic and have a plan*—one that highlights your priorities as a writing program, or, in other words, prioritizes treating your people well.

Table 6.2 PARS and Agile Values in Online Writing Instruction

PARS Letter	Agile Value	Application for the Future of OWI
Personal (P)	Individuals and interactions over processes and tools	Consider having resources, shells, and samples ready for instructors who may be new to teaching online. Make this kind of sharing part of the program's culture, so that instructors know they don't have to start from scratch when shifting modalities of teaching.
Accessible (A)	Working software over comprehensive documentation	Incorporate accessibility into existing resources, as well as add ways of checking for accessibility in different areas and materials for the course. Have an awareness of the limits of teachers and students in terms of learning new software.
Responsive (R)	Customer collaboration over contract negotiation	Identify the strengths of instructors and the writing program team, alongside performing continuous assessment of what instructors are comfortable with and what areas they can continue to learn about. Give instructors ways to self-assess their classes and collaborate with students over course design.
Strategic (S)	Responding to change over following a plan	Hold continuous assessment and discussions of the program's goals in terms of instructors, teaching modalities, and tools available to teachers and students. Make sure that everything the program does serves a purpose.

References

Beavers, M. (2021). Administrative rhetorical mindfulness: A professional development framework for administrators in higher education. *Academic Labor: Research and Artistry, 5*(1). https://digitalcommons.humboldt.edu/alra/vol5/iss1/9.

Beck, K., Beedle, M., Bennekum, A., Cockburn, A., Cunningham, W., Fowler, M., Grenning, J., Highsmith, J., Hunt, A., Jeffries, R., Kern, J., Marick, B., Martin, R., Mellor, S., Schwaber, K., Sutherland, J. & Thomas, D. (2001). *Manifesto for Agile software development.* https://agilemanifesto.org/.

Borgman, J. & McArdle, C. (2019). *Personal, accessible, responsive, strategic: Resources and strategies for online writing instructors.* The WAC Clearinghouse; University Press of Colorado. https://doi.org/10.37514/PRA-B.2019.0322.

Hesse, D. (2012). Writing program research: Three analytic axes. In M. Sheridan & L. Nickoson (Eds.), *Writing studies research in practice: Methods and methodologies* (pp. 140–157). Southern Illinois University Press.

Lang, S. M. (2016). Taming big data through agile approaches to instructor training and assessment: Managing ongoing professional development in large first-year writing programs. *WPA: Writing Program Administration, 39*(2), 81–104. https://www.wpacouncil.org/aws/CWPA/pt/sp/journal-archives.

Pope-Ruark, R. (2014). A case for metic intelligence in technical and professional communication programs. *Technical Communication Quarterly, 23*(4), 323–340. https://doi.org/10.1080/10572252.2014.942469.

Pope-Ruark, R. (2017). *Agile faculty: Practical strategies for managing research, service, and teaching.* University of Chicago Press.

Pope-Ruark, R. (2022). *The agile academic.* Rebecca Pope-Ruark. https://theagileacademic.com/.

Posner, M. (2022). Agile and the long crisis of software. *Logic Magazine, 16.* https://logicmag.io/clouds/agile-and-the-long-crisis-of-software/.

Purdy, J. P. (2014). What can design thinking offer writing studies? *College Composition and Communication, 65*(4), 612–641.

Ristich, M., McArdle, C. & Rhodes, J. (2021). Assessing the limits of program strategy: "Archi-Strategy" in an age of disruption. *Programmatic Perspectives, 12*(1). https://cptsc.org/wp-content/uploads/2021/07/Ristich-et-al._-Archi-Strategy-perspectives_.pdf.

Smith, A., Chernouski, L., Batti, B., Karabinus, A. & Dilger, B. (2021). People, programs, and practices: A grid-based approach to designing and supporting online writing curriculum. In J. Borgman & C. McArdle (Eds.), *PARS in practice: More resources and strategies for online writing instructors* (pp. 83–96). The WAC Clearinghouse; University Press of Colorado. https://doi.org/10.37514/PRA-B.2021.1145.2.05.

Strickland, D. (2011). *The managerial unconscious in the history of composition studies.* Southern Illinois University Press.

Yerace, M. (2022). New priorities in strange times: How writing programs navigated emergency remote teaching. *Computers & Composition Online.* http://cconlinejournal.org/dec_2022/Yerace/Codedocs/index.html

Appendix: Participant Descriptions

Andrea is a graduate assistant and doctoral candidate at a public research university with about 17,000 students. She works with the writing across the curriculum (WAC) program at her university.

Barry is a tenure-track professor at a flagship state university with about 34,000 students. As of March 2020, he was the director of composition, working with teaching faculty and GTAs, and with at least one graduate assistant on staff. Barry's program had never offered courses online before March 2020.

Chantal is a tenure-track professor at a small liberal arts college with about 6,000 students, where she oversees first-year writing, their writing-intensive WAC courses, and is the English department chair.

Dexter is a tenure-track professor at a public research university of over 30,000 students. As assistant chair for the department, he oversaw training of new GTAs, including their practicum courses. He works with a staff member, the director of writing, who handles scheduling concerns and other business for the program.

Erin is a non-tenure-track professor and writing program administrator at a community college with about 11,000 students and a large Hispanic student population.

Fernand is a tenure-track professor and coordinator for the graduation writing assessment requirement, which involves upper-division writing requirements. He works alongside a colleague who oversees the lower-division writing courses.

Gabrielle is a tenure-track professor at a regional comprehensive university of about 7,400 students, where she oversees writing-to-learn courses and runs assessment for the first-year writing program.

Humberto is a tenure-track professor at a public research university of about 19,000 students. He was the director of the university writing program in 2020 and worked on a team with a teaching faculty associate director, a graduate assistant director, and a permanent staff member.

Imelda is a tenure-track professor at a public land-grant research university of over 30,000 students, where she is the director of composition. Her team includes two associate directors, at least one of whom is also a faculty member.

Karen was a non-tenure-track professor working at a regional comprehensive institution of about 6,000 students in March 2020. As the writing programs director, she also trained GTAs.

Melissa is a tenure-track professor at a public land-grant research university with about 50,000 students. As of March 2020, she was the interim director of the writing program and worked with TAs as part of that role.

Olga is a tenure-track professor at a regional comprehensive university of about 21,000 students, where she directs first-year writing.

Rebekah is a tenure-track professor who became the associate director of the writing program in the summer of 2020. She works at a public university of about 18,000 students.

Get Into Your Rhythm!

All golfers are part of a larger group or team, even though golf is actually an individual sport. Golfers have teams that include coaches, trainers, mentors, and their families, and these teams cheer them on, help them improve, and hold them up when they're feeling low or not playing well.

Writing program leaders need teams too. It's more productive and fun to work together and get an activity completed. Additionally, multiple perspectives usually always make the end product stronger.

What we like about Lourdes Fernandez et al.'s chapter is that they introduce this idea of collaboration in regards to hybrid online writing courses and research. We also like that this chapter is so focused on meeting the needs of instructors and supporting instructors in a continuous fashion as they teach online.

Chapter 7. Research is a Team Sport: A Collaborative PARS Approach to Sustainable Hybrid and Online Writing Instruction Development

Lourdes Fernandez, Ariel M. Goldenthal, Kerry Folan, Jessica Matthews, and Courtney Adams Wooten
George Mason University

Abstract: In this chapter, we demonstrate how the PARS (personal, accessible, responsive, and strategic) framework can be applied to collaborative research that is sustainable for all participants over the long term. By strategically selecting instructors whose interests in hybrid and online writing instruction (OWI) vary, developing a thoughtful timeline and research scope that allows participants to self-select tasks that they are most interested in, and creating feedback loops that are both iterative and multidirectional to respond to instructor needs, our team has been effective and prolific in its research. This chapter includes a thorough overview of our research team's development and practice as well as recommendations and a timeline to help others create and sustain their own research team.

Keywords: research, collaboration, writing program administration, professional development, hybrid

In their book *Personal, Accessible, Responsive, Strategic: Resources and Strategies for Online Writing Instructors*, Jessie Borgman and Casey McArdle (2019) use golf as an overarching metaphor to frame their approach for teaching writing online. Not only is the title an acronym (PARS) that plays upon the vocabulary of golf, but also the nature of the game itself serves as a useful analogy for what online writing instruction involves. We see the connection for sure. Though golf is technically an individual sport, most golfers will tell you that they're in it as much for the social and collaborative aspects as they are for the personal challenge. Similarly, though the traditional image of an academic researcher may be a tweedy professor holed up alone in a musty office, we have found that academic research can be just as effective as a "team sport." Collaborative research can keep faculty invested, help maintain manageable workloads, and support consistent progress.

In this chapter, we describe the work of a team of seven faculty and writing program administrators (WPAs)—the Hybrid Task Force—who in fall 2019 began addressing the needs of instructors teaching hybrid writing courses in a writing program at a mid-Atlantic R1 institution. Our program is large: about

100 faculty teaching around 9,000 students a year in approximately 450 sections. It supports four general education composition courses: a one-semester first-year-writing-intensive course, two different first-year-writing-intensive courses designed to support multilingual and international pathways students, and a 300-level advanced composition course.

Our institution first began offering hybrid writing courses in 2017, spurred in part by the need to offer students flexible learning options and in part by growing constraints on available classroom space. By 2019, the program offered around ten percent of its composition courses, mostly advanced composition, in the hybrid mode; however, the COVID-19 pandemic quickly led to a plethora of distance learning options, including various models of hybrid courses, which continue to be offered in the program. Needless to say, shifting from a fully face-to-face (F2F) model of instruction to a partial distance learning (DL) model between 2017 and 2019 and then to a fully DL model during the pandemic was a challenge, and we assume it was a bit like helping golfers learn to play virtual golf like a professional in just a couple months.

Though we didn't consciously set out to do it at the time, our task force has developed an effective and replicable model for OWI professional and course development. The original task force was a strategically selected group of instructors with a self-reported interest in OWI, but with varying levels of hybrid teaching experience. By working collaboratively and pairing more and less experienced faculty together, we effectively conducted secondary and primary research; shared findings internally and externally through workshops, conferences, and peer-reviewed papers; fostered internal faculty expertise beyond the original members of the task force; and extended into the external sharing of resources outside our institution. This approach mirrors a community of practice (CoP) model that Lydia Hilliard (2021) discusses, which is evidenced-based, sensitive to local need, implementable with limited funding, and concerned with keeping faculty workloads in mind (Adams Wooten et al., 2022).

To better understand our approach, it might be useful to think of a biological feedback loop. As the task force shared original findings with fellow instructors, colleagues integrated these takeaways into their own teaching practices. Over time, they built on and complicated the original findings through feedback and additional research, which was in turn reintegrated into the task force's work. In this way, we avoided a rigid, top-down approach to knowledge-building and instead adapted the Borgman and McArdle (2019) PARS framework, recognizing that all faculty are members of the professional community and respecting their contributions to the conversation.

In the following sections, we provide a plan and research timeline that can help programs interested in a similar approach sustainably collect data, develop teaching resources, refine training and workshops, create new online and hybrid materials, and adapt existing course design approaches through the collaborative research model.

Theory and Practice
Our Task Force Team: A Framework for Sustainable Collaboration

The composition program established the hybrid task force with the main charges of gathering existing scholarship relevant to writing-intensive hybrid courses, developing teaching resources, and supporting faculty teaching hybrids in the program. Faculty teaching hybrid courses, particularly before the pandemic, were assigned them for a variety of reasons, including classroom availability and scheduling issues, and faculty teaching hybrids sometimes had training and experience and sometimes did not. In our program (before the pandemic), hybrids were taught with one in-person meeting a week and the rest of the material delivered asynchronously online. Since the pandemic, hybrid courses are also taught virtually, with one class meeting per week via Zoom and the rest of the work completed asynchronously, as well as hybrid synchronously, with one in-person session in a classroom and one via Zoom. The program also offers fully synchronous courses, where both weekly meetings are in-person via Zoom. While in 2019 the focus was understanding and supporting the hybrid, in-person course, the task force has developed materials that support all multimodal courses now offered.

To convene the task force, the program recruited writing faculty who were interested in learning more about hybrids or had experience teaching hybrid and/or online courses. As part of a quality enhancement plan (QEP) at the time, the program had access to funding to support undergraduate research, which included how to teach undergraduate research in our advanced composition courses, in particular through hybrid course design. This funding, which was only available until summer 2020, and that we augmented through our much smaller program budget through spring 2021, allowed the program to support the initial activities of the task force, providing a stipend to each faculty member.

During fall 2019, the team gathered scholarship and wrote a literature review, developed teaching resources for our internal website, and decided to formalize a research study to fill in gaps in hybrid writing pedagogy research. The team developed the institutional review board (IRB) protocol with survey and interview questions, and we decided to conduct the study in spring 2020, so we focused on securing funding for data coding in the summer. A central consideration was our ability to feel like the work was fair and sustainable, since the pay would not really cover all of the work involved. We conducted interviews with 14 faculty in spring 2020 as the pandemic was just beginning.

In the years since, we have collaboratively and iteratively worked to develop resources, analyze data, publish and present on the data, develop training and workshops based on the data, and make recommendations to the program on how to develop faculty expertise. We have also secured external grant funding to conduct a second study, this time focused on student experiences of hybrid courses. That study will follow a similar timeline as the original study.

The task force itself has remained stable, and the work has been sustainable, despite the lack of funding in the last two years of the work. The task force has become a site of mentoring and professional development for its members. Below, we describe the concrete steps we took to recruit and to establish sustainable participation in the task force; we also include our advice on how to coordinate a task force of this kind and a project timeline. The collaborative model used has allowed for flexibility, versatility, and agency that other groups of faculty could use as a sustainable model. An important consideration is the research timeline, particularly when funding, time, and workloads constrain faculty participation. Over time, our team's research timeline remained sensitive to those constraints. Table 7.1 shows our research timeline and the activities the team has conducted since 2019.

Table 7.1. Research Timeline

Semester and Year	Research Activities Conducted
Summer 2019	Develop goals and a schedule for the task force. Invite select faculty with experience for the task force.
Fall 2019	Members of the task force conduct a review of the literature, craft a research report with short- and long-term recommendations for the program and institution, and create teaching resources to be shared with faculty in the program.
Spring 2020	Draft first research protocol and submit for IRB approval. Conduct surveys and follow-up interviews.
Summer and Fall 2020	Code interviews and discuss findings. Outline potential academic papers based on findings. Begin drafting articles.
2021	Continue drafting and revising articles after submission. Apply for continued funding.
2022	Publish articles. Develop schedule for phase two of research. Draft second research protocol and submit for IRB approval. Create public-facing website with teaching resources.
Ongoing activities 2021–2022	Present at local and national conferences. Draft curricular teaching resources. Revise teaching resources based on new research. Facilitate departmental workshops.

Starting the Team: Recruit and Develop Faculty Expertise

An essential component of building a team is to strategically recruit faculty who can grow in a variety of ways and faculty who need or want different experiences so that their contributions are complementary and change over time. Building on the idea from PARS that personal administration involves respecting faculty and recognizing that they are members of the professional community, the team pulled in a variety of faculty members with different stakes in hybrid teaching, including non-tenure track (NTT) faculty and graduate teaching assistants (GTAs). Members of the team would meet regularly and choose which aspects of the project they were most interested in developing, including teaching resources, programmatic resources, pedagogical workshops, conference presentations, peer-reviewed articles, and grant applications. In brainstorming sessions and email threads, the team discussed priorities and project preferences, and team members would choose what they wanted to do. If there were not enough team members interested in pursuing a grant or submitting a proposal for a conference, then the team did not pursue that opportunity. For more manageable tasks, some members of the team would collaborate, while others would join at a different juncture, or not at all. Those with shared interests worked together on projects, and the decision-making process on what opportunities to pursue developed organically through discussion.

During the recruitment process, we invited faculty with a wide range of experiences and motivations to participate. We wanted faculty with experience teaching hybrids, but we also wanted faculty interested in developing expertise in hybrids. Additionally, we wanted to provide development opportunities for graduate students in the program. Faculty members chose to join for varied reasons, including to learn more about hybrids, to extend their expertise with online courses, to deepen their experience with qualitative research and managing research projects, and to extend their research interests in online teaching and disability studies scholarship.

The original members of the task force did not include the WPA, who is the only tenure track (TT) faculty member in the program. The task force received support from the program and supported program initiatives, and the director provided the space for task force members to do the work independently and at their own pace. An assistant director in the program, who was full-time NTT faculty, took on the coordination role, focusing on the logistics of facilitating, rather than overseeing, the work. This facilitated, delegated model has been essential to the collaborative process and has enabled a high degree of iteration.

Sustaining the Team: Strategic Collaboration and Iteration

Making sure the process is iterative and flexible is essential when funding is scarce and workloads are high. One way the task force engaged faculty expertise was by creating mechanisms where faculty could do more or less work depending on their interests, time, and expectations. Faculty could also work in pairs or alone and fold into larger group discussions as desired. Here are two examples of how this dynamic has developed:

- One faculty with creative writing and digital design experience is not as interested in the research components of the study (coding data, analyzing data, publishing in peer-reviewed journals). This faculty is interested in the teaching resources piece, so they participate more intensely when the work is related to design and implementation of teaching resources and the creation of workshops for the program. The instructor has contributed incredible teaching resources, conducted workshops, and coined the term *braiding*, which has helped us frame the findings from the study. In the next iteration of the study, the faculty will work more closely with the data but still decide when and how to contribute.
- One faculty with a background in creative writing and linguistics originally focused on teaching resources and workshops but has also become increasingly embedded in the research studies. To develop methods expertise, they were paired with someone with coding experience during the initial data coding portion of the study and learned how to develop codebooks, settle on themes, and write analysis. At the same time, as peer-reviewed articles were being written, the faculty moved from support for the first two articles to lead writer of the third article. The process has been intensively iterative, flexible, and collaborative, modeled on development and mentorship.

In order to facilitate sustained, collaborative faculty engagement, we have focused on cultivating fluid team dynamics that support different branches of work. One coordinator manages logistics and the timeline using a facilitated model that allows for different entry points into the work. The coordinator manages the back-end logistics, including sending reminders about timelines and opportunities, but does not manage all aspects of the research, writing, and resource and training development process. This approach allows for other faculty to lead portions of the work as desired or needed and gives the coordinator the space needed to help the task force stay on track without directly managing it.

This coordinator approach was only possible because the director of the program joined the work when the first round of peer-reviewed publications was beginning and after initial data analysis had been completed. The director has been thoughtful about how to engage as a member of the task force without replicating the hierarchical structures that her role would imply. That collaborative, delegated leadership model has ensured faculty can work without feeling they are working directly for the director while still seeing the work as supporting the program.

Motivating the Team: From Strategic Iteration to Strategic Versatility

To understand the work of the task force over the last three years, as suggested previously, it is helpful to visualize the work as a biological feedback loop, interconnected and engaged in multiple, simultaneous processes. While the initial research study and initial resource development were completed by members of the task force, members of the task force have at different points networked with other faculty, shared resources formally through workshops and training sessions as well as informally through casual interactions and conversations, and brought back the feedback to the work of the task force. Simultaneously, task force members have continuously incorporated findings from the data, revisions from peer-reviewed articles, and feedback from conference presentations into the aims and work of the task force. Figure 7.1 shows these feedback loops.

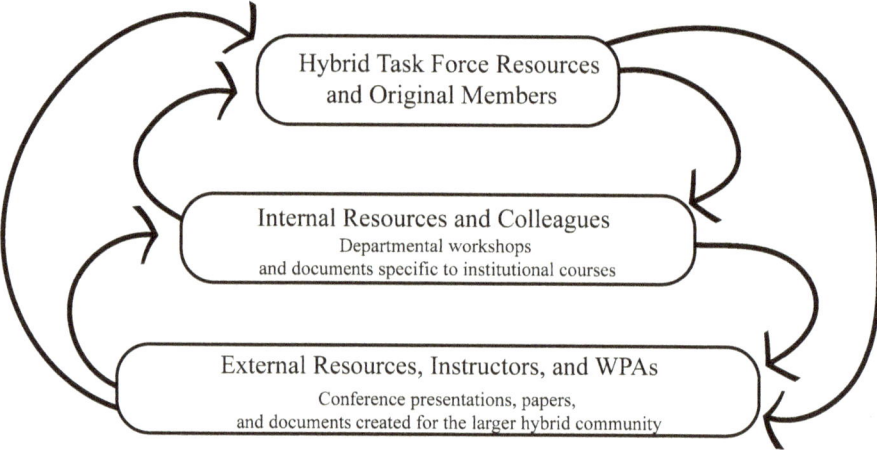

Figure 7.1. Iterative research and feedback process (image created by Ariel M. Goldenthal).

Accessible administration, according to PARS, involves listening to and supporting faculty, including with students and technical support. Throughout the team's work, we have used data to reshape the frequency and format of faculty professional development, to revise the program-developed online templates, and to make better course design and scheduling decisions. Because of the complicated nature of teaching hybrid courses, our team began its work wanting to know more about how faculty experience these courses and how our program could better support faculty who teach them. Our group found that feedback strategies in hybrid courses change in small but important ways, and we have begun rethinking how students access feedback and how faculty can make feedback more visible for students in LMSs (Goldenthal et al., 2022). Our team also developed resources about how to "braid" together the online and face-to-face components of hybrid courses that help faculty scaffold and support students' learning experiences in hybrid courses (see publicly available resources at https://hybridtl.org).

The pandemic accelerated this process of branched iteration, and the task force has become increasingly versatile in how it synthesizes new feedback and develops new material and interventions. PARS discusses responsive administration in several ways, including supporting faculty without exploiting them and supporting faculty and program needs broadly. We convened our team in response to faculty and student needs as our program increased the number of hybrid courses offered without explicitly supporting faculty through programmatic or institutional professional development. The pandemic changed the scope of the task force's work and made some of the work more urgent. As we were conducting interviews, the university went fully online in March 2020. Suddenly, the faculty who we were interviewing to learn more about how they teach hybrids were teaching fully online, often keeping the hybrid model but with a virtual, synchronous weekly meeting. The protocol we had designed asked faculty to speak of hybrids generally, but the pandemic inflected some of the responses with this pivot. As a result, we had data showing how faculty adapt to online environments in a crisis; how they use prior knowledge, current expertise, and peer-to-peer networks to adapt; and how workloads impact access to training and professional development.

From slow iteration, we moved to multidirectional response, both to address immediate concerns and to develop durable teaching resources that would support multimodal teaching that uses different elements of hybrids and online technologies. During the second and third year of the project, as the pandemic created new exigencies, the task force developed several initiatives to respond to short-term and long-term issues. As we analyzed data, we used some of the findings to immediately develop workshops focused on workload-aware feedback strategies and on strategies to provide explicit transitions to students enrolled in hybrid courses. The team also continued to analyze the data to support requests for additional support for courses and to prepare for conferences and peer-reviewed articles. The multiple directions of the task force allowed members options to share their knowledge and expertise and the chance to try new things (e.g., writing an academic paper, analyzing interview data) while developing materials and training to better support and respond to faculty needs as the pandemic progressed and the program offered additional course delivery methods, including virtual hybrid and synchronous online courses.

As feedback from multiple sources has been folded into the work, and as data has been used recursively to aid decision-making and to develop faculty mentoring roles, new areas of concern have also developed. The data, feedback from training and workshops, and response from the program have opened conversations about the role of access in hybrid writing courses. Access originally meant how faculty accessed resources easily, but the conversation now includes student access to learning in hybrid modalities, including multilingual students and students with disability accommodations. The pandemic created a pivot towards more variations of our traditional hybrid modality, which further accelerated this conversation. One main result of these multidirectional feedback loops is that we are beginning to center accessibility throughout other program initiatives and conversations. This feedback loop now informs the second stage of the research study, which will focus on student experiences in hybrids. The survey and interview protocols will include questions about accessibility and inclusion, and students will be asked to describe their experiences using technology; accessing and implementing feedback; and engaging with the space, time, and place differences in the hybrid modality.

Conclusion and Takeaways

Building Your Own Team

Given our group's experiences building a collaborative and sustainable research and teaching model, in Table 7.2 we offer some lessons learned that others can take up in developing similar approaches to building collective knowledge about online writing instruction (or other changes in a writing program).

Table 7.2. Lessons for Developing Collective Knowledge About OWI

Lesson Learned	Discussion
Have a basic and flexible strategic plan in place.	Determine what members want out of the group (e.g., experience with academic collaboration, teaching resources they and others can use) and what they want to create (e.g., teaching resources, journal articles, presentations). These can then be scaffolded into a timeline, and different clusters of group members can participate as they want. The plan should be flexible enough to evolve over time and to reflect a collaborative approach to goal setting.
Use a pilot to launch new initiatives and task forces.	Constrain the work, work closely with a small team, and figure out resources, including funding, time, and support for sustainable workflow, before scaling the work. Allow for slow uptake of the work throughout the program, as faculty working in the pilot can then become part of training teams.
Assemble a small group of faculty already doing or interested in exploring the same idea to make launching an initiative focused and sustainable.	Scope work to be tightly constrained and framed around a smaller goal to support development of expertise and to promote careful expansion that keeps in mind workloads.

Lesson Learned	Discussion
Be intentional about group size.	The group has to be big enough to allow for members to step in and out of tasks they care about within the larger project. The group should have faculty with overlapping strengths but with enough room for individual professional development.
Consider individual expertise and how it matters in the context of collaboration.	Although starting with common interest in hybrids and different areas of expertise, as the team has collaborated, new expertise has developed, individual contributions have changed, and some redundancy of expertise has been built. This, in turn, has changed who leads a task, who steps out, etc.
Pair faculty strategically to build expertise and group cohesion.	Pairing more experienced group members with less experienced group members on particular tasks builds mentorship into the group and allows opportunities for group members to develop as teachers, researchers, and program leaders. This can take more time than assigning members to tasks they already know how to do, but it is an integral part of the group's development.
Develop work slowly and commit to collaboration.	Allow time for activities such as thinking, processing, and listening that Laura Micciche (2011) argues can build "slow agency." Unless an external exigence demands speedy work, a workflow that accounts for group members' schedules and evolves around these will make collaborative efforts most sustainable over time, even if it does mean changes based on the work are slower in developing across a writing program.
Use a fluid, facilitated coordination model.	Allow for group collaboration and collaboratively-developed goals. The work should never exceed what the team is willing to do at any given time, and this commitment to collaboration requires a facilitated, rather than a directive, coordination style. If a WPA is involved in the group, consider whether they are the best person to lead the group.
Build a sustainable research timeline to help manage expectations and workload.	To prioritize collaboration, research should be sensitive to workload. Different types of work can be completed at different times, with periods of intense, focused work and periods of very little research-related work. For instance, research tasks such as data collection can be interspersed with workshops and training that are informed by ongoing, partial data analysis.
Be flexible with available funding.	If funding is available, then it should also be strategic. Rather than tying funding to group members doing work overall, funding can be tied to what people want to do and contribute. This supports group members who want to say no to some tasks, while still supporting those who are doing particular tasks that support the writing program as a whole.
Build faculty expertise iteratively across the program.	As the group gains expertise and builds knowledge, leverage this new expertise to iteratively build faculty expertise across the program. With our group, this involved group members facilitating workshops and sharing resources that other faculty then learned from and began modifying on their own.

Although academic research is often framed as a solitary endeavor, we have found that approaching it as a team sport has allowed for our group to gain individual and collective skills and knowledge that have led to further growth in hybrid pedagogies across our program. The lessons we learned can serve as a game plan for others who want to design and implement a collaborative research task force of their own. We see two major takeaways from these lessons: 1) Use a model that allows research and analysis to expand by branching rather than moving linearly from the top down to cultivate a creative environment for faculty inquiry, and 2) give each team member the freedom to dive deeply into the position they "play" because it strengthens the collective expertise of the team overall.

Adapting this type of model can be useful in many different settings, where the team assembled can define their own goals and how to collaboratively work towards them. With an area of research such as hybrid writing pedagogies, where the scholarship in the field is less-developed, this type of model also provides a pathway for cyclical knowledge-building from scholarship, from a group's own research, and from the development of resources that can be both internally and externally shared and further extended. As new innovations and pedagogical strategies emerge in online writing instruction (for instance, through HyFlex instructional modalities), building collaborative and recursive research groups in and between institutions will be an important part of our field's developing further knowledge of how to best support students and faculty who teach and learn in online spaces. This model offers one flexible approach that can help the field accomplish this work in sustainable ways.

References

Borgman, J. & McArdle, C. (2019). *Personal, accessible, responsive, strategic: Resources and strategies for online writing instructors*. The WAC Clearinghouse; University Press of Colorado. https://doi.org/10.37514/PRA-B.2019.0322.

Goldenthal, A. M., Matthews, J., Wooten., C. A., Fitzpatrick, B. & Fernandez. (2022). Feedback practices in hybrid writing courses: Instructor choices about modality and timing. *Journal of Response to Writing 8(2), 40–72*. https://scholarsarchive.byu.edu/journalrw/vol8/iss2/3.

Hilliard, L. (2021). Using PARS to build a community of practice for hybrid writing instructors. In J. Borgman & C. McArdle (Eds.), *PARS in practice: More resources and strategies for online writing instructors* (pp. 209-223). The WAC Clearinghouse; University Press of Colorado. https://doi.org/10.37514/PRA-B.2021.1145.

Micciche, L. (2011). For slow agency. *WPA: Writing Program Administration, 35(1)*, 73–90. https://wpacouncil.org/aws/CWPA/pt/sp/journal-archives.

Wooten, C. A., Fitzpatrick, B., Fernandez, L., Goldenthal, A. M. & Matthews, J. (2022). Drown[ing] a little bit all the time: The intersections of labor constraints and professional development in hybrid contingent faculty experiences. *Academic Labor: Research and Artistry, 6(1), 1–26*. https://digitalcommons.humboldt.edu/cgi/viewcontent.cgi?article=1079&context=alra.

Appendix: Suggested Readings

Borgman, J. & McArdle, C. (Eds.). (2021). *PARS in practice: More resources and strategies for online writing instructors*. The WAC Clearinghouse; University Press of Colorado. https://doi.org/10.37514/PRA-B.2021.1145.

Caulfield, J. (2012). *How to design and teach a hybrid course*. Stylus.

Fitzpatrick, B., Fernandez, L., Goldenthal, A., Matthews, J., Wooten, C. A. & Biller, B. (2022). When communities of practice fail to form: Perceptions of peer-to-peer networks and developing competence in hybrid course design. *WPA: Writing Program Administration* 46(1), 77–96. https://wpacouncil.org/aws/CWPA/pt/sp/journal-archives.

Garrison, D. R. & Vaughan, N. D. (2007). *Blended learning in higher education: Framework, principles, and guidelines*. Jossey-Bass.

Paull, J. N. & Snart, J. A. (2016). *Making hybrids work: An institutional framework for blending online and face-to-face instruction in higher education*. National Council of Teachers of English.

Snart, J. A. (2010). *Hybrid learning: The perils and promise of blending online and face-to-face instruction in higher education*. Praeger.

Keep Your Focus!

All golfers get training, whether it's working with a golfing coach regularly, taking lessons occasionally, or having a full-out caddie and golf coach like professional golfers do; everyone needs training to hone their skills.

Online writing instruction design and facilitation is no exception. Over the past decade, preparation and training have continued to be an issue facing OWI at institutions across the country. What we like about Bethany Mannon's chapter is that she has laid out a clear, replicable, and holistic training course for new and existing online writing instructors. Her use of the hyperdoc to keep the training organized is innovative, and we really like how she focuses on ongoing professional development for her staff.

Chapter 8. Transitioning Online Writing Instruction from Crisis to Sustainability

Bethany Mannon
APPALACHIAN STATE UNIVERSITY

Abstract: This chapter advocates for online writing instruction (OWI) training that responds to the specific needs of a writing program, grows out of faculty perspectives, and aims to create a sustainable approach to online teaching. To make this case, I outline how I implemented such an approach at Appalachian State University. Part I describes a place-based study of rhetoric and composition (RC) faculty who launched online writing courses at App State in response to the COVID-19 pandemic. These interviews aimed to understand how faculty perceive student growth and achievement in OWI and how our RC program should train and support faculty teaching these classes. Part II describes four professional development modules to support future OWI instruction that I developed following those interviews. I also share results of a pilot in which twelve OWI faculty completed the modules and assessed their effectiveness. Part III proposes implications of this research for other writing program administrators (WPAs). I contend that professional development, assessment, and writing curricula grounded in program self-study serve the needs of faculty and support effective instruction.

Keywords: online first-year writing, writing program administration, faculty perspectives, writing pedagogy, professional development, assessment

Historically, my rhetoric and composition (RC) program resisted teaching first-year writing online. When I joined Appalachian State University in 2018, writing faculty and writing program administrators (WPAs) worried that online spaces would not allow collaboration and connection among students and faculty, and therefore would not support effective teaching. Moreover, they saw little student or faculty interest in online first-year writing (OFYW). When we all converted our courses to synchronous or asynchronous online modalities in spring 2020, we viewed this shift as a short-term response to the COVID-19 pandemic. In fact, student and faculty demand for OFYW persisted that semester and beyond. As faculty discovered that online teaching actually suited them quite well, and as students flocked to online sections, we as a program saw a call to assess our established practices and envision a new direction for our future.

This rapid shift to online instruction caused an interruption and an opportunity to research the factors that support faculty and student success in online writing classes (OWCs). The research I describe in this chapter was initially a response to a global health crisis, but our questions about online writing instruction (OWI) matter beyond that context. Natural disasters or regional emergencies are possible, even likely, to interrupt face-to-face course delivery in the future. We saw this happen in 2019 when a hurricane caused flooding that closed another campus in our state for several months. Even more important, though, our shift online propelled critical self-reflection from our teachers and program-wide conversations. As Phoebe Jackson and Christopher Weaver (2018) argue in the introduction to *Writing in Online Courses*, "the online environment calls into question the 'givens' of the traditional classroom and opens them up for interrogation and analysis" (p. xviii). Our RC program saw a need for ongoing professional development and an intentional, sustainable approach to OWI that would be personal, accessible, responsive, and strategic. We envisioned a time when faculty could instead elect to teach in this modality because of its advantages in pedagogical and work-life balance. They could thoughtfully design their OWCs rather than adapting their materials with short notice.

This chapter describes a self-study of the online pedagogy and curriculum in the RC program I direct. This project has two takeaways for readers. First, it will provide WPAs, especially new ones like myself, with a model for studying OWI and building professional development in their programs that can then equip them to advocate for program self-direction. Second, it brings attention to faculty experiences and perspectives, important sources of insight into OWI. I contend that professional development, assessment, and writing curricula can best serve the needs of faculty and support effective OWI when they are grounded in faculty experience.

Theory and Practice

In fall 2020, I designed a place-based study of RC faculty who launched online writing courses at Appalachian State University that semester. This project responded to our program's need for an OFYW curriculum, but my own goals as a teacher and WPA motivated the study and shaped its design too. Unlike many of my colleagues, my prior experience had convinced me that these courses could be fruitful for faculty and students. At previous institutions (including the university that Stuart Selber, Daniel Tripp, and Leslie Mateer describe in their chapter in this collection-chapter 5), I had seen online students collaborate with each other enthusiastically, thrive through one-on-one interaction with me, and connect with our material in ways that were personally meaningful and academically rigorous (Mannon, 2019). I sang the praises of OWI to anyone who would listen.

As I planned this study, I sought to align the research with my professional goals. I was in my first semester as the director of composition (and in my first year on the tenure track), and I wanted opportunities to get to know my fellow teachers. As a relative newbie to the WPA role, I hesitated to move forward with my agenda—convincing the RC program that OWI can be great for teachers and students—without first learning what my colleagues thought of online teaching.

I also wanted to start involving undergraduates in research. I pictured a study of online teaching as a project to which undergraduates could contribute in authentic and integral ways.

Along with my own perspective and goals, two questions steered this study:

1. How do faculty perceive student growth and achievement in online first-year writing?
2. How can our writing program effectively train and support faculty in OWI?

I focus on faculty perceptions of student learning, though there are certainly other productive ways to frame study of OWI. For example, scholars have considered how the online environment affects writing and learning (Bourelle et al.,2016; Jackson & Weaver, 2018) or students' self-assessments of their own learning (Boyd, 2008; Litterio, 2018). Others have described course designs that facilitate student participation and community (Borgman & McArdle, 2019; Mannon, 2019), and the field has established effective practices for course design and implementation (CCCC OWI Committee, 2013). While features of the online environment and student perceptions of the online modality do come up in my research—because faculty mentioned them—I prioritized faculty perspectives and experiences. What did they see happening in their classes?

To explore how faculty implement best practices and their perceptions of student learning online, I interviewed 17 faculty members who had taught a full semester of OFYW during fall 2020. Some were teaching online for only the first or second time. Others had years or semesters of OWI experience but were, of course, responding to students' evolving needs. Broadly, my goal was to understand their experiences so I could make that information the basis of our professional development and curriculum going forward.

We asked our interviewees the following questions, which we provided in advance:

> In your OFYW courses, where did you see students growing as writers meeting course goals and outcomes? List as many areas as you want.
> - Did that growth happen at particular points in the semester or throughout?
> - What aspects of the course were challenging for students? List as many as you want.
> - Did they encounter that difficulty at particular points in the semester or throughout?
> - Which assignments did your OFYW include?
> - Did you feel you could connect with students successfully?

- Were there times in your OFYW course when your teaching was particularly effective?
- Which parts of the course were challenging for you to teach?

In your online courses, did you observe any differences in how students met course goals and outcomes compared to face-to-face classes?

For first-time teachers: what was it like for your first semester to be online?

In the future, when you can choose between face-to-face, hybrid, or fully online courses, what experiences from this fall will help you make that decision and design that course?

These interviews balanced open-ended questions with focused or directive ones, a balance designed to elicit both concrete information and narrative responses.

I say "we" as I talk about this research design, and that "we" includes three talented undergraduate researchers. Ali and Elliot completed human subjects training and then scheduled interviews, interviewed faculty, checked transcripts, and helped code our data to identify where faculty experienced successes and struggles. A third undergraduate, Georgia, had assisted me with interview-based research in the past. I asked her to join this study to train our new researchers in interviewing and coding. In fact, I designed the study around interviews, rather than class observations or assessments of student writing, because undergraduate researchers could contribute to this stage even as they were honing their interview skills. I would recommend a similar design to other faculty planning to study OWI.

These interviews provided the major findings I would go on to use in professional development. Initially, we coded deductively using the *Position Statement of Principles and Example Effective Practices for Online Writing Instruction* (2013). We turned each principle into a code and noted where speakers alluded directly or indirectly to the principle, and what they said about it. We initially planned to do two "passes" through the transcripts, with two researchers checking each other's work (Saldaña, 2013). However, we noticed that the codes based on *Effective Practices* overlooked the most interesting parts of our interviews. These codes did not, in practice, help us understand the challenges and successes our faculty encountered.

This bump in the research process actually redirected us to analysis that aligned more closely with the PARS principles than with the CCCC statement. We switched gears to re-code inductively based on the important or recurring points we found in the interviews. Those codes included the following:

discussion, technology, flexibility, community, connection, judgment, feedback, essential knowledge, student engagement, peer review, course structure, writing as a process, reflection, inclusion, and planning. This was a helpful and necessary shift away from program structure and toward the PARS focus on faculty practices and course design.

Reading and coding these interview transcripts revealed the following trends in faculty experiences with OWI:

- Faculty rarely observe spontaneous moments of enthusiastic discussion or exploration of ideas. That is, they rarely felt the lively, surprising environment of a face-to-face classroom at its best. However, an intentional, even scripted style of teaching that suited online modalities could still support discussion and exploration.
- Our faculty like teaching online! They find it fits their teaching style and allows work-life balance, which is especially valuable for some non-tenure-track lecturers teaching four (or more) sections.
- Faculty hypothesized that the online environment has advantages for student learning. In their experiences, students felt autonomy and ownership over their writing, and they transferred skills from low-stakes writing to high-stakes writing more readily than in face-to-face classes. One instructor reported that students participated in discussions of power, privilege, and social justice more openly in online discussion boards than they had done in face-to-face classroom spaces.
- Faculty developed multiple, varied, largely successful strategies to make their courses personal and collaborative.

These findings are surely just the tip of the iceberg. The advantages to students and faculty (points 2 and 3) are particularly pertinent to research, course design, and professional development, and merit follow-up in a future article.

With these initial findings in mind, with funding from a Conference on College Composition and Communication (CCCC) Emergent Researcher grant, and with mentoring from Casey McArdle and Jessie Borgman, I created professional development modules to support OWI. I aimed to create a training that would a) meet a gap in the online instruction landscape, b) fit a community with a wide range of interests, preparation, and availability, and c) respond to the experiences and material constraints of our program. I discuss each of these goals in the following sections.

Meet a Gap in the Online Instruction Landscape

Several of our faculty had participated in in-depth, months-long (and sometimes expensive) training for online teaching that came from national organizations or our state university system. Others had completed professional development on campus. My colleagues and I knew these trainings were available, but we saw drawbacks in each one. Only rarely did these workshops focus specifically on OWI;

more often, they reviewed technology or guided participants in thinking about online teaching apart from the content or pedagogy of their discipline. The existing on-campus trainings tended to be one-off events lasting an hour or an afternoon. To address this gap in the OWI professional development landscape, I envisioned a sequence of modules that would ask participants to think about teaching writing and develop materials rooted in the PARS philosophy—and do so over a timeline of weeks. My review of research in the field and my conversations with Jessie and Casey confirmed that I wouldn't be "reinventing the wheel" with this design.

Be Flexible Enough for Faculty with a Wide Range of Interests, Experiences, and Available Time

My interviews showed me that some faculty would have time and energy to delve into effective online pedagogy; others would complete readings and activities in the slivers of time between their responsibilities as teachers and caregivers. This training needed to be explicitly useful and customizable, responsive to the fact that future participants might have previous experience (both positive and negative) and training.

Reflect the Experiences of our Faculty and Material Constraints of our Program

When I embarked on this study in fall 2020, my RC program had already done professional development and self-study around diversity, equity, and inclusion. Workshops by our own faculty and external speakers had explored alternative assessment and other ways of moving away from syllabi based on standard academic English. Many of our faculty had built social justice and rhetorical ethics into their classes, and I hoped that an OWI training could reflect that work and add to those conversations.

This training was also motivated by a desire to maintain RC program autonomy in the areas of curriculum, qualifications, and professional development. In fall 2020, our campus had no required qualifications to teach online courses. At the same time, communication from campus and system administration expressed concern about the quality of online courses and told us that students wanted to be back in the classroom (these concerns were vague and had unclear foundations, as our faculty senate pointed out). I hoped developing an in-house OWI training could help us get ahead of any top-down requirements for or limits on online teaching. Fortunately, such limits never materialized, as I will discuss in my next section, but this research did help keep some of our autonomy.

Based on my goal of a flexible, responsive OWI training, I created a hyperdoc divided into four "detachable" modules (see Figure 8.1). Faculty could complete them in or out of sequence, together or individually, according to their needs and preferences.

Online Writing Instruction for Expository Writing & Writing Across the Curriculum at Appalachian State		
Introduction Welcome to OWI Training in the App State RC program! 1 hour	Using this hyperdoc: Over these four modules you'll discuss key concepts for teaching online and create materials for your online writing courses. We'll have a mix of synchronous and asynchronous activities focused on: • Thoughtful online course design • Adapting RC course goals for an online modality • Inclusive online teaching • Effective writing assignments We'll start by introducing ourselves to our colleagues and thinking about how we'll introduce ourselves to online students.	
	Create: Instructor information and bio	Readings & Resources: App State Vertical Writing Model
Module 1: Course Design (synchronous) Goals & Outcomes 4–6 hrs., depending on prior experience	Activities: Reflect on experience & knowledge and set goals for this training Participate in 1 hr. synchronous Zoom discussion of instructor backgrounds and PARS model Create: Online writing course syllabus	Readings & Resources: PARS Model Overview "Hybrid and Fully Online OWI" from Foundational Practices of Online Writing Instruction Learn more (optional): Access and Design in the Online Writing Classroom OWI Effective Practices & Principles
Module 2: RC Course Goals (asynchronous) Goals & Outcomes 4 hours	Activities: Discussion forum: Pedagogical tools Workshop: Provide feedback on your team's syllabi Reflect: Impressions of synchronous and asynchronous learning, team-based discussions Create: Informal assignment	Readings & Resources: "Beyond the Discussion Board" - Kevin De Pew Kevin's ignite talk handout Kevin's ignite talk slides "Cohort-based Discussion Forums" Research findings: Building Community in Online Courses
Module 3: Accessibility & Anti-racist Pedagogy (synchronous) Goals & Outcomes 2–3 hours	Activities: Collaborative reading: Performing Antiracist Pedagogy 1 hr. synchronous discussion of inclusive, antiracist writing pedagogy online	Readings & Resources: Performing Antiracist Pedagogy Research findings: Inclusive Teaching Online "Antiracist Practice in the Online Writing Classroom" - Jude Miller Jude's ignite talk handout Jude's ignite talk slides

Online Writing Instruction for Expository Writing & Writing Across the Curriculum at Appalachian State		
Module 4: Assignments & Syllabi (asynchronous) Goals & Outcomes 3–4 hours	Create: Formal Assignment 1 Activities: Discuss: Explore an assignment from a colleague's course Reflect: How effective is your own assignment?	Readings & Resources: Assignment Gallery Syllabus Gallery Spreadsheet: Assignments you can reference and App State resources you should know
Going Forward	Research Cohort: Feedback on Modules Mid-Semester Check-in End-of-Semester Check-in	Readings & Resources: Meet RC Course Coordinators

Figure 8.1. Online writing instruction hyperdoc.

I piloted this training in December 2021 and January 2022 in order to assess its effectiveness and offer professional development to interested faculty. A cohort of 12 full- and part-time RC lecturers completed the modules and provided anonymous feedback on the format, activities, and resources immediately after finishing. They gave feedback again in May 2022 after teaching a full semester of OWI and implementing ideas from the training. Here are their assessments of the training, which might be helpful for fellow administrators looking to create OWI professional development:

1. The training was relevant and "good at covering the basics," as one respondent put it. However, another stated that the modules made the most sense for people new to online teaching. Others seemed to agree, based on their requests for more readings on innovative practices and activities to encourage critical thinking about teaching.
2. Participants liked Modules 2 and 4, in which they created and shared syllabi, assignments, and activities. They confirmed what I had anticipated: that creating and workshopping immediately useful course materials would make this training responsive to the limited time and possibly extensive prior experience of faculty.
3. Similarly, participants liked the easy-to-navigate hyperdoc. "The design was visually easy to see the workload," one reported. Others expressed interest in using our learning management system (LMS) rather than Google Docs and folders. I had purposely avoided incorporating the LMS because new faculty are sometimes unable to access it right after they're hired. I will make this consideration explicit for future cohorts, and I take those participants' point about using dynamic online spaces.

4. Finally, participants commented on the limited interactivity of the training. I designed modules to give participants a feel for asynchronous and synchronous activities, Zoom conversations and discussion boards, and the roles of both teacher and student. To facilitate discussions and feedback on materials, I placed participants in teams of four; several responded positively to this format.

The majority of participants asked for more interaction between participants and with the facilitator (me, in this case). One reported that "Others didn't participate as much, from burnout, which made some assignments hard to complete." They offered specific recommendations for increased interaction: more small group activities, opportunities to see one another's LMS sites, and opportunities to continue connecting with their small group cohorts after the training is over. One participant shared that they would like to learn more about others' passions.

These assessments of the training modules made me rethink my initial goals. Does our professional development aim to ensure a certain level of quality teaching? Create community? Think creatively and innovate course materials? My "a bit of all of the above" approach led to limited interaction among this cohort and limited engagement with new, innovative ideas. As an online teacher, I discovered that cultivating community and collaboration at times has more value than covering content. I see a parallel with faculty development. My next step is to fine-tune this training for a target audience of knowledgeable teachers looking to connect and collaborate with one another.

These interviews and pilot training suggest a future direction for OWI at Appalachian State. As I discussed earlier in this chapter, we are invested in teaching online because of the clear benefits to faculty and to students. I met my goal of getting to know the program, and I found that faculty had already seen that OWI could be successful and rewarding. However, the interviews and pilot ultimately showed me how additional steps could continue to create a sustainable OWI curriculum:

1. Assessment of student writing could put interview findings in conversation with concrete observations about student learning in OFYW. In May 2022, five faculty who had done interviews joined me in reading portfolios from online sections and evaluating how they met course goals and outcomes. We returned to a longstanding question in OWI research—assessing student learning—with an explicit interest in how those findings align with or diverge from faculty experiences and perceptions.

2. We are ready for pointed discussions about our online identity and qualifications to teach online. In spring 2023, a team of online teachers is meeting biweekly to have these conversations, mediated by a longtime friend of the program in the university's Center for Excellence in Teaching and Learning for Student Success.

Conclusion and Takeaways

My research showed that when we moved online faculty responded to complex challenges in creative and thoughtful ways that reshaped our writing program. They became more intentional in creating opportunities for students to bring their personal selves to their writing, and more attuned to student autonomy and voice. They considered the elements of their online course design and, in many cases, became more conscious of the personal challenges and circumstances that affected students' work in OFYW. These faculty members elected to teach online out of necessity, not preference. However, they had a more positive experience of online teaching than existing research led me to expect, perhaps because of the autonomy and support in our program.

The study and pilot presented in this chapter have three implications for WPAs. First, I offer a model for WPAs looking to study and guide OWI in their programs. Fellow WPAs are welcome to consult or borrow from the modules (the hyperdoc) that I share. I hope they also push back against my approach to design and implement professional development that reflects the specific needs of their programs and advances in OWI and writing studies—especially as these fields expand their consideration of diversity, equity, and inclusion (DEI) in online courses.

Second, this research helped our program advocate for online courses when administration urged us to go back to exclusively face-to face classes. While top-down requirements for qualifications to teach online never arose, RC had to defend our right to decide how many online and hybrid FYW courses we offer. A fellow WPA and I successfully made this case by pointing to my external grant from CCCC, our research, and our in-house professional development. Assessing student writing and pairing those findings with faculty perspectives will help us to continue making a strong case for offering a number of composition sections online.

I continue to advocate for including faculty perspectives in OWI research. Whether that research takes place in internal self-studies or in data collection for outward-facing articles, it should inquire into faculty experiences and perceptions of student learning. Faculty have deep knowledge of strategies to minimize the obstacles to connection and collaboration, and their experiences help WPA researchers place these pedagogical strategies in the reality of instructors' lives. I am thinking particularly of the intense and growing demands of responding to first-year students who come to us with heightened mental health issues and spotty writing, reading, and thinking skills after multiple semesters of high school online. At many universities, faculty knowledge is rarely included in making decisions and policies for online courses. OWI research can avoid making that same oversight and instead tap into one of our richest sources of insight about the online writing classroom.

References

Almjeld, J. (2014). A rhetorician's guide to love: Online dating profiles as remediated commonplace books. *Computers and Composition, 32*, 71–83. https://doi.org/10.1016/j.compcom.2014.04.004.

Borgman, J. & McArdle, C. (2019). *Personal, accessible, responsive, strategic: Resources and strategies for online writing instructors.* The WAC Clearinghouse; University Press of Colorado. https://doi.org/10.37514/PRA-B.2019.0322.

Bourelle, A., Bourelle, T., Knutson, A. V. & Spong, S. (2016). Sites of multimodal literacy: Comparing student learning in online and face-to-face environments. *Computers and Composition, 39*, 55–70. https://doi.org/10.1016/j.compcom.2015.11.003.

Boyd, P. W. (2008). Analyzing students' perceptions of their learning in online and hybrid first-year composition courses. *Computers and Composition, 25*, 224–243. https://doi.org/10.1016/j.compcom.2008.01.002.

CCCC OWI Committee for Effective Practices in Online Writing Instruction. (2013). *A position statement of principles and effective practices for online writing instruction (OWI).* https://www.owicommunity.org/owi--distance-education-resources.html.

Gold, D., Garcia, M. & Knutson, A. V. (2019). Going public in an age of digital anxiety: How students negotiate the topoi of online writing environments. *Composition Forum, 41*. https://compositionforum.com/issue/41/going-public.php.

Jackson, P. & Weaver, C. (2018). Introduction: Why do you teach online? In P. Jackson & C. Weaver (Eds.), *Writing in online courses: How the online environment shapes writing practices* (pp. 1–13). Myers Education Press.

Lannin, A. A., Cisco, J., Philbrook, J. & Philbrook, M. (2017). "How do you know that works?": A mixed methods approach to writing program assessment. *WPA: Writing Program Administration, 40*(2), 52–76. https://wpacouncil.org/aws/CWPA/pt/sp/journal-archives.

Litterio, L. M. (2018). Uncovering student perceptions of a first-year online writing course. *Computers and Composition, 47*, 1–13. https://doi.org/10.1016/j.compcom.2017.12.006.

Mannon, B. (2019). Digital selves: Personal narrative pedagogy in the online writing course. *Currents in Teaching and Learning, 11*(1), 7–19.

Saldaña, J. (2013). *The coding manual for qualitative researchers.* SAGE.

Loosen Up!

All golfers, whether professional or not, know that things don't always go their way. Sometimes shots don't land where they want them to, sometimes water or sand get the best of them, and sometimes their game is just off. That's why it's important to have empathy and compassion with one's self as a golfer and as an online writing program leader.

We like how Rachael Groner and Tania Islam's chapter focuses on empathy and how administrators can adapt their practices to maintain a sense of empathy and compassion in their writing program community. With hectic schedules, upper-level pressure to produce, and student and faculty issues, sometimes being a program leader can be hard. Groner and Islam's chapter reminds us that empathy is important, and they provide clear strategies and practices to keep an empathic mindset.

Chapter 9. Sustaining Empathy and Community in a Large First-Year Writing Program

Rachael Groner and Tania Islam
Temple University

Abstract: The practice of empathy in a writing classroom is not a novel concept. This chapter explores empathy and community as sustainable practices for writing program administrators. We argue that it is the responsibility of writing program administrators to implement sustainable policies and strategies that maintain a sense of empathy and community. We acknowledge that most writing program administrators agree that this is a key responsibility. But aligning with the PARS model and articulating an adaptation of Lisa Blankenship's "rhetorical empathy" as an administrative stance, we describe insights gained during the COVID-19 pandemic that deepened our practices and understanding of administrative work, and we argue for strategies to assess and seek resources for this work to be sustainable for administrators as well. Our chapter, thus, is a timely reminder to writing program administrators to focus our energies on maintaining and fostering this sense of empathetic community amongst first-year writing faculty.

Keywords: empathy, community, writing program administration (WPA), labor-based grading, faculty development

Empathy is a complex word. It is protean in nature, changing its meaning according to place and circumstance. For the purpose of this chapter, we are defining empathy as the ability to understand, feel, and share the feelings and emotions of another person. In relation to first-year writing program administration, empathy recognizes the heterogeneity of the faculty body and relies on implementing inclusive policies to support instruction. Of course, this working definition does not encompass the enormity of the concept, but it is utilitarian and has helped the authors of this chapter immensely to run the day-to-day administration of a large first-year writing program at an urban R1 university.

Our first-year writing (FYW) program consists of faculty at various ranks and employment statuses, including part-time adjunct faculty, full-time non-tenure-track faculty, Ph.D. and MFA graduate students, and full-time tenure-track or tenured faculty. In a given semester, we have approximately 60 faculty members teaching various FYW courses. As a program, we offer courses in multiple modalities—asynchronous online, synchronous online, hybrid (both online and in-person), and fully in-person—and we have separate sections dedicated to unique student populations, such as ESL and honors students. But despite the many differences among our instructors and the courses they teach, we have historically built and maintained a community through two main approaches:

3. a consistent schedule of faculty development sessions, and
4. the use of small, instructor-led teaching circles that allow informal opportunities to discuss teaching and share ideas.

In addition, our instructors see each other on campus often because our classes are scheduled in nearby blocks of classrooms, our schedule runs off-matrix (and thus our classes change at times different from the rest of the university schedule), and our faculty office spaces are organized in pods.

While some online and hybrid instructors have always been less able to take advantage of these many points of contact and community because they are not as physically present on campus, our online instructors have almost all been full-time faculty or graduate students who had at least one in-person course and/or were on campus for other reasons. All together, these approaches to build and sustain an empathetic community are consistent with Jessie Borgman and Casey McArdle's (2015) virtual community (The Online Writing Instruction Community: www.owicommunity.org) and their PARS approach to designing, administering, and instructing online writing courses. We have adapted the PARS approach for our administrative work as follows: It enables us to maintain a *personal* connection with our faculty, it enhances the *accessibility* of our course materials and teaching tools, and it allows us to be *responsive* to instructors and available to faculty and each other throughout the semester, and combined, it offers us *strategic* and creative ways to support our faculty and our curriculum.

Even though we were confident about our approaches to building and sustaining community, the COVID-19 pandemic challenged us to consider the sustainability of our faculty community and administrative support systems. In 2020, when faculty were suddenly sent home to learn how to teach fully online and when our usual places and opportunities became strained, we realized that we needed to build new approaches to supplement our community and ensure sustainability and empathy, both during the pandemic and beyond. These interventions were geared towards addressing the immediate pandemic-related concerns, and they have now become mainstays in our program and will continue to be reengineered and reconfigured as needed. As writing program administrators, we used the unfortunate opportunity of the pandemic to reevaluate strategies that had worked but now needed to improve. In that vein, we hope our chapter will contribute to ongoing conversations about PARS-inspired writing program administration being flexible and committed to supporting faculty no matter what challenges arise. The pandemic may be our most recent crisis moment, but other crises are certainly coming.

Theory and Practice

The value of empathy and community has been explored widely by composition scholars, and it undergirds the PARS approach. While it would be unwieldy to review the literature in full, we want to highlight a few of the theories that frame our field-specific understanding of these important ideas. Krista Ratcliffe's (1999) practice of rhetorical listening suggests that readers and writers benefit most from listening to others' views without aiming to simply agree or disagree. Through adopting a "stance of openness," Ratcliffe (2005) suggests that rhetorical listening requires us to "question ourselves—our attitudes and our actions—to determine whether we need to affirm, revise, or reject them" (p. 210). Ratcliffe (1999) goes on to say that if we become uncomfortable in the process, "good" because "such discomfort simply signifies already existing problems and underscores the need for standing under the discourses of ourselves and others—and listening" (p. 210). Lisa Blankenship (2019) goes further to suggest that writing instructors adopt a curriculum of "rhetorical empathy" in which we encourage students and ourselves to engage with personal stories and feelings as integral to academic reading and writing, not separate from it. Blankenship argues that we must shift "the focus of rhetoric from (only) changing an audience to changing oneself (as well) and extending rhetorical listening in new directions by accounting for the role of the personal and the emotions in rhetorical exchange" (p.18). In a writing classroom, for instance, a writer should imagine not only what their audience might think in response to their text but what the audience might *feel* when they read it. As Blankenship explains, "rhetorical empathy results in an emotional engagement that can disarm; it asks for vulnerability from the speaker or writer that can, at times, promote it in return" (p. 16). While there may be constraints to rhetorical empathy, such as the potential for emotion to seem manipulative or the ways that being vulnerable is different for those in privilege and power than for those not, it is possible to work through these constraints if we are open to acknowledge and explore their impact. As writing teachers, we strive to teach from a rhetorically empathetic stance.

The scholarship on empathy as an administrative practice, however, is less well developed. There were many calls in the *Chronicle of Higher Education* and similar outlets for faculty to be empathetic toward students during the early months of the pandemic. Many of us also received emails from our university employers recommending self-care and suggesting we be generous with our struggling students. While these calls for empathy were well-intentioned, they often felt unhelpful because they failed to recognize that faculty were already working at capacity and had little time and few resources to practice self-care. Further, many of us were already being generous with students and could not incorporate additional labor without a decrease in class sizes or other structural changes (few of which were available). As Kaitlin Clinnin (2020) notes in her article about being a writing program administrator (WPA) after a local mass shooting that killed and injured hundreds of people in Las Vegas, WPAs may not be trained as emergency first responders, but in a crisis, "WPAs perform similar emotional labor" (p. 137) and are often the ones who send out meaningful emails about the crisis and field questions and concerns that are specific to our instructors and students. Clinnin also notes that she felt responsible as a WPA to model "the response I hoped [instructors] would use with their own students: a combination of empathy for students and clear, logical guidance to support the eventual return to routine" (p.137). We, too, felt an enormous pressure to model what we hoped our newer or less experienced instructors would offer to themselves and their students. We also appreciate the collection in which Clinnin's chapter appears, the excellent *The Things We Carry: Strategies for Recognizing and Negotiating Emotional Labor in Writing Program Administration* (Navickas et al., 2020). In their introduction, Kristi Costello and Jacob Babb (2020) trace theories of emotional labor that are most relevant to WPAs and suggest that their collection is intended to begin a conversation about "giving readers tools while also recognizing that the act of negotiating emotional labor is an ongoing process that is not intended to eliminate emotions" (p. 11).

We would also note that publications about online learning have been incredibly helpful, such as Rhonda Thomas, Karen Kuralt, Heidi Skurat Harris and George Jensen's chapter in *PARS in Practice: More Resources and Strategies for Online Writing Instructors* (2021), which describes how to build community among faculty who are teaching all or mostly online (p. 201, in particular). And, as a program with a large number of non-tenure-track faculty, we often ask and attempt to answer questions such as those posed by Ann M. Penrose (2012) in "Professional Identity in a Contingent-Labor Profession: Expertise, Autonomy, Community in Composition Teaching." We appreciate her insistence that faculty be treated as autonomous professionals who make many contributions as opposed to treating non-tenure-track faculty as underlings or defining us in the negative by what we are not expected to do, i.e., research. Julie Lindquist's *Conference on College Composition and Communication* (CCCC) address in 2021 on the isolation of the pandemic has prompted us all to reflect deeply on why a sense of community as writing instructors is so important. Lindquist quotes one of the 2020 CCCC documentarians, Gabrielle Kelenyi, who points out that a constraint many of us have faced is that if we don't keep working and being productive, we might let down our communities, but of course, as she says, "it's those same communities who help me get unstuck and regain my confidence" (p. 194). Indeed, being an academic in a writing program is often to navigate multiple communities, all of which are essential to our being and yet which we cannot serve well in every situation. We agree wholeheartedly that one of the best functions of working within a community is getting "unstuck" when necessary, and it is valuable for administrators and faculty alike.

Our Vision for a Sustainable Practice of Empathy and Community

Our main strategies for practicing empathy and creating community in our composition program stem from long-standing policies developed by several WPAs over the last 20+ years but feature a few small innovations and shifts toward a practice of sustainability and rhetorical empathy developed during the pandemic that we will continue in the future to some extent. Our long-standing policies are not necessarily unique and are likely similar to those of many writing programs, but in this section, we highlight what we believe constitutes an administrative practice of rhetorical empathy.

Existing Structures of Support: Faculty Development and Teaching Circles

We have long offered three faculty development sessions each semester to bring our faculty together and encourage ongoing discussion and support for their work in the classroom. Topics range from instructors sharing best practices for classroom activities to presentations by partners from around the institution, such as the writing center or the counseling center, to invited speakers from writing studies to educate ourselves about trends in the field. Full-time faculty are required to attend two of the three meetings, and part-time faculty and graduate students are warmly invited but are not required to attend. These meetings are often social events, in part, which helps us meet the P (personal), and the content orientation of these sessions is also geared toward meeting the A (accessible) elements of the PARS approach. Pre-pandemic, we offered breakfast or lunch as an incentive for participation, and unless a presentation or workshop was planned for the entire time, we usually allowed for at least thirty minutes of each meeting to be time for people to catch up. We wish that we could offer compensation so that our part-time faculty were able to attend; we have been moderately successful at attracting faculty at all levels because our topics are practical and speak to their needs and interests. During the pandemic, when these meetings were conducted on Zoom, speaker permission was duly noted for recording. If we didn't get consent, the FYW administrators would take notes and send an email to the listserv summarizing the event and key takeaways.

In March 2021, we had the privilege of inviting Dr. Lisa Blankenship as a guest speaker at one of our faculty development meetings. She spoke about her book *Changing the Subject: A Theory of Rhetorical Empathy* and how rhetorical empathy relates to hierarchical relationships within the classroom. This session generated robust conversation in which our FYW faculty agreed and posed intellectual challenges to Dr. Blankenship's model, especially junior faculty and teacher assistants (TAs) who already have tenuous "authoritative" positions in the classroom to begin with. As WPAs, we never try to monitor or censor our faculties and their opinions during such faculty development sessions. The only community guideline is for faculty to be genial and to disagree (if it comes to that) respectfully. As hosts, we always try to make our speakers feel welcomed, but not at the expense of our faculty's right to question what is being said.

Our other long-standing policy is that all faculty teaching a writing course are assigned to a small (3–5 instructor) teaching circle each semester, and each circle meets three times a semester. This is part of a FYW faculty member's teaching responsibility at Temple, so there is no additional compensation offered for attending these teaching circle meetings. The graduate assistant arranges the teaching circles and collects short reports from them to get ideas for future faculty development sessions and generally make sure that the circles are meeting and staying on track. The first meeting is intended to be a casual opportunity to talk about our syllabi and share anything new or interesting we are doing in our courses. The second meeting is similar but also includes an exchange of one or more student papers for the purposes of discussing our grading rubric in anticipation of the third meeting, which takes place during our finals week when instructors have already collected their students' final portfolios. At the third meeting, we read each other's student portfolios to ensure that grades are similar across sections, to offer suggestions when a portfolio is on the cusp of two grades, and to support each other in evaluating portfolios that are potentially failing. Our instructors always have the final say about their students' grades, but teaching circles allow us to contextualize grades within conversations about the grading rubric and the practices of the program.

Teaching circles are instructor-led, and leadership rotates among circle members throughout the semester to equitably distribute responsibility for the circle's success. This policy has been in place for a long time, since at least 2003, and while there are minor complaints from the faculty about the time these meetings take or about the rare instances in which communication breaks down in a particular circle, such concerns are far outweighed by the benefit of having a sense of community and a place to seek advice when needed. As our graduate assistant in 2020-2021, Tania noticed that informal teaching circle reports were more focused than ever before on being micro-support systems in which instructors were engaging in conversation and a free exchange of ideas. We ask that after each meeting the leader reports back on topics of interest in case we administrators note a pattern or an interest that could lead to a faculty development workshop, and the pattern throughout the pandemic in these reports was: We are collaborating and sharing ideas, and we are glad to have our teaching circles. These teaching circles have also been a meeting place of faculty across ranks, which has further bolstered this sense of community in our program. Junior faculty (new hires and TAs) have always appreciated the opportunity to meet other FYW instructors and engage with them in discussions on curriculum and pedagogy.

No-agenda, Optional "Release Valve" Meetings

In March 2020, we encouraged instructors to do what they could to finish the remaining weeks of the semester by moving teaching circle meetings to Zoom instead of in-person. We also moved the third and final faculty development session online, and thus our usual policies of support were largely able to continue as planned. But even with these supports in place, there seemed to be a need for even more support and community because the campus shutdown was both sudden and uncertain (that is, would we stay online for the rest of the semester, or was it really a two-week shutdown?). We offered an additional level of support by adding fully optional, agendaless, and unrecorded meetings on Fridays via Zoom. Structured as virtual "brown bag" sessions, these Friday meetings were informal, and faculty were encouraged to join in to keep the sense of community alive. As WPAs, we recognized that it was unhealthy for faculty to teach fully online without an opportunity to meet other members of the FYWP and partake in regular social interaction. In fact, there were numerous news items mentioning how "cabin fever" was resulting in severe depression and reduced productivity in working professionals. We did not want our faculty to feel isolated and unsupported. These meetings were, and still are, agendaless open meetings. We usually begin with a simple and friendly "hey, how's it going?" and then let the conversation flow organically. One can think of the vibe as "fireside chat meets brown bag meetings." During the pandemic, they functioned initially as a "release valve" where instructors could vent about how difficult it was to flip online and how much they missed having hallway conversations or just a chance to talk to adults other than those in their families or close circles, even if it wasn't about teaching or our careers. But these meetings also functioned as opportunities for instructors to ask questions or get/give advice or suggestions for best practices, especially related to online teaching and instructional technology.

Sometimes, instructors used time during these "release valve" meetings to critique university policies or what they perceived as a lack of action in supporting students. It was useful to hear those critiques because as administrators, we could bring their concerns to our upper-level meetings at the dean's office and vice provost levels to provide feedback to central administrators outside of our unit and most likely not in touch with teaching faculty on a regular basis. We also found that instructors offered critiques of our policies and practices as program administrators, and we were open to those critiques and used them as opportunities to become deeply reflective about where and how we could do better. For instance, some faculty voiced concern about our recommendation in the fall of 2020 to use complete/incomplete grading for the process work component of the course's final grade, such as in-class writing, online discussion posts, and quizzes. Before the pandemic, these elements were assessed as "participation" and tracked by instructors in idiosyncratic and varied ways. Some instructors kept careful notes throughout the semester, some wrote occasional reports for students so that they knew roughly where this portion of their final grade might stand, and yet "participation" made up roughly 30 percent of the final grade and had the potential to swing a student's grade up or down by one grade level. As administrators, we felt strongly that it would be more empathetic to convert this grade into something more transparent because so much of the student experience seemed uncertain due to the pandemic.

We were also inspired by ongoing discussions in the field, such as those around Asao Inoue's 2019 argument for labor-based grading schemes and texts such as Susan Blum's (2020) *Ungrading: Why Rating Students Undermines Learning*, and we felt that shifting toward labor-based grading was fully compatible with our existing practice of only giving students feedback on drafts during the semester and grading their progress and final drafts in a portfolio at the end of the semester. We communicated with the faculty about these changes in several ways, including sharing a version of the new syllabus with comments in the margins explaining our thinking behind the changes and offering a range of options in those comments if someone wished to adopt some of our ideas but not all, for instance. We also wrote an additional "debate" document in which we invited faculty to write on the document and make comments of their own as an ongoing conversation, and this document remained "live" over several months. Our intention was that faculty should not feel as though they were debating with us but that this conversation was open to all and that they could speak to their peers and generate ideas in real time. We held several meetings in the summer of 2020 when these changes first rolled out to answer questions and address concerns, and we acknowledged that indeed, these changes were significant, particularly for long-time faculty who had developed their own pedagogical systems and practices that could be hard to revise while living through a pandemic.

One of the strengths of rhetorical empathy as an administrative practice is that it allows us to compassionately speak up to the institutional pressures and structural barriers with which all writing programs must contend. Blankenship (2019) is right that the practice of rhetorical empathy will "change the subject of discourse—both the content of discourse and its agent [on both sides], and as a result it holds the potential for bridging difficult rhetorical impasses" (p. 16). That is, we hope that our practices will influence others at the university to act in similar ways, and together over time, we may slowly challenge the institution to become a better place. We strive to be the kind of administrators we would have wanted and often did not have when we were graduate students and in the early years of our career. In our own early years, we raised concerns or encountered institutional barriers and were shut down or marginalized as a result. Ethical leadership must be grounded in the sharing of stories, feelings, and perspectives in order to treat colleagues as respected professionals who will do their best work if they feel supported and heard. But as Blankenship (2019) acknowledges, we should assess rhetorical empathy as a[n administrative] practice by "the degree to which it leaves the door open for future engagement and gradual shifts rather than [to judge whether or not it produced] immediate change" (p. 123).

While we scaled back the number of these optional, no-agenda meetings from eight in the fall of 2020 to five in 2021–2022, they have continued in Zoom even though our campus has largely returned to in-person instruction. They still encompass our feeling of camaraderie and function as a virtual safe space for faculty to freely discuss various issues and concerns that they are facing in their classrooms, and we have noticed that some in-person conversations are now intentionally continued in these virtual meetings, which is a lovely development that demonstrates how multiple spaces for discussion and collegial interaction are necessary. One or two spaces or times for faculty to engage in meandering dialogue are not enough. As administrators, we continue to have no expectations from these meetings except the proliferation of friendship and community in our program.

One-on-One Email Messages

Even though our teaching circles and extra meetings offered many points of contact for faculty if they chose to seek them out, we were aware that our part-time and graduate student instructors might find additional meetings burdensome and that the teaching circles, while useful, might not be as supportive as if they were in person. Early in the pandemic, Rachael (with significant assistance from Tania and the other members of our admin team, Cate Almon and Anne Horn) sent long emails to everyone to share information, invite faculty to ask questions, and urge faculty to discuss ideas or challenges through the program listserv. But we worried that these emails to everyone would not be enough, so our third and final strategy was to reach out individually to faculty members through targeted emails aligned with the P (personal) and the S (strategic) elements of the PARS approach. These emails were casual in tone, written in a spirit of solidarity, and featured an invitation to engage in conversation if the faculty member so desired. We copied and pasted, but we added individual notes where appropriate. For example, if someone had already expressed that they were technologically challenged, we would add a brief reminder that we could set up a Zoom meeting with them to go over how best to use ed tech in their classes.

The director and the FYW advisor split the duty of reaching out to the full-time faculty, the associate director reached out to the part-time faculty, and the graduate assistant reached out to the graduate student TAs. These individual emails opened a one-on-one line of communication where faculty could communicate needs that were specific to them and their situation, such as if they were involved in different or increased caretaking in their homes while also trying to handle their job responsibilities. Though only a few faculty members responded with questions or a need for help, many faculty responded positively to say that they were okay and appreciated the check-in. We felt that these emails were an important initiative that replaced some of what instructors were able to do pre-pandemic by walking into the first-year writing office or finding one of us in the halls or in between classes. We had some concerns about sending these emails, such as whether instructors would feel targeted in any way (and so we crafted an email that made it very clear that everyone was receiving the same message and that we were not writing only to them). We were also concerned about whether these emails would in any way feel like surveillance or prompt additional work, such as causing an instructor to feel obligated to respond and then spend too much time and energy doing so (and so we included several lines to insist that we would not read anything into a non-response and that no response was necessary). We acknowledge that we could not fully prevent these latter concerns in every case, but we decided it was better to take these calculated risks and reach out than not.

Conclusion and Takeaways

In conclusion, what we are advocating for in this chapter is an empathetic approach to FYW administration by focusing on the *strategic* and *responsive* aspects of the PARS model. These strategies and methods grounded in the PARS model and adapting theories of empathy and community as administrative practices are not necessarily groundbreaking. But they helped us as administrators feel as though our work was intentional, as was particularly important during the pandemic's heightened sense of crisis and uncertainty, and they encouraged us to think deeply about how our existing decentralized, instructor-run program was, in fact, working relatively well and did not need radical reform in order to support instructors and provide an atmosphere in which they and their students could succeed. We plan to continue prioritizing empathy and the sharing of experiences and stories in all our administrative decisions, and we will continue to foster a sense of community in our writing program, no matter what the future has in store for us.

We acknowledge that there are lingering concerns about how feasible it is to practice an administrative form of rhetorical empathy and/or to see community building as central to our jobs as WPAs. For instance, it is important to remember that just as the pandemic has resulted in student disengagement, faculty are also suffering from disengagement and/or disillusionment. Quite a few academics and faculty members at our institution and in higher education in general have begun to question their roles in the classroom, and many of us are exhausted. Further, we are keenly aware of the news that there is an enrollment cliff coming, that students may choose to go directly into the workforce instead of coming to college right away, and that these dynamics might change the conditions of our employment and work. As WPAs, it is vital that we work towards allaying this sense of gloom and doom, and this is where our bold description of this work as "sustainable" may be aspirational, at best. In addition, what we have described here is focused on what WPAs should do, and we have not discussed how WPAs should take care of their own needs in the process. Who will have empathy for the WPA? We suggest that a network of fellow WPAs may be the answer, but when we are all stretched thin, this resource may not be fully available to us, even when we are in most need.

Also, empathy itself is a process attuned to specific readers, writers, and listeners, and it is not as though we can suggest one kind of empathy to fit all situations. Nor can we or anyone suggest ways to build community that work in every program or institution because community and its structure(s) of feeling are, too, specific and contextual. Rather, we envision that our administrative practice of sustainable empathy and community will always be open, flexible, and context-specific. Nonetheless, we hope this chapter offers the following key takeaways:

- We strongly suggest that WPAs let faculty know that rhetorical empathy is a key aspect of your approach, and that your door is open to discuss administrative practices if anyone has questions or ideas for improvement. If you do not already have a policy or set of strategies for instructors on how to touch base with you, developing one proactively is a good idea. It can be frustrating to send missives and receive no or few responses, and we acknowledge the limitations of email communication as unreliable. As we have said many times to our new graduate student teachers, if a message is truly important, we should say it to students at least three times and in three different modes, if possible, and this is good advice in almost any context. For large departments or programs such as ours, we recommend developing a deep bench of communication modes and opportunities.
- Find a safe and meaningful way to allow faculty to speak back to administrators. Our use of a "release valve" set of meetings each semester has worked well, but it may not work well forever, so we also recommend planning for multiple avenues in which faculty can engage with WPAs, especially in a crisis. There are many ways that our faculty participate in the work of the program (i.e., curriculum committees, an executive committee, awards committees), but our recommendation is for something less "work" related and more focused on listening to and sharing in discussions about the feel and experience of teaching in the program. Also, when faculty complain or raise concerns in any venue, listen and take notes that intend to gather impressions without tracking who said what. Then, sit with their complaints or concerns, and reflect on them within your administrative team (if you have one, and if you do not, we suggest building one, even if it is only one additional person, such as an associate director or graduate assistant). If there is an immediate problem to be fixed, do it, but most likely, these complaints and concerns have stories

that undergird their existence, and the more you listen to those stories, the more you are likely to have genuine empathy for your faculty and their working conditions.
- Do not spend too much time reinventing the wheel. Once you have good policies and processes in place, conduct assessments and make simple adjustments when necessary. As Mike Ristich et al. (2021) argue, having good policies in place and avoiding the tendency to administrate reactively makes a writing program particularly nimble when massive challenges such as a pandemic arise. It can be difficult to assess if there is enough empathy or community within a writing program, but we have found that if you ask about these qualities in a safe, open environment supported by consistent, long-term practices of empathetic administration, you'll get useful answers.
- Be kind, always. At the risk of sounding preachy, please remember that faculty members are human beings who apart from teaching the FYW courses also have personal lives and very real, complex needs and wants outside of work. We would not include this in our list of takeaways if we had not been on the receiving end of unkindness more than once. Empathy from a writing program administrator is of paramount importance.
- Lastly, as Clinnin and others in *The Things We Carry* suggest, remember that all of the above is essential emotional labor that should be included in end-of-year reports, merit pay requests, or any other opportunity in which administrators document their work for deans or provosts. This work is as laborious as any other aspect of the WPA position, and it should be recognized and duly compensated. It is easy to say this, of course, and in a time of slashed budgets and worries about the future, it may be a difficult ask of WPAs and their supervisors. Still, we call to normalize the documentation of emotional labor and community building.

The work of a WPA is often challenging, but we have found it easier and more rewarding to align our administrative practices with core values such as empathy and kindness. We hope that this chapter empowers future administrators to adopt similar practices, and we look forward to seeing administrative rhetorical empathy develop within our field and throughout higher education.

Notes

We wish to thank Cate Almon and Anne Horn, both of whom were instrumental in developing these ideas and were co-presenters of an earlier version of this work at the 2021 Philadelphia Writing Program Administrators (PWPA) Spring Conference. We have no conflicts of interest to disclose. Correspondence concerning this article should be addressed to Rachael Groner at rachael.groner@temple.edu.

References

Blankenship, L. (2019). *Changing the subject: A theory of rhetorical empathy*. Utah State University Press.

Blum, S. (2020). *Ungrading: Why rating students undermines learning (and what to do instead)*. West Virginia University Press.

Borgman, J. & McArdle, C. (2019). *Personal, accessible, responsive, strategic: Resources and strategies for online writing instructors*. The WAC Clearinghouse; University Press of Colorado. https://doi.org/10.37514/PRA-B.2019.0322.

Borgman, J. & McArdle, C. (2015). *PARS*. The online writing instruction community. https://www.owicommunity.org/.

Clinnin, K. (2020). And so I respond: The emotional labor of writing program administrators in crisis response. In K. Navickas, K. M. Costello, J. Babb & C. A. Wooten (Eds.), *The things we carry: Strategies for recognizing and negotiating emotional labor in writing program administration* (pp. 129–144). Utah State University Press.

Costello, K.M. & Babb, J. (2020). Introduction: Emotional labor, writing studies, and writing program administration. In C.A. Wooten, J. Babb, K.M. Costello & K. Navickas (Eds.), *The things we carry: Strategies for recognizing and negotiating emotional Labor in writing program administration* (pp. 3–16). University Press of Colorado. https://www.jstor.org/stable/j.ctv18oh76t.

Inoue, A. (2019). *Labor-based grading contracts: Building equity and inclusion in the compassionate writing classroom*. The WAC Clearinghouse; University Press of Colorado. https://doi.org/10.37514/PER-B.2019.0216.0.

Lindquist, J. (2021). Writing and teaching in a time of COVID: Uncommon reflections on learning and loss. *College Composition and Communication*, 73(2), 184–205.

Navickas, K., Costello, K. M., Babb, J. & Wooten, C. A. (2020). *The things we carry: Strategies for recognizing and negotiating emotional labor in writing program administration*. Utah State University Press.

Penrose, A. M. (2012). Professional identity in a contingent-labor profession: Expertise, autonomy, community in composition teaching. *WPA: Writing Program Administration*, 35(2), 108–126. https://wpacouncil.org/aws/CWPA/pt/sp/journal-archives.

Ratcliffe, K. (1999). Rhetorical listening: A trope for interpretive invention and a "code of cross-cultural conduct". *College Composition and Communication*, 51(2), 195–224. https://doi.org/10.2307/359039.

Ratcliffe, K. (2005). *Rhetorical listening: Identification, gender, whiteness*. Southern Illinois University Press.

Ristich, M., McArdle, C. & Rhodes, J. (2021). Assessing the limits of program strategy: "Archi-strategy" in an age of disruption. *Programmatic Perspectives*, 12(1), 127–151.

Thomas, R., Kuralt, K., Skurat Harris, H. & Jensen, G. (2021). Create, support and facilitate personal online writing courses in online writing programs. In J. Borgman & C. McArdle (Eds.), *PARS in Practice: More resources and strategies for online writing instructors* (pp. 185–207). The WAC Clearinghouse; University Press of Colorado. https://doi.org/10.37514/PRA-B.2021.1145.2.11.

Only Birdies!

Every once in a while, golfers need to step back and assess their play. Whether it's their putting, chipping, or driving of the ball, taking some time to assess their play allows golfers to improve.

Many program leaders know that assessment is part of what improves a program and keeps it working. Assessment also allows for determination of success in the program goals and practices. Jennifer Trainor and John Holland's chapter lays out their program self-assessment based on the PARS framework to help readers engage in their own conversations about student writing and their faculty's professional development.

What we like about Trainor and Holland's chapter is that it is so focused on student perspectives and taking into consideration what their student users are saying about their courses. But along with this student focus, they don't forget faculty, and they discuss how important it is to assess one's faculty professional development on an ongoing basis in order to fill gaps and improve instructor performance and satisfaction.

Chapter 10. Personal, Accessible, Responsive, and Strategic Assessment: Creating a Faculty Community of Practice

Jennifer Trainor and John Holland
SAN FRANCISCO STATE UNIVERSITY

Abstract: In this chapter, we apply the PARS framework (Personal, Accessible, Responsible, Strategic) to a program self-assessment we designed and implemented for faculty teaching first- and second-year writing courses. We explain how we used our institution's request for an assessment of student writing to build a community of practice in which teachers meet regularly to read and interpret end-of-semester student reflections. Our goal has been to transform traditional assessment of student writing into an opportunity to engage with faculty in regular conversations about our pedagogical approaches, seeking to close the loop by noticing what parts of our teaching connect with students and what gaps we need to fill with professional development.

Keywords: assessment, professional development, community of practice, rubrics, faculty engagement

You know how to play the game. It is program assessment time, and the game is a kind of paint-by-rubric. Judge and rate student writing, and the result, as everyone already knows, will be filed away in a committee report too divorced from context to be useful to anyone, let alone the teachers dutifully ranking the students' writing.

As both writing teachers and leaders in our writing program (John, a full-time lecturer faculty who has led program and campus-wide initiatives related to online learning; Jennifer, a professor of composition who has served as writing program administrator (WPA) and regularly teaches first-year writing), we have been highly skeptical of this game: rubrics that flatten student learning, boilerplate descriptors of "good" academic writing, norming sessions that paper over students' writing process and raters' reading process, results that feel to teachers like a condemnation of their work. The assessment game is always followed by "business as usual" when we return to our classrooms.

And on our campus, as is the case in writing programs across the country, "business as usual" can feel very isolating. We sit alone in our offices. Schedules are aligned so that office mates do not work on the same day; doors can be closed to avoid distractions. Most writing teachers work at multiple campuses, the proverbial freeway fliers in an urban landscape where two-hour commutes are not unusual. We fly solo. We teach solo. Assessment, in this context, is not grounded in listening, reciprocity, or community, and judgments about student performance can land hard on vulnerable students and teachers working without job security or institutional enfranchisement.

Theory and Practice
Rethinking Assessment with PARS

In 2019, we began using the PARS framework to refocus assessments, looking beyond rubrics and judgments of student writing and toward the longer view, positioning ourselves in opposition to the standard rules of play. We needed an approach to assessment that were asset-based and equity-focused, that broke down teaching silos, and that led to meaningful changes and growth among teachers. To use Jessie Borgman and Casey McArdle's (2019) golf analogy, we needed an assessment process that focused less on the score and more on how and why we practice and play the game.

As researchers, our strengths complemented each other: John brought expertise in online pedagogy and a strong sense of design at all levels (from hole-in-one evidenced-based workshops that could change how teachers understand their work to an understanding of research methods to a sense of how to facilitate online teacher learning). Jennifer brought a commitment to accessibility, social justice, and community-building. Together, we set out to create a different assessment game in our program— one imbued with long-range vision; rooted in a stronger sense of teamwork, collaboration, social justice, and community; accessible via multiple modalities; and drawing on faculty expertise and experience.

Our personal, accessible, responsive, and strategic approach has resulted in evolution, even a revolution. We have moved from silos and empty hallways to a community of practice—a model of collaborative leadership and collaborative operational work in our writing program that takes place across multiple modalities. Our work has shown us that just as PARS shifted teachers' and administrators' perceptions of online education—from transactional and linear to human-centered and process-oriented—it can similarly change how we approach assessment, which is often initiated in a top-down way by those who view education, including literacy education, as transactional and skills-based. Faculty tend to resist such assessment because they perceive it as divorced from the complexities and relational aspects of teaching and learning they value. PARS helped us to construct an organic, contextual, local approach to assessment that reflected the faculty's experience, promoting improvements in curriculum and pedagogy while removing the silos teachers had been working in.

In the following sections, we share key takeaways as a blueprint—of sorts—for using PARS to create a meaningful assessment. Our assessment was personal in that it brought faculty together for weekly discussion and reflection, accessible in that it transformed assessment from obscure rubric language and acontextual scoring of anonymous students driven by administrative need to a faculty-owned and faculty-led process of transparent interpretation and improvement, responsive in that we adapted our assessment continually to meet emerging faculty and program needs, and strategic in that we have continued to garner funding for the program by bridging our goals with university priorities.

Personal Assessment: Identify Program Values

Scholars in writing studies argue that assessment should be locally controlled, context-sensitive, rhetorically based, and accessible (i.e., transparent to all interested parties) and that assessments should be consistent with contemporary theories about language, learning, and literacy (Moore et al., 2009). Most importantly, they argue that assessment must involve teachers— "Members of the community are in the best position to guide decisions about what assessments will inform that community" (Conference on College Composition and Communication, 2022)—and that it must focus on *closing the loop* and creating meaningful changes in teacher practice.

We saw connections between these scholarly perspectives on assessment and our PARS-driven approach. Following Broad (2003) and Gallagher and Turley (2013), we designed a self-study assessment project that would engage as many faculty as possible in the process of reflecting on and expressing their educational aims, creating an iterative process in which the resulting knowledge became part of our ongoing inquiry. We invited a team of teachers to meet each week as part of a self-study assessment project. In the first year of the project, we asked teachers to reflect on their pedagogical goals and to bring in class samples from students who they deemed to be strong writers as well as from those who they considered to be struggling.

Rather than requiring teachers to submit student work for assessment, we invited teachers to talk together about what they value in student writing. Each week, we discussed a different teacher's struggling and strong students. These conversations were a tough, but critical, shift for all of us. For most teachers, assessment meant objective judgment (think about those rubrics to judge student writing). Instead, we encouraged an interpretive process focused on teachers' perceptions of their students and classrooms—what was working, where they and their students were struggling, and what success looks like for them. In the ensuing discussions, silos began to dissolve as teachers listened to one another and identified our shared teaching values and goals.

While assessment is usually focused on the performance of broad indicators of academic writing (appropriate use of thesis statements, source citation, analysis), teachers on our assessment team revealed in these early discussions that for them, "success" was indicated by signs of student growth over time—e.g., when teachers saw that students had learned something new, tried something new, took a risk, showed ownership and independence in their literacy practices, gained a new perspective, grew in confidence and self-efficacy, overcame negative experiences or associations with writing. These signs of success were not reflected in typical outcomes-based rubrics, but they are central to how teachers in our program think about their teaching and their students' learning.

Identifying these values was slow work, involving weekly meetings as an assessment team for an entire year. At times, the meetings felt aimless, more like a graduate seminar than an assessment. Nevertheless, we took notes on emerging themes and questions throughout the process. As a result, by the end of the year, we could articulate a set of organic program values that were rooted in community and personally meaningful to teachers. Next, we codified those values into assessment tools—a critical move that made assessment *accessible*.

Try This!	<ul><li>What typifies a strong writer, in your view?</li><li>What characterizes a struggling writer?</li><li>What evidence in this piece of writing tells you that a student is struggling or strong?</li></ul>

Accessible Assessment: Use Local Tools Designed by Faculty

Borgman and McArdle (2019) point out that "mitigating confusion is central to accessible design" (p. 45). As they write, the best way to encourage student success is to design materials that are transparent, intuitive, and meaningful to students. We quickly discovered that the same principle applies to assessment practices with faculty. Too often, assessment materials are couched in alien and distancing, if not obscure and confusing, terms. Rubrics, for example, are often tautological or assume shared understandings of rhetorical and writing terms that in reality do not exist.

To avoid these problems, we wrote threshold concepts (TCs) that embodied teachers' values and created a kind of learning map of the growth teachers told us they looked for in their students. The learning map consisted primarily of teachers' descriptions of typical students' progress toward understanding the threshold concepts rather than mastery of outcomes. Our TCs and learning map were both derived from the values and goals that emerged in the first year of our community-based assessment project. We wanted to ensure that the assessment language we were using was familiar—that it came from teachers themselves.

We ultimately created seven TCs describing teachers' learning goals and 35 (five for each TC) descriptions of students' unfolding development in relation to those learning goals. These descriptions were essential because they represented teachers' core value when they read and assessed student writing: growth over time. Ultimately, these tools gave us an accessible language for talking about the student writing we were starting to collect for a more formal phase of our assessment.

Try This!	Ask faculty to map typical students' journeys toward learning goals: • Where do students begin? How would you characterize students at the beginning of the semester in relation to each learning goal? • How would you characterize students' location in relation to each learning goal by the end of your course? • What do students still need to learn?

In the second year of our assessment, teachers developed, beta-tested, and revised the threshold concepts and learning map we used to analyze student writing. The learning map, although it resembles a rubric, is different in several key ways. For example, rather than leading assessors to a judgment about student writing, the map prompts assessors to consider learning and literacy development over time. Rather than student performance, the map focuses on aspects of literacy that support performance, such as reading and writing processes and metacognition, as well as attitudes about literacy and school. Rather than focus on one moment of student performance, the map captures growth and change over time and articulates typical milestones that students meet in their first year of college. Finally, the map describes students' understanding of the seven threshold concepts at the beginning of their college journey and articulates learning goals that we expect students to meet by the time they finish their upper-division writing-in-the-disciplines courses.

As discussed in the next section, we used these teacher-created assessment tools to create a *responsive* assessment, listen to students' experiences of our courses, and create a community of practice among faculty.

Responsive Assessment: Listen to Students and Teachers

For Borgman and McArdle (2019), responsive means that online instructors are available to respond to and collaborate with students [faculty] (p. 51). In the context of our assessment practices, responsive meant listening—both to students and teachers—while attending to what we hear. Our assessment began with listening to teachers describe their values and goals. As we moved into data gathering, we similarly prioritized listening to students. Instead of collecting student papers, we created a reflection assignment that asked students to tell us about their literacy learning and growth. From there, we asked faculty interpretive questions about those student reflections: How do students experience our courses? How do they develop as students and as writers? What do they struggle with? What do they learn?

Our reflection assignment asks students to choose two from a list of the learning goals we identified in the first year of our assessment and to write a 400-word reflective mini-essay for each. We collect the students' reflections (anonymously and with permission) and archive them. Teams of teachers then meet weekly for a semester to discuss student reflections and place the student using our learning map.

Our assessment is *responsive* in that teacher growth emerges from collaborative interactions between faculty. These interactions create community and offer teachers a rare space to talk freely about their teaching. As Lynn Hilliard (2020) says, faculty need permission to be vulnerable as a precursor to building mutual respect and trust: "We need a place where we can share what's happening in our classes—including what isn't working—without fear of retribution" (p. 210). Our assessment teams are the backbone of the larger community of practice in our program; our weekly meetings function as a space for teachers to reflect on their teaching and to see their teaching reflected through the eyes of students.

Participants in our assessment program have consistently told us that our weekly meet-ups were the highlight of their work week, a time to put the day-to-day stress of teaching on the shelf to talk with colleagues about student writing, reflect on their practices, and begin to alter their perspectives about writing assessment. "It's like a weekly graduate seminar for practicing teachers," said one of our recent participants. "What's different," said another participant, "is that our sessions are built around a focused heuristic for close reading and close discussion of student work."

Try This!	Here are the discussion questions we use to structure our weekly assessment meetings: • What learning goals did the student focus on? • What does the student say they learned? What evidence (reasons, examples) do they cite to support their claims about what they learned? • What evidence of learning or growth do you see in their writing? Using your skills of textual analysis, close reading, and interpretation, how would you characterize the student's reflection? • Place the student on our threshold concept learning map. Why did you place the student as you did? • Thinking about this student's reflection, what do you think is working in our classrooms, and what do you think we need to change or improve?

This process is grounded in responsiveness: a cycle of listening in which students reflect on their experiences, faculty listen closely to students and each other as they discuss their interpretations of student learning, and WPAs collaborate with faculty, listening to both students and faculty about what is working in the program and what gaps need to be filled.

We facilitated most of the sessions in much the same way as we would lead class discussions in a graduate course. Each week, we began by asking one or two participants to share a sample from the student reflections they read that week. The sample can be one that surprised, intrigued, confused, or impressed them. The discussion takes off from there. These are not norming sessions; instead, we encourage teachers to read student work with an interpretive lens as we try to understand a particular student's learning journey through our course. Through this process, our weekly meetings build community, as trusting relationships emerge via discussion of students' growth, learning, and experiences.

Try This!	Our Self-Study Team Wrap-up Questions: • How would you characterize the most meaningful takeaways from our work this semester? These takeaways might be about your own curriculum, or about our program. • Our focus has been on mapping student understanding (via TCs and student reflection) rather than assessing their skills and/or their written products. How can this approach inform your teaching? • What has it been like for us to not judge student writing? • What would be most beneficial for our program regarding our following faculty professional development session [state the date] for 20 minutes of seed planting? • What do we want to share about our self-study experience at back-to-school meet-ups in the Fall semester?

Strategic Assessment: Tie Teachers' Perspectives to University Priorities

Our assessment process has morphed into professional development as teachers on our semester-long assessment teams formed communities of practice and as we took insights gleaned from their discussions back to the larger program, creating workshops and learning opportunities for faculty that drove program improvement.

Turning assessment into meaningful professional development required us to be *strategic*. First and perhaps most importantly, every teacher who has participated in our assessment for the past three years has been paid in either stipends or course releases for their work. Securing this funding required that we continually tie our internal goals and values, as well as teachers' perspectives and experiences, to university priorities. For example, in our third year of this assessment project, we focused on equity gaps and drop, fail, withdraw (DFW) rates, both of which are high priorities on our campus. We proposed to use our assessment teams and protocols to conduct a deep dive into the issues that impede student success. But we grounded this proposed deep dive in our teacher-driven assessment practices.

We asked faculty on our assessment team to identify and analyze a current student who was struggling in some way. Our team then filled out a shared Google Doc with notes and reflections about each student. We tracked interventions and success across the semester, creating case studies of students, some of whom made it successfully through our courses, and some of whom did not. At the end of the year, we wrote a report that reflected the insights we gained from these case studies, including the professional development we identified as necessary to improving our program's efforts to support struggling students. Sharing these insights with the campus and administrators helps bridge the gap between administrative focus on student success data and teachers' experiences and expertise. Strategically, such bridging helps administrators better understand our work and strengthens our ability to secure future funding.

Try This!	Consider strategically translating university priorities into issues and language that faculty care about. In our case, for example, we translated the "bean-counting" aspects of our university's focus on equity and student success (e.g., numbers of DFWs in first-year courses, equity gaps presented as percentages) into questions that faculty value and respond to:
	• What do you see/don't you see re: this student that worries you?
	• Where is this student on our threshold concept map so far?
	• Student-Reported Struggle - What have they told you/not told you? What do you surmise (unknowns)?
	• Your Response to the Struggle: How do you hope to support the student? What kinds of interventions might help?
	• Post-Script - (mid-term check-in): What happened with the student? What were the results of your intervention?
	  ▪ Where are they now?
	  ▪ What can we learn from your interaction/experience with this student?

Conclusion and Takeaways

While most of us in writing studies would agree that assessment can feel like a burden, our PARS approach has transformed this burden into an active, vibrant community of practice. We hope we can inspire other programs to chart a similar course by sharing our process here. Aligning assessment practices with PARS has increased teacher collaboration, agency, and ownership of our program. It has helped us understand students' learning in a more fine-grained way, which helps us create curricula and classroom strategies that address where students are in order to move them toward more profound learning and a deeper relationship to literacy.

Most importantly, it has provided us with a constructive set of practices to build and sustain teachers' professional communities in our program, and it has contributed to larger changes in the culture of assessment on our campus. Our Center for Teaching Excellence now offers workshops on anti-racist classroom assessment, for example, and there is a movement afoot to find more holistic ways to evaluate teaching, moving away from over-reliance on teacher evaluation surveys given at the end of the semester.

Both teachers and students themselves need support in resisting narrow definitions of assessment. As Doug Downs (2020) writes, a college writing classroom should function as "a space, a moment, an experience—in which students might reconsider writing apart from previous schooling and work, within the context of inquiry-based higher education" (p. 50). Aligning our assessment practices to match this definition of our work has, more than any other professional development, created supportive communities of practice in our program and created a culture of meaningful improvement in our classrooms. Here are some final thoughts:

- Get personal with your writing faculty. Ask faculty to articulate their assessment goals and create meaningful assessment tools. Find your own local lens on what your program values in student writing.
- Promote accessible outcomes by transforming your assessment practices from a top-down acontextual mandate (standard rubrics) to a faculty-owned and faculty-led process of interpretation and improvement.
- Be responsive in designing institutional assessment mandates by listening to your teachers and students.
- Design strategic assessment practices that leverage university dictates with faculty values and student voices.

References

Adler-Kassner, L. (1999). Just writing, basically: Basic writers on basic writing. *Journal of Basic Writing*, 18(2), 69–90. https://www.jstor.org/stable/43741055.

Adler-Kassner, L. & Wardle, E. (Eds.). (2015). *Naming what we know: Threshold concepts of writing studies*. Utah State University Press.

Adler-Kassner, L. & Wardle, E. (Eds.). (2019). *(Re)Considering what we know: Learning thresholds in writing, composition, rhetoric, and literacy*. Utah State University Press.

Borgman, J. & McArdle, C. (2019). *Personal, accessible, responsive, strategic: Resources and strategies for online writing instructors*. The WAC Clearinghouse; University Press of Colorado. https://doi.org/10.37514/PRA-B.2019.0322.

Broad, B. (2003). *What we really value: Beyond rubrics in teaching and assessing writing*. Utah State University Press. https://doi.org/10.2307/j.ctt46nxvm.

Conference on College Composition and Communication. (2022, May 4). *Writing assessment: A position statement*. National Council of Teachers of English. https://cccc.ncte.org/cccc/resources/positions/writingassessment.

Downs, D. (2013). What is first-year composition? In R. Malenczyk (Ed.), *A rhetoric for writing program administrators* (pp. 50–63). Parlor Press.

Estrem, H. (2015). Threshold concepts and student learning outcomes. In L. Adler-Kassner & E. Wardle (Eds.), *Naming what we know: Threshold concepts of writing studies* (pp. 89–104). Utah State University Press.

Gallagher, C. W. (2012). The trouble with outcomes: Pragmatic inquiry and educational aims. *College English, 75*(1), 42.

Gallagher, C. W. (2016). What writers do: Behaviors, behaviorism, and writing studies. *College Composition and Communication, 68*(2), 238–265.

Gallagher, C. W. & Turley, E. D. (2012). *Our better judgment: Teacher leadership for writing assessment*. National Council of Teachers of English.

Hilliard, L. (2020). Using PARS to build a community of practice in hybrid learning. In J. Borgman & C. McArdle (Eds.), *PARS in practice: More resources and strategies for online writing instructors* (pp. 209–223). The WAC Clearinghouse; University Press of Colorado. https://doi.org/10.37514/PRA-B.2021.1145.

Moore, C., O'Neill, P. & Huot, B. (2009). Creating a culture of assessment in writing programs and beyond. *College Composition and Communication, 61*(1), W107.

National Writing Project. (n.d.). *Programs & services*. https://www.nwp.org/what-we-do/programs-services.

Halfway Through the Course!

Part of being a professional or amateur golfer is practice and training. Golf is a lifelong sport and one that you continue to improve upon the more you play, practice, and train.

You've heard us say many times that we see online writing instruction (OWI) similarly to golf: the more you do it the better you get at it. We feel the same about leading a program: the more you run into as an administrator, the longer you've done it, and the more you put into it, the more you get better at the job.

Training and professional development is especially important for newer OWI instructors and those functioning as graduate teaching assistants (TAs). What we like about Miranda Egger's chapter is that she clearly states the long-standing problem of training and preparation as related to OWI that has existed for over a decade. Egger's chapter illustrates how program leaders could adapt some of her practices to get their instructors more OWI-specific training.

We really like Egger's insistence on OWI-specific scholarship, especially considering the recent COVID-19 pandemic and shift to emergency remote instruction. At this time, many taught writing online with little or no training and little to no OWI-specific training. Egger's chapter makes the case that the decade+ of OWI-specific scholarship is vastly important in training new instructors and graduate TAs to teach writing online.

Chapter 11. Professionalizing from the Fringe: Informally Supporting Teaching Assistants via (and Welcoming Them Into) the OWI Community

Miranda L. Egger
UNIVERSITY OF COLORADO DENVER

Abstract: Teaching assistants (TAs or GTAs) are our field's newest emerging teacher-scholars, graduate students who commonly move through a training protocol to help them confidently enter the first-year composition (FYC) classroom. These TAs are typically supported by a small cohort of peers, experienced faculty, collaboratively engaging with grounding, evocative theory—and participating in a practicum course that helps bring this network of supportive components together. It's not uncommon for those same TAs to go on to teach online iterations of FYC, but this time from the fringe—with no new practicum, no new cohort, no new formalized faculty support, and no additional scholarship to support their practice. At best, the implication is that the learning they did about current scholarship in composition studies during the practicum automatically translates to the online learning environment. At worst, this lack of new training leaves these novice teachers to struggle and to assume that online writing instruction (OWI) scholarship doesn't exist, doesn't matter, and isn't necessary to foster student success. Those of us fully immersed in OWI know otherwise, and many teacher-scholars have made the call for OWI training for new (and new-to-online) educators. I echo that call, but in this chapter, I present and illustrate the benefits of an informal Practicum+ model for doing so in light of competing priorities for resources.

Keywords: writing program administration, OWI, training, support, teaching assistants

I taught my first college-level class in 2000. I was 24 years old, far more concerned about the performance of teaching—rather, how badly my hands might shake in front of the students—than about successful facilitation of content using the available means within a specific learning environment. I wanted to succeed, but to my novice self, *succeed* meant not tripping on computer wires or panicking in response to a student question. The only thing that woke me up from my hyper-focused attention on superficial performance was the opportunity to see the wider world of rhetoric, composition, and writing studies (RCWS) via the graduate practicum course. I was still nervous each time I stepped up to the podium, but I began to feel supported by the hint of a tradition guiding me along the way. When I taught my first asynchronous online composition course in 2010, I was (to extend the golf metaphor that Jessie Borgman and Casey McArdle often use with PARS) back to teeing up to hit a ball towards a green I couldn't see, with someone else's equipment, alone, and without a sense of a foundation holding me firm. I hadn't seen any professional community for online writing instruction (OWI), and nothing indicated—not colleagues, not Conference on College Composition and Communication (CCCC) sessions—that OWI scholarship and supportive professional communities existed. Absent that kind of community, I relied on my own limited reasoning, which led me to believe that the best ways to teach in the traditional, synchronous classroom would also be the best ways to teach in the asynchronous classroom and that any changes in performance were due to students' abilities or an inherent deficiency in asynchronous learning spaces, not my inexperienced facilitation. This is a common shortsighted trope, widely expressed in articles about the damned nature of online learning, even today.

These days, I serve as assistant director of composition at the University of Colorado Denver—a public, urban, Hispanic-serving research university with roughly 15,000 students,[1] often dubbed a "commuter" campus to indicate the high proportion of nontraditional students. My responsibilities include supporting composition teachers, especially our latest graduate teaching assistants (TAs). Additionally, I recently took on the role of English department liaison for online writing instruction and, as such, my responsibilities extend specifically to *online* writing instruction. That means, of course, that I have a reason to closely examine the barriers that our OWI faculty face, especially our graduate teaching assistants who *might* take on an online course and find themselves floundering, swinging their own brand-new clubs towards a green they cannot clearly see, *still* not recognizing that a network of OWI-specific professional support does exist. The effect of this support-free transition to OWI is not only struggling online students and classes dogged with high DFW[2] and attrition rates[3] but also an ongoing reluctance to teach in online environments and a habit of perpetuating tired myths that online instruction is inherently less effective than traditional face-to-face (F2F) courses. This all means that, despite the growth in OWI research and scholarship, we are continuing to send teacher-scholars into the broader field of RCWS with no clear sense of OWI as a thread of scholarship worth pursuing.

---

1. At my home institution, 49 percent of freshmen are first-generation college students, and 42 percent of students identify as Black, Indigenous, People of Color (BIPOC).

2. DFW refers to the rate of students who do not successfully meet core competency standards and cannot pass this core requirement because they have earned a grade less than C— a D, F, or a W.

3. In our composition classes, online classes have more than double the attrition rates of traditional F2F classes.

At this point, after 30 years, we may have validated OWI as a field of study and practice, but are we sharing that tradition in replicable ways with our newest teacher-scholars? And, have we designed training protocols that connect local sites to the larger network of support in visible ways that honor personal teaching styles but buttress them with foundational, shareable principles—like PARS and the 13 OWI principles in the 2013 CCCC OWI Position Statement? In this chapter, I describe a Practicum+ model as an informal means to support new OWI TAs and help better professionalize a new generation of OWI teacher-scholars.

Theory and Practice

The theoretical foundation that ties our individual local contexts to a broader, connective network of better practices is already well established. I didn't have to look far to find sets of values necessary to design online facilitation that is particular to all local contexts and individual teacher styles: the four elements of **P**ersonal, **A**ccessible, **R**esponsive, and **S**trategic, coupled with the Principles of OWI (2013), provide a comprehensive picture of OWI-centric values to aim for as we posture ourselves at the first tee of a new course.

My own local context is not at all atypical. Every fall, a new cohort of graduate students teach a first-year composition course, the first of a two-course core sequence requirement. The TAs learn and build their own teaching practice during a four-day, pre-semester orientation crash course in composition studies and throughout the fall practicum, which is a credit-bearing, in-person graduate seminar. My writing program administrator (WPA) colleague, Dr. Rodney Herring, and I have experimented with variations of the composition pedagogy to hand to new TAs but have aimed for a balance between structure and autonomy. The assignment sequence is set for them in advance, and all TAs use the same textbook; beyond that structure, then, is where instructor autonomy begins to take shape: each new TA adapts the major assignments, chooses the controversy as a course theme and the readings related to that controversy, and designs daily class activities that help students successfully achieve the goals of each separate assignment.

While my department is highly supportive in the preparation of new teachers generally, that support hasn't yet yielded formal resources for new-to-online professional development.[4] Still, the department has an emerging interest in studying and improving the learning experience in online spaces amid increasing demands for online course options as well as a growing concern that equity gaps are expanding and rates of success are disproportionately low within online learning spaces. In alignment with the circumstances that dominate most students'

---

4. As is common in most large universities, CU Denver has a dedicated ODE (Office of Digital Education) that serves many faculty professional training needs when it comes to online education, but there is no OWI-specific professional development.

decisions to take online classes (Wu & Hiltz, 2004), our students typically report that flexibility is key to the decision to enroll in an online course. The students at my home university are often working full-time or holding down multiple jobs, taking care of family, and managing their own health issues—meaning online courses are often their only viable option. Consequently, the number of students enrolled in online learning spaces is rising rapidly (Martinez et al., 2020). See Figure 11.1 for online enrollment growth at my home institution since 2013.

In spring 2020 (just before the COVID-19 pandemic), 33 percent of all the English courses in my home department were offered online to meet student demand, and, like at most large public universities, the demand for online courses has far outpaced the professional support structures (Allen & Seaman, 2013). Students aren't the only ones who increasingly demand online options yet report dissatisfaction with their experience. According to the CCCC Committee for Best Practices in Online Writing Instruction's 2011 *Report of the State of the Art of OWI*, faculty are also dissatisfied with the departmental support, which leads to "poor teaching, low expectations [for students and for online courses] and insufficient retention of experienced instructors," despite the growth in demand (CCCC State of the Art, 2011, p. 12; CCCC State of the Art, 2021). Students and faculty are experiencing a growing list of demands on their lives, their health, and their financial well-being, and the problem is only growing more and more urgent. Those demands mean that online courses are ideal for many students; however, their experiences aren't yet aligning with the students' and faculties' reported satisfaction with the online learning experience (Hewett et al., 2011). We clearly have a problem to solve in OWI and an opportunity to invite and support new-to-online educators into this field of study more effectively.

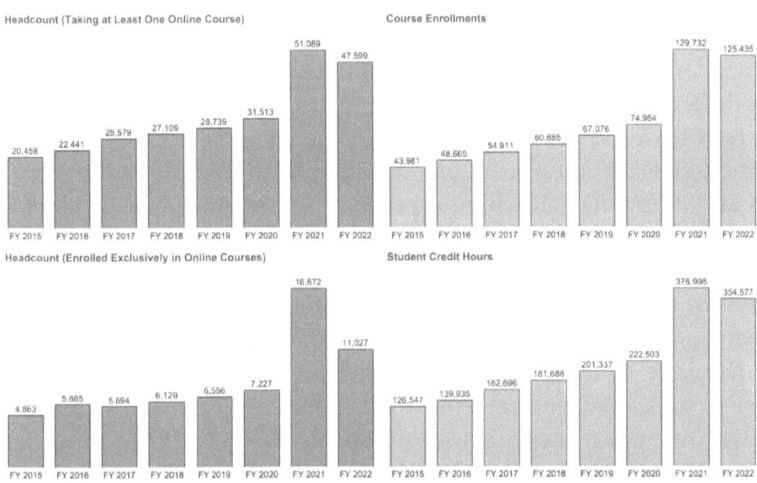

Figure 11.1. Online enrollment figures. Data retrieved from https://www.cu.edu/online-enrollment.

Addressing the Problem

I'm not the first teacher-scholar who has sought to meet the growing demand and mitigate dissatisfaction by designing opportunities to support new and new-to-online instructors in OWI. Since training for new online teachers is non-existent at many institutions (Borgman & McArdle, 2019; Bourelle & Hewett, 2017; Hewett & Ehmann, 2004; Mechenbier, 2015), these teacher-scholars have creatively forged their own brand of local support. For example, Tiffany Bourelle's (2016) eComp was designed as a seminar that their GTAs could opt into after successfully completing the traditional practicum course and teaching F2F for one full semester. Likewise, N. Claire Jackson and Andrea Olinger (2021), Kelli Cargile Cook (2007), and David Grover et al. (2017), in lieu of a formal graduate seminar, designed a certificate-based, six-week mini-course in OWI. GSOLE (the Global Society of Online Literacy Educators) offers a similar certification process, designed by experts in the field and open to all interested OWI educators, that includes eight modules designed to be engaged over a full semester with a small cohort.

Despite the value of these responsive efforts, the circumstances at my own institution demand a less formal solution, one that could work concurrently with the traditional practicum. The initial opportunity presented itself in the Fall 2018 semester. We had three new TAs that, for reasons beyond our control, agreed to teach Core Composition I in an asynchronous online classroom, using Canvas (our institution's learning management system [LMS]). These three graduate students were new to teaching and especially new to *online* teaching (none had even taken an online course before). Each was enrolled in the typical practicum, along with nine graduate student peers, but the typical practicum was not designed to support this new *online* teaching challenge. Dr. Herring and I decided to add a new component to the practicum—an additional one hour/week meeting time that was dedicated solely to online writing instruction mentorship. I have since come to refer to this model as Practicum+.

For the university administrators, this pilot OWI TA program offered new teachers an intermediary teaching experience in order to gain the confidence they needed to transition to the traditional, in-person classroom. However, for me, this was the opportunity I'd been hoping for—a chance to design and use professional development materials to best support brand-new teachers as they solve the "theoretical, pedagogical, and technological puzzles of . . . online courses" (Cargile Cook, 2005); present best practices; and provide the tools necessary to make pedagogical choices of rhetorical awareness, writing, reading, access, and equity in digital learning spaces. For me, the new Practicum+ model was not a stepping stone to serve more traditional learning environments but an end in and of itself—one that could be designed for flexibility and sustainability.

I found two elements key to this Practicum+ model:

- an asynchronous OWI guide that introduces practical PARS-based tips for practice, complete with citations that show a wide foundational range of scholarship
- weekly informal meeting space with the OWI TAs to share practical concerns with OWI-related instruction and co-construct weekly activities

The OWI Guide

I kept my more subversive goals of permanently adding an OWI component to our graduate training to myself but designed the materials with that larger goal in mind. The material of this guide was not based solely on the lore that Beth Hewett and Scott Warnock (2015) argue commonly governs such novice endeavors (though I believe strongly in that lore). Rather, the goal was to illustrate, in a snapshot, that there is a strong OWI community of scholarship from which to draw practical tips. Drawing primarily from foundational values, like the OWI principles (2013) and PARS (Borgman & McArdle, 2019), I designed a new and new-to-online faculty reference guide.

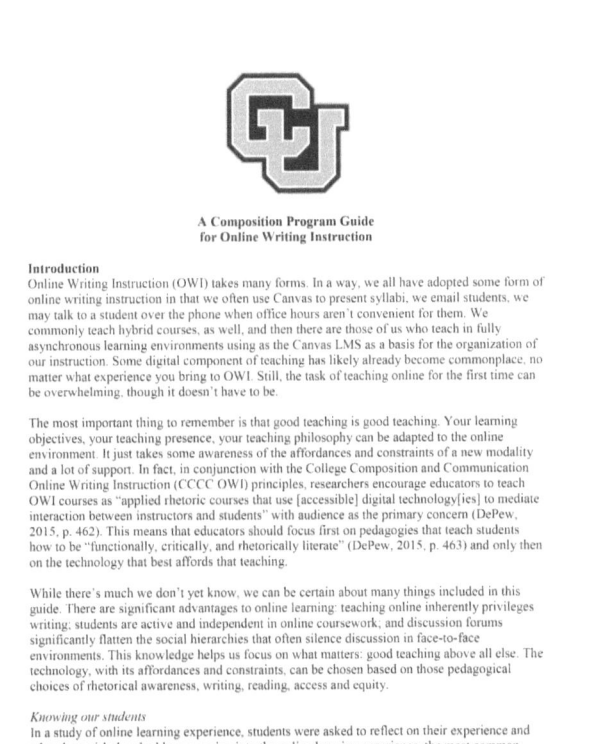

Figure 11.2. This image is the first page of the OWI Guide, where its purpose is described.

> Your presence is important to the online learning environment and is forged, in large part, by facilitating discourse (Anderson et al., 2001). This purpose includes discourse that helps students challenge misconceptions and guide them to higher levels of thinking, reflective practice, and examining assumptions (Strategic). Further, facilitating discourse (through discussion) is essential to maintain interest, motivation, and engagement of students, to make their learning active, and to maintain teacher presence (Personal).
>
> Your presence can look different, depending on the goals of the discussion (Strategic). You might act as: Generative Guide, Conceptual Facilitator, Reflective Guide, Personal Muse, and/or Mediator (Warnock, 2009, p. 73–74).

Figure 11.3 Addressing Asynchronous Discussions

The guide goes on to offer practical tips for engaging students in online discussions, inviting OWI educators to consider themselves thoughtful designers in seven key areas of consideration: Introduction (purpose of the guide, knowing our local students), OWI Principles and PARS, Designing for Accessibility and Inclusivity, Designing for Multilingual Students, Designing for Multimodality, Designing Asynchronous Discussions, and Building Relationships in Online Spaces. These seven key areas draw content from the myriad scholarship already present among scholars in the field, but they were chosen to reflect local values and pedagogical principles. Figure 11.4 from the OWI Guide lists tips specific to designing for accessibility and was adapted from a variety of sources—some within OWI (e.g., Coombs, 2010) and some from disability studies (e.g., Oswal, 2015; Vidali, 2021).

Practicum+ Weekly Meetings

This guide was merely a starting point, a static resource to ground discussions in OWI scholarship. The strength of the Practicum+ model for supporting new OWI TAs lies in the weekly meetings that ran concurrent with their first OWI experience. These meetings were our way to honor the OWI principles' (2013) efforts to provide experienced OWI mentorship (Principle 7), satisfying interaction among new TAs (Principle 7) and ample opportunities for reflection (Principle 15), and to make the application of the PARS values common and natural within discussions of pedagogical design.

To that end, Dr. Herring and I met with the three OWI TAs once a week for one hour, in addition to the traditional practicum course meeting time. In those meetings, we co-designed weekly OWI activities within the already-built infrastructure (i.e., three major assignments and a final portfolio), offered guidance to better align weekly objectives with major course outcomes, and aligned pedagogical goals with technical *tools* to best achieve those goals.

> Rather than perpetuating a "deficit" model by retrofitting course design for a student brave enough to disclose a disability to a system that will judge them, we should facilitate our OWI course in a way that flexibly presents information and reduces common barriers.
>
> Tips for providing access to students with disabilities:
> - Be STRATEGIC & make it ACCESSIBLE:
>   - Include a disability statement on your syllabi up front (not buried at the end; Vidali, 2021).
>   - Vary modes of content delivery, including feedback (consider asynchronous audio or video feedback as well as text-based feedback). Include a combination of text and images to best serve all readers (Schriver, 2013).
>   - Caption all videos (YouTube provides auto-captioning that can be edited for accuracy) and post audio lecture scripts for all audio lectures.
> - Make it PERSONAL & be RESPONSIVE:
>   - Don't forget to simply ask the student what they might need to facilitate the best possible learning experience. Disabled students, like all students, have diverse needs and skill levels that necessitate addressing their learning individually (Oswal, 2015).

Figure 11.4 Designing for Accessibility

We built general sketches of weekly activities together, yet each TA had the autonomy to choose how to fashion those weekly assignments according to their own voice, their own style. For example, after discussing the value of peer review and the technological affordances of this digitally based exercise, each TA took those goals and designed an online peer review prompt that suited their own style (see Figures 11.5–11.7).

While a semester-long, graduate seminar would have been ideal, the circumstances didn't allow for such ideal measures. We had to be careful not to design the Practicum+ as a credit-bearing course, with assigned texts, time to write about OWI teaching philosophies, or even time to explore theory. Instead, I wrote that collection of scholarship into the guide and used the scholarship to craft my own questions and tips in response to the practical concerns brought up by the OWI TAs in the Practicum+ meetings. For example, I knew that when online students were asked to reflect on their experience and what they wish they had known going into the online learning experience, the most common answer given was a clear sense of "instructor expectations" (Bozarth et al., 2004), so we reviewed assignment sheets and rubrics for clear expectations together. We also know that students often just stop attending when they feel overwhelmed with the confusion of having multiple courses using varied online learning systems with varied goals.

Revising and Editing (ER1)

Begin this week by reading chapter 9 "Revision" (pp. 107-117) and chapter 10 "Style" (pp. 121-130) in your textbook. Understanding what revision is - as opposed to editing - and why both are crucial will lead us into the next major assignment: Revision Project.

For this project, you will select one of the major papers, either the Rhetorical Analysis or Entering the Conversation, and see again what you've done and how it can be improved. While you can choose either, it may be best to choose the Rhetorical Analysis since you already have feedback on it. However, don't let this limit you. If you would like to revise the Entering the Conversation paper, let me know and I will return comments to you as quickly as I can.

For this assignment, use the following questions to begin editing the paper you have chosen for revision. Don't merely answer these questions, but open your paper and highlight problem areas for later revision.

Begin with **paragraph level** and focus on content:

1. Re-read your **thesis**. Are you able to locate your thesis clearly and easily? Does your thesis accurately represent what your paper is trying to argue? Highlight your thesis in red. If your thesis is unclear or needs modification after a re-reading, fix this during the revision process.

2. Within each body paragraph, you should have a **topic sentence** or claim that you remain focused on. Highlight each claim in orange. If you stray from this claim, highlight this sentence in yellow to edit later, move elsewhere, or delete entirely.

3. All claims should also have **evidence**, highlight each piece in green. If a paragraph or claim does not have evidence/highlight, come back to add support during revision.

4. Finally, all evidence should have **analysis** that ties the evidence to the thesis. Highlight where you analyze the evidence in blue. If you do not have analysis/highlight, come back and analyze your evidence during revision.

Now, focus on **sentence level** and focus on word choice:

1. Is your word choice accurate? Are you being **precise** and saying exactly what you mean? Are you being **concise**? Are there any areas where you could reduce the amount of words for better presentation and clarity? If you see word choice that needs to be edited, highlight them in purple.

2. Find areas where you use **passive voice**. How can you restructure the sentence to use **active voice** instead? Highlight passive voice in pink.

3. Do you **transition** between paragraphs smoothly? If not, highlight these areas in grey.

The goal of this assignment is to end up with a clear goal of revision. Your highlighted areas should show that you where to begin with your editing process on both a sentence and paragraph level. Submit your highlighted paper here, but keep a copy for yourself to use when you revise your paper for the Revision Project.

Figure 11.5. Revision assignment, TA 1.

Editing (ER2)

For this weeks assignment, read chapter 9 "Revision" (pg. 107-117) and chapter 10 "Style" (pg. 121-130) in your textbook. This assignment will have two parts, a self-evaluation and a reverse outline. To receive credit, you must complete **both** parts of this assignment by Sunday (11/11).

Part One: For this week, you will look towards revising one of your major assignments. It would be the most beneficial to revise your Rhetorical Analysis assignment, since you already have a grade for this assignment. Remember, you are able to revise one of your major assignments to replace your original grade--so take revision seriously.

Answer the following questions about your paper using the strategies you read in your textbook:

- Review your **conclusion**. Are you merely summarizing what you've already stated? How can you connect your assertions in the larger scope of this conversation?
- Does your **thesis statement** cover all of your assertions in your body paragraphs? Do all of your topic sentences make a claim in support of your thesis? How can you revise your thesis to cover your entire argument?
- How can you make your sentences more **precise**? Are you being unnecessarily wordy? Can you simplify the meaning of your sentence? Does this sentence contribute to your claim/analysis in that particular paragraph?
- Pick a sentence that uses passive voice. How can you make changes in it to be in **active voice**?
- Examine each of your body **paragraphs**. Does your topic sentence make a clear claim in support of your thesis? Do you move between each idea using a transition word? Do you use evidence and then analyze and unpack that evidence? Do you use transitional phrases throughout each paragraph to help your reader seamlessly understand your point?

Figure 11.6. Revision assignment, TA 2.

Reverse Outline (ER3)

Reverse Outline

You will be completing a reverse outline. Use the paper you will be revising for this. For this outline, use what you have written in your paper, not what you *should have* written. This will help you identify problem areas. A reverse outline identifies the elements of a piece of writing that is already written. In your reverse outline, highlight or underline each of the indicated elements in the correct colors. Be prepared to upload this as a word document or google doc.

- Looking through each sentence, highlight in yellow places in which you've used the passive voice
- Thesis: Highlight your Thesis in red
- Main ideas: Highlight or underline each main idea used to support thesis in purple
- Evidence: Highlight each piece of evidence that supports these main ideas in green
- Audience: Highlight in pink all of the places where you write about the audience
- Transitions: Highlight each transition word or phrase in red

Once you have completed the reverse outline, write the following reflection: Overall, how well do you think your thesis was supported in this paper? How well did you follow the parameters of the assignment? According to your analysis of your writing, how strong are your claims? Respond in 250-300 words.

Figure 11.7. Revision assignment, TA 3.

With this in mind, we collaboratively examined our course navigation, technical expectations, decisions about where and how to submit work and how to offer consistent and transparent feedback, and worked to build in redundancies via multiple channels. We also knew that the best online instruction happens when teachers are engaged; when they demonstrate interaction and intervene at strategic times (Edwards et al., 2011); and when they succeed with motivation, self-discipline, communication, and commitment (English, 2014), so together we sought any and all opportunities to deliver, interact with, and design pedagogy that honored these findings.

To support the technical learning curve (as that is a major source of struggle for new OWI educators, by many measures), I had access to the TAs' Canvas course shells along the way and visited each shell before the Monday morning publishing deadline to review directions, check technical settings, and troubleshoot any other issues I could detect and advise on in advance.

Benefits of Practicum+ Meetings

For our program, this Practicum+ model worked in expected, and even more unexpected, ways. We drew four primary advantages derived from the weekly meetings and the extensive post-semester interview with each OWI TA.

OWI TAs increased discussions of effective teaching with technology as well as heightened discussions of multimodality, inclusivity, and access.

For the OWI TAs, teaching online opened up the opportunity to think more critically about pedagogical design for all their TA cohort. Hewett and Warnock (2015) tell us that "OWI principles can be applied broadly to the motivation and the exigencies for composition writ large . . . beneficial for all modes of teaching" (p. 553). This Practicum+ model substantiated this claim dramatically. We saw this "writ large" motivation most clearly in the teaching demonstrations. We were all uncertain how the purely OWI demonstrations might go over with the other traditional TAs. In fact, when the OWI TAs presented to the whole cohort, they were timid and had mistakenly assumed the other teachers wouldn't be interested. What we all discovered, however, was that the opposite was true. The traditional TAs eagerly asked for the demonstration materials to be shared. They had thoughtful, engaging questions for the OWI TAs and requested more demonstrations of online teaching and learning. They all discussed, as a result of these OWI demonstrations, ways to move some class discussions/activities to online spaces (finding their own way to Jose Bowen's *Teaching Naked* [2012] assertions), new ways to guide more active digital reading, or ways to more effectively use online tools to help students recall course materials.

The OWI TAs found their OWI experience helpful to their future F2F pedagogical design as well. One OWI TA in this pilot Practicum+ model was an interesting case because she taught both F2F and online sections. She struggled with classroom management online, but she also saw more possibilities with her online as well as F2F classes *because* she taught online. For example, when asked what she'd do differently teaching this class next time around, she said, "I'd allow them to engage in multimodal elements more so next time. All my students can demonstrate their understanding of rhetoric better using multimodal elements and using Canvas." When I asked which class this response applied to, she hesitated, then admitted "both." She felt like her new experience using technologies to do good pedagogical work illustrated a possibility to do better in every learning environment.

Having strictly OWI TAs in the practicum mix, in fact, encouraged the other nine TAs to critically engage issues of access (e.g., providing help videos for struggling students) and inclusivity (e.g., making a digital discussion forum for students who didn't get a chance to speak up in class). Up to this point, these were not conversations that came up so organically (that is, unprompted) in prior traditional TA cohorts.

> *The Practicum+ sessions both supported TAs through, and heightened our awareness of, the need for technical support.*

While the research calls for us to move beyond professional development that narrowly focuses on technical support for the LMS (Taylor & McQuiggan, 2008), I found that technical uncertainties still dominated the concerns the OWI TAs brought to our weekly meetings. However, the issues weren't primarily about technical ignorance; rather, they were concerns over how to make technology serve pedagogy. The TAs told us that they felt strongly supported by the dedicated time to talk through—with us and with each other—those concerns. These meetings were specific to their OWI experience and focused on what they needed most, in the moments when they needed it most, each and every week: collaboratively planning the weekly assignments, brainstorming how to use the technology thoughtfully, troubleshooting issues with student engagement, testing the limits of the LMS, practicing creative means of feedback, and reflecting on what moves worked best.

My having full access to the OWI TAs' course shells and reviewing the settings and prompts before each module opened helped me to intervene on the numerous technical problems with the LMS before they became visible. Also, allowing the TAs access to one another's course shells was deemed helpful, since they borrowed from one another and helped catch technical errors early. Sharing such pedagogical spaces can be challenging for many teachers; there is a tendency to be territorial with our classrooms—digital or F2F—and pedagogical design. To honor that, I was careful to check for technical concerns (e.g., consistent due dates, point values, submission directions, gradebook setup), not to critique prompts, response times, or grade distributions. This restraint helped foster a necessary trust in having me visit their course shell.

> *OWI TAs showed an increased awareness and acceptance of OWI as rigorous and viable.*

These pilot OWI TAs are typical in that they entered this pilot program reflecting common attitudes toward OWI. In fact, two (of the three) expressed deep doubts that online environments were ever really conducive to learning. But by the end of the Fall 2018 semester, after being immersed in OWI and supported through their own online-specific course-design processes, all three ended the semester with a strong feeling that OWI *can* work when designed thoughtfully, that it was a distinct boost to accessibility, and that OWI was overall a strong and viable mode of education.

> *The Practicum+ meetings provided much-needed emotional support and a long-term view of the value of online education.*

This effort (and my work to support faculty through the COVID emergency transition) has brought another element of OWI training to my attention. The presence of an experienced mentor and a supportive cohort who can help guide the co-design process and troubleshoot issues is largely an emotional endeavor. As I reflect, I notice that much of what I have done is provide emotional support for the risk these new and new-to-online educators are taking on: sometimes playing with a new interface, sometimes smoothing over any mistakes, mostly calming the nerves that accompany new risks.

When taken altogether, these results of the Practicum+ model for supporting new OWI TAs proved effective. Having and supporting OWI TAs with a new Practicum+ model was not only a benefit to the online TAs but a benefit to *all* TAs—especially around multimodality, inclusivity, and accessibility—regardless of the classroom environment. Beyond that, however, this effort to weave OWI-specific scholarship and professional development proved beneficial to more than the TAs and their students. As a result of the Practicum+ model, our CU Denver English department and the field of rhetoric, composition, and writing studies now have a few new teachers mentored specifically in OWI. Further, a new precedent has been set for training new OWI TAs through informal grassroots means, not just to solve some problem of underprepared graduate students, but to honor OWI as "stimulating and nourishing learning spaces in their own right," not the "impoverished replicas of traditional classroom spaces" (Cargile Cook, 2005, p. 65).

Limitations of the Practicum+ Model

I acknowledge that this approach falls short of ideal and warrants ongoing reflection. In one final interview with the OWI TAs at the end of the Fall 2018 semester, I culled together tips for redesigning this program. While the three novice OWI instructors left feeling uncertain about the kinds of things all TAs wrestle with—the fairness of assessment, the value of written feedback, how to teach to such a disparate group of abilities—some of their concerns were specific to OWI, such as engaging and successfully interacting with struggling students who don't respond to emails; balancing the text-heavy tendency of OWI course design with videos and audio links; and the steep learning curve of doing so with a focus tuned to accessibility, making better use of multimodal opportunities to engage learners, and time management. These OWI TAs essentially echoed what Lisa Meloncon and Heidi Skurat Harris (2015) and Wanda Worley and Lee Tesdell (2009) warned us about: Online teaching requires an expansion of your own literacies, much as it does for students' literacies, and that means that OWI instructors' time and energy are heavily taxed as developing an online course takes an enormous amount of time and research. As one OWI TA put it, "Online is deceptive. You think you can do more than you can, faster than you can." The truth of this leaves WPAs to more carefully consider the tentative balance between allowing TAs to have pedagogical freedom and the pragmatic concerns of being a new teacher and supporting those concerns with the transcontextual theory they need—all while simultaneously offering the emotional and logistical support they might not yet know they need. I found the need for tuning into such a balance even more pronounced among OWI TAs.

Further, the issues of WPA labor are problematic. The design and implementation of the Practicum+ model was not stipended but should have been. I'd encourage other programs to make a better case for supporting the additional labor—both for the WPAs designing the OWI guide and hosting the weekly meetings (in the form of a stipend, service credit, or a course release) as well as the graduate TAs (in the form of an additional stipend or credit towards their degree).

Conclusion and Takeaways

Ultimately, this pilot Practicum+ model[5] taught us the same lessons the field has learned from expanding into myriad threads of scholarship (e.g., disabilities studies, queer studies, multimodal studies): When we seek to learn about a new and seemingly different way to teach, we are all empowered to expand our tools for inclusivity. Now, with a Practicum+ program that makes room for OWI-specific pedagogies, values, and scholarly support, we can prepare teachers for the rigors of teaching via digital media, merged with the practical instantiation of the theories and best practices presented in the growing body of OWI research. That focus on OWI specifically improves teaching for us all, in every learning environment, and maximizes learning among our students.

I suspect I'll always feel nervous when I begin a new class, a new module, a new activity, whether online or F2F. But, after years of searching for a professional support network, I lean on the traditions of OWI scholarship that I can now see. I find that scholarship eases my mind, gives me a head start, and supports a focus

---

5. In two subsequent years, this informal attempt to professionally develop new TAs in OWI had to shift to a Spring-semester series of informal weekly meetings, disconnected from the practicum. I continued to meet with new OWI TAs, concurrent with their first semester of online instruction, proving the model is portable, flexible, able to be applied to any semester where new TAs (or instructors new to OWI) can participate without designing a new course or re-arranging the graduate curriculum.

of online pedagogical design that rests firmly on rigor, support, and student-centric learning. I wish I'd seen that glimpse of a professional network sooner, but I hope efforts like this one (and so many others, in varied circumstances) help continue the good work.

For others looking to do something similar, tailored to their own local contexts, the key takeaways of the Practicum+ program are to collect key concerns among scholarship that meet their programmatic values (in an OWI guide, easily shared with all interested educators) and, more critically, designate an experienced (and enthusiastic) OWI educator to meet with new (and new-to-online) faculty each week for practical weekly discussion and collaborative design concurrent with their first OWI teaching experience.

The future will ideally involve more choice for both teachers and students who are free to determine the best learning environment for their needs. That same ideal future will offer all TAs the opportunity to try teaching (and learning) in varied classroom environments, if they choose, and be prepared and supported as they design F2F, asynchronous online, remote, hybrid, and HyFlex facilitation. Until that day, these informal efforts at professional development might be the best way forward for those of us who are slowly building a case for dedicated OWI TA training in their home departments.

References

Allen, E. I. & Seaman, J. (2013). *Changing course: Ten years of tracking online education in the United States*. Babson Research Group. http://www.onlinelearningsurvey.com/reports/changingcourse.pdf.

Anderson, T., Rourke, L., Garrison, D. & Archer, W. (2001). Assessing teaching presence in a computer conferencing context. *Journal of Asynchronous Learning Networks*, 5(2), 1–17. https://doi.org/10.24059/olj.v5i2.1875.

Baran, E. & Correia, A. P. (2014). A professional development framework for online teaching. *TechTrends*, 58(5), 95–101. https://doi.org/10.1007/s11528-014-0791-0.

Borgman, J. & McArdle, C. (2019). *Personal, accessible, responsive, strategic: Resources and strategies for online writing instructors*. The WAC Clearinghouse; University Press of Colorado. https://doi.org/10.37514/PRA-B.2019.0322.

Borgman, J. & McArdle, C. (2021). *PARS in practice: More resources and strategies for online writing instructors*. The WAC Clearinghouse; University Press of Colorado. https://doi.org/10.37514/PRA-B.2021.1145.

Bourelle, T. (2016). Preparing graduate students to teach online: Theoretical and pedagogical practices. *Writing Program Administration*, 40(1), 90–113. https://wpacouncil.org/aws/CWPA/pt/sp/journal-archives.

Bourelle, T. & Hewett, B. (2017). Training instructors to teach multimodal composition in online courses. In E. A. Monske & K. L. Blair (Eds.), *Handbook of research on writing and composing in the age of MOOCs* (pp. 348–369). IGI Global.

Bowen, J. B. (2012). *Teaching naked: How moving technology out of your college classroom will improve student learning*. Jossey-Bass.

Bozarth, J., Chapman, D. & LaMonica, L. (2004). Preparing for distance learning: Designing an online student orientation. *Educational Technology and Society*, 7(1), 87–106. https://eric.ed.gov/?id=EJ851992.

Cargile Cook, K. C. (2005). An argument for pedagogy-driven online education. In K. C. Cook & K. Grant-Davies (Eds.), *Online education: Global questions, local answers* (pp. 49–66). Routledge.

CCCC Online Writing Instruction Standing Group. (2021). *The 2021 state of the art of OWI report*. Conference on College Composition and Communication. https://sites.google.com/view/owistandinggroup/state-of-the-art-of-owi-2021.

CCCC Committee for Best Practices in Online Writing Instruction. (2013). *A position statement of principles and example effective practices for online writing instruction (OWI)*. https://www.owicommunity.org/owi--distance-education-resources.html.

Conference on College Composition and Communication Committee for Best Practices in Online Writing Instruction. (2011). *Report of the state of the art of OWI*. https://www.owicommunity.org/owi--distance-education-resources.html.

Coombs, N. (2010). *Making online teaching accessible: Inclusive course design for students with disabilities*. Jossey-Bass.

Edwards, M., Perry, B. & Janzen, K. (2011). The making of an exemplary online educator. *Distance Education*, 32(1), 101–118. https://doi.org/10.1080/01587919.2011.565499.

English, J. (2014). *Plugged in: Succeeding as an online learner*. Cengage.

Grover, S. D., Cargile Cook, K., Skurat Harris, H. & DePew, K. E. (2017). Immersion, reflection, failure: Teaching graduate students to teach writing online. *Technical Communication Quarterly*, 26(3), 242–255. https://doi.org/10.1080/10572252.2017.1339524.

Hewett, B. L. & Ehmann, C. (2004). *Preparing educators for online writing instruction: Principles and processes*. National Council of Teachers of English.

Hewett, B. & Warnock, S. (2015). The future of OWI. In B. L. Hewett & K. E. DePew (Eds.), *Foundational practices of online writing instruction* (pp. 547–563). The WAC Clearinghouse; Parlor Press. https://doi.org/10.37514/PER-B.2015.0650.

Jackson, N. C. & Olinger, A. R. (2021). Preparing graduate students and contingent faculty for online writing instruction: A responsive and strategic approach to designing professional development opportunities. In J. Borgman & C. McArdle (Eds.), *PARS in practice: More resources and strategies for online writing instructors*. The WAC Clearinghouse; University Press of Colorado. https://doi.org/10.37514/PRA-B.2021.1145.2.13.

Martinez, D., Mechenbier, M. X., Hewett, B., Melonçon, L., Harris, H. S., St.Amant, K., Phillips, A. & Bodnar, M. I. (2020). A report on a U.S.-based national survey in online writing courses. *Research in Online Literacy Education Journal*. http://www.roleolor.org/a-report-on-a-us-based-national-survey-of-students-in-online-writing-courses.html.

Mechenbier, M. (2015). Contingent faculty and OWI. In B. L. Hewett & K. E. DePew (Eds.), *Foundational practices of online writing instruction* (pp. 227–249). The WAC Clearinghouse; Parlor Press. https://doi.org/10.37514/PER-B.2015.0650.2.07.

Melonçon, L. & Harris, H. (2015). Preparing students for OWI. In B. L. Hewett & K. E. DePew (Eds.), *Foundational practices of online writing instruction* (pp. 411–438). The WAC Clearinghouse; Parlor Press. https://doi.org/10.37514/PER-B.2015.0650.2.13.

Oswal, S. (2015). Physical and learning disabilities in OWI. In B. L. Hewett & K. E. DePew (Eds.), *Foundational practices of online writing instruction* (pp. 253–289). The WAC Clearinghouse; Parlor Press. https://doi.org/10.37514/PER-B.2015.0650.2.08.

Schriver, K. (2013). What do technical communicators need to know about writing? In J. Johnson-Eilola & S. Selber (Eds.), *Solving problems in technical communication* (pp. 386–427). University of Chicago Press.

Taylor, A. & McQuiggan, C. (2008). Faculty development programming: If we build it, will they come? *Educause Quarterly, 31*(3), 28–37.

Vidali, A. (2021). Lecture. Delivered 10.12.2021.

Warnock, S. (2009). *Teaching writing online: How and why*. National Council of Teachers of English.

Worley, W. & Tesdell, L. (2009). Instructor time and effort in online and face-to-face teaching: Lessons learned. *IEEE Transactions on Professional Communication, 52*(2), 138–151. https://doi.org/10.1109/TPC.2009.2017990.

Wu, D. & Hiltz, S. (2004). Predicting learning from asynchronous online discussions. *Journal of Asynchronous Learning, 8(2)*, 139–152. https://doi.org/10.24059/olj.v8i2.1832.

Reset, Refocus, Recharge!

Almost all professional golfers have a coach who works with them to improve their swing, short game, or even mental game. As good as you might be, there is always room for improvement. There are different golf courses—some with lots of water, some with lots of bunkers, some built for the long game, and some that are all about the short game. The point is, you have to tailor your game to each golf course, and you need help with that. Even when you know the course and have played it a bunch of times, you can always have surprises pop up. We see this with online course design too. You can have the best online course design and students can still get tripped up locating something they need.

What we like about this chapter is that Joseph Bartolotta, Anthony Yarbrough, and Tiffany Bourelle discuss instructional design theory that is centered via five steps: analyze, design, develop, implement, and evaluate. The authors give administrators and faculty a chance to engage in more conversations about how the changing educational landscape (student population, technology, program goals, etc.) can be met with a more agile framework of iteration.

We like the focus on design in this chapter because it's not something that gets discussed often and many writing program leaders with little to no experience in OWI are often faced with designing online courses. Bartolotta et al.'s chapter gives program leaders a clear framework to use when thinking about design.

Chapter 12. Professional Development for Online Writing Instruction: The Place of Instructional Design

Joseph Bartolotta
HOFSTRA UNIVERSITY

Anthony Yarbrough
UNIVERSITY OF NEW MEXICO

Tiffany Bourelle
UNIVERSITY OF NEW MEXICO

Abstract: This chapter describes ways to incorporate theories of instructional design into online writing practica and other professional development for online writing instruction. Specifically, we discuss creating an online training practicum (or professional development workshop) structured in a way that mimics the Collaborative Mapping Model (CMM) of instructional design, combined with Analyze, Design, Develop, Implement, and Evaluate (ADDIE) and Backward Design principles, where the teacher-trainer works with online writing instructors to create effective online writing instruction environments. In this model, trainees are immersed in a course guided by these methods while learning how to structure their own online courses using similar design approaches. This immersive model also suggests a constructivist approach to learning, guiding trainees to better understand how to facilitate a collaborative, active learning atmosphere for online student success.

Keywords: instructional design, training, Analyze, Design, Develop, Implement, and Evaluate (ADDIE), Collaborative Mapping Model (CMM), backward design, program administration

Training writing instructors used to be a straightforward affair. In a time before learning management systems (LMSs) and online tools, administrators could get by with training instructors in creating assignments, scaffolding activities, and implementing best pedagogical practices in the writing classroom. As classrooms moved online, the work of designing the classroom environment fell more upon teachers themselves, many of whom had not been trained in delivering writing instruction online. It is no longer enough to simply be an instructor of writing; we must also curate digital classroom spaces for instruction within the parameters set by higher education institutions and online learning service providers.

In other words, online writing instructors must be at once teachers and instructional designers (Blythe, 2001). Without training, they were sent into design roles. We want to refocus on what training in instructional design for online writing instructors could look like and provide a framework that builds a training structure that gives instructors an eye for instructional design.

Scholars have long been calling for training in online writing instruction (OWI) pedagogy (Bourelle & Hewett, 2017; Cargile Cook, 2007; Hewett & Ehmann, 2004; Hewett & Powers, 2007), and the COVID-19 pandemic has made clear that training in online writing instruction will become an important part of professional development for *all* writing instructors. Indeed, in *Teaching Writing in the Twenty-First Century*, Beth Hewett, Tiffany Bourelle, and Scott Warnock (2022) argue that composition in the digital era means that all communication is multimodal and all teaching is online in some capacity, with instructors using an LMS and various media to teach within onsite, hybrid, remote, and fully asynchronous classrooms. This shift means administrators must balance theories and pedagogies of teaching writing with the newly essential tool of acuity toward digital instructional design. Many interwoven theories including content strategy (Borgman, 2019, 2020; Borgman & McArdle, 2019), web design (Snart, 2021), course mapping (Ambrose et al., 2010), backward design (Wiggins & McTighe, 2005), and the analyze, design, develop, implement, and evaluate (ADDIE) model of instructional design (Morrison, 2010), as well as tools such as usability testing and user-centered design more broadly (Bartolotta et al., 2017; Bartolotta, 2021) offer useful ways to develop online writing classes. With all this in mind, how do writing administrators wade through theories of online pedagogy and course design to create a compact and trainable approach to preparing the next generation of online writing instructors?

Hewett et al.'s (2022) observation about the changing nature of online writing instruction indicates a clear need to reconceptualize training to include pairing instructional design methods with the best practices of online writing instruction. The PARS approach offers a workable framework to imagine what this sort of training can look like. This chapter discusses the "Strategic" element of PARS by offering a theoretical background for such training, as well as a "how-to" guide for administrators and instructors alike to follow when structuring similar training for online writing instructors based on their institutional context.

Theory and Practice

Online writing instruction scholarship varies in terms of approaches to creating curriculum, with Warnock (2009) suggesting instructors can migrate what they do in the onsite classroom to the online environment and Beth Hewett and Christa Ehmann Powers (2004) arguing that instructors need training in reconsidering their curricula for the online environment. However, scholars do agree that instructors must consider the needs of their students and what might work best for the context of their institutions before building their courses. In *Writing Together: Ten Weeks Teaching and Studenting in an Online Writing Course*, Scott Warnock and Diana Gasiewski (2018) discuss the online writing class from both the instructor and student point of view. As Warnock's student, Gasiewski gives insight into the material, prompting Warnock to consider how his students interact with the course material; such insight provided in their collaborative book offers instructors a starting point for creating and potentially revising their online curriculum accordingly.

Curriculum design that considers the students' impressions and experiences is also in line with more recent scholarship on user-centered design in teaching, which calls for the need to consider all students and their access needs and challenges in the online space (Borgman, 2019; Borgman & Dockter, 2018). Another approach to student-centered design includes usability testing of online courses, where the instructor asks a student a series of questions regarding what they like in the course, what they don't like, what was useful, what wasn't—all to better understand how students are interacting with the material (Bartolotta et al., 2017). Similarly, Joseph Bartolotta (2021) offers a way for instructors to conduct their own usability testing with their own students using PARS as a lens to ground that approach.

In *Writing Together*, Warnock and Gasiewski (2018) posit that the approaches and suggestions they provide are "platform-neutral" (p. xix), arguing for an instructor's focus to remain on pedagogy, including the curriculum they build and the ways in which they interact with the students on a daily basis. We agree that developing one's pedagogy is perhaps the most important aspect of teaching, but we do want to extend the conversation to include the LMS, as we believe such platforms are never as neutral as we hope. For instance, in "Preparing for the Rhetoricity of OWI," Kevin DePew (2015) argues for the rhetoricity of online education, asserting that instructors should never just use technology for technology's sake. We take this to mean that instructors need to carefully consider their courses and how they approach the curriculum, offering a variety of content that includes text, sound, video, animation, and so on (McClure & Mahaffey, 2021). The LMS inherently will impact how the course is delivered and how students interact with the material, depending on what resources or technologies are available through that platform. In what follows, we discuss how teacher-trainers can work with trainees to consider their pedagogies, how these pedagogies will translate to the online classroom, and further, how they can work within the constraints of the LMS to deliver the best possible content for student success.

Success can only be achieved when students have opportunities to interact with the curriculum, which can be affected by the constraints and affordances of the LMS. To build a successful online writing course, we suggest using instructional design approaches that allow for the consideration of the curriculum and how it works in conjunction with the LMS. Specifically, we discuss the instructional models of analyze, design, develop, implement, and evaluate (ADDIE);

the Collaborative Mapping Model (CMM); and backward design, combining the three to provide instructors with a comprehensive guide for considering course design. In "The Collaborative Mapping Model: Relationship Centered Instructional Design for Higher Education," Jason Drysdale (2019) notes that the ADDIE model has become "widely characterized as the traditional industry-standard model of instructional design" (p. 58). Since then, other instructional design methods have been developed, including CMM and backward design, focusing on the process of course design based on student achievement of course outcomes. In this text, we use ADDIE as the overarching structure of how we shape instructional design training, but we find CMM and backward design to be important concepts that add nuance to how we operationalize ADDIE in practice. When process and student learning outcomes are the focal points of composition, these methods are useful for online writing course development in that the collaborative, outcome-focused process aligns with what instructors will ask of their students in a typical composition course.

Table 12.1 Critical Concepts of Backwards Design, CMM, and ADDIE

Critical Concepts	
Backward Design	An approach to designing instruction where the designers start with the results they'd like to see (i.e., achieving student learning outcomes) and then work backward to find methods, activities, and resources that help achieve those results (Wiggins & McTighe, 2005).
Collaborative Mapping Model (CMM)	An approach to instruction design where instructional designers work with instructors who are experts in their field to develop high-quality learning experiences for students (Drysdale, 2019). In this chapter, we recognize that not all institutions have the resources to make instructional designers available to instructors, so as we imagine it here, the teacher-trainer fills the role of instructional designer.
ADDIE	Standing for "analyze, design, develop, implement, and evaluate," ADDIE is a systematic approach to course design that allows administrators and instructors alike to strategize, assess, and revise instructional design (Morrison, 2010).

How-To: Structuring Professional Development

In this section, we offer ways that teacher-trainers—often writing program administrators or faculty who are well versed in online education principles—can create online teaching professional development opportunities that could be delivered through practicum courses or a series of workshops. We see the practicum class being a semester-long training endeavor; however, an intensive week-long workshop can also be structured if a practicum is not possible (we recommend compensating faculty for their time spent in the training workshops). Regardless of format, we suggest that the training is structured in such a way that mimics the

CMM of instructional design. However, we know that many schools do not have instructional designers who are available for guidance in course design. In these cases, teacher-trainers must assume the mantle of instructional designers. In such training, the teacher-trainer works from the CMM to collaborate with instructors (the trainees) to learn of their pedagogical goals and to use the LMS to facilitate learning. Trainees are essentially immersed in the CMM while building their own course maps and content, with immersion being an established effective practice for online training (Grover et al., 2017; Hewett & Ehmann, 2004). In other words, the trainees are immersed in an online course guided by these methods while learning how to structure their own online courses using similar design approaches. Through such hands-on experiences, trainees learn which instructional design strategies align best with their pedagogical goals, which strategies facilitate and hinder learning for their own students, and which strategies they can implement appropriately into their course design. This immersive model also suggests a constructivist approach to learning, guiding trainees to better understand how to facilitate a collaborative, active learning atmosphere for online student success.

During the practicum or workshops, trainees first develop their teaching pedagogies through readings and discussions of multimodal composition (Cui, 2019; DePalma & Alexander, 2015; Lauer, 2009; Palmeri, 2012; Shipka, 2011); multiliteracies (Khadka, 2019; New London Group, 1996; Serafini & Gee, 2017), including critical, functional, and rhetorical (Selber, 2004); and online writing pedagogies (Borgman & McArdle, 2019; DePew & Hewett, 2015). The training is practical as well, as the trainees also develop their online courses using their institutional LMS, aligning their course with their teaching pedagogies.

The first major project asks trainees to develop a multimodal assignment prompt they would teach in their online course, using the principles they learned through the readings and discussions. They are then asked to swap with a peer and complete each other's assignments as if they were students in the course. After completion of the project, they leave their peer feedback using screen capture technology (such as Camtasia), and both trainees then revise their assignment prompt and reflect on why they made the changes. The peer review, including all communication between trainees, is conducted in asynchronous formats. The entire project from start to finish gives the trainees not only insight into what students might experience when creating the project, but it also gives them experience creating video feedback, which scholars have suggested is important to establish teaching presence in the online classroom (Harris & Greer, 2021). Lastly, because the peer review is conducted through asynchronous formats, the trainees gain a greater sense of how peer review will work from a student perspective in their own online courses.

The final major project is the creation of an online course the trainees can teach from in subsequent semesters. Combining CMM with ADDIE and backward design principles, the teacher-trainer works with trainees to create a map of the course, starting with identifying the course outcomes and then imagining assignments that allow students to experience those outcomes. Through backward design, the trainees take their multimodal assignment prompt and draft out a map that outlines activities, quizzes, small writing assignments, and other exercises that support the assignment. The map links each activity to the institution's student learning outcomes for first-year writing. After outlining their course map, trainees are then prompted to think through the specifics of their curriculum and how the LMS can best support these activities. In the following list, we provide an example of what the final project looks like through the ADDIE model of instructional design. Although we are presenting this sequencing in a linear fashion, in reality, much of what the trainees are learning about comes throughout the course and is reiterated in the final project.

Analyze

Trainees should refer to evaluative data from previous and current iterations of the course; they should also research the students as the audience for their curriculum. Trainees consider their course prerequisites and, using available educational and demographic data, ascertain students' learning needs or technological challenges. This phase is arguably the most important, as trainees will be conducting analysis of their students before starting the course design, throughout their teaching of their course, and after the course is complete. We suggest trainees first research and understand the students at their institution and gather whatever data is available. For example, the University of New Mexico (where all of the authors of this text have taught) is a Hispanic-serving institution. Indeed, our outcomes for first-year writing reflect the need for students to understand and value languages, dialects, and registers beyond standardized English. Further, the university is experiencing high growth of students from across different backgrounds and cultures, with the university reporting in 2021 "a 26 percent increase in [Native American] students, a 65 percent increase in African American students, and a 7.5 percent increase in Hispanic students in the freshman class compared with last year. International student enrollment increased by 74 percent" (Jones, n.p.). Trainees are encouraged to choose readings from authors with diverse, intersectional backgrounds and interweave the readings throughout the course, not just in one unit, to illustrate that diversity, inclusion, and access are integral and valued aspects of the course (Diab et al., 2016).

Analysis should look not just at demographics but access as well. From the latest study of internet access in New Mexico, we know that at least 26 percent of residents throughout the state do not have access to broadband internet, and 15 percent do not have access to a computer (Duran, 2019). Aligning with our institutional and state data, trainees read Rochelle Rodrigo's (2015) "OWI on the Go" and Michael Gos' (2015) "Nontraditional Student Access to OWI" to learn how students access the course from their cell phones and how internet access might affect students' participation and overall success in the course. Trainees also read Daniel Anderson's (2008) "The Low-Bridge to High Benefits" and Joy Robinson et al.'s (2019) "State of the Field: Teaching with Digital Tools in the Writing and Communication Classroom," where they learn to include low-bridge software as options for multimodal composition, as requiring high-bridge technology such as web design software can potentially marginalize students who have limited resources or internet bandwidth concerns.

In his article "A Broad-Based Multiliteracies Theory and Praxis for a Diverse Writing Classroom," Santosh Khadka (2018) suggests that "[a] course or a course sequence crafted around such a framework i.e. around an array of literacies such as essayist, rhetorical, multimodal, visual, and intercultural, can encourage students to use their native cultural, linguistic and media resources in the class while preparing them for complex composition and communication challenges of the globalized world" (p. 96). While the practicum readings are structured around teaching first-year students the literacies Khadka includes, learning to integrate these into an online curriculum is often a tall order for trainees, especially when many of them are first-time instructors who have limited experience in onsite teaching let alone in online environments. Thus, it is imperative that the teacher-trainer works with the trainees to guide them in deconstructing readings, formulating their pedagogical goals, and connecting them to the course outcomes or objectives. Trainees must *analyze* why they are including certain readings and activities by considering their connection to course outcomes; we discuss fostering this connection in the next element of design.

Design

Trainees should plan their courses for optimal student engagement by creating opportunities for higher-order thinking strategies, peer-to-peer interaction, and variety in activities. The key word in the previous sentence is *plan*: In the design phase, trainees simply map their course through a bare-bones outline, aligning the course activities with their pedagogical goals, the course outcomes, and the students' needs and challenges that were researched in the analyze phase. Using backward design principles, trainees create assignments that best assess evidence of understanding for outcomes on unit and course levels, and they consider the resources that may be required to complete each assignment. Trainees are encouraged to use the course calendar as the "map" that allows them to create a basic outline of the course. The calendar is constructed like a table, with columns for activities, outcomes, and points that can be attained for completion of each activity.

Trainees also learn the instructional design method of "chunking," which is based on the idea that similar content should be grouped together in an online course (Schuessler, 2017). Trainees learn to chunk their courses into units that correspond to the major writing assignments; they also learn to break down each week in the unit into small, manageable tasks that work toward scaffolding the major writing assignments. This sketching also considers repetition and redundancy (Warnock, 2009), where trainees create units that look similar and follow the same format for each week (i.e., the first week in each unit asks students to take a short quiz on the assignment and corresponding readings; the second week in each unit asks students to participate in two discussion boards, and so on, where every unit follows this structure). Trainees can think of designing or chunking the content in the LMS to mimic what is found in the calendar map. In other words, each unit in the LMS should be clear, with the same number of weeks, aligning with the calendar structure. Trainees will then take their outline and fully develop the activities in the next phase before adding the content to the LMS.

Develop

Trainees now create course materials using the insights generated in the previous steps, considering how the learning outcomes align with course material on semester, project, and weekly levels. At the develop phase, trainees are encouraged to create their content through word processing software for easy copy into the LMS. They draft out the wording for discussion boards, journals, small writing assignments, and quizzes—anything they sketched out in the previous phase. The teacher-trainer must encourage trainees to think from the student seat again and anticipate questions they might receive:

- Have they thought about how students will respond, including word count and number of times to peers in the course?
- Have they asked students to use a variety of multimedia throughout the course to establish student presence?
- Have they offered low-bridge options at all levels, not only at the small and major writing assignment level but also at the discussion board post level?

Trainees can work together to review each other's scaffolding, but the teacher-trainers, who are likely experienced online instructors, should guide trainees to reconsider their content before the next phase of implementation.

Implement

Trainees take what they drafted in the develop phase and build these activities in various ways. Teacher-trainers should give feedback on the course scaffolding during the develop phase so that during the *implement* phase, trainees are now reviewing the LMS and searching for effective tools to teach the course content. The current LMS at UNM is Canvas, and trainees are provided several workshops to help them learn the features before they start building (teacher-trainers should research their own institutions to learn of LMS training opportunities or find tutorials on their LMS to guide trainees). At the same time, trainees are also encouraged to find and create various media to teach course concepts. Trainees build their own tools, such as a video that goes along with an assignment prompt or a short screen capture that shows students how to use the library databases; they are also encouraged to find and utilize prebuilt tools such as videos on YouTube, podcasts, sound bites, and other media. Lastly, trainees listen to webinars such as "Equity-Minded and Culturally Affirming Teaching and Learning Practices in Virtual Learning Communities" by Frank Harris III and J. Luke Wood (2020), who posit that the online course should be a mirror for students to see themselves represented. At the implement phase, trainees find media that represents *themselves and their students,* based on the analyze phase that asked them to research the students at their institution.

Evaluate

Trainees should review the course curriculum and structure to ensure the connection of their course design to established best practices of online writing pedagogy. The data gathered in the *evaluation* phase can be used to inform both the current and subsequent iteration of the ADDIE cycle. At the end of the training workshop or practicum, trainees should evaluate the actuality of the online curriculum they developed with their initial analysis and course vision, making adjustments if necessary. At the end of the training course, trainees are encouraged to use whatever institutional accessibility and assessment protocols are appropriate, such as the newest rubric from the Online Learning Consortium (OLC) or Quality Matters (QM), to review their courses. If their courses do not meet the QM standards, they can develop an action plan for meeting the criteria and make changes before the semester begins. They are also encouraged to use the OLC's rubric, which discusses design with more depth than the QM rubric, focusing on use of white space, font size and color, flashiness of media used, and other design elements that must be considered when using various LMS templates.

While the teacher-trainer should guide trainees to review their own courses, they should also provide overall feedback on the course to ensure that the course meets the programmatic goals. They should observe the course during the semester in which it is taught. They can screencapture their "observation," noting what they see and where the instructor can make improvements. Teacher-trainers should share the screencapture observation with the instructor (no longer a trainee) and open up a conversation, allowing the instructor to respond and share their own impressions of the course (Bourelle et al., 2022; Mechenbier & Warnock, 2019). At this point, the instructor can develop an action plan for revising the course based on the teacher-trainer's feedback and whatever feedback they have received from students at the midway point. This plan can be expanded upon the conclusion of the semester. Collaboration should not stop when the training course is over; the teacher-trainer should continue mentoring the instructors, offering feedback and future training as program outcomes and the field of composition change and evolve. In actuality, evaluation should occur throughout the teaching of a course and not just at the end. Instructors can use surveys, real-time student feedback, course evaluations, and feedback from colleagues and administrators to determine whether the course is effectively meeting student learning needs, making course revisions as necessary.

Conclusion and Takeaways

Not all teacher-trainers will be well versed in instructional design theory, and they do not have to be. However, we hope that our chapter has provided a starting point for more discussions regarding integrating instructional design with online writing pedagogy, and we also hope that our chapter offers avenues for more scholarship on the subject for readers who are interested in understanding how instructional design functions and how the LMS can work in conjunction to enhance, not hinder, online writing instruction. Finally, we hope our readers can take our model and reconsider their teacher-training practices; we also hope that instructors without access to similar training methods can utilize some of what we've provided to create their own curriculum with an eye toward designing their courses, using the LMS to its fullest digital capacity. As we noted at the beginning of this chapter, the pandemic made it so that all instructors have taught online in some fashion; therefore, it is now more important than ever to return to teacher training with, as we have argued, an eye toward instructional design theory to guide us to better understand how course design within an LMS works to facilitate learning.

References

Ambrose, S. A., Bridges, M. W., DiPietro, M., Lovett, M. C. & Norman, M. K. (2010). *How learning works: Seven research-based principles for smart teaching*. Wiley & Sons.

Anderson, D. (2008). The low bridge to high benefits: Entry-level multimedia, literacies, and motivation. *Computers and Composition, 25*(1), 40–60. https://doi.org/10.1016/j.compcom.2007.09.006.

Bartolotta, J. (2021). Usability testing for OWI instructors. In J. Borgman & C. McArdle (Eds.), *PARS in practice: More resources and strategies for online writing instructors* (pp. 305–315). The WAC Clearinghouse; University Press of Colorado. https://doi.org/10.37514/PRA-B.2021.1145.2.18.

Bartolotta, J., Bourelle, T. & Newmark, J. (2017). Revising the online classroom: Usability testing for training online technical communication instructors. *Technical Communication Quarterly, 26*(3), 287–299. https://doi.org/10.1080/10572252.2017.1339495.

Blythe, S. (2001). Designing online courses: User-centered practices. *Computers and Composition, 18*(4), 329-346. https://doi.org/10.1016/S8755-4615(01)00066-4.

Borgman, J. (2019). Creating a user-centered experience in online courses through content strategy. In G. Getto, J. Labrioloa & S. Ruszkiewicz (Eds.), *Content strategy in technical communication* (pp. 154–170). Routledge. https://doi.org/10.4324/9780429201141.

Borgman, J. (2020). *An investigation of the content practices of online writing instructors and administrators* [Doctoral dissertation, Texas Tech University]. TTU DSpace Repository. https://ttu-ir.tdl.org/bitstream/handle/2346/86509/BORGMAN-DISSERTATION-2020.pdf?sequence=1.

Borgman, J. & Dockter, J. (2018). Considerations of access and design in the online writing classroom. *Computers and Composition, 49*, 94–105. https://doi.org/10.1016/j.compcom.2018.05.001.

Borgman, J. & McArdle, C. (2019). *Personal, accessible, responsive, strategic: Resources and strategies for online writing instructors.* The WAC Clearinghouse; University Press of Colorado. https://doi.org/10.37514/PRA-B.2019.0322.

Bourelle, T. & Hewett, B. (2017). Training instructors to teach multimodal composition in online courses. In E. A. Monske & K. L. Blair (Eds.), *Handbook of research on writing and composing in the age of MOOCs* (pp. 348–369). IGI Global.

Bourelle, T., Hewett, B. L. & Warnock, S. (2022). *Administering writing programs in the twenty-first century.* Modern Language Association of America.

Boyd, D. (2016). What would Paulo Freire think of Blackboard: Critical pedagogy in an age of online learning. *The International Journal of Critical Pedagogy, 7*(1), 165–185. https://libjournal.uncg.edu/ijcp/article/view/1055.

Cargile Cook, K. (2007). Immersion in a digital pool: Training prospective online instructors in online environments. *Technical Communication Quarterly, 16*(1), 55–82. https://doi.org/10.1207/s15427625tcq1601_4.

Cui, W. (2019). Rhetorical listening pedagogy: Promoting communication across cultural and societal groups with video narrative. *Computers and Composition, 54*, https://doi.org/10.1016/j.compcom.2019.102517.

DePalma, M. J. & Alexander, K. P. (2015). A bag full of snakes: Negotiating the challenges of multimodal composition. *Computers and Composition, 37*, 182–200. https://doi.org/10.1016/j.compcom.2015.06.008.

DePew, K. E. (2015). Preparing for the rhetoricity of OWI. In B. L. Hewett & K. E. DePew (Eds.), *Foundational practices of online writing instruction* (pp. 439–467). The WAC Clearinghouse; Parlor Press. https://doi.org/10.37514/PER-B.2015.0650.2.14.

Diab, R., Godbee, B., Ferrel, T. & Simpkins, N. (2016). Making commitments to racial justice actionable. In F. Condon & V. A. Young (Eds.), *Performing antiracist pedagogy in rhetoric, writing, and communication* (pp. 19–39). The WAC Clearinghouse; University Press of Colorado. https://doi.org/10.37514/ATD-B.2016.0933.2.01.

Drysdale, J. (2019). The Collaborative Mapping Model: Relationship-centered instructional design for higher education. *Online Learning, 23*(3), 56–71. https://doi.org/10.24059/olj.v23i3.2058.

Duran, J. A. (2019). Bringing broadband to the desert: Rural New Mexico, fiberoptic cable, and electric utility cooperatives. *New Mexico Law Review, 49*(2), 384–401. https://digitalrepository.unm.edu/nmlr/vol49/iss2/9/.

Gos, M. W. (2015). Nontraditional student access to OWI. In B. L. Hewett & K. E. DePew (Eds.), *Foundational practices of online writing instruction* (pp. 309–346). The WAC Clearinghouse; Parlor Press. https://doi.org/10.37514/PER-B.2015.0650.2.10.

Grover, S. D., Cook, K. C., Harris, H. S. & DePew, K. E. (2017). Immersion, reflection, failure: Teaching graduate students to teach writing online. *Technical Communication Quarterly, 26*(3), 242–255. https://doi.org/10.1080/10572252.2017.1339524.

Harris, F. & Woods, J. L. (2020). *Equity-minded and culturally affirming teaching and learning practices in virtual learning communities*. Center for Organizational Responsibility and Advancement (CORA), Northern Illinois University. https://www.niu.edu/flexteaching/workshops/equity-in-virtual-learning.shtml.

Harris, H. S. & Greer, M. (2021). Using multimedia for instructor presence in purposeful pedagogy-driven online technical writing courses. *Journal of Technical Writing and Communication, 51*(1), 31–52. https://doi.org/10.1177%2F0047281620977162.

Hewett, B. L. & Ehmann, C. (2004). *Preparing educators for online writing instruction: Principles and processes*. National Council of Teachers of English.

Hewett, B. L. & Ehmann, C. (2007). Guest editors' introduction: Online teaching and learning: Preparation, development, and organizational communication. *Technical Communication Quarterly, 16*(1), 1–11. https://doi.org/10.1080/10572250709336574.

Hewett, B., Bourelle, T. & Warnock, S. (2022). *Teaching writing in the twenty-first century*. Modern Language Association of America.

Jones, B. (2021). *UNM new student numbers increase substantially*. The University of New Mexico. https://news.unm.edu/news/unm-new-student-numbers-increase-substantially.

Khadka, S. (2018). A broad-based multiliteracies theory and praxis for a diverse writing classroom. *Computers and Composition, 47*, 93–110. https://doi.org/10.1016/j.compcom.2017.12.002.

Khadka, S. (2019). *Multiliteracies, emerging media, and college writing instruction*. Routledge.

Lauer, C. (2009). Contending with terms: "Multimodal" and "multimedia" in the academic and public spheres. *Computers and Composition, 26*(4), 225–239. https://doi.org/10.1016/j.compcom.2009.09.001.

McClure, C. I. & Mahaffey, C. (2021) Finding the sweet spot: Strategic course design using videos. In J. Borgman & C. McArdle (Eds.), *PARS in practice: More resources and strategies for online writing instructors* (pp. 101–117). The WAC Clearinghouse; University Press of Colorado. https://doi.org/10.37514/PRA-B.2021.1145.2.06.

Mechenbier, M. & Warnock, S. (2019). A collaborative method for observing/evaluating online writing courses. *College Composition and Communication, 71*(1), A8-A16.

Morrison, G. R. (2010). *Designing effective instruction* (6th ed.). Wiley & Sons.

New London Group (1996). A pedagogy of multiliteracies: Designing social futures. *Harvard Educational Review, 66*(1), 60–92.

Palmeri, J. (2012). *Remixing composition: A history of multimodal writing pedagogy*. Southern Illinois University Press.

Robinson, J., Dusenberry, L., Hutter, L., Lawrence, H., Frazee, A. & Burnett, R. E. (2019). State of the field: Teaching with digital tools in the writing and communication classroom. *Computers and Composition, 54*. https://doi.org/10.1016/j.compcom.2019.10251.1.

Rodrigo, R. (2015). OWI on the go. In B. L. Hewett & K. E. DePew (Eds.), *Foundational practices of online writing instruction* (pp. 493–516). The WAC Clearinghouse; Parlor Press. https://doi.org/10.37514/PER-B.2015.0650.2.16.

Schuessler, J. H. (2017). "Chunking" semester projects: Does it enhance student learning? *Journal of Higher Education Theory and Practice, 17*(7), 115–120.

Selber, S. A. (2004). *Multiliteracies for a digital age*. Southern Illinois University Press.

Serafini, F. & Gee, E. (Eds.). (2017). *Remixing multiliteracies: Theory and practice from New London to new times*. Teachers College Press.

Shipka, J. (2011). *Toward a composition made whole*. University of Pittsburgh Press.

Snart, J. (2021). Online writing instructors as web designers: Tapping into existing expertise. In J. Borgman & C. McArdle (Eds.), *PARS in practice: More resources and strategies for online writing instructors* (pp. 243–254). The WAC Clearinghouse; University Press of Colorado. https://doi.org/10.37514/PRA-B.2021.1145.2.14.

Warnock, S. (2009). *Teaching writing online: How and why*. National Council of Teachers of English.

Warnock, S. & Gasiewski, D. (2018). *Writing together: Ten weeks teaching and studenting in an online writing course*. National Council of Teachers of English.

Wiggins, G. & McTighe, J. (2005). *Understanding by design*. Association for Supervision and Curriculum Development.

Hit 'Em Long and Straight!

There are many golf courses out there that have been designed and built for specific audiences with no real goal of being inclusive when it comes to inviting players from all over. Those are exclusive and embody the problem we both see when it comes to expanding the game and connecting with new audiences.

Far too often, classes are designed for only teachers and not students. Very few organizations that build content management systems (CMSs) used by institutions take the time to engage with students about how they view and interact with course content. Students are the primary users of these spaces, not instructors.

We really like how Abram Anders and colleagues utilize a user-centered model to develop pre-designed courses. It focuses on collaboration as a means to support faculty within the development of pre-designed courses while exploring an iterative course development approach with tasks and timeframes for each role. We think this is an excellent way of supporting current faculty who want to be more engaged with their students as well as new faculty who need support as they begin teaching. What we also like is that by default this level of care and detail that Anders et al. explore actually aids the faculty in focusing on the student users, that is, their courses become user-centric by default, and that's a very good thing!

Chapter 13. Strategic Administration for Online Courses in Communication and Writing Programs

Abram Anders, Jenny Aune, Katharine Fulton
IOWA STATE UNIVERSITY

Anne Kretsinger-Harries
UNIVERSITY OF KANSAS

Amy Walton, Casey White
IOWA STATE UNIVERSITY

Abstract: The strategic administration of online courses in communication and writing programs depends on a balance of standardization and flexibility to meet the needs of diverse stakeholders. Based on experiences managing online courses in three large communication and writing programs, the authors of this study argue that exercising collaborative leadership and using iterative development principles to create pre-designed courses can support a sustainable approach to creating user-centered learning experiences for both students and instructors. In addition to providing a research-based rationale and sharing situated examples, this study provides specific recommendations to help programs promote collaborative leadership and integrate elements of the PARS framework—personal, accessible, responsive, and strategic—into the iterative development of pre-designed courses.

Keywords: collaborative leadership, iterative development, PARS framework, pre-designed online courses, strategic administration, writing program administration

Reflecting on the administration of online writing courses or programs, Jessie Borgman and Casey McArdle (2019) warn that a lack of strategy and adequate support for faculty and students "increases the likelihood that online and hybrid courses will become cycles of despair and dysfunction, where faculty blame underprepared students and students give up on poorly executed online courses" (p. 81). The danger of this type of failure became critically apparent for communication and writing programs across the nation when the COVID-19 pandemic necessitated an abrupt shift to online instruction for multiple semesters without the possibility of upfront strategic planning.

The pandemic was a crucible for many communication and writing programs and for their capacities to approach online writing instruction (OWI) in ways that emphasized strategic investments in instructor- and student-centered design and support. If a lack of strategy leads to a "cycle of despair and dysfunction," we argue that a strategy embracing collaborative leadership and the iterative development of pre-designed courses for instructor- and student-centered experiences can promote a cycle of continuous improvement and innovation. This strategy is based on these principles:

- collaborative leadership for human-centered innovation
- pre-designed courses that emphasize instructor- and student-centered experiences
- iterative development processes that enable responsive design and support

Following previous research of interdisciplinary collaboration, these principles offer a distillation of insights produced through "developing highly specialized best practices to guide specific projects" and are offered as a heuristic that can be adapted by other programs, teams, and leaders (McMullin & Dilger, 2021, p. 488). Using these principles, communication and writing program leaders can work with their stakeholders to strengthen their collective capacities for continuous improvement and innovation.

The authors of this chapter have experience as the leadership team for three large-scale communication and writing programs in the English department at Iowa State University. We share the unique perspectives and insights generated through our experiences exercising shared leadership as we adapted to the challenges of the COVID-19 pandemic and prepared our programs for sustained adaptability and innovation in online learning for the future.

Theory and Practice

We found inspiration in the "model of lean programmatic work" developed by Meredith Johnson et al. (2017, p. 17). Based on theories of lean manufacturing and lean startups, this model for communication and writing program administration helped us orient ourselves to lead through our strengths and make disruptive circumstances the occasion for strategic innovation. In alignment with the tenets of lean programmatic work, we focused on addressing the local needs of our stakeholders and exercising social responsibility during an era of heightened challenges for teaching and learning. We also emphasized efficiency, sustainability, and visibility to ensure that we could continue to perform at a high level while prioritizing our accountability to students and instructors. In particular, we sought to navigate the tensions between standardization and flexibility articulated in the model of lean programmatic work. Johnson et al. (2017) highlighted the relevance of this tension for curricular development, noting that standardization can protect "vulnerable populations," such as inexperienced contingent faculty, by limiting the amount of preparation required to teach while also providing a consistent and user-centered experience for undergraduate students. Standardization can also enable the efficient use of program resources. However, flexibility is equally important for enabling innovation and disruption: "Experimental approaches can invigorate programs in unexpected ways and propel them forward" (Johnson et al., 2017, p. 31). Ultimately, strategic approaches to curricular development will balance the benefits of standardization with the need to exercise flexibility for innovation in both responsive and planned ways.

Previous research has found that pre-designed courses—which offer complete implementations of shared curricula, including major assignments and developmental learning activities—can provide consistent, user-centered experiences for students and allow instructors to focus on course delivery and assessment (Mitchum & Rodrigo, 2021). Pre-designed courses create space for instructors to focus on presence and student engagement and provide a balance of cognitive, social, and teaching presence (Garrison et al., 2010). Though standardized courses can limit instructor autonomy, it is important to recognize that thoughtful, accessible, navigable online courses require extensive investments of time and expertise to develop (Remley, 2013). Pre-designed courses not only save instructors preparation time, but they can help instructors develop online pedagogical expertise through structured practice with well-designed online instructional content and learning activities (Rodrigo & Ramírez, 2017). Furthermore, Jo Mackiewicz and Jeanine Aune (2017) have argued that pre-designed courses can become a platform for collaboration between program leaders and faculty as they engage in idea-sharing through communities of practice. Thus, shared curricula implemented in pre-designed courses can be standardized to consistently support students and instructors *and* foster the type of serendipitous experimentation that promotes creativity, adaptability, and innovation.

Building on this work, our programs implemented the PARS framework and its "personal, accessible, responsive, and strategic" elements in our shared design process (Borgman & McArdle, 2019, 2021). Through iterative development involving multiple overlapping collaborative design teams and multiple forms of assessment, we were able to make significant and timely changes in our pre-designed courses to address evolving instructor and student needs as we moved through different stages of the pandemic. Our efforts are aligned with previous research demonstrating that collaborative approaches to online curriculum design can promote a balance of standardization and flexibility and enable the development of accessible online teaching and learning experiences for both instructors and students (Smith et al., 2021).

Above all, we sought to bring a user-centered mindset to designing for our students and instructors. As Michael Greer and Heidi Skurat Harris (2018) argue, "A user-centered mindset returns students to the center of the conversation, energizing and improving professional development in which teachers and students, not technology, shape learning experiences" (p. 23). Toward this end, our approach has been inspired by human-centered design and design thinking processes as we oriented ourselves to design as a form of creative problem-solving and treated our pre-designed courses as prototypes to be successively revised (Leverenz, 2014; Wible, 2020).

Program Context

Iowa State University enrolls 25,000 students in more than 80 undergraduate programs across six colleges: Agriculture and Life Sciences, Design, Engineering, Human Science, Liberal Arts and Sciences, and the Ivy College of Business. The university's vision to "lead the world in advancing the land-grant ideals of putting science, technology, and human creativity to work" includes a communication proficiency policy requiring all students to be able to communicate effectively in written, oral, visual, and electronic (WOVE) mediums (Iowa State University, n.d.).

The Department of English has three multicourse programs that support Iowa State's communication proficiency policy (see Table 13.1). ISUComm Foundation Courses (FComm) offers a sequence of two multimodal composition courses. ISUComm Speech Communication (SpComm) offers two public speaking and professional speaking courses. ISUComm Advanced Communication (AdvComm) offers four upper-division professional communication and writing courses. In total, these three programs employ over 100 instructors, ranging from first-semester graduate teaching assistants (GTAs) to faculty with more than 30 years of experience, and provide communication instruction to upwards of 12,000 students in 450 sections every academic year. As of spring 2022, 21 percent of all program sections were taught online.

As Table 13.2 illustrates, prior to the pandemic, each program had varied approaches to online learning and different levels and forms of instructional design and technology support. At the start of the pandemic, as our entire institution moved to online learning, each program capitalized on its unique resources to quickly support instructors and students. As the pandemic endured, our programs continued to make iterative improvements to their online courses. During the 2020–2021 academic year, our program leaders began to collaborate more frequently and worked together to address challenges that emerged for all of us.

Collaborative leadership across programs during the pandemic became essential to help us triage problems and develop a unified approach for offering faculty support and resources. In the following sections, we will share the strategies we developed and our recommendations for implementing the PARS framework to support the strategic administration of online courses in large-scale communication and writing programs. These sections include recommendations for collaborative leadership, pre-designed courses, and iterative development that come from our shared experiences of collaborating across programs.

Table 13.1. Communication and Writing Programs at Iowa State

FComm **ISUComm Foundation Courses**	SpComm **ISUComm Speech Communication**	AdvComm **ISUComm Advanced Communication**
Multimodal composition 2 course sequence ENGL 150: Critical Thinking and Communication ENGL 250: Written, Oral, Visual, and Electronic Composition	Public and professional speaking 2 course options SpComm 212: Fundamentals of Public Speaking SpComm 312: Business and Professional Speaking	Professional communication and writing 4 course options ENGL 302: Business Communication ENGL 309: Proposal and Report Writing ENGL 312: Science Communication and Public Engagement ENGL 314: Technical Communication
225 Sections 61 instructors 5,500 students 18% online (spring)	45 sections 24 instructors 2,000 students 11% online (spring)	180 sections 32 instructors 4,000 students 39% online (spring)

Note. Statistics are based on AY 2021-2022.

PARS for Strategic Program Administration

Prior to the pandemic, the directors of our three programs largely focused on their own courses and faculty, engaging in sporadic, as-needed collaboration. This changed as our program leaders found themselves navigating similar challenges created by the pandemic:

- How might we create student-centered online courses tailored for undergraduate students without experience with online learning?
- How might we make the workload manageable for our teaching faculty, who teach multiple sections per semester, and our graduate students, who teach on top of their own graduate work?
- How might we provide training for instructors with varying levels of online teaching experience?
- How might we remain adaptable and supportive as primary delivery modalities shift throughout different phases of the pandemic?

Multiple iterations of our collective approach to online course development provided rich opportunities to evaluate the strengths and weaknesses of courses and program processes. Additionally, our increased collaboration and responsiveness to feedback resulted in a shared, iterative process for course creation and shared capabilities for instructor support and training.

Table 13.2. A Developmental Timeline for ISUComm Programs

Pre-Pandemic Independent Growth	Spring 2020 Emergency Transition	AY 2020–2021 Iterative Development	AY 2021–2022 Collaborative Leadership
AdvComm Developed online courses in 2015 and initiated Quality Matters review	AdvComm Pivoted to pre-designed online courses with all sections using Blueprint delivery process	AdvComm, SpComm, FComm Engaged in iterative development to address instructor workload and student engagement	AdvComm, SpComm, FComm Continued to refine pre-designed courses and promote instructor engagement and creative collaboration
SpComm Developed hybrid courses in 2014 with no plans for fully online courses	SpComm Created online course modules based on pre-designed hybrid courses	SpComm, FComm Developed and tested pre-designed online courses and enhanced instructor support	
FComm Developed online learning activities with an online course pilot initiated in fall 2019	FComm Created online course modules based on pilot online courses		
Collaborative Created online learning team (OLT) and online learning coordinator (OLC) roles	Collaborative Led design sprints with OLC and OLT support	Collaborative Implemented Blueprint delivery process for all programs; developed shared process for iterative course design, review, and delivery with OLC and OLT support	Collaborative Developed flexible versions of pre-designed courses for both in-person and online course delivery

Over time, we became more strategic in our focus and began to think about how to sustain the continuous improvement of our programs. We began to ask a new set of questions:

- How might we build on our established success and keep our online pre-designed courses vibrant and evolving?

- How might we sustain instructor engagement and provide flexibility as they work with our standardized curriculum and pre-designed course materials?
- How might we more directly involve the expertise and creativity of our instructors in the design of new instructional material and activities?

Above all, we sought to employ user-centered approaches to better integrate the expertise and perspectives of our stakeholders into the iterative design process and to ensure more diverse, inclusive, and equitable outcomes. It has been extremely gratifying to be able to iteratively address instructor and student concerns, semester by semester, and to see those issues become resolved and give way to new challenges.

Collaborative Leadership

Our experiences demonstrated that collaboration and invention could thrive in the right environment and with dedicated support. We recognized that a collaborative approach to leadership should occur among program leaders and with our faculty and staff. During the early phases of the pandemic, close collaboration between program leaders and a commitment to seeking feedback through multiple stakeholder channels served our programs extremely well. Our program leaders met frequently and shared the feedback and issues that were reported by instructors, which included questions and concerns raised by students. Working together, we were able to identify patterns and prioritize global concerns, such as helping students with time management and clarifying communication expectations for instructors. With the support of our design teams, we were able to develop and implement new instructional content and provide on-demand support for our courses to meet these needs.

Our approach to collaborative leadership also involved internal collaboration with faculty and staff. For example, during our emergency transition to online instruction in the spring of 2020, the FComm program convened a design team that consisted of the program director, assistant directors, online learning coordinator, and the two lead instructors from our online course pilot. This small team, with its well-situated members, was able to provide a fairly robust and diverse sample of instructor feedback and reported student concerns that represented both instructor and GTA perspectives in our two courses. The director and assistant director solicited feedback from first-year GTAs in our mentoring program, the online learning coordinator reported feedback from experienced term faculty, and the lead instructors shared feedback from a pilot team that included experienced online instructors. This approach to collaborative leadership helped us create responsive incremental changes, and it informed more impactful changes to our standardized curriculum and pre-designed courses insofar as it informed our extended, team-based design sprints over the summer.

Our programs emerged from the early stages of the pandemic with stronger pre-designed courses, a shared process for iterative development, and a more collaborative approach to leadership with more clearly defined roles and integration of stakeholder contributors (see Table 13.3):

- Program directors and assistant directors lead curriculum development and instructional design and provide professional development as well as course-specific support for instructors.
- An online learning coordinator and the online learning team of GTAs support the development and design of Canvas course sites and provide on-demand online learning and technical support for instructors.
- Program instructors engage in collaborative design teams and communities of practice and contribute to program assessment activities.

Moving forward, we sought to cultivate ecosystems of innovation and idea-sharing for our programs. Our leadership teams experimented with diverse formal and informal approaches to collaboration and worked to create communities founded on trust, support, and visibility. Once the groundwork for collaboration was established, faculty and staff leaders were able to thrive in a variety of contexts, from program-sponsored work teams to organized communities of practice to informal social networks of colleagues. Our programs involved instructors in shared leadership using a spectrum of collaboration strategies (see Table 13.4). These collaboration strategies helped integrate the expertise and perspectives of diverse faculty and staff into design processes and offered individual instructors opportunities to directly shape leadership decisions that impact their courses.

Table 13.3. Collaborative Leadership and Shared Capabilities

FComm	SpComm	AdvComm
ISUComm Foundation Courses	ISUComm Speech Communication	ISUComm Advanced Communication
Director	Director	Director
Assistant Director		Assistant Director
Shared Support Program Support Staff Online Learning Coordinator Online Learning Team		
Shared Processes Regular program directors' meetings with program staff Iterative development and review process for pre-designed courses		

Table 13.4. Collaboration Strategies to Support Innovation

Context	Strategies
Emergent Leaders	Create informal and formal leadership roles for instructors who make valuable contributions to design teams and communities of practice.
	Empower experienced instructors who are willing to share expertise and instructional materials with peers and provide suggestions for improvement.
Design Teams	Use extended-project design teams to support the iterative development of instructional designs with in-depth engagement and real-time feedback.
	Use brief, highly structured design sprints to involve diverse instructors in shaping curriculum, policies, and instructional designs.
	Use research assistants to discover research-informed approaches to challenges and prepare scaffolding for design teams.
	Recruit collaborators who can contribute diverse perspectives and bring expertise from multiple programs and contexts.
Training and Professional Development	Use orientations and graduate teaching assistant proseminars to offer situated instruction and curated development resources.
	Use a formal mentoring program and/or mentoring circles to support professional development and promote engaged social learning.
	Provide on-demand training materials to support experienced instructors with the transition to online teaching and learning.
Communities of Practice	Lead experimental teaching teams to pilot and provide feedback on new instructional designs and/or thematic content.
	Lead professional development opportunities that feature diverse community perspectives and expertise and provide opportunities for informal idea-sharing and collaboration.
Social Networks	Create informal opportunities for co-creation and idea-sharing such as lesson-planning co-working sessions.
	Create informal opportunities for mutual support and idea-sharing such as grading co-work sessions.
	Offer opportunities to build relationships through unique learning opportunities and teaching assignments such as learning communities or shared theme sections.
	Promote backchannels for informal sharing and surface challenging feedback, such as peer-to-peer social media groups.

Recommendations for Collaborative Leadership Aligned with the PARS Framework

Promote *personal* leadership by offering inclusive collaboration opportunities for instructors and by integrating student feedback.

- Create opportunities for diverse instructors to shape and contribute to curricular development and course designs and integrate student feedback to frame and focus collaboration activities.
- Create accessible collaboration opportunities with greater and lesser time commitments from intensive experiences like design teams to expansive experiences such as social learning events.
- Use co-creation and social learning activities as the occasion for leaders to connect with instructors to build rapport, trust, and shared purpose.

Promote *accessible* leadership through the alignment of curricula, policies, and pre-designed course formats across programs.

- Design program policies to be user-centered and aligned across programs to create clarity and consistency for both instructors and students and to address global issues in holistic and sustainable ways.
- Design courses using consistent and aligned organizational and formatting patterns; the use of repeated module structures and weekly schedules can lower cognitive load not only for students but also for instructors. With less time needed to anticipate the flow of instruction and student work, instructors can focus on personalizing instruction and delivery.

Promote *responsive* leadership by offering instructors timely learning opportunities and support.

- Provide opportunities for learning and idea-sharing that are specific, situated, and timely to increase engagement, and provide instructors the support they need when they need it. For example, a community of practice could meet just before a module begins to review learning objectives, share ideas for adapted activities, and share strategies for assignment-specific formative feedback.
- Provide on-demand support with clear guidance for how different types of questions can be addressed to different contacts and resources—program leaders, program staff, online learning specialists, institutional information technology, etc.
- Communicate timely and reiterated invitations for instructors to seek support for sensitive issues such as working with students who are disengaged, disruptive, and/or experiencing mental health issues.

Promote *strategic* leadership by collaborating across programs and creating shared capabilities for collaboration and idea-sharing.

- Connect, coordinate, and share ideas with leaders of similar programs in your department or institution. Collaboration with peer leaders can provide valuable perspectives and lead to the creation of shared approaches and resources that can strengthen all programs.

- Create shared processes and technology-based platforms for exchanging ideas and content.
- Create curriculum-aligned design and instructional materials—such as assignment, activity, and lesson-planning templates—to make it easier to share, reuse, and build each other's work.

Pre-Designed Courses and Standardized Curricula

To support our instructors and students, all three programs have developed pre-designed online courses that implement standardized curricula based on a shared syllabus, major assignments and grading rubrics, and supporting learning activities. Common features of our pre-designed courses include:

- brief lecture videos focused on key concepts and skills
- discussion activities that promote social learning and engagement
- process and micro-drafting activities to apply concepts and make progress on major assignments
- structured draft workshops that use discussion activities and collaborative writing applications to facilitate sharing peer and instructor feedback
- video-based presentations that integrate rehearsal and peer feedback activities

These courses are delivered as fully ready-to-use course sites using the Blueprint course functionality of the Canvas learning management system (LMS). The Blueprint functionality allows the creation of one primary Blueprint or template course, which can be connected to Canvas sites for each course section. Blueprint allows for efficient Canvas site creation and the capacity to "push" on-demand updates and fixes to all connected sites. Each program also provides pre-semester workshops and orientations for all instructors as well as comprehensive text- and image-based course setup guides. These courses integrate features aligned with the PARS framework (see Table 13.5).

Promoting personal approaches to delivery and a sense of instructor ownership is a fundamental challenge for using pre-designed courses. While these courses can support instructors in many ways, they can also be perceived as restrictive of autonomy and demotivate instructor engagement (Mackiewicz & Aune, 2017; Mitchum & Rodrigo, 2021; Remley, 2013). To mitigate these issues, it is important to involve instructors in course development processes and to promote opportunities to adapt and customize instructional content and activities (Rice, 2015; Stewart et al., 2016). Course development processes can offer valuable opportunities for professional development in which instructors can develop and contribute their professional expertise while collaborating with peers toward common goals (Penrose, 2012; Rodrigo & Ramírez, 2017). Ideally, pre-designed courses can also integrate dedicated spaces for adaptation and customization, such as open activity slots with recommended activity options.

Pre-designed courses can be developed using universal design principles and implemented across all sections to consistently offer accessible learning experiences for all students in the program (Oswal & Melonçon, 2014; Womack, 2017). In addition, pre-designed courses can be readily available for instructors even when instructors are assigned to courses close to the beginning of the semester. A consistent overall design can also help provide a programmatic feel across multiple program levels, helping instructors and students who interact with the courses.

Through the integration of instructor guidance and design resources, pre-designed courses can also promote responsive and strategic approaches to course delivery. Pre-designed courses can offer a space to share raw materials—slideshow files, video transcripts, weekly overview announcements—for instructors to personalize and organize within a course. Programs can also directly integrate "just-in-time" information for "how to do things" for both instructors and students and could include tutorials and instruction sets, pre-scheduled and/or templated course announcements, or even an unpublished instructor resources module.

Ultimately, pre-designed courses allow programs to implement vision and values into routines and structures across all courses and sections. This approach can ensure comparable learning experiences for all students in a program and support robust approaches to program and learning assessment. Pre-designed courses can also facilitate information-sharing with institutional partners and for accreditation efforts. While there are many benefits, it is undeniable that creating pre-designed courses takes a great deal of time and effort and high levels of collaboration and coordination. As we will discuss further, a structured iterative development process can be essential for sustaining continuous improvement and ensuring coherence, consistency, and alignment in pre-designed courses.

Table 13.5. Example Features of Pre-Designed Courses Aligned with the PARS Framework

Personal	Accessible
A personalizable homepage featuring an instructor photo, email, and student (office) hours information can help create instructor presence and promote student engagement.	Instructional videos can be made more accessible for students and instructors by providing downloadable transcript and slideshow files. Dedicated design teams can implement these types of accessibility features in a consistent and aligned way.
Responsive	Strategic
A pre-designed welcome message can provide both students and instructors with timely guidance and up-to-date information. Pre-designed messages can be provided through an LMS as pre-scheduled announcements or unpublished message templates.	Instructor resources can be directly integrated into pre-designed courses as an unpublished module and provide convenient access to guidelines for planning and delivery as well as adaptable instructional content.

Recommendations for Pre-Designed Courses Aligned with the PARS Framework

- Promote *personal* instruction by integrating spaces for adaptation and customization in instructional content and learning activities.
- Provide modular spaces within courses where instructors are encouraged to create or cultivate their own materials to make it easy for instructors to adapt course sites without fear of breaking course functionality.
- Promote ownership of instructional content by providing copies of slideshows and transcripts for instructional videos and alternative versions of learning activities that can be adapted by instructors.
- Provide training for creating instructor presence in the course, but also be explicit about workload expectations and time management strategies for online teaching (e.g., explain the difference in grading practices between major assignments and low-stakes learning activities such as weekly discussion boards).
- Promote *accessible* and user-centered learning experiences by creating pre-designed courses based on design principles and user feedback.
- Use design teams to develop and review courses to ensure the use of universal design principles for accessibility.
- Create course designs with strong alignment and consistency in structure, layout, and instructions for different assignment and activity types.
- Integrate user feedback and address "pain points" in user experiences.
- Provide *responsive* support by integrating just-in-time guidance and information for instructors and students.
- Create pre-designed messages using LMS capabilities for pre-scheduled announcements or unpublished message templates to integrate timely guidance for instructors and students. Messages could include welcome announcements, weekly overviews, and timely instructions for specific activities, such as draft workshops.
- Provide integrated materials to support instructors' delivery, such as an unpublished resource module or integrated assignment and activity alternatives.
- Provide *strategic* support by creating instructor guides for planning, adapting course content, and delivery.
- Provide resources that explain course designs and delivery expectations for new and returning instructors. Ideally, this will include both asynchronous reference materials and synchronous training, workshop, or orientation events.
- Provide a pre-semester checklist to help instructors prepare for the semester.
- Provide pre-designed course setup guides emphasizing required and optional customizations to promote a personal approach to instruction.

Iterative Development

For pre-designed courses to remain effective, iterative course development is essential. While smaller updates are made to the pre-designed course sites following each semester, more extensive redesign projects occur between the spring and fall semesters. Beginning with evaluation, we gather instructor and student feedback on issues ranging from the curriculum to usability and accessibility within the LMS. We then form a small team of course directors and experienced instructors to decide on revisions and updates and establish a plan for completing the work. Once major revisions are complete, another team dedicated to technology support reviews the course for other key issues, such as accessibility, usability, and correctness. For a detailed overview of our iterative course development process, see Table 13.6.

Table 13.6. Example Timeline for Iterative Course Development

Role	Task	Timeframe
Program Directors and Assistant Directors	Solicit feedback on fall and spring courses using methods such as instructor surveys and focus groups and review of student course evaluations.	April/May
Online Learning Coordinator	Create initial course sites by copying last-used course content into new sites.	June
Program Directors, Assistant Directors, and Design Teams	Develop new course content and improvements to address instructor and student feedback.	July
Design Teams and/or Volunteer Instructors	Review course sites for problems, and provide feedback on areas for improvement.	Mid/late July
Program Directors and Assistant Directors	Update course sites to address the recommendations of reviewers. Promising new ideas may be identified and piloted by design teams and volunteers before inclusion in pre-designed courses.	Late July
Online Learning Team	Review course sites from a technology perspective, address accessibility issues, check for broken links and settings, etc.	Early August
Online Learning Coordinator	Coordinate with Iowa State's Center for Excellence in Learning and Teaching to push course template content to all attached section sites.	August
Program Directors and Assistant Directors	Lead pre-semester workshops to review curriculum, policy, and course updates, and provide resources and support.	Week before the semester begins

Role	Task	Timeframe
Online Learning Coordinator and Online Learning Team	Provide on-demand support and forward curricular design issues and pedagogical questions to program directors.	Week before the semester and first two weeks of the semester
Directors and Online Learning Coordinator	Fix and push updates for any critical issues.	As needed

We have found that this iterative design process affords benefits to all stakeholders, resulting in a higher-quality teaching and learning experience for instructors and students alike. By being actively involved in the design and revision process, instructors see that their voices are heard by program leaders and are valued because suggested changes are reflected directly in the course materials used across all sections. This also allows program leaders to personalize their online courses for the specific team of instructors with which they work.

Having a dedicated time period over several weeks to determine and address major needs makes it easier to follow through on course revisions. For instance, accessibility pain points can be readily prioritized and addressed with a sense of global importance and impact on different stakeholders. Furthermore, challenging changes that would be difficult for individual instructors to address can be made by design teams. This process also allows for prioritization, making it easier to follow through on suggestions provided by instructors and other stakeholders. Some suggestions may be easily and quickly implemented, whereas others could be put on the agenda for a future iteration of the course.

For example, in AY 2020–2021, our instructors reported that they and our students were experiencing workload and time management pressures as they adapted to fully online learning. All three programs conducted self-studies to better understand instructor and student workload and subsequently implemented changes that addressed concerns unique to each program. For spring 2021, our programs made immediate changes which included streamlining the number of weekly process assignments and clarifying grading and feedback expectations for instructors. Over the summer, each program was able to implement additional changes that included more consistent approaches to the organization of modules and weekly activities to communicate expectations more clearly and enable time management for both instructors and students.

Recommendations for Iterative Development Aligned with the PARS Framework

- Promote *personal* engagement through transparent decision-making and clear explanations of updates and changes.

- Provide resources for instructors that highlight any changes to the course design. For small updates, a pre-semester email is sufficient. For more extensive changes, consider creating a shared resource within the LMS or a file-sharing service such as Google Docs or Box.
- For curricular changes, provide context as to why the change was implemented. For example, if a major assignment has been updated with new goals, prompts, grading criteria, or other important content, briefly explain how that decision was arrived at (e.g., instructor feedback, student evaluations, stakeholder needs, pedagogy research).
- Highlight the contributions of collaborators to share credit and model opportunities for instructors to help shape curriculum and course designs.
- Develop expertise to support *accessible* and user-centered online design and delivery.
- Create, if possible, dedicated roles or teams to assist with course development, technical support, and instructor training. Ideally, individuals in these roles would have or receive training in instructional design and/or online instructional standards such as Quality Matters.
- Recruit experienced faculty to participate in course design projects, and utilize institutional resources to support relevant professional development opportunities.
- Partner with institutional resources to develop expertise and processes that ensure accessibility and universal design of instructional materials.
- Foster a *responsive* iterative design process to build community and shared responsibility.
- Actively seek to involve stakeholders with diverse perspectives in the design process, and solicit multiple forms of feedback that best suit instructor groups. For example, for courses largely taught by GTAs, there may be more frequent informal opportunities for feedback during regular meetings and other interactions with course directors, while experienced instructors with higher teaching loads may provide feedback more readily through a survey or email.
- Encourage instructors to report issues and make suggestions, both large and small, as they interact with the pre-designed courses. Acknowledge suggestions and implement them if appropriate and possible.
- Address persistent issues, such as instructor workload, through responsive course design and iterative improvement.
- Develop a *strategic* process map including timeline, roles, and responsibilities.
- Integrate the full scope of the design process: feedback on the previous iteration, design phase, revision and feedback phase, and support phase. It is important to continually "close the loop" to promote the benefits of iterative design.

- Make sure the design process accounts for different aspects of course design, including curriculum, LMS setup, universal design, and accessibility. For example, once the full course has been developed, have an individual or task force review the shell to check specifically for accessibility.
- Use *strategic* approaches to collect feedback throughout the design process.
- Embrace prototyping and create "good enough" initial prototypes of new assignment and learning activities designs; conduct focus groups or pilot tests with small groups of instructors to get feedback and identify where more instructional material, scaffolding, or changes are needed.
- Involve instructor volunteers to review course sites before using tools like Blueprint to push new content out to all instructors.
- Review and revise to sustain curricular alignment and universal design. It's easy to introduce inconsistencies when creating new material, especially when diverse contributors are involved.

Conclusion and Takeaways

Our collective experiences have demonstrated that pre-designed courses can support a strategic approach to ensuring accessible and student-centered instructional designs (see Table 13.7). Pre-designed courses can allow instructors to focus on personal and responsive aspects of course delivery and develop expertise through practice. When developed using iterative design principles and collaborative leadership, pre-designed courses can also become instructor-centered platforms for integrating diverse expertise and enacting shared responsibility for offering high-quality learning experiences.

Furthermore, we have found that strategic administration can be supported by investing in collaborative approaches to leadership that promote idea-sharing and comparison and contrast across programs as well as enable decision-making based on a wider range of experiences and expertise. Collaborative leadership depends on creating inclusive communities in which collaborators at every academic rank, including contingent faculty and GTAs, are empowered to take on leadership opportunities and share feedback. Our programs were fortunate to have program leaders that represented both tenure-track and contingent faculty perspectives, and our design teams almost universally included representation from all instructor ranks, including contingent faculty and GTAs.

Embracing a collaborative leadership approach requires that program leaders invest in building trust and rapport with stakeholders to make them feel comfortable and motivated to share feedback and contribute to design. Trust can be built by proactively seeking, accurately representing, and responsively addressing feedback. Rapport can be created by embracing and implementing the best ideas no matter who suggests them. Leaders themselves have to give up a certain version of top-down control and let the process and feedback play a significant role in decision-making. This can include listening to and acting on uncomfortable, critical feedback. Ultimately, collaborative leadership can support human-centered innovation through iterative development and the transparent collection of stakeholder feedback precisely because it can make programs accountable to stakeholders in both highly challenging and highly productive ways.

Table 13.7. Summary Recommendations Aligning with the PARS Framework

Collaborative Leadership	Pre-Designed Courses	Iterative Development
Promote personal leadership by offering inclusive collaboration opportunities for instructors and by integrating student feedback.	Promote personal instruction by integrating spaces for adaptation and customization in instructional content and learning activities.	Promote personal engagement through transparent decision-making and clear explanations of updates and changes.
Promote accessible leadership through the alignment of curricula, policies, and pre-designed course formats across programs.	Promote accessible and user-centered learning experiences by creating pre-designed courses based on design principles and user feedback.	Develop expertise to support accessible and user-centered online design and delivery.
Promote responsive leadership by offering instructors timely learning opportunities and support.	Provide responsive support by integrating just-in-time guidance and information for instructors and students.	Foster a responsive iterative design process to build community and shared responsibility.
Promote strategic leadership by collaborating across programs and creating shared capabilities for collaboration and idea-sharing.	Provide strategic support by creating instructor guides for planning, adapting course content, and delivery.	Develop a strategic process map including timeline, roles, and responsibilities. Use strategic approaches to collect feedback throughout the design process.

References

Borgman, J. & McArdle, C. (2019). *Personal, accessible, responsive, strategic: Resources and strategies for online writing instructors*. The WAC Clearinghouse; University Press of Colorado. https://doi.org/10.37514/PRA-B.2019.0322.

Borgman, J. & McArdle, C. (Eds.). (2021). *PARS in practice: More resources and strategies for online writing instructors*. The WAC Clearinghouse; University Press of Colorado. https://doi.org/10.37514/PRA-B.2021.1145.

Garrison, D. R., Anderson, T. & Archer, W. (2010). The first decade of the community of inquiry framework: A retrospective. *Internet and Higher Education*, 13(1–2), 5–9. https://doi.org/10.1016/j.iheduc.2009.10.003.

Greer, M. & Harris, H. S. (2018). User-centered design as a foundation for effective online writing instruction. *Computers and Composition, 49,* 14–24. https://doi.org/10.1016/j.compcom.2018.05.006.

Iowa State University. (n.d.). *Mission and vision.* https://las.iastate.edu/mission/.

Johnson, M. A., Simmons, W. M. & Sullivan, P. (2017). *Lean technical communication: Toward sustainable program innovation.* Routledge.

Leverenz, C. S. (2014). Design thinking and the wicked problem of teaching writing. *Computers and Composition, 33,* 1–12. https://doi.org/10.1016/j.compcom.2014.07.001.

Mackiewicz, J. & Aune, J. E. (2017). Implementing routine across a large-scale writing program. *The WAC Journal, 28*(1), 75–105. https://doi.org/10.37514/WAC-J.2017.28.1.04.

McMullin, M. & Dilger, B. (2021). Constructive distributed work: An integrated approach to sustainable collaboration and research for distributed teams. *Journal of Business and Technical Communication, 35*(4), 469–495. https://doi.org/10.1177/10506519211021467.

Mitchum, K. & Rodrigo, R. (2021). Administrative policies and pre-designed courses (PDCs): Negotiating instructor and student agency. In C. K. Theado & S. NeCamp (Eds.), *Working with and against shared curricula: Perspectives from college writing teachers and administrators* (Vol. 17, pp. 29–44). Peter Lang.

Oswal, S. K. & Melonçon, L. (2014). Paying attention to accessibility when designing online courses in technical and professional communication. *Journal of Business and Technical Communication, 28*(3), 271–300. https://doi.org/10.1177/1050651914524780.

Penrose, A. (2012). Professional identity in a contingent-labor profession: Expertise, autonomy, community in composition teaching. *WPA: Writing Program Administration, 35*(2), 108–126. https://wpacouncil.org/aws/CWPA/pt/sp/journal-archives.

Remley, D. (2013). Templated pedagogy: Factors affecting standardized writing pedagogy with online learning management systems. *Writing and Pedagogy, 5*(1), 105–120. https://doi.org/10.1558/wap.v5i1.105.

Rice, R. (2015). Faculty professionalization for OWI. In B. L. Hewett, K. E. DePew, E. Guler & R. Z. Warner (Eds.), *Foundational practices of online writing instruction* (pp. 389–410). The WAC Clearinghouse; Parlor Press. https://doi.org/10.37514/PER-B.2015.0650.2.12/

Rodrigo, R. & Ramírez, C. D. (2017). Balancing institutional demands with effective practice: A lesson in curricular and professional development. *Technical Communication Quarterly, 26*(3), 314–328. https://doi.org/10.1080/10572252.2017.1339529/.

Smith, A., Chernouski, L., Batti, B., Karabinus, A. & Dilger, B. (2021). People, programs, and practices: A grid-based approach to designing and supporting online writing curriculum. In J. Borgman & C. McArdle (Eds.), *PARS in practice: More resources and strategies for online writing instructors* (pp. 83–96). The WAC Clearinghouse; University Press of Colorado. https://doi.org/10.37514/PRA-B.2021.1145.2.05.

Stewart, M. K., Cohn, J. & Whithaus, C. (2016). Collaborative course design and communities of practice: Strategies for adaptable course shells in hybrid and online writing. *Transformative Dialogues: Teaching & Learning Journal*, 9(1), 20. https://www.kpu.ca/sites/default/files/Transformative%20Dialogues/TD.9.1.9_Stewart_et_al_Collaborative_Course_Design.pdf.

Wible, S. (2020). Using design thinking to teach creative problem solving in writing courses. *College Composition and Communication*, 71(3), 399–425.

Womack, A. M. (2017). Teaching is accommodation: Universally designing composition classrooms and syllabi. *College Composition and Communication*, 68(3), 494–525.

Stay Out of the Bunkers!

Often you can capitalMarize on how you have played courses in the past and use that knowledge when playing a new course that is similar. For example, if you play a course that is filled with bunkers one week, you can use that game plan to build a strategy for the next course that is swarming with bunkers. Why replicate work when you have already done the labor? Save that energy for the course ... and maybe those bunkers!

We like this chapter because Catrina Mitchum takes a user-centered approach to pre-designed courses that allows faculty to put students first when it comes to designing and deploying content. Using Kenneth Burke's (1969) idea of rhetorical agency, Mitchum provides a framework to support faculty who might be used to just plugging and playing with whatever content they are forced to use. Mitchum reminds readers that pre-designed courses can be structures used to engage students with content rather than exclude and that they can aid instructors in powerful choices that promote agency and ownership.

Chapter 14. Promoting Instructor Agency and Autonomy with Pre-Designed Courses

Catrina Mitchum
University of Maryland Global Campus

Abstract: This chapter focuses on creating an online writing program ecology that uses pre-designed courses (PDCs) as a starting point. In order to be personal, accessible, responsive, and strategic (Borgman & McArdle, 2019), an online writing program that utilizes PDCs in an effort to reduce instructor labor needs to also consider instructor agency and autonomy. This chapter articulates instructor agency in terms of Kenneth Burke's (1969) rhetorical agency, with a specific focus on asking questions and acting on answers as a framework for creating an online writing program that uses PDCs as a space for instructor autonomy based on instructor choice (which can vary from one instructor to the next). We know that instructor autonomy is important in online writing instruction (OWI) because it creates a sense of ownership over course curriculum and connection to students and the larger program (Penrose, 2012). This chapter provides examples and samples to show and tell how that balance has been created in one particular context.

Keywords: Pre-designed courses, PDCs, shared curriculum, online writing program administrator, OWPA, instructor agency

Pre-designed courses (PDCs) have a bad reputation. This is largely due to their top-down nature. While they do have the potential to be a hindrance to instructors, students, and learning in general, if an ecology is built around them, there is a lot of potential for them to be a space of shared curriculum that is responsive to the needs of various stakeholders (mainly, students and instructors). Ideally, these PDCs would have a subject matter expert (SME) that is also the instructional designer (or at least works closely with one) because these particular courses require an approach different from a traditional asynchronous online course.

Over the last 14 years, I've taught online with various institutions that gave me varying levels of "control" over the course shell, what was taught, how it was taught, and how I delivered it. For example, at some institutions, I designed and taught my own courses; at some institutions, I designed for others; some institutions didn't allow me to do anything but grade and make announcements; others tracked how many days I logged in and how many discussions I posted; still others started to require that I use their slide deck and stick to their script when leaving feedback and leading synchronous sessions. This chapter comes out of my shift from this type of teaching experience to being an administrator, or OWPA, of an online writing program (OWP) over the last three years as well as multiple conversations with my friend and colleague, Chvonne Parker, who had similar teaching experiences.

The online writing program that I administered at University of Arizona has used pre-designed courses (PDCs) since shortly before I started as an non-tenure track (NTT) lecturer in 2017. There is value in having an online course built for you; the number of hours that goes into designing and maintaining an online course is overwhelming as a contingent faculty member. Previous scholarship has argued for utilizing PDCs in an effort to mitigate that labor (Rodrigo & Ramírez, 2017) and give instructors a starting point as they professionalize as online teachers (Mitchum & Rodrigo, 2021). However, creating an online writing ecology doesn't stop at designing a course and offering professional development. These things have to be done with specific considerations in mind, and the PARS framework, with its focus on personal, accessible, responsive, and strategic teaching and administrative approaches (Borgman & McArdle, 2019), can help us consider instructor users as we try to strike a balance between support of labor, instructor agency, and work-life for the administrator.

We know that instructor autonomy is important in online writing instruction (OWI) because it creates a sense of ownership over course curriculum and connection to students and the larger program (Penrose, 2012). To promote instructor agency and autonomy, online writing programs that utilize PDCs need to be personal, accessible, responsive, and strategic. Kenneth Burke's (1969) pentad, a framework for understanding motivation developed by the rhetorical theorist, can help us understand how to define agency and make considerations for increasing it in an effort to increase instructor motivation when teaching a PDC. Burke's work is particularly useful in the case of instructor agency in PDCs because it's about motives. What motivates a program to use PDCs and what motivates instructors to be invested in using and adapting them? In his introduction to a *Grammar of Motives*, Burke (1969) says, "any complete statement about motives will offer some kind of answers to these five questions: what was done (act), when or where it was done (scene), who did it (agent), how he did it (agency), and why (purpose)" (p. xv). This chapter will answer and complicate some of these questions because the focus of an online writing program that uses PDCs is about the balance of motives between co-agents (Burke uses "co-agent" to define friends who help the "agent" or "hero" on the journey [p. 229]; here, "co-agents" is reciprocal as responsibility shifts between designer and deliverer of the course).

Theory and Practice

PARS and Burke for Negotiating Co-Agency

For our purposes here, we're assuming PDCs are being used in asynchronous online courses, and so we have the act and the scene: the act for the instructor of the course is delivery (for the admin it's the design), and the scene is asynchronous online writing courses. The agent, agency, and purpose can help us take the next steps to find the places in our programs where PARS—Jessie Borgman and Casey McArdle's (2019) personal, accessible, responsive, and strategic framework for teaching and administrating online—can be applicable as administrators using PDCs.

Specifically, asking questions and acting on answers provides us with a method for enacting a PARS approach in creating an online writing program that uses PDCs as a space for instructor autonomy based on instructor choice (which can vary from one instructor to the next). I was an interim administrator of the online writing program at University of Arizona from January 2020 until January 2023. The program has approximately 50 sections a semester of first-year and professional technical writing (PTW) courses that fall under the purview of the online writing program, and the online campus grew at a rate of approximately 20 percent each year during that time. Supporting that many faculty teaching from the same PDC is no small feat. In answering the larger PARS (personal, accessible, responsive, strategic) questions below, in terms of Burke's Pentad, I'm pulling from both experiences as an instructor and as an administrator in order to help find a balance between support and agency for instructors without drowning in the labor yourself.

How do you make a PDC program personal to instructors?

You leave space and guidance for personalization. We know that students online are retained and more successful when they connect with their instructors (Boston et al., 2009). We know this can be done through instructor delivery of the course by creating an authentic persona (Garrison et al., 1999; Meyer et al., 2009), but we also know that in each course we teach (regardless of modality) we have different students in front of us (Powell, 2013). Borgman and McArdle (2019) say "Personal administration begins with treating your faculty with respect and acknowledging that they are contributors to the larger field of writing studies even if they are just instructors and not producing scholarship or presenting at conferences" (p. 27). Instructors need to have space and know-how to personalize a curriculum they didn't design. This is about finding balance. A pre-designed course is a tool; there needs to be enough structure that instructors don't need to build but not so much restriction that there's no space to own it.

This requires both giving choice to instructors and giving guidance and suggestions for where, how, and why to both add their personalization as well as be personal in their courses as they deliver them. As the administrator of an online program that utilizes PDCs, that space needs to be created in the design and instructors need to understand the design to deliver it well. Leaving the space isn't quite enough; the space needs to be identified. The flex points, the choices, and the spaces need to be articulated through the strategy of instructor guides. Personalizing comes from a smooth transition between agents: The agent shifts from designer (or admin in my case) to instructor. Without transitions, the new agent isn't aware of the agency they have or the purpose behind what's been designed. This can result in getting lost on the ride.

How do you make a PDC program accessible for instructors?

The PDCs themselves should of course be accessible to students, but also to instructors; jumping into a curriculum that's not yours can be overwhelming (especially in an accelerated online format). It's important to remember that instructors might have disabilities, neurodiversities, or mental health conditions just like students. Instructors who teach from these courses might also be teaching a split prep, at multiple institutions, or all of the above. The content and its support need to be accessible and easy to navigate. Iterative user-experience design is necessary.

When we start to give students choices, which we should be doing (Cavanagh, 2016), we start to run the risk of overwhelming instructors. To help find balance between student need and instructor need for accessibility and motivation, we, as co-agents, need to provide student choices in ways that the delivering instructor can guide. This, again, involves designing an instructor guide that articulates the how and the why behind the choices but also provides reasonable choices with sufficient support built in.

Personally, I give my students open reign on the technology they use. However, in the PDC I managed for the program, the final ePortfolio currently has two options built in. Normally, I try not to put my literal voice into the courses, but to provide support, there are four videos (two for each technology option) that walk students through setting up and adding materials to the portfolio. I selected two programs that are also supported by the institution, so that if the materials I provide aren't enough, instructors have additional support. This is key: I'm one person; the more I can pull from the support that already exists at the institutional level, the more feasible giving choice becomes. So, in this case, I've given students the choice between two programs that are turned in the same way without putting additional burden on the instructor for supporting the technology beyond knowing where the resources are located. This example, however, wouldn't go smoothly without providing an instructor guide that explains this and being available for support. These support mechanisms are crucial to shifting agency to your co-agent in a way that makes the content easy for instructors to understand. Opening up a fully designed course can be overwhelming, and so articulating the how (not necessarily the how for instructors but the how for students) and the why can help instructors own the curriculum.

How do you make a PDC program responsive to instructors and students?

The interesting thing about Burke and his pentad is that it's not just about each of the terms (act, scene, agent, agency, and purpose) but also about the interactions between these elements. PARS is similar in that there is a lot of "speaking" between the pieces of the framework. Administrators in an online writing program need to design PDCs that leave space for instructors to be responsive but also need to be responsive to instructors' needs and experiences. As Borgman and McArdle (2019) have noted, the PARS elements work together and are interconnected, so any online program ecology that is personal and accessible *has* to be responsive. If it's not, then it's not personal or accessible. Online PDCs are responsive by creating feedback mechanisms, including forms for minor errors (broken links are the worst), forms for larger suggestions, and frequent spaces for real-time feedback (Mitchum & Rodrigo, 2021). Don't ask for feedback if you're not going to do anything with it. As an instructor using the materials as a requirement or voluntarily, feeling like you're not heard can lead to not bothering to give feedback. This is also the point at which shared curricula truly become shared. Instructors should be encouraged to garner feedback from students and share it along with their own experiences so that the courses can be improved for everyone. Managing multiple online courses that you're not teaching *has* to be a team effort or the courses stagnate. Responsiveness is crucial. Being responsive in a program that uses a shared PDC can also look like, as Borgman and McArdle suggest, providing professional development that can give instructors ideas for how to fix what isn't working in the courses and that they're interested in. To be responsive, you need to make communication a two-way street.

Finally, as an administrator in an online writing program that uses PDCs, it's important to provide both support you anticipate (like getting-started materials) as well as just-in-time support. For example, I had built the onboarding website, but I also offered open labs for course preparation. If enough instructors are asking for the same type of help, then it becomes a help video on the website (because there's clearly a gap). Something that's important to remember when being a responsive administrator is to find your own responsive support. For example, knowing when and where the campus resources are for some of the tech concerns that are more general.

How do you act strategically when creating a PDC online writing program?

I'd argue this is the lynchpin. If you don't have a strategy that comes from a place of collaborative inclusion, then we become everything that makes us balk at the idea of a PDC. Borgman and McArdle (2019) remind us that it all comes down to strategy and that everyone needs to make strategic moves when designing, instructing, or administrating online courses. Understanding the why (purpose) of the design (agency) can provide the instructor (our co-agent) space to articulate the why (purpose) through delivery (agency). You can't just give a PDC to instructors and assume that all will be well; instructors need guides. Guides for getting started, guides for transparency that articulate why certain choices were made, and support for professionalization. Without these guides, instructors, no matter how experienced they are, can't make informed choices. They also can't explain the breadcrumbs of the scaffolding to the students the first time around if we don't provide a map and a compass. This is where framing administrators and instructors as co-agents, per Burke, is useful. As co-agents, we should be helping each other in the scene of online teaching and learning. We can't ethically ask instructors to teach a course they didn't design (even if it helps reduce labor) if we don't explain to them the pedagogical undercurrents of what they're teaching. Therefore, without guides, it is impossible for instructors to develop knowledgeable personas or actually take autonomous ownership of the course.

Practical Application

Up until January of 2023, I worked, both as an NTT faculty member and then as an administrator, to create these necessary elements of an online writing instruction ecology. When I started at the institution, we had a Google doc that had some explanation for a few of the deadlines. However, it was largely about places that needed to be updated (like inserting links, adding instructor bios, etc.). In fall 2019, without an administrator title, I created, with the administrator's approval, a series of instructor guides directly within the LMS. Those guides started as a series of reminders (like putting students into groups) as well as a "heads up" to instructors for places students struggle. Over the last few years, as I shifted into administration and became a different agent in the same co-agent relationship, both the structure and the content have better adapted to instructor needs by using feedback mechanisms as usability tests.

Turning a course over to be used is the space where Burke's agent shifts from being the course designer to the course instructor and that handoff needs transition the same way a play or writing does. In the program, I built that transition in three places:

1. A course map
2. A shared curriculum website that focuses on onboarding and support
3. An instructor guide that is built into the LMS at each deadline

The Course Map

The course map is part and parcel of designing an online course. As a designer, it gives you a bird's-eye view or outline of the activities and the outcomes those activities are helping students reach. I'd also argue that a map should have the purpose of each activity articulated so instructors can follow the madness behind the methods. The key, though, is sharing it. As I've learned recently, it's also about explaining how to use it. The course map can give instructors an idea of where to personalize (based on the activities they know students will be completing and the outlined purpose for students), and the overview makes the course arc accessible to instructors in ways that a fully fleshed out LMS can't. Having the purpose laid out this way can give instructors agency over their personalization of the course. Figure 14.1 is a very small piece of the course map created for the same deadline that the instructor guide is for. (See the instructor guide in Appendix B.)

Due Date	Goals	Student Learning Outcomes (SLOs)	Activity	Purpose
XX/XX	Goal 1	1A. Analyze a text's genre and how that influences and guides reading and composing practices. 1C. Apply knowledge of rhetorical options in reading practices.	DD2HW1: What Is a Genre? (Discussion Topic)	Start exploring what a genre is in order to understand the genre of literacy narratives.
	Goal 2	2B. Support ideas or positions by discussing evidence from multiple sources.		
	Goal 4	4A. Adapt composing and revision processes for a variety of technologies and modalities. 4D. Identify the collaborative and social aspects of writing processes.	DD2HW2: Understanding Literacy and Project #1 (Discussion Board)	To begin understanding literacy and to understand what is being asked of you in Project #1
	Goal 5	5A. Narrate their processes and progress as writers throughout Foundations Writing courses.		

Figure 14.1 A Piece of the Course Map

This can take time, but all asynchronous online courses should have a course map anyway (in instructional design, this is a mapping of course activities to the course outcomes). Taking the time to add the purpose to each activity and sharing the map and its uses is an easy first step to creating an accessible curriculum that can be personalized.

The Website

The website starts with instructions for getting started that are particular to the LMS and program size. Instructors request their own course shell and copy the PDCs into their own classes. Instructors are then guided to their particular courses, where the website includes the following sections for each (I've included sample text for our ENGL101 course and website, designed for accessibility, in Appendix A):

- **The course:** This section of the course page gives an overview of what the course arc is. There's a statement of how many projects, what those projects are, and how they connect.

- **Updates:** This section gives instructors information about bigger changes made to the course and the timeframe in which they were made. This is for the instructors who have taught these courses before.
- **What You'll Find:** This section articulates the two spaces where instructors will find course materials and what they'll find in each space. The online courses use Google Drive to both give students space to ask live questions on major projects and have a central storage location. This section articulates what "things" live where.
- **D2L Walkthrough and Eli Review Walkthrough:** This section contains two screencast, captioned videos that provide a walkthrough of what instructors will find in the LMS and how Eli Review (the peer review program we use) integrates and weaves with our LMS.
- **Course Content Preview:** This section gives links to the LMS and the GDrive folder in case instructors want to take a look. These courses are available for our instructors who teach face-to-face to use, and so they might want to look through the materials before deciding what to copy. This section also gives instructions on where to find the next steps and various support materials.

The website content is about orienting instructors to the how and why of the course as a whole. The website provides an overview of the course arc, of the course map, and the overall structure. It also provides a series of short help videos and documents specific to both the course setup and potential issues instructors might encounter. The goal here is to remember that you and the instructor are co-agents and articulating the overarching purpose is key in transitioning agency from your position as administrator/designer to the instructor as the deliverer/facilitator of the content.

The Instructor Guide

The instructor guide is the next level of transition. The guide has a "Start Here" section that provides more information about the initial steps for setup like copying all the Google elements and where to update the links, the sections of the course that need to be updated with instructor information, etc. Then, every deadline in the course (referred to as due dates) has a guide built in with reminders, to-dos, and things to look out for. You can find an example in Appendix B, where I've included the instructor guide for the second deadline of the course in which students are asked to explore the concept of genre in a discussion board and explore their literacies.

As you can see in the sample, there are a few key elements to help translate the course to the delivering instructor:

1. **Overarching reminders:** These can be things to remember to return to outside of the LMS (like Google or Eli Review), reminders for students

(like support, signing up for notifications, etc.), things to consider when creating their videos or announcements to overview the deadline to students.
2. **Activity-specific information:** Each activity has information about what students are being asked to do, why they're being asked to do it, and how it plays into the rest of the course.

The LMS instructor guide also contains two feedback forms. The Error Report Form is a form used to report small errors like broken links, places where rubrics are incorrect, typos, etc. It lives as a Google form that I receive notifications for. It's important to skim the forms as they come in in case there's a large issue (like when *Writing Commons* did a re-org or the OWL at Purdue redid its website) that should be addressed on a larger scale. Other small stuff can wait until the end of term. The Module Suggestion Form is a form used for instructors to suggest larger revisions based on their experiences teaching the course. This can be completed anonymously (see Mitchum & Rodrigo, 2021 for more details).

The information in the guide is updated right along with the course and has had edits based on instructor questions and feedback since its initial implementation. These guides are about orienting instructors to the details of the course content. Again, it's about articulating the purpose to instructors in finer detail so that instructors, as co-agents, can enact their agency (through delivery of the course). It's important to have this information "physically" close to the content for students so instructors both remember the tool is there and can access it easily; this is done through "hiding" content from students in the LMS.

Wish List

Creating this online teaching and learning ecology was a lot of work. More work than I care to admit, but it also makes a good argument for having a team. I was lucky enough that our lecturers, of which I was still one, have service, and some were willing to dedicate that service time to helping improve the courses through feedback on the curriculum, but also on the support being offered. Even with that support, there are still places where more support could be offered by the institution. In an ideal world with a full team to work on it, creating slide decks with a script for instructors who want to adapt something instead of starting from scratch when they record would be fantastic.

Labor

While the initial setup is a lot of work, having these support tools has helped to mitigate repetitive labor. For example, each time I was asked how to do something new, it became a video that lives on the website. The overview videos can be watched as many times as instructors need, and this has reduced the amount of time that I spent in one-on-one meetings. This work isn't about automating (these videos still need to be recreated periodically) but creating tools that make the information more accessible to instructors (they have faster access to a video when it's convenient for them than they did to me).

Finding ways to mitigate administrative labor is important because the overall goal here is to relieve instructor labor. Many instructors who teach online writing courses have no other support because they're adjuncts, graduate teaching assistants (GTAs), or NTT lecturers. They also aren't paid for the serious uptick in labor that designing an online course well requires. When OWPAs create PDCs, it's a good first step in relieving that labor, but let's not create more work by not giving them support.

Conclusion and Takeaways

In this chapter, I've attempted to show how, while implementing a PDC as an OWPA, you might create a collaboratively inclusive shared curriculum by answering those very important PARS questions in a way that considers and balances the idea of instructor agency using Burke's Pentad. It requires accepting that we're co-agents (who do the design and curriculum) with instructors who teach (deliver) the class and so need to keep them in mind as we transfer agency during the lifecycle of a PDC. In order to do this, though, you need a team that's both dedicated to improving the experience and also fairly compensated for it.

In conclusion, here are a few things to remember:

- Improving the instructor experience improves the student experience.
- Support should be provided in various ways at various times because we're all on the same team.
- You need support as well.

References

Borgman, J. & McArdle, C. (2019). *Personal, accessible, responsive, strategic: Resources and strategies for online writing instructors.* The WAC Clearinghouse; University Press of Colorado. https://doi.org/10.37514/PRA-B.2019.0322.

Boston, W., Diaz, S. R., Gibson, A. M., Ice, P., Richardson, J. & Swan, K. (2009). An exploration of the relationship between indicators of the community of inquiry framework and retention in online programs. *Journal of Asynchronous Learning Networks, 13*(3), 67–83. https://doi.org/10.24059/olj.v13i3.1657.

Burke, K. (1969). *A grammar of motives.* University of California Press.

Cavanagh, S. R. (2016). *The spark of learning: Energizing the college classroom with the science of emotion.* West Virginia University Press.

Garrison, D. R., Anderson, T. & Archer, W. (1999). Critical inquiry in a text-based environment: Computer conferencing in higher education. *The Internet and Higher Education, 2*(2–3), 87–105. https://doi.org/10.1016/S1096-7516(00)00016-6.

Meyer, K., Bruwelheide, J. & Poulin, R. (2009). Why they stayed: Near-perfect retention in an online certification program in library media. *Journal of Asynchronous Learning Networks*, 13(3), 129–145. https://doi.org/10.24059/olj.v10i4.1747.

Mitchum, C. & Rodrigo, R. (2021). Administrative policies and pre-designed courses (PDCs): Negotiating instructor and student agency. In C. K. Theado & S. NeCamp (Eds.), *Working with and against shared curricula: Perspectives from college writing teachers and administrators* (pp. 29–44). Peter Lang.

Penrose, A. M. (2012). Professional identity in a contingent-labor profession: Expertise, autonomy, community in composition teaching. *WPA: Writing Program Administration*, 35(2), 108–126. https://wpacouncil.org/aws/CWPA/pt/sp/journal-archives.

Powell, P. R. (2013). *Retention and resistance: Writing instruction and students who leave*. Utah State University Press.

Rodrigo, R. & Ramírez, C. (2017). Balancing institutional demands with effective practice: A lesson in curricular and professional development. *Technical Communication Quarterly*, 26(3), 314–328. http://doi.org/10.1080/10572252.2017.1339529.

Appendix A: Sample Text English 101 Course

The Course

The ENGL101 PDC has 3 major projects. The project flow builds off of the Students' Guide concept of "a genre you know" and "a genre you don't know." The first project is a genre literacy narrative, and students are asked to write a narrative about how they became literate in particular genres that they know well. The second project is a genre analysis. Students are asked to do secondary research and primary research in order to learn about a new genre. The final project is an ePortfolio that students have been working toward during the term.

Updates for AY21–22

In addition to the updates made for the academic year, the following updates were made for Summer 22:

- Module 1 shifted to 8 due dates and framing it as learning the genre of literacy narrative together.
- Module 2 gained a due date, divided up the secondary research notes, and streamlined the 2 options.
- Module 3 was updated with all new support materials for students to choose between Adobe Express or Google Sites.

For Fall 2021-Spring 2022, the ENGL101 asynchronous online sections will return to using the pedagogical tool Eli Review (instructions are located in D2L). Some additional updates to the course for AY21–22 are:

- More accurate estimated work times. Each reading, video, and step has an estimated time associated with it. The reading times were calculated with a reading speed of 200 words per minute. Many writing tasks were given concrete time limits within which to write.
- More specific rubrics. Rubrics were shifted to a 1/0 point scale and required elements were broken down into small, observable pieces.
- Improved scaffolding in Module 1.
- Shift in Module 2 away from multiple reports to asking students to take notes on secondary and primary sources in order to articulate the way the community uses the genre. You will have the choice between two deliverables: a report or an infographic. You will need to delete the Module 2 option that you don't want to use.
- Module 3 has shifted away from requiring an essay and instead asks students to integrate and weave their reflections throughout their portfolios.
- Removal of images with a box to better divide up the text of the assignments as well as the inclusion of more linked videos and updated program videos.
- Eli Review assignments have been updated and improved upon based on an assessment of student reviews in Eli during 2020–2021 academic year.
- 197B is now just one section instead of two.
- Updated SLOs and textbook links.

What You'll Find in GDrive and D2L

After you copy the course over, within the D2L course, there is an instructor manual in each module. To access materials, you need to help you set up your class, you'll want to click on **Content>START HERE Due Date 1>Instructor Manual** in the course. It will have everything you need to prep the course. However, if you want to explore the course and the projects before copying over, you can do that using the links on this page.

In addition to the content in the PDCs, there is content in a shared GDrive folder where you will find major assignment prompts that you need to copy in order to update the links in D2L to your own copies and the "Getting to Know You" Survey. You will also find a course map and suggested schedules for each course length. The course map indicates which assignments you need to make sure you update with your own preferences or information. Those elements are in red text in the D2L assignments, but the course map helps you to quickly identify the areas that need your attention. The D2L shells and GDrive folder are linked below.

D2L Walkthrough & Eli Review Walkthrough

These are both captioned videos that provide a walkthrough of the two different course pieces.

Course content preview

Below, you'll find the link to the PDC and a link to the GDrive Folder content. Feel free to use the PDC link to orient yourself to the course; however, copying over is a different process that is outlined in the Copy Your Course video. Use the title next to the link to search for the correct course. You can find more videos, suggestions, and guidance on the Support page.

Appendix B: Instructor Guide

Read Before Due Date 2

Be sure to check the Project 1 Google Doc to answer any questions/comments students have posted. If you click on Comments in your document, you can select how/if you receive notifications that comments have been made.

Remind everyone to be logged into their UA Gmail to work with/access course materials (I've gotten many requests for access; almost all come from regular Gmail accounts).

Post an overview for both the module and the DD. Also remind them to allow time for a response if they email you questions. This might also be a good time to set up your office hour scheduling (you might use the free version of Calendly or Google Calendar Appointments). This due date is all about getting students thinking about the two big concepts of the literacy narrative: narrative as a genre and what literacy is. It might be helpful to make that connection for students here so they see how this work is going to help them reach the SLOs and work toward the project.

HW1: This discussion is students' first introduction to the concept of genre. Since the course focuses on understanding genres within their contexts, this is a critical first discussion. You might want to do a bit more explanation of how the writing program thinks of genre (we define it broadly) and be sure to keep a close eye and give feedback on this particular discussion so you can correct misconceptions of genre and try to prompt them to make connections to previous reading, writing, and working experiences. Be very present in this particular discussion board (however, don't feel like you have to do it for every discussion board).

HW2: This is asking students to explore the concept of literacy and apply it to the literacy narrative. Share a Google Doc version of the Project 1 assignment instructions with ability to comment and be sure to change the link in the activity prompt. Make sure you read and respond to questions on the Google doc. In DD3HW3, students will be asked to consider their own literacies, so they will have another activity that asks them to think about literacy. This, though, is a good time to make sure, again, students are starting to think of literacy broadly.

Make sure you also update the link under the "Syllabus and Major Assignment Quick Links" area

Before and/or after this due date, consider posting this message about tech support.

Remember that if you run into tech troubles with <institutional system>, please start with:
- <LMS> Support: <LMS Support URL>
- General IT (Non-Bookstore Software): <IT URL>
- Contact the 24/7 IT Support Center at <insert phone number> for issues related to non-Bookstore downloads: <URL>
- <institution> Library Software: Contact the <institution> Library at <phone number> via Live Chat <URL>, or complete a webform <URL> for issues related to <institution> Library Software or Databases.
- <institution> Bookstore Software: Contact the <institution> Bookstores Licensing at <phone number> or email <email> for issues related to <institution> Bookstores software licenses.

Keep It in the Fairway!

Having a game plan on how to approach a certain golf course is crucial to having a low score for the round, as well as having fun playing the game! There are some courses where you know you won't be hitting your driver off the tee because of hazards, or certain pin placements you know you won't aim for because if you miss by just a little, your ball is going for a swim.

What we like about this chapter by Dylan Retzinger and Kellie Sharp-Hoskins is how they use PARS to develop a structure for pre-designed courses that emphasizes making such structures personal, accessible, responsive, and strategic. All of this is grounded via design that is inclusive and not exclusive. It asks faculty and administrators to embrace the personal nature of teaching and become a leader. All of these moves are difficult, but with a plan in place, you can be creative while building new and supportive relationships in and out of your classrooms.

Chapter 15. Third Personal, U Variable: Complicating PARS and UX in Pre-Designed OWI Courses

Dylan Retzinger and Kellie Sharp-Hoskins
NEW MEXICO STATE UNIVERSITY

Abstract: In this chapter, we consider how a PARS approach to online writing instruction (OWI) takes shape in the context of pre-designed or "master" courses, which are courses designed by those who may not be teaching them and taught by instructors who cannot substantively change or personalize them. In the context of our own university, and within the constraints of Quality Matters, we reflect on the ways our conceptualization of PARS principles shifted in creating pre-designed courses. We document these shifts in relation to each element of PARS—personal, accessible, responsive, strategic—identifying how the difficulties designing courses for others can invite creative strategies in OWI that do not sacrifice ethical or pedagogical commitments. We offer concrete strategies developed in our own context, modeling for those with a similar charge how they might enact PARS principles in circumstances heavily constrained by institutional expectations and multiple layers of administrative oversight. We end with four guiding principles for implementing PARS for pre-designed courses: focus on relationships, create opportunities for personalized assessment, build from commonplaces, and get creative.

Keywords: pre-designed courses, master courses, online writing instruction, user experience, administration, Quality Matters

In 2020, our R2, land grant, Hispanic-serving institution (HSI) teed up U-O (University Online). Aiming to increase enrollment and revenue by offering fully online degree programs directed toward adult learners who need more flexibility when pursuing their education, U-O was conceived of as an administrative division responsible for leveraging campus resources to create fully online programs. Such resources as related to general education writing courses were initially imagined by U-O in terms of instructor sharing, wherein academic departments, and in our case, the writing program, would send recommendations for adjunct instructors to U-O to teach pre-designed courses (PDCs)—ready to go courses, complete with syllabi, schedules, assignments, and gradebooks that needed only an instructor to deliver. In practice this meant that we were being asked to staff PDCs that U-O had created without us. In the writing program (WP), we had a different vision: If the courses were going to be taught by our instructors, they should be informed by our curriculum. Negotiations ensued.

We wanted instructor agency and a localized, place-based curriculum—or in Jessie Borgman and Casey McArdle's (2019) PARS terms, the ability for instructors to *personalize* the learning and teaching experience in ways that are culturally and materially *accessible, responsive,* and *strategic*. As a WP in an HSI and land-grant institution, we recognize how body and geopolitics shape learning experiences and understand the value of meeting students where they are by building on (and building in) instructor and student literacies. Our WP currently (and historically) offers writing courses in person and online; framed by common goals, they are designed and taught by graduate assistant, adjunct, college-track, and tenure-track instructors, who have access and contribute to shared resources, textbooks, and professional development opportunities. Programmatically, this means that our curriculum is discursively shaped by a community of instructors who ultimately design their own courses in a manner that not only reflects their pedagogical commitments and personalities, but also facilitates opportunities for reflection and revision. We view this agency and responsibility as being instrumental to the professional development of our instructors and to the goal of creating learning experiences for students that are personalized in terms of content and design.

U-O, by contrast, wanted consistency and repeatability—what they see as the keys to accreditation and successful user experience (UX)—so that no matter who the instructor or student, the course would be strategic and accessible in the same ways. This consistency was articulated primarily around course design and interface and realized through accordance with Quality Matters (QM) standards.[1] Courses should *look* the same, with information in (online) places that can be anticipated by the student across courses, promoting accessibility and eliminating confusion. For U-O, consistency means that students don't need to learn a new logic for each course in their program of study; instead, they learn one time how the *interface* works and can then focus on the *content* of the course. Content and usability are imagined as unrelated.

These differences in commitments shaped many conversations, but by spring 2022, we agreed to create two pre-designed writing courses (first-year composition and introduction to technical and professional communication [TPC]) for U-O. Aside from being pre-designed, U-O's expectations and our writing program's constraints for the courses were that they needed to

- be eight weeks long,
- use asynchronous delivery,

---

1. QM is a for-profit organization that helps affiliated institutions certify the "quality" of their online courses by implementing course development processes (such as a "course map" that facilitates developing a schedule and aligns learning outcomes with assignments) and evaluating courses based on a rubric of standards (i.e., Course Overview and Introduction, Learning Objectives, Assessment and Measurement, Instructional Materials, Learning Activities and Learner Interaction, Course Technology, Learner Support, Accessibility and Usability).

- meet QM standards,
- have a five-year shelf life,
- be taught primarily by adjuncts,
- use e-books only, and
- be co-designed and peer reviewed by U-O.

Such expectations flew in the face of many of our commonplaces and practices (16-week terms, discipline-oriented standard, constant reflection and revision, to name a few) and so—to extend Borgman and McArdle's (2019) golf analogy—the task of creating two pre-designed online writing (OW) courses was *a lie in the rough*. Simply *put(t)*, we had to learn a new style of PARS for the course. In this chapter, we describe our experience navigating this new terrain and our reimagining of the PARS principles for PDCs. *Fore!* It gets complicated.

Theory & Practice

Reimagining PARS Principles

In *Personal, Accessible, Responsive, Strategic: Resources and Strategies for Online Writing Instructors*, Borgman and McArdle (2019) create "a distinct approach to OWI . . . that encompasses the theory and practice from decades of previous research" (p. 5). More specifically, grounded in user experience (UX) theory as a humanizing vehicle (see also Greer & Harris, 2018), the PARS principles help OW instructors navigate issues related to building relationships with students (personal), designing usable student learning experiences (accessible), affirming the presence of students and instructors in learning management systems (responsive), and a host of administrative concerns (strategic). From another vantage, PARS is a situated alternative to rubrics like QM, whereby PARS refashions generalized checklists or rescales QM "standards" (see Oswal & Melonçon, 2017) as principles for the unique contexts of OWI. Whereas QM treats online education as a question of interface, focusing almost exclusively on countable, measurable features of pedagogical delivery, PARS is principle-based, encouraging pedagogical decisions that consider complex relationships between students, teachers, institutions, *and* interfaces. Borgman and McArdle (2021) even point out that PARS is not a checklist: "To be clear, the PARS approach is not a checklist—it is a holistic approach to online instruction that acknowledges the complexity of course design and its facilitation in digital spaces" (p. 4). Zooming out, whereas both PARS and QM can be seen as efforts to address an ongoing stigma of online education—namely, that online courses are the faux counterpart to face-to-face classes—the latter can unwittingly reify the stigma, equating effective teaching with effective interface design. Historically, this stigma is especially pertinent to the territory of this chapter, PDCs, or what Shelley Rodrigo and Cristina Ramírez (2017) identify as

> master online courses, fully developed online courses that are used to teach multiple sections of the same course . . . sometimes referred to pejoratively as template or "canned" courses with ready syllabi, assignment and activity prompts, scaffolded course schedules, and gradebook categories predesigned for instructors who merely deliver the course. For many instructors, *delivery* literally includes making announcements and grading work. (p. 317)

For OW instructors, PARS is an approach that creates a community and a heuristic to help them navigate and better articulate the traps and bunkers of a stigmatized game by focusing on the UX of students through the lens of teachers as UX designers. But what happens when the game being played is, in fact, a canned UX? Borgman and McArdle begin to answer this question in their 2019 introduction to PARS and 2021 edited collection, *PARS in Practice*. Building on their work, in this chapter we share our experiences creating pre-designed writing courses and articulate strategies for negotiating the hazards along the way.

When we began designing courses that others would teach, unknown persons in an unknown timescale, we recognized that the "personal" element of PARS organizes the relationships among the other terms (accessible, responsive, and strategic) and to student and instructor users. This is perhaps, in the words of Borgman and McArdle (2019), because "being personal is one of the most important things you can do as an online writing instructor. Personalizing the classroom, your instruction, or (if you're in administration) the way that you handle your writing instructors is key to success" (p. 17). Indeed, student satisfaction and retention in online writing courses are highly correlated with instructor presence, rapport, and interpersonal relationships (Glazier, 2021; Glazier & Harris, 2020, 2021; Ruecker, 2021). Yet in the context of the PDCs intended to prioritize repeatability via *de*-personalized design, we struggled to apply this principle: How could we make a course personal when neither of our persons would be involved? How could we make the experience of teaching and taking a PDC *personal* for students and instructors?

As we further considered personalization, we began to better understand how the "personal" of PARS is also highly relational and political. For example, our design choices affect the presence (see Gunawardena, 1995) of the instructor and students, our instructional language creates a persona (see Warnock, 2009) that shapes the relationship between students and instructors, and the politics of our content choices—e.g., assignments related to race (see Bomberger, 2004)—create learning contexts that not all instructors might be comfortable with or capable of navigating. At the same time, we didn't want to create sterile courses that pandered to what Sushil Oswal and Lisa Melonçon (2017) described as "ideologies of normalcy" (p. 63) in online writing courses. We recognized that users, personas, and presences—i.e., affects of our online identities (Nakamura, 2002)—are embodied through our language, content, and design choices, and we came to see that personal was the transgressive principle, i.e., designers are people, too. With the politics of persons in play, we recognized that *personal* never exists outside of larger, including institutional, contexts and relationships. In this capacity, we propose that online writing instruction built on the personal is successful when teachers and students are welcome to engage as whole persons, to bring their expertise and idiosyncrasies, their languages and literacies, to their presence, interactions, and assignments in the course. When a course invites this type of engagement—no matter who designed it—it *feels* personal.

Inspired by this shift, we began to *responsively* rethink PARS principles as a situated politics of relation—or, in other words, as the framework through which relationships (between teacher, students, course content, university, and place) can emerge. In the following sections we thus attend to each principle in turn, first explaining how we reframed it for our context before offering suggestions and strategies for others.

(Third) Personal

One of the biggest obstacles for embedding the personal in a PDC was that we would not be participants in the course. In our own courses (that we design *and* teach), students get to know us through our assignments, instructions, and feedback, but how does that translate in PDCs? In this section we identify three shifts in our thinking about what it means to "personalize" a course and how we implemented each in the context of pre-design.

[1] Designers are People, Too

While a PARS approach centers the person of students, teachers, and (to a lesser extent) administrators, in its earlier articulations the *designer* is often synonymous with the teacher (or sometimes, administrator). In our context, however, creating a PDC for U-O meant design by team. This included three curricular designers (the WP team that we assembled) and one U-O designer, who was in practice a QM guide and U-O's representative for quality control. Working with an instructional designer from U-O and acting as instructional designers ourselves, however, we began to see designers as unmarked persons shaping the course. Indeed, even a course pre-designed by a textbook company, for example, draws on people—content experts, instructional designers, and usability testers—to create a successful product. Whereas such products might be rhetorically styled to depersonalize content (away from its designers), we considered how as designers we might "show up" in the interface in concrete ways. Accordingly, we

- recognized the importance of creating a diverse design team (in terms of institutional positions, embodiments, and experiences);
- created an "About This Course" page (see Figure 15.1) to introduce ourselves and the WP;

- drew on readings that we would use in our own classes;
- used our expertises to shape descriptions, explanations, and assignments,
- adopted a conversational tone; and
- used pronouns like "we" and "us" to better relate to students and instructors.

With these (simple) strategies, we hoped to create familiarity for students and teachers, so despite the unilateral direction of design and communication (from us to them), they would have a sense of the people who built the class. We also wanted to avoid creating an ethos based on a disembodied and distant "master teacher"; as much as possible, we wanted the course to represent the diversity of our program so that instructors wouldn't feel like they would be "filling in," so to speak, for an unidentified "expert." Instead, we wanted to create opportunities for instructors to relate to and identify with course content and design.

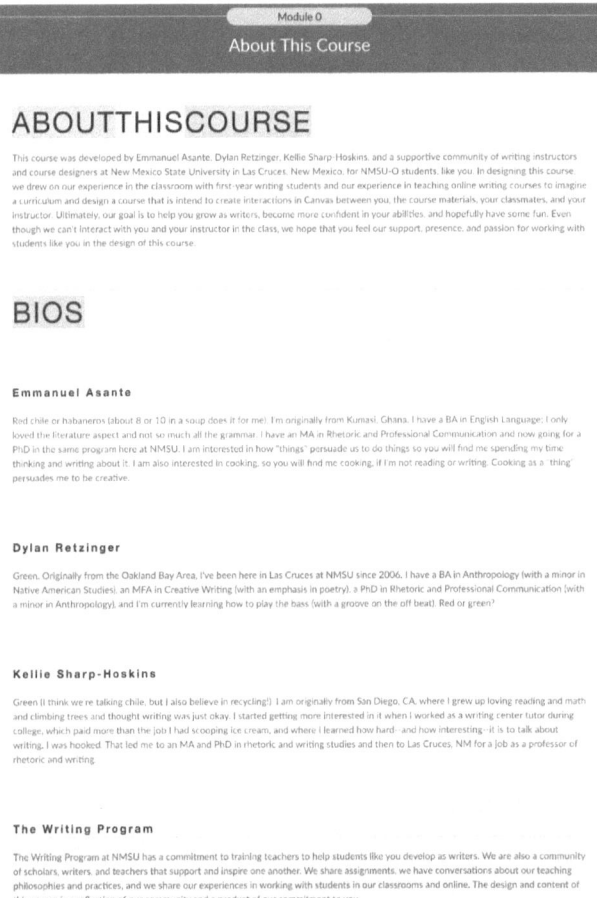

Figure 15.1. "About This Course" page.

[2] Making Personal Space(s)

While we initially imagined personalization as the effect of the *people* who populate a course (students and teachers), in the context of PDCs we had to consider how the *spaces* of the LMS (in our case, Canvas) could invite people to engage *as* individuals. In this context, we also had to acknowledge the need for personal space; that is, while we sought the affordances of personalization, we did not want to require participation that would threaten personal boundaries or privacy. One aspect of pedagogy *feeling* personal is about people making choices (rather than being conscripted). Without knowing the preferences or personalities of the teachers *or* students, then, we created assignments, activities, and assessments that offered options for personalization. For example, we

- invited students to invoke or reflect on personal and professional literacies *of their choosing* (throughout the semester),
- asked students to consider their personal relationships to prompts and subject matter as a prewriting exercise that would not necessarily show up in their writing (explicitly),
- alerted students ahead of time to any assignments that would be shared with peers,
- created different ways for students to relate to course content, e.g., giving students the opportunity to interact with the authors of the course textbook,
- used different spaces and modalities (e.g., discussions, peer reviews, images, videos) to vary peer interactions,
- created different ways for instructors to provide feedback and be present to students (e.g., through announcements, summative feedback, rubrics, participation in discussion boards), and
- added a little color to the U-O aesthetic, giving spaces distinct visual personalities.

[3] Post-Design Implementation & Personalization

The expectations of U-O meant that changing the design, content, assignments, and assessments of the course *in situ* would be unavailable to instructors, in effect eliminating key options for personalization, but as long-time writing teachers, we know that much of the relational work of writing instruction emerges as students turn in work and get instructor and peer feedback. For us, this meant shifting focus away from personalized *design* and toward personalization in practice. To support this shift, we

- discussed with instructors how—and where—the workload of teaching this class changes, away from lesson and assignment prep and toward more frequent and consistent engagement with student writing; and

- used significant scaffolding to encourage students and teachers to see drafting and revision work as opportunities for discussion and deliberation.

By helping teachers reimagine their allocation of time and energy, we see opportunities for instructors to affirm and engage with student experiences, ideas, literacies, and writing in ways that are *personal*. Where one line of professional development (curriculum design) might be blocked by PDCs, another line (personalized assessment) opens.

Accessible (for Who?): U Variable

"Accessible for who?" was the driving question for adopting PARS in our PDCs. Whereas in an instructor-created course, accessibility is centered around the UX of students (Borgman & Dockter, 2018), in creating a PDC we had to negotiate accessibility for students *and* instructors, each of whom access course interfaces, concepts, and assignments from particular embodied, culturally-situated perspectives (St.Amant & Sapienza, 2011). Stability was replaced by heterogeneity: Our users became one of many variables. Additionally, notions of accessibility were mediated by the requirements of U-O and, in particular, their deference to QM standards, which disarticulate content and form (in ways that don't always account for the situated peculiarities of OWI). While scholarship in OWI rightly critiques QM metrics, which articulate accessibility in terms of a checklist instead of in terms of dynamic, relational embodiment (Oswal & Melonçon, 2017), in this section we discuss ways in which we approached accessibility for our different audiences in the context of PDCs that *would* ultimately be assessed by QM standards.

[1] Instructors

Borgman and McArdle (2019) advocate for courses to be designed for students, as students are the primary users, but we had to design these courses with the instructor in mind. We thus considered instructors—rather than students—to be our first audience since they would have to understand the course content, logic, and design in order to teach the class. Instructor accessibility in our context is (importantly) complicated by the diversity of our instructors and by our own pedagogical commitments; as designers, we were mindful to account for variables in position, academic background, experience teaching, digital/learning management system literacy, pedagogy, linguistic, and cultural/embodied identities. We recognized that while many instructors would be teaching these courses with expectations reflecting prior (online/teaching) experience, others might be relatively new to the learning management system (LMS), the institution, or to teaching online. As course designers with our own histories, experiences, and commitments, we had to remind ourselves that we would not be the primary users of the PDCs; the courses might be staffed by instructors with backgrounds in literature, creative writing, or English studies, who might imagine the courses—or interpret their learning outcomes—much differently than we do. In order to make our courses accessible to instructors we

- created an "Instructor Guide" module to help instructors anticipate some of the quirks and logistics of the course,
- requested major assignments from instructors (from our main campus programs) with different levels and kinds of experience teaching writing,
- used collected assignments to brainstorm and craft the PDCs,
- used textbooks and readings shared by main-campus courses, and
- created a design team that represented different contingencies of the WP, each with different relationships to teaching and disciplinary knowledge.

By drawing on resources from a variety of teachers, we shifted away from our specific expertises and toward a more commonly held programmatic expertise. We saw this as a way to make the courses accessible not only to main-campus teachers who might take on a U-O class but to an even broader range of teachers that might staff U-O in the future.

[2] Students

When thinking about what accessibility means for students in a PDC, one key complication is that instructors may not be able to readily answer questions about the course content or design (especially if it would be their first time teaching the course). Student questions or confusion, of course, can range from issues of clarity, instruction, and design to issues of expectation: What does the teacher expect? What is the goal of the assignment? Our goal was to, as much as possible, anticipate the needs and questions of students in order to take that burden off of instructors. This took shape in several ways as we

- contextualized word choice/jargon to account for our specific disciplinary training,
- linked to supplemental handouts to explain terms that instructors might take for granted (i.e., words like "concept" and "idea"),
- specified expectations for length and format of *every* assignment (from quick activities to longer, more formal projects) to eliminate ambiguity,
- formally integrated expectations into grading criteria for each assignment,
- modeled format expectations for every assignment, and
- focused on consistency within courses, using different assignment types to create weekly rituals, and across courses, so that once a student took our composition course the structure of the TPC course would feel familiar.

[3] Quality Matters

As writing instructors, we understand accessibility in capacious terms—as referring to physical and digital infrastructure and interfaces as well as linguistic and cultural concepts and commonplaces. U-O, by contrast, relies on QM standards to assess the accessibility of its courses in more bounded terms that prioritized the interface. In practice, this meant that the resources U-O shared with us (like course templates and course maps) modeled accessibility in formal ways. Rather than attempt to use those forms, we found it necessary to *build* a structure recognizable to QM standards *and* to our writing teachers; we thus

- created overviews and introductions at *each* level of the course: module, assignment, activity, etc.;
- correlated named assignment *types* with specific weekly due dates to create patterns and a pace for the class (i.e., "Reading Discussions" due Monday, "Writing Exercises" due Tuesday, etc.); and
- inserted grading criteria with specific requirements for each assignment.

While this course design appears *motivated* by QM, in practice, our conversations and internal review practices centered our pedagogical values and the students' needs, rather than QM standards explicitly. That is, even though we knew QM review was imminent, we made online writing instruction and student accessibility (in its complexity) preeminent in our conversations.

Responsive (by Design)

Like the other elements of PARS, the responsiveness of a course fundamentally shifts in a PDC, and this, of course, is by design. Whereas a course designed and delivered by the same person might *become* responsive in practice, as instructors respond to the students in the class, or as administrators to the needs of faculty (Borgman & McArdle, 2019), a PDC does not have the same flexibility because decision-making is less kairotic. As Rodrigo and Ramírez (2017) suggest, PDCs intentionally reduce the number of decisions an instructor has to make, supporting them by giving them specific boundaries. In our particular context and from our purview, the ability of our administrators to be responsive was also reduced because the courses are ultimately under the administration of U-O, who not only hire the teachers but also authorize and allocate funding for us to design and update the course. While restrictive, the limitations invited us to conceive of different *kinds* of response by design.

[1] Embedding Responsiveness

In the design of our PDCs, we tried to think of ways responsiveness could be considered a feature of course, i.e., responsive *architecture*. Such features included

- readings and assignments that are place-based and culturally sensitive, i.e., responsive and local to the region;
- instructions (embedded within activities and assignments) directing students to ask questions of their instructors in order to promote a responsive relationship;
- required drafts spaced out to ensure sufficient time for instructor response feedback;
- assignments and activities centered on student perspectives and experiences in response to curricular content;
- reflective writing assignments, inviting students to respond to their experience of the course; and
- structured but flexible due dates that respond to the varying schedules of students and teachers (see Figure 15.2).

Due Dates

There will be three due dates each week (one for each assignment type), as follows:

- Tuesday 11:59 pm (Reading Responses)
- Wednesday 11:59 pm (Professional Identity)
- Thursday 11:59 pm (Technical Situations)

This structure is designed to spread the workload out over the course of the week. With some variation, you can expect the same amount of work each due date and a consistent schedule for the course of the class. Further, the assignment sequence build on one another; one assignment prepares you for the next and reinforces the previous. As much as possible you are encouraged to stick to the due dates by completing one assignment a day.

That said, all assignments in a given module can be turned in by Sunday of a given module:

- Sunday 11:59 pm (Grace Period)

In other words, while not encouraged or recommended is possible to complete all the on the weekend. All assignments turned in after Sunday will be counted and graded as late. Please refer to the course syllabus for more on the course design and the late work policy.

Module Structure (A Daily Representation of the Course Design)

Monday	Tuesday	Wednesday	Thursday	Sunday
Module Opens (by 11:59 am)	Reading Response Due (11:59 pm)	Professional Identity Due (11:59 pm)	Technical Situation Due (11:59 pm)	"Grace Period" Module Closes (11:59 pm)

Figure 15.2. A paced but flexible due date system.

By thinking about the ways that activities of the course could facilitate response, we disarticulated it from the *person* or *personality* of the instructor, embedding it in the course itself. Such embedding work invites students and instructors to enact responsiveness, prompting them to engage with one another in a variety of ways.

[2] Narrating Responsiveness

As OWI researchers with significant online teaching experience, we recognize the importance of responsiveness in our own classes. In fact, responsiveness is not only a best practice but also one of our values. One of the challenges we became aware of in the context of a PDC is that while we might be able to design for responsiveness as a practice, we had the responsibility of communicating our values. To do this we

- highlighted features of the course (in the assignment prompts and instructor guides) where responsiveness was *built in*, inviting instructors to (re)consider how and when they could respond to their students;
- shifted expectations for where (and on which activities) instructors would spend their time in a PDC (versus another course): less need for "prep" but more need for consistent interaction and more opportunities for responding to individual student writing (informal and formal);
- emphasized response as a dialogue between instructor and students (rather than one-way communication of instructor expectations) by using individualized/personalized questions to prompt such dialogue; and
- along with U-O, promoted opportunities to interact with students *outside* of response to assignments—through virtual or synchronous office hours, email and chat check-ins, announcements, etc.

In these capacities, we became aware of our responsibility to not only design the course but also to shape the narrative—to be aware of and account for the pedagogical arguments that we were making by design.

[3] Administering Response

At an administrative level, being responsive in PDCs is generally understood as being attentive to both the experiences of students and instructors (Borgman & McArdle, 2019). However, our contexts meant that we couldn't be responsive in ways that might be expected by students or instructors. We had to consider multiple levels of administration of these courses, which include, in our case, not only the WP, Department of English, and College of Arts & Sciences—administrative levels with which we were familiar—but U-O and its preferred metric for evaluating course design, QM. Our charge to enact responsiveness, then, became one of negotiating multiple layers of administration in order to allow the course to feel responsive to students and instructors. This required specific *strategies*, to which we turn below.

Strategic (to Use)

If being strategic is ultimately about pulling every*thing* together (Borgman & McArdle, 2019), when it comes to PDCs, we found that it must also revolve around pulling every*one* together. This means getting administrators, designers, and instructors to support one another in ways that are responsive to the experiences of students and instructors. One of the ways in which this can happen is to create UX feedback mechanisms and long-term plans. In this section, we discuss ways that administrators, designers, and instructors can strategize maintaining and updating pre-designed courses while working within their institutional constraints.

[1] Negotiating with Administration

When we began negotiating with administrators across multiple units and with varying degrees of administrative authority, it quickly became apparent that we had different visions in mind. Our initial game plan was to create an assignment catalog that left room for U-O instructors to personalize their courses, while U-O wanted QM-certified PDCs—an idea to which we were initially resistant. When we eventually came to terms with the expectations (understanding that they would be created with or without us), we quickly moved toward identifying strategies to work within the constraints. These strategies included

- organizing meetings for administrators across levels of scale,
- articulating and reiterating online writing instruction as a discipline with history and expertise *beyond* QM,
- requesting existing U-O PDCs (this included writing courses and courses outside of our discipline) so that we could better conceive of a range of possibilities,
- affirming the disciplinary and pedagogical expertise of instructors (at every meeting),
- coming to terms with the constraints of QM,
- learning how to work with the expertise of U-O's designer, and
- narrating our goals in terms valuable to U-O: Because we knew strategy and accessibility were values held in common, we leveraged them to make our position and expertise legible to administrators.

The key to administration (at all levels), of course, is to put everyone in a place to succeed, to understand what students and instructors are experiencing, and to allocate resources. To this end, being strategic about the administration of a PDC necessitates relationship building, forethought, and planning for uncertainties.

[2] Building Relationships

One of the biggest obstacles for our WP was that, like instructors of our PDCs, we lost a degree of autonomy and agency. As online writing instructors who value UX, we try to respond to the experiences of our students in a timely fashion (if something isn't working, we try to identify the issue and correct it). The challenge in PDCs becomes twofold: (1) any revisions or updates require communication, approval, funding, and coordination with another administration; (2) our UX feedback loop is structurally removed, relocated, and delayed. In other words, instead of being able to see for ourselves how students or instructors are experiencing the course, we need to work with instructors and U-O administrators to solicit that information and make changes. At an administrative level, this makes having strong relationships with instructors and administrative counterparts crucial. To build these relationships, we

- solicited assignments from instructors;
- consulted with instructors as usability testers;
- communicated, rather than concealed, the constraints and affordances of the courses with instructors; and
- learned and translated disciplinary and administrative jargon in meetings (to highlight different expertise without sacrificing communication).

Of course, the challenge of any relationship is that things are subject to change.

[3] Anticipating New Exigencies, Planning for Uncertainties

As OW instructors, we are used to iteratively revising and updating our courses to keep things fresh (e.g., drawing on current events to give ideas and practices exigency) and responsive (e.g., to the energy/personality of students, to the material conditions/seating arrangements of a classroom, or the introduction of new technology in an LMS). When it comes to PDCs, especially ones that are expected to have an extended shelf life, it's important to keep in mind that current events can go stale, the student makeup of a given course is unpredictable and complex, and LMSs themselves are updated. While we can't anticipate the news, plan for LMS updates, or predict changes in our student body, we can

- design to LMS features that are least likely to change,
- create exigencies for students to speak to current events and personal experiences, and
- choose readings with longer shelf lives.

Ultimately, we recognize that uncertainties and unanticipated experiences are not only to be expected but the vehicle for change. Since our experiences are still in the formative stage, in the conclusion we offer four overall strategies to shape the design and administration of PDCs.

Conclusion and Takeaways

Identifying strategies, as we have done in the previous sections, for creating successful PDCs, we understood that our work, in fact, was not only to learn how to *play* the course—which woods (assignments) and irons (activities), or how much force to put in our swing (design)—but how to collaboratively *build* one within our limitations, around the existing administrative, material, and temporal obstacles, and with respect to the contours of our university's terrain. Others who create PDCs will have different constraints. They, like us, will have to move beyond PARS as a generalized practice and imagine PARS for *their* course. While the play may vary, based on our experience, we close with four approaches to help others drive, wedge, and putt PDCs that are personal, accessible, responsive, and strategic:

- *Focus on relationships*: Assemble a team that represents the diversity of your program (so that your PDCs reflect and are welcoming to that diversity); develop strong working relationships with administrators and designers on multiple levels to create conditions for negotiation and shared expertise; take time to articulate shared goals and distinct expertises; and leverage those relationships to create feedback loops.
- *Focus on personalized assessment*: If you have concerns about PDCs stunting the development and agency of instructors (e.g., because they don't get to design the course or because their pedagogical expertise goes to waste), remember that personalized instructor *feedback* is not only one of the most important dimensions of any writing course (i.e., what students are likely to remember and learn from) but also a theory and practice that instructors can cultivate and exercise.
- *Build from commonplaces*: Create PDCs that reflect your WP's or department's theory *and* practices—understand how a variety of instructors individually (and in turn programmatically) approach the course, and draw on your team's expertise to integrate and synthesize *existing* resources into your PDC. This allows the experience and expertises of teachers to show up in the design and mitigates a top-down ethos of "master classes."
- *Get creative*: Be open to collaborating on assignments and using content that you might not have thought about or used in your own class; try to see administrative expectations and constraints as opportunities to support students and their writing.

Finally, PDC or DIYC (do-it-yourself course), we hope that our complicating of PARS serves to illustrate for all the importance of recognizing and accounting for the political and relational dimension of *personal* and more generally of OWI. Building a course for others to play means strategically setting them up for success, so they see themselves as players with style and skills welcome in the clubhouse and on the green, primed to take their best shots.

References

Bomberger, A. (2004). Ranting about race: Crushed eggshells in computer-mediated communication. *Computers and Composition*, 21(2), 197–216. https://doi.org/10.1016/j.compcom.2004.02.001.

Borgman, J. & Dockter, J. (2018). Considerations of access and design in the online writing classroom. *Computers & Composition, 49*, 94–105. https://doi.org/10.1016/j.compcom.2018.05.001.

Borgman, J. & McArdle, C. (2019). *Personal, accessible, responsive, strategic. Resources and strategies for online writing instructors.* The WAC Clearinghouse; University Press of Colorado. https://doi.org/10.37514/PRA-B.2019.0322.

Borgman, J. & McArdle, C. (2021). Introduction: PARS and online writing instruction. In J. Borgman & C. McArdle (Eds.), *PARS in practice: More resources and strategies for online writing instructors.* The WAC Clearinghouse; University Press of Colorado. https://doi.org/10.37514/PRA-B.2021.1145.

Glazier, R. (2021). *Connecting in the online classroom: Building rapport between teachers and students.* Johns Hopkins University.

Glazier, R. & Harris, H. S. (2020). How teaching with rapport can improve online student success and retention: Data from empirical studies. *Quarterly Review of Distance Education, 21*(4), 1–17.

Glazier, R. & Skurat Harris, H. (2021). Instructor presence and student satisfaction across modalities: Survey data on preferences in online and on-campus courses. *International Review of Research in Open and Distributed Learning, 22*(3), 77–98.

Greer, M. & Harris, H. (2018). User-centered design as a foundation for online writing instruction. *Computers & Composition, 49*, 18–24. https://doi.org/10.1016/j.compcom.2018.05.006.

Gunawardena, C. N. (1995). Social presence theory and implications for interaction and collaborative learning in computer conferences. *International Journal of Educational Telecommunications, 1*(23), 147–166.

Nakamura, L. (2002). *Cybertypes: Race, ethnicity, and identity on the internet.* Routledge.

Oswal, S. K. & Melonçon, L. (2017). Saying no to the checklist: Shifting from an ideology of normalcy to an ideology of inclusion in online writing instruction. *WPA: Writing Program Administration, 40*(3), 61–77. https://wpacouncil.org/aws/CWPA/pt/sp/journal-archives.

Rodrigo, R. & Ramírez, C. (2017). Balancing institutional demands with effective practice: A lesson in curricular and professional development. *Technical Communication Quarterly, 26*(3), 314–328. https://doi.org/10.1080/10572252.2017.1339529.

Ruecker, T. (2021). Retention and persistence in writing programs: A survey of students repeating first-year writing. *Composition Forum, 46*. https://compositionforum.com/issue/46/retention.php.

St.Amant, K. & Sapienza, F. (Eds.). (2011). *Culture, communication, and cyberspace: Rethinking technical communication for international environments.* Routledge.

Stewart, M. K. (2021). Social presence in online writing instruction: Distinguishing between presence, comfort, attitudes, and learning. *Computers and Composition, 62.* https://doi.org/10.1016/j.compcom.2021.102669.

Warnock, S. (2009). *Teaching writing online: How and why.* National Council of Teachers of English.

Don't Throw Your Clubs!

There are a variety of rules and regulations associated with golf when it comes to equipment and the game. And while these are almost the same across the board, almost everyone revises or personalizes their putter. Whether it is a new comfortable grip or lead tape on the head to make it heavier, the club was once standard, and everyone was able to buy it off the shelf. Now, making those adjustments to the putter is a personal act, and everyone has different preferences and strategies for the design and use of their putter. It is how the golfer uses the putter that helps to form a connection to hopefully see better results.

Pre-designed courses offer instructors and administrators a variety of options when it comes to standardizing content, learning outcomes, and experiences for students. Mariya Tseptsura's chapter lays solid groundwork for creating accessible and usable spaces for students to engage and learn. What we like about Tseptsura's chapter is that it lays the groundwork for how to collaboratively develop a pre-designed course that meets the program goals, course goals, student goals, and instructor goals. It provides a solid structure for faculty and administrators to examine the personal nature of course and curricular design.

Chapter 16. Pre-Designed Courses and Instructor Autonomy: Emphasizing the Personal in Course Design

Mariya Tseptsura
University of Arizona

Abstract: While pre-designed online courses, or PDCs, are becoming more common across writing programs, concerns over their use are far from subsiding. This chapter argues that many of these concerns, and particularly the debates over the loss of instructor autonomy, can be addressed by applying the PARS framework and putting a strategic emphasis on the personal elements of the PDC. The chapter describes one approach to creating a PDC that provided instructors with multiple curricular choices, easily customizable elements, and course assignments that facilitated personal connections and communication. The chapter further argues that in order to make the best use of PDCs, writing instructors must be able to modify their courses and have sufficient training in personalizing the PDCs.

Keywords: pre-designed courses, course design, personal, online writing instruction, OWI training

Pre-designed courses, or PDCs (also known as "master," "template," or "canned" courses), were once commonly used mostly in for-profit higher education institutions but have become a staple in many writing programs across the nation. According to the Conference on College Composition and Communication's (CCCC) *2021 State of the Art of OWI Report*, 19 percent of the respondents in the most recent survey of online writing instruction (OWI) practitioners indicated that they were given PDCs to teach from, and 28 percent responded that they had received training for working with the PDCs. At the same time, scholars and practitioners continue to raise valid concerns over the use of PDCs, most notably regarding the loss of instructor autonomy: as Samantha NeCamp and Connie Theado (2021) put it, many instructors find PDCs "limiting and impersonal" (p. 1). While these concerns remain justified, this chapter argues that they can be addressed by applying the PARS (personal, accessible, responsive, strategic) framework designed by Jessie Borgman and Casey McArdle (2019) and specifically by emphasizing the *personal* element of the framework in course design and use. This chapter describes one writing program's approach to building a PDC with a *strategic* emphasis on giving instructors opportunities to make the course *personal* and offers an overview of specific curricular and design strategies and course materials.

Theory and Practice

One of the more serious points of criticism of PDCs is that these courses remove instructor autonomy and control over course content and design. Indeed, teaching from a PDC seemingly goes against the *CCCC* OWI Principle 5 that argues that "Online writing teachers should retain reasonable control over their own content and/or techniques for conveying, teaching, and assessing their students' writing in their OWCs" (CCCC A Position Statement, 2013). Losing instructor autonomy can lead to dissatisfaction on the part of composition instructors who might already feel disenfranchised by the structure of the discipline or resent that their roles were seemingly reduced to maintenance and grading (Mechenbier, 2015; Penrose, 2012; Rice, 2015). Being limited in how and how much they can modify a course severely curtails instructors' ability to make it personal: not only are the instructional materials designed by someone else, but lack of ownership and autonomy might lead instructors to feel less willing to go the extra mile to project their personality into the course or to make the course more personal for their students. Using PDCs might also limit how responsive the course is to students' needs, as the disconnect between those who design online courses and the students who take them (Rogers et al., 2007) is further exacerbated.

While these criticisms are not unjustified, universities and writing programs are becoming increasingly reliant on PDCs not only because of their desire to capitalize on the easy expansion methods promised by the PDCs but also because these courses provide some level of necessary standardization and instruction quality in situations where, just as learning management systems (LMSs) are becoming more complex, writing programs often rely on contingent workforce and are unable to provide adequate OWI-focused training in order to prepare their instructors to be proficient course designers. Developing a pedagogically sound, technologically up-to-date, accessible, and visually appealing course takes a high level of expertise in a number of fields from writing pedagogy to instructional design and digital technology. As Shelley Rodrigo and Cristina Ramírez (2017) argued,

> It is unfair to accept, then, that all writing studies scholars have the knowledge, design, and technological expertise to design their own online courses. Further, it is unreasonable and unethical to assume that less experienced scholars and instructors, such as graduate student teachers and lecturers, are prepared to design their own online course. (p. 316)

It is not surprising that under such conditions, instructors feel overwhelmed and exploited (Stewart et al., 2016); for instance, online instructors in Peter Shea's study (2007) named the increased workload of online "course development, revision, and teaching" (p. 84) as the main demotivating factor for choosing to teach online, with many pointing out that their institutions were unwilling to acknowledge this increased workload. Furthermore, there are some valid concerns about quality of online instruction; for instance, the CCCC's *2021 State of the Art of OWI Report* revealed that "Only 37% of respondents offered more text-based communication for ESL students, and only 48% viewed their courses as ADA compliant" (p. 11). While lack of attention to accessibility is a serious concern that can potentially create barriers for multiple groups of students, these statistics further confirm that it is unreasonable to expect all online writing instructors to be expert course designers.

By creating a PDC, writing programs can alleviate the additional workload writing instructors have to tackle when teaching online and can offer them an *accessible* course, *strategically* designed based on the best practices in OWI and educational technology. The resources typically available to writing programs far outweigh individual instructors' design ability, especially as a team model of course development has become increasingly common. For example, the design of the course described in this chapter involved a team of six: three experienced composition instructors, an instructional designer, a graphic designer, and an educational technology specialist, not to mention a video production team and a slew of technology available through the university's office of online education. Shared curriculum and PDCs can alleviate the burden of course development and help instructors focus on the needs of their students instead of content creation, leading to "instructional growth and greater student success" (Thompson, 2021, p. 79). PDCs can provide the benefits of a well-designed, strategic, and accessible course, but it might seem that by their very definition, they are doomed to remain impersonal. However, this doesn't have to be the case: this limitation can be addressed through a strategic focus on the personal elements of the course through specific strategies described below.

To make a course personal, though, instructors need to have the freedom to modify course content whenever needed. Different programs have different levels of restrictions when it comes to modifying course content. Some programs limit the scope of changes instructors can make, and some do not allow instructors to make any changes at all. As Rodrigo and Ramírez (2017) pointed out, sometimes these restrictions are necessitated by external factors like the Quality Matters (QM) certification limitations that require that individual courses be taught with minimal modifications if they want to maintain the QM certificate. However, in other cases, these restrictions seem to communicate a lack of trust in instructors' abilities and might lead to feelings of resentment or "a sense of disempowerment over their own work" (Ruiz, 2015). And of course, stricter restrictions make it more difficult to make the course personal. The negative outcomes of restricting instructor autonomy outweigh potential benefits of retaining greater control over course content. Instead of restricting instructors' ability to modify their courses, writing program administrators (WPAs) should encourage it and train instructors on how to customize their courses in the most effective and efficient ways. Working with the PDCs can then become a professional development opportunity at a time when opportunities for building OWI expertise are still (regrettably) rare: the CCCC's *2021 State of the Art of OWI Report* indicated that only 29 percent of instructors teaching online courses received mandatory training (with 77 percent of those responses indicating their training was limited to working with the LMS), and 27 percent indicated that they did not receive any training for teaching online. Using and adapting a PDC can become a valuable OWI training opportunity, and furthermore, such training can then be directed back towards course development, allowing the PDC design team to incorporate instructors' feedback into continuous course revision. In what follows, this chapter describes one writing program's approach to creating a PDC with enough strategically built-in flexibility to be personal and responsive.

Developing English 101 PDC

The writing program at the University of Nevada, Las Vegas (UNLV) serves approximately 9,000 students each year and offers a two-semester composition sequence (English 101 and 102). At the time I joined the program in my position as the associate director of composition in charge of the program's online courses in the fall 2019, the program offered 10–12 sections of online composition courses per semester. The program's director had recently developed a PDC for English 102, but there was no PDC for English 101, and instructors were routinely given online courses to teach with little support in developing or delivering them. During my first round of online teaching observations, it became clear that many of our highly qualified, accomplished instructors were struggling with moving their traditional face-to-face (F2F) teaching strategies into online spaces. Considering that at the time, the writing program (WP) was not able to offer extensive OWI training, creating a PDC for English 101 became one way to support our online instructors and lighten the heavy load of designing a course (Melonçon, 2017). I developed the first iteration of the English 101 PDC in fall 2019, and it was used in individual sections of the course for the first time in spring 2020—just in time for the COVID-19 pandemic transition to emergency remote instruction.

The development of the PDC also dovetailed with some broader standardization initiatives in the writing program. The standardization efforts included a required course portfolio assignment, a common timeline for major assignment due dates, and some aspects of the curriculum such as course structure (three main units culminating in major writing projects), as well as a list of required reading assignments and common themes and genres for the major writing projects.

The English 101 PDC included these standardized elements too, and the course was scaffolded following the principles of backward design (Wiggins & McTighe, 2005) so that each unit contained a major writing project and a series of smaller assignments, discussions, quizzes, and reading materials that all built on each other, leading students towards each unit's learning outcomes. In creating the major assignments, I collaborated with two of our most experienced online instructors; three course development specialists from the UNLV Office of Online Education supported me through the entire process of course development. The course was built following accessibility and universal design principles, as well as the needs of our highly diverse, multilingual student population (Amorim & Martorana, 2021; Miller-Cochran, 2015). For instance, all course documents and online materials were reviewed for compliance with the university's accessibility standards (e.g., all videos included closed captions and all course materials were accessible to screen readers and other assistive technology tools as well as displayed consistently in web and app versions of the LMS). Finally, to lighten the literacy load for our students, the course featured multiple multimodal components, such as introductory video lectures for each of the reading assignments and major writing assignments.

It took a semester of team efforts and labor to build the PDC and make it into a well-designed course that was strategic in helping students achieve the program's learning outcomes. Similar to other programs (e.g., Rodrigo & Ramírez, 2017), we made the English 101 PDC a requirement for all instructors teaching online for the first time. We also held a two-hour OWI orientation prior to the start of each semester and conducted teaching observations that gave us a chance to provide more individualized support. We gave our instructors complete control over their courses: They were welcome to modify any part of the course on the condition that they followed the program's curriculum guidelines and did not drastically alter student workload. Finally, instructors who had taught the course online before were able to opt out of the PDC and use their own materials instead; often, they preferred to reuse a version of the PDC they had modified before.

During a year and a half of using the PDC across our online sections of English 101, I surveyed our instructors on how they were using the course and what changes they would like to see.[1] From the instructor surveys, I received many positive comments about the course, and a majority responded that they made only minimal modifications to the course. Only less than a quarter of instructors said they used the course as a rough draft and modified it significantly; some changes I observed included introducing different major assignments and alternative reading materials. However, I was curious as to why most of the instructors chose not to modify the course, considering they were free to do so. In informal conversations with instructors, many of them voiced the concerns that they were not familiar enough with the curriculum to modify it, or that they did not have enough time to make significant changes.

---

1. At the time, it was beyond our capacity to survey the students as well; the program had plans for implementing a few student surveys and user data collection tools in the upcoming years, after this chapter was written. The course development team relied on the combined expertise and extensive online teaching experience of its composition instructor members to determine the best ways to accommodate our students' needs.

Perhaps not surprisingly, none of the instructors teaching online for the first time wanted to modify the course, instead trusting in the program's expertise and taking their time to gain more experience. However, in some ways, the PDC itself felt restrictive as instructors could not see easy pathways to modifying and personalizing its content: because each small part was designed to be connected to a larger whole, they were hesitant to change anything lest they trigger a domino-like collapse of a curricular unit. It was evident that instructors needed clearer guidelines on how to personalize the course, both in the instructor manual that accompanied the course and in the course materials themselves. Finally, when asked about future changes they would like to see in the course, the most common answer was adding alternative assignments or units to diversify the course curriculum.

To address these concerns, I directed a team of three experienced instructors to revise the PDC in the summer of 2021. Below is a description of some of the major elements of the course that were introduced in order to help our instructors take greater ownership of their courses and make them feel more personal, as well as forge better personal connections to their students. As Borgman and McArdle (2019) stated, "Personalization of the classroom doesn't have to be a huge endeavor, small steps go a long way" (p. 30); some of the revisions might seem small-scale individually, but together, they accumulated to create a noticeable change in how easily the PDCs could be personalized.

Alternative Curricular Units

One of the main goals of our revisions was to create alternative units that would allow instructors to exercise greater control over their own curriculum. We designed five alternative units (see Table 16.1 for an overview of course curriculum and alternative units), each complete with a major writing project prompt and a series of lower-stakes activities and reading and writing assignments that helped students advance towards the unit's outcomes. Our approach was similar to what Allegra Smith et al. (2021) described as a grid-based course design where instructors could choose between different assignments and genres that would best suit their pedagogical approaches. Jacqueline Amorim and Christine Martorana (2021) described a similar approach that they called a "drag-and-drop" model that let instructors choose between different assignment options to include into their course modules.

Because of the limitations of our particular LMS (Canvas), we built these alternative units as separate modules inside a course shared with our cohort of online instructors: each module included all of the instructional materials needed to replace a default module with an alternative one, preceded by a set of step-by-step directions on how to do it. Instructors just needed to "import" the alternative materials and delete the old ones from their courses. Not only did instructors have greater autonomy over their curriculum, these alternative units also made it explicit how the different pieces of the curriculum puzzle fit together in the PDC, pointing to a clearer way to revise and personalize the course materials. Finally, diversifying curriculum can help alleviate some of the concerns over academic honesty, as students can potentially recycle their papers when re-enrolling in a different section of the course (Mitchum & Rodrigo, 2021).

Table 16.1. Course Curriculum for All Sections of English 101 and in the PDC

	Unit 1: Weeks 1–5	Unit 2: Weeks 6–9	Unit 3: Weeks 10–14	Unit 4: Weeks 15–16
Common major project genres recommended by the writing program:	Literacy narrative Memoir Response essay	Opinion or letter to the editor Brochure or infographic Review Commentary	Rhetorical analysis Genre analysis Textual analysis	Course portfolio
PDC major assignment options:	Literacy narrative Language memoir "This I Believe about Writing" essay "Place of Memory" memoir	Opinion piece with infographic Letter to the editor with a brochure or flier	Rhetorical analysis Genre analysis	Course portfolio

Focusing on Personal in Course Design

As Rhonda Thomas et al. (2021) remind us, "Being personal in online classes isn't simply having a good personality" (p. 187). In the context of online courses, "personal" goes beyond simply reflecting the instructor's personality, although the course should include enough opportunities for instructors to do that as well. Thomas et al.'s (2021) research indicates that students need to feel "a 'personal connection' to the course and the instructor," which they define as "distinct moments in a course when students recognize links between their ideas and identities and those of the instructor" (p. 188). Arguably, it is easier to design a course that would focus on the personal aspect if the instructor were the designer of the course. When designing a PDC though, course designers need to be strategic about building in the personal elements in two ways: 1) they can include intentional blank spots to be filled in by individual instructors, such as an instructor introduction page placeholder, course announcement templates, or personalized course policies, and 2) they can build elements of the course that would help humanize instructor and students alike and help students establish personal connections to the course materials, their classmates, and their instructor. In our course design, we pursued these two lines of personalization with a range of elements described below (for an overview of these elements, see Table 16.2.

Table 16.2. Overview of PDC Design Strategies for Course Personalization

Curricular Design Elements	Personalizable "Blank Space" Elements	Elements Promoting Personal Connections
Multiple alternative curricular units and assignments	Instructor introduction template (with supplemental support for developing multimodal introductions) Course announcement templates Customizable instructor policies "Welcome" and "First Steps" pages featuring short instructor introductions Short, visually distinct annotations on course materials and assignments that provide supplemental instructor commentary	Icebreaking introduction discussion Confidential student introduction survey Informal surveys at mid- and end-points of the semester Informal, ungraded "checking in" discussions and surveys Short assignments (e.g., open-ended quiz questions) that serve as comprehension checks and initiate student-instructor communication Assignments encouraging students to make connections between course concepts and their lives Optional multimodal elements in course assignments Group projects and discussions promoting a sense of community

From the start, our English 101 PDC included an "Instructor Introduction" page template that left space for instructors to add their photo or video and share a few professional and personal details about themselves. In addition to the template page, the course manual included directions to the existing university resources for creating a professional introductory video. The home page of the course also included a short personal welcome video that featured the author of this chapter as one of the composition program directors. In addition, the course "Welcome" and "First Steps" pages also featured short instructor introductions that could be easily modified.

Besides the introduction page and videos that would help students get to know their instructors as people, instructors were encouraged to participate in the icebreaking introductory discussion and respond to the prompt's questions the same way their students would. The questions invited students to share details about their backgrounds and academic and personal interests as well as their beliefs about writing; students were also asked to attach a photo or video of themselves to enhance their introduction. Such icebreaking discussions are very helpful in personalizing the course (Borgman & McArdle, 2019); furthermore, they can be used to establish course cohorts (Sibo, 2021) or form small groups for future activities. However, the public nature of such discussions may discourage some students from sharing more personal details that might help their instructor be better prepared to assist them. Understandably, some students might not want to publicly share their linguistic, age, or cultural and national backgrounds. Some students might only want to share very minimally; it is perhaps not surprising that some studies (e.g., Matsuda et al., 2013) have shown that online instructors feel like they don't always know who their students are.

To help instructors get to know their students beyond the introduction discussion, we included a confidential student survey that invited students to share more private details about their backgrounds, such as their age or spoken languages, and also asked about students' past experiences with writing and online courses and the challenges they were anticipating that semester. Besides the initial questionnaire, the course also included a mid-semester informal survey asking students for feedback on how the course was going, their reflections on the instructor's feedback, and any other concerns or suggestions they might have. The course also featured an ungraded "Checking In" public discussion in the second half of the semester, designed to let students voice any thoughts and concerns about the course or the current writing project and find some help and advice from their instructor and classmates.

Most of the course assignments also prompted students to make personal connections to the course themes. For the first unit, for instance, we designed four major assignments that instructors could choose from: a literacy narrative, a language memoir, a "This I Believe about Writing" essay, and a place-centered memoir assignment. All of these assignments asked students to use their personal experiences with language, writing, and literacy to reflect on larger social or cultural trends. The course also promoted a sense of community through multiple small-group assignments, discussions, and peer reviews.

Moreover, the course included strategically placed check-in elements that facilitated better communication between instructors and students; as Thomas et al. (2021) points out, "Creating a personalized experience for students requires layers of strategic and purposeful communication with each student" (p. 191). Thus, after the introduction of each of the four major writing assignments, students took a quiz that asked them to submit a question about the assignment to their instructor. In my personal experience, students often hesitate to ask questions via email or do so at the last moment before a major due date. Prompting students to ask questions early on helped make sure that they considered the prompt carefully and asked questions at an appropriate time. It also opened one more channel of communication between students and their instructor, as the LMS allowed students to comment on instructor's feedback (and the instructor was also able to respond to students' comments or questions that way too).

Finally, some assignments in the course invited students to make use of multiple modalities by, for instance, creating an audio post or a short screencast video in response to a discussion prompt. Mindful of potential impediments students might face when it comes to using technology (Bancroft, 2016), these multimodal components were not required but highly encouraged as an additional means to bring students' personality into the course and lessen its literacy load. Additionally, we looked for more ways to make it easier for instructors to add their own voice to the course materials. Videos are a great tool for infusing instructors' voices and personalities into the course, but creating them can be time-consuming and technologically challenging. One aspect of F2F instruction that is often lost in online spaces is the verbal commentary instructors often share with the class when discussing new writing or reading assignments. We sought to replicate that aspect with a series of annotations that appeared as yellow sticky notes placed on top of course materials such as assignment prompts or reading guides. These notes contained instructor commentary on the assignments and materials; by default, they explained some of the rationale behind the curriculum and gave students additional studying tips (e.g., a note on one of the first discussion assignments read, "Remember that to earn full credit, you need to come back to the discussion and respond to your peers' posts. It will be even more awesome if you can come back once or twice after that to check if your responses got any replies"). The instructor manual that accompanied the course emphasized that these sticky notes were an easy place where instructors could give students additional directions, explanations, or metacommentary—especially if instructors have taught the course before or if they noticed common challenges or confusion that students were experiencing in the current course.

Conclusion and Takeaways

In the aftermath of the COVID-19 campus closures, it is clear that not only is the demand for online courses unlikely to subside but that writing programs should have sufficient resources for scaling up their online offerings when needed. PDCs can be an invaluable tool in alleviating the heavy workload of course development that often falls on individual instructors without adequate training or compensation. PDCs can also provide supplemental OWI training, although it should be stressed that OWI training should never be limited to providing PDCs alone. Reportedly, most instructors appreciate having this form of support (e.g., Rodrigo & Ramírez, 2017), but the potential negative effects of PDCs should not be overlooked. In the worst-case scenario, PDCs can feel restrictive and impersonal and can turn instructors away from online teaching. To make better use of the PDCs' potential and mitigate their limitations, course designers need to place strategic emphasis on the personal elements of the course. This chapter described three main ways our program sought to make our PDC more personal (see Table 16.2 in the previous section offers an overview of the main strategies in each of the three categories):

1. offering alternative curricular units and assignments that allowed instructors more control of their own course,
2. building in blank spaces to be filled in by the instructors, bringing forth their personality and voice, and
3. including activities that facilitated students' personal connection to the course and helped build a sense of community.

More importantly, however, implementing these strategies rests on the underlying principle of granting instructors more freedom in modifying and personalizing their courses. "Locking in" course content can not only spark dissatisfaction and resentment towards PDCs but can ultimately make the course worse by keeping it impersonal. Instructors should also have sufficient training and resources for navigating and customizing the PDC in addition to the recommended OWI professional development. By building multiple ways for instructors to customize their courses and giving them the freedom to make these courses their own, we can ensure that PDCs remain personal as well as responsive, strategic, and accessible (as Borgman and McArdle remind us, these four elements are always interconnected). Finally, WPAs and course design teams need to be responsive to instructors' and students' needs and actively seek their feedback; regular surveys and focus groups should be used for continuous PDC revision and updates.

References

Amorim, J. & Martorana, C. (2021). Online teaching, linguistic diversity, and a standard of care. In C. K. Theado & S. NeCamp (Eds.), *Working with and against shared curricula: Perspectives from college writing teachers and administrators* (pp. 13–28). Peter Lang Publishing.

Bancroft, J. (2016). Multiliteracy centers spanning the digital divide: Providing a full spectrum of support. *Computers and Composition, 41*, 46–55. https://doi.org/10.1016/j.compcom.2016.04.002.

Borgman, J. & McArdle, C. (2019). *Personal, accessible, responsive, strategic: Resources and strategies for online writing instructors.* The WAC Clearinghouse; University Press of Colorado. https://doi.org/10.37514/PRA-B.2019.0322.

CCCC Committee for Best Practices in Online Writing Instruction. (2013). *A position statement of principles and example effective practices for online writing instruction (OWI)*. National Council of Teachers of English. https://www.owicommunity.org/owi--distance-education-resources.html.

CCCC Online Writing Instruction Standing Group. (2021). *The 2021 state of the art of OWI report*. Conference on College Composition and Communication. https://cccc.ncte.org/wp-content/uploads/2022/05/2021SoAFullReport.pdf.
Matsuda, P. K., Saenkhum, T. & Accardi, S. (2013). Writing teachers' perceptions of the presence and needs of second language writers: An institutional case study. *Journal of Second Language Writing, 22*, 68–86. https://doi.org/10.1016/j.jslw.2012.10.001.
Mechenbier, M. (2015). Contingent faculty and OWI. In B. L. Hewett & K. E. DePew (Eds.), *Foundational practices of online writing instruction* (pp. 233–255). The WAC Clearinghouse; Parlor Press. https://doi.org/10.37514/PER-B.2015.0650.2.07.
Melonçon, L. (2017). Contingent faculty, online writing instruction, and professional development in technical and professional communication. *Technical Communication Quarterly, 26*(3), 256–272. https://doi.org/10.1080/10572252.2017.1339489.
Miller-Cochran, S. (2015). Multilingual writers and OWI. In B. L. Hewett & K. E. DePew (Eds.), *Foundational practices of online writing instruction* (pp. 297–313). The WAC Clearinghouse; Parlor Press. https://doi.org/10.37514/PER-B.2015.0650.2.09.
Mitchum, C. & Rodrigo, R. (2021). Administrative policies and pre-designed courses (PDCs). In C. K. Theado & S. NeCamp (Eds.), *Working with and against shared curricula: Perspectives from college writing teachers and administrators* (pp. 29–43). Peter Lang.
NeCamp, S. & Theado, C. K. (2021). Working with and against shared curricular: An introduction. In C. K. Theado & S. NeCamp (Eds.), *Working with and against shared curricula: Perspectives from college writing teachers and administrators* (pp. 1–13). Peter Lang Publishing.
Penrose, A. M. (2012). Professional identity in a contingent-labor profession: Expertise, autonomy, community in composition teaching. *WPA: Writing Program Administration, 35*(2), 108–126. https://wpacouncil.org/aws/CWPA/pt/sp/journal-archives.
Rice, R. (2015). Faculty professionalization for OWI. In B. L. Hewett & K. E. DePew (Eds.), *Foundational practices of online writing instruction* (pp. 389–410). The WAC Clearinghouse; Parlor Press. https://doi.org/10.37514/PER-B.2015.0650.2.12.
Rodrigo, R. & Ramírez, C. D. (2017). Balancing institutional demands with effective practice: A lesson in curricular and professional development. *Technical Communication Quarterly, 26*(3), 314–328. https://doi.org/10.1080/10572252.2017.1339529.
Rogers, P. C., Graham, C. R. & Mayes, C. T. (2007). Cultural competence and instructional design: Exploration research into the delivery of online instruction cross-culturally. *Educational Technology Research and Development, 55*(2), 197–217. https://www.jstor.org/stable/30221239.
Ruiz, C. A. (2015). *Job satisfaction of adjunct faculty who teach standardized online courses* [Doctoral dissertation, University of South Florida]. Digital Commons at USF. https://digitalcommons.usf.edu/cgi/viewcontent.cgi?article=6968&context=etd.
Shea, P. (2007). Bridges and barriers to teaching online college courses: A study of experienced online faculty in thirty-six colleges. *Journal of Asynchronous Learning Networks JALN, 11*(2), 73. https://doi.org/10.24059/olj.v11i2.1728.

Sibo, A. (2021). The literacy load is too damn high!: A PARS approach to cohort-based discussion. In J. Borgman & C. McArdle (Eds.), *PARS in practice: More resources and strategies for online writing instructors* (pp. 71–81). The WAC Clearinghouse; University Press of Colorado. https://doi.org/10.37514/PRA-B.2021.1145.2.04.

Smith, A., Chernouski, L., Batti, B., Karabinus, A. & Dilger, B. (2021). People, programs, and practices: A grid-based approach to designing and supporting online writing curriculum. In J. Borgman & C. McArdle (Eds.), *PARS in practice: More resources and strategies for online writing instructors* (pp. 83–95). The WAC Clearinghouse; University Press of Colorado. https://doi.org/10.37514/PRA-B.2021.1145.2.05.

Stewart, M., Cohn, J. & Whithaus, C. (2016). Collaborative course design and communities of practice: Strategies for adaptable course shells in hybrid and online writing. *Transformative Dialogues: Teaching and Learning Journal, 9*, 1–20.

Thomas, R., Kuralt, K., Harris, H. S. & Jensen, G. (2021). Create, support, and facilitate personal online writing courses in online writing programs. In J. Borgman & C. McArdle (Eds.), *PARS in practice: More resources and strategies for online writing instructors* (pp. 185–207). The WAC Clearinghouse; University Press of Colorado. https://doi.org/10.37514/PRA-B.2021.1145.2.11.

Thompson, H. (2021). From skeptic to believer to advocate: How I came to understand the benefits of shared curricula writing programs. In C. K. Theado & S. NeCamp (Eds.), *Working with and against shared curricula: Perspectives from college writing teachers and administrators* (pp. 75–90). Peter Lang Publishing.

Wiggins, G. & McTighe, J. (2005). *Understanding by design*. Pearson.

Go Low!

While having a plan is always great when it comes to playing golf, you also have to do your research to better understand how the course works in terms of layout, speed of the greens, wind, weather, and other factors. This is where a caddy can aid in your research and give you the chance to not only prepare but also feel confident to improvise.

We like this chapter by Julie Watts because it explores how online student orientations (OSOs) can be complex, but when working with students to prepare them for courses and expectations, this hard work at the front of the semester will alleviate more headaches down the line. Utilizing community of inquiry (CoI), Watts engages in building and maintaining relationships between students, content, and learning in a way that is structured but also rewarding for those involved.

Chapter 17. Fairway Finder: Implementing an Online Student Orientation

Julie Watts
University of Wisconsin-Stout

Abstract: A course-embedded, learning-focused online student orientation (OSO) can be consequential for online learners, helping them to take ownership of their path through a course and enabling them to use OSO strategies and skills in subsequent online classes. Drawing from an OSO used in an online technical and professional communication graduate program (Watts, 2019) and using the community of inquiry theory (Garrison, 2016), this Fairway Finder OSO helps students identify behaviors and skills they need to succeed as online learners and what behaviors and skills they should expect from peers and the instructor. Interactive learning opportunities are provided that enable students to continuously reflect on how they can move beyond surface learning and achieve deep learning (Phillips & Graeff, 2014). The Fairway Finder OSO helps instructors to achieve PARS—personal, accessible, responsive, strategic—learning experiences for students (Borgman & McArdle, 2019).

Keywords: online learning, online student orientation, community of inquiry, deep learning

While research has eroded misconceptions about the "digital native," illustrating that working and playing online are not the same as learning online (Brumberger, 2011), we are only beginning to understand how to best prepare students for online writing classes (Stewart, 2021). One often-overlooked strategy is the online student orientation (OSO; Melonçon & Harris, 2015). OSOs showing online students how to navigate their learning management system (LMS) or discover university resources are prevalent (Taylor et al., 2015; Wozniak et al., 2012), yet OSOs providing strategies for becoming informed, reflective online learners are less common (Cho, 2012). A course-embedded, learning-focused OSO can be consequential, becoming (to extend Jessie Borgman and Casey McArdle's golf analogy) a "fairway finder"—strategies helping students chart their path through a course.

Drawing from a study about an OSO developed for an online technical and professional communication graduate program (Watts, 2019), students identify behaviors and skills they need to succeed as online learners and those they should expect from peers and instructors, using the community of inquiry (CoI) theory as a framework (Garrison, 2016). The OSO's interactive learning opportunities enable students to continuously reflect on and devise how to move beyond surface learning and achieve deep learning (Phillips & Graeff, 2014).

This chapter describes what I call the Fairway Finder OSO, analyzing how it helps instructors craft personal, accessible, responsive, and strategic (PARS) learning experiences (Borgman & McArdle, 2019). The Fairway Finder OSO prepares students "to learn how to learn" online and is useful for students with all levels of online course experience (Levy, 2006, p. 226).

Theory and Practice

The 2021 State of the Art of OWI Report shows that OSOs for online learners are not widely offered, with only 22 percent of respondents reporting any orientation to online writing courses (CCCC Online Writing Instruction Standing Group, 2021, p. 34). Typically, online programs requiring OSO participation identify overcoming technological barriers or discovering university resources as OSO goals. OSOs based on learning theories, helping students learn *how to learn* online are less prevalent (Wozniak et al., 2012).

OSOs addressing technological barriers often prompt students to complete LMS tasks, helping mitigate high course-withdrawal rates and buoying student satisfaction (Taylor et al., 2015). Such OSOs coupled with student services information also contribute to student satisfaction (Jones, 2013). While face-to-face orientations have long acknowledged complex social development and learning issues (Perigo & Upcraft, 1989) and despite literature characterizing differences between online and face-to-face learning environments (Baker, 2010; Gerlock & McBride, 2013; Moore, 1993), OSOs orienting online students tend to focus on easy-to-assess and remediate LMS and resource issues.

Yet learning-focused OSOs—especially the course-embedded variety, which contribute to higher rates of course and program completion (Taylor et al., 2015)—provide online students benefits. Philipa Levy (2006) embedded a two-week OSO into the beginning of a 17-week online course and incorporated OSO tasks throughout the semester. Students wanted more orientation tasks at the beginning of the semester, more synchronous communication throughout the semester, and those tasks that focused on "critical reflection and dialogue" were particularly important for developing students' "'learning to learn' capabilities" (Levy, 2006, p. 236). Studies show that theory-driven OSOs tackling students' challenges learning in online environments not only improve student satisfaction but impact learning outcomes (Watts, 2019; Wozniak et al., 2012).

Community of Inquiry (CoI) Theory

The Fairway Finder course-embedded OSO uses CoI theory, encouraging students to identify and nurture behaviors and skills they need to cultivate and ask for in others to succeed as online learners (Garrison et al., 2000). Online courses

258 Watts

should be communities of inquiry—places where students move beyond surface learning (characterized by rote memorization) to achieve "deep and meaningful learning" in which they synthesize concepts and apply ideas (Rourke & Kanuka, 2009, p. 23). A vibrant CoI features members working to achieve social, teaching, and cognitive presence (see Table 17.1).

Table 17.1. CoI Social, Teaching, and Cognitive Presences

Social Presence	Acknowledges that engaging with others fosters learning (Wang & Wang, 2012)
	CoI members cultivate social presence by sharing beliefs and values, cooperating to create trusting learning environments, and collaborating around common intellectual tasks (Swan et al., 2009).
Teaching Presence	Accomplished through course design, discourse facilitation, direct instruction (Anderson et al., 2001), and timely, constructive feedback (Shea et al., 2010)
	Students contribute to teaching presence by self-regulating their learning (Zimmerman, 2008) and participating in coursework (Akyol & Garrison, 2011).
Cognitive Presence	Characterized by students' sustained interaction with, reflection about, and application of course content; students "question their existing assumptions" and need to "construct" and apply "new knowledge" (Stewart, 2017, p. 71)
	Instructors scaffold students' critical inquiry by setting up complex problems, helping students explore and integrate relevant information and apply/test ideas (Garrison & Cleveland-Innes, 2005).

Instructors and students can ask questions like these to analyze their own and others' behaviors and activities relevan Photo of a very hilly golf course fairway. There is tall rough brown grass in the front and to the left. There are many ominous looking blue and white clouds in the sky. t to these presences:

- How do my actions and messaging help cultivate *social presence*?
- What behaviors related to *teaching presence* is my instructor enacting, and how can I take advantage of these?
- How can I complete coursework to develop my *cognitive presence*?
- How can I scaffold coursework, enabling students to practice and achieve *cognitive presence*?
- How can I assign student groups intellectual tasks to cultivate productive *social presence*?

Students with varying degrees of online learning experience find the OSO helpful:

> Prior to learning about this model, I could recognize that something in an online course was not working, but struggled to articulate or even really pinpoint the cause. Now I have both a framework and a vocabulary to not only identify what works

and does not work in an online course but to discuss it. (Watts, 2019, p. 263)

While the Fairway Finder OSO is structured in a 15-week semester course, it also could be integrated into shorter courses or stand alone.

Fairway Finder OSO and the PARS Framework

The Fairway Finder OSO features a PARS sensibility. Its activities are *strategic*(S) in that students grapple with online learning concepts before wrestling with course content and then twice more during the semester. The balance of individual and group activities is an *accessible* (A) way for students to tackle OSO concepts, working individually and collaboratively to devise meaning and test their knowledge. Students receive *responsive* (R) peer feedback and individualized instructor feedback. The OSO is a *personal* (P) learning journey set within a community: Each participant is responsible for their own and others' teaching and learning.

Week 1: Discovering and Defining the CoI

Week 1 introduces the Fairway Finder OSO, with few other activities scheduled. Students recognize the OSO importance and are incentivized to complete the activities (see Table 17.2).

Students view a slideshow lecture explaining CoI, illustrating the theory to them not as an abstract concept but as a tool they can *use*—helping them to identify, measure, and reflect on their own and others' activities and behaviors. To apply CoI, students read a blog article and post to a discussion board. Students share their experiences and position themselves expressively, focusing on the work (the presence) one needs to invest to collaboratively create a CoI. In the individual response papers, which receive instructor feedback, students further comment on CoI applications.

Table 17.2. OSO Week 1 Learning Goals and Activities

Week 1 Learning Goals	Learn about the CoI theory.
	Discover how social, teaching, and cognitive presences can be manifested by CoI members.
Week 1 Activities and Materials (Appendix A)	View a ten-minute slideshow explaining CoI. *
	Read "Five-Step Strategy for Student Success with Online Learning" (Morrison, 2015), and post to a discussion board about how the article strategies inculcate the presences.
	Write an individual response paper analyzing "CoI Framework: Establishing Community in an Online Course" (Lambert & Fisher, 2013) to illustrate the application of CoI.

*If you teach graduate students, consider also assigning Chapter 2 "Theoretical Foundations" and Chapter 3 "Community of Inquiry," found in E-Learning in the 21st Century (Garrison, 2016).

Week 8: Applying Community of Inquiry Concepts to Learning

During Week 8, students return to the Fairway Finder OSO, using CoI to reflect on and self-monitor their skills and behaviors while providing feedback to others (see Table 17.3). Students write a CoI reflection and plan, which receives instructor feedback, encouraging reflection about how they have cultivated (and could improve) cognitive and social presence and how they could better leverage teaching presence.

Students participate in a discussion board sharing features of their plans, stimulating whole-class discussion. To critique CoI behaviors and activities, students need to feel part of a safe, trusting learning environment. Schedule this critique after members have established trust, and integrate student reflection and instructor feedback into the course before Week 8 to further this "trusting influence" among CoI members (Peacock & Cowan, 2019).

Table 17.3. OSO Week 8 Learning Goals and Activities

Week 8 Learning Goals	Apply CoI concepts to course activities.
	Check in with CoI members to provide feedback about their CoI behaviors and skills.
	Devise self-improvement plans to help CoI members achieve the presences.
Week 8 Activities and Materials (Appendix B)	Write a 750- to 1,500-word CoI reflection and plan.
	Participate in a discussion board analyzing plan features and ideas.

Week 15: Reflecting on Our Community of Inquiry

Students revisit the reflection and plan and devise a final response, discussing how the presences were practiced and achieved (see Table 17.4). Responses can be paired with portfolios including revised coursework that indicate where presences are evident:

- *Teaching presence.* Essay that received useful instructor feedback.
- *Cognitive presence.* Poster project displaying survey data analysis.
- *Social presence.* Collaborative proposal project illustrating various student contributions.

Final responses and portfolios can be used in course or program assessment (Watts, 2017).

CoI members are responsible for student learning, and instructors take the OSO journey with students. This shared experience distinguishes the Fairway Finder OSO from others that simply orient students to technology or university resources. The Fairway Finder OSO encourages instructors to cultivate their teaching presence and guides students as they practice achieving social and cognitive presence.

Table 17.4. OSO Week 15 Learning Goals and Activities

Week 15 Learning Goals	Apply CoI concepts to course activities.
	Analyze how students have "learned how to learn online."
Week 15 Activities and Materials (Appendix C)	Submit a final response paper to the instructor. Students use CoI concepts analyzing how they have "learned how to learn online."
	Compile a portfolio containing selected, revised coursework. Students reflect on their learning journey and point to places in their work where presences are evident.

Conclusions and Takeaways

Students should be responsible for their learning but also know that they can succeed by participating in a community of learners. The Fairway Finder OSO gives students a vocabulary to analyze and reflect on their learning, helping them succeed. Consider the following takeaways to implement the Fairway Finder OSO:

1. *Integrate the CoI framework* variously, "naming" cognitive, social, and teaching presence when explaining readings, tasks, and assignments. When I use audio feedback to respond to student work, I explain that I use this medium to cultivate teaching presence. When assigning collaborative projects, I state that this cultivates social and cognitive presence.
2. *Incentivize OSO activities* by awarding points, providing feedback, and engaging in CoI activities throughout the semester.
3. *Ensure OSO activities are collaborative*, so CoI members share ideas and provide and receive feedback. Students should receive peer feedback and individualized instructor feedback.
4. *Continue to update the OSO*, allowing instructors to consider how PARS allows for different iterations of orientation content.

The Fairway Finder OSO prompts CoI members to experience a *personal* (P) learning journey that occurs within a community. Activities characterized by instructor and peer feedback help students grapple with OSO concepts in an *accessible* (A) way—they work on their own and with others to devise meaning and test their knowledge. Students receive *responsive* (R) peer feedback and individualized instructor feedback, showing the value of student contributions and enabling them to learn from others. CoI members participate in *strategic* (S) ways: Activities are assigned throughout the semester and culminate in a semester-end reflection. This course-embedded, learning-focused OSO orients students to online learning environments, giving them ownership of their path through the course.

References

Akyol, Z. & Garrison, D. R. (2011). Assessing metacognition in an online community of inquiry. *Internet and Higher Education, 14*, 183–190.

Anderson, T., Rourke, L., Garrison, D. R. & Archer, W. (2001). Assessing teaching presence in a computer conferencing context. *Journal of Asynchronous Learning Networks, 5*(2), 1–17.

Baker, C. (2010). The impact of instructor immediacy and presence for online student affective learning, cognition, and motivation. *The Journal of Educators Online, 7*(1), 1–30.

Borgman, J. & McArdle, C. (2019). *Personal, accessible, responsive, strategic: Resources and strategies for online writing instructors*. The WAC Clearinghouse; University Press of Colorado. https://doi.org/10.37514/PRA-B.2019.0322.

Boykin, D., Hower, A., Kepler, D., Marling, J., Pittman, J. & Walters, J. (2015). Orientation programs: CAS contextual statement. In J. B. Wells (Ed.), *CAS professional standards for higher education* (9th ed.). Council for the Advancement of Standards in Higher Education. http://www.cas.edu.

Braxton, J. M., Doyle, W. R., Hartley III, H. V., Hirschy, A. S., Jones, W. A. & McLendon, M. K. (2014). *Rethinking college student retention*. Jossey Bass.

Brumberger, E. (2011). Visual literacy and the digital native: An examination of the millennial learner. *Journal of Visual Literacy, 30*(1), 19–47.

CCCC Online Writing Instruction Standing Group. (2021). *The 2021 state of the art of OWI report*. Conference on College Composition and Communication. https://sites.google.com/view/owistandinggroup/state-of-the-art-of-owi-2021.

Cho, M-H. (2012). Online student orientation in higher education: A developmental study. *Educational Technology Research and Development, 60*, 1051–1069.

Garrison, D. R. (2016). *E-learning in the 21st century: A community of inquiry framework for research and practice*. Routledge.

Garrison, D. R., Anderson, T. & Archer, W. (2000). Critical inquiry in a text-based environment: Computer conferencing in higher education. *The Internet and Higher Education, 2*(2–3), 87–105.

Garrison, D. R. & Cleveland-Innes, M. (2005). Facilitating cognitive presence in online learning: Interaction is not enough. *American Journal of Distance Education, 19*(3), 133–148.

Gerlock, J. A. & McBride, D. L. (2013). Managing online discussion forums: Building community by avoiding the drama triangle. *College Teaching, 61*, 23–29.

Jacobs, B. C. (2003). New student orientation in the twenty-first century: Individualized, dynamic, and diverse. In G. L. Kramer (Ed.), *Student academic services: An integrated approach* (pp. 127–146). Jossey-Bass.

Jones, K. R. (2013). Developing and implementing a mandatory online student orientation. *Journal of Asynchronous Learning Networks, 17*, 43–45.

Lambert, J. L. & Fisher, J. L. (2013). Community of inquiry framework: Establishing community in an online course. *Journal of Interactive Online Learning, 12*, 1–16.

Levy, P. (2006). 'Living' theory: A pedagogical framework for process support in networked learning. *ALT-J, Research in Learning Technology, 14*, 225–240.

Melonçon, L. & Harris, H. (2014). Preparing students for OWI. In B. L. Hewett & K. E. DePew (Eds.), *Foundational practices of online writing instruction* (pp. 417–444). The WAC Clearinghouse; Parlor Press. https://doi.org/10.37514/PER-B.2015.0650.2.13.

Morrison, D. (2015). Five-step strategy for student success in online learning. *Online Learning Insights: A Place for Learning about Online Education*. https://onlinelearninginsights.wordpress.com/2012/09/28/five-step-strategy-for-student-success-with-online-learning/.

Moore, M. G. (1993). Theory of transactional distance. In D. Keegan (Ed.), *Theoretical principles of distance education* (pp. 22–38). Routledge.

Peacock, S. & Cowan, J. (2019). Promoting sense of belonging in online communities of inquiry in accredited courses. *Online Learning Journal*, 23(2), 67–81.

Perigo, D. J. & Upcraft, M. L. (1989). Orientation programs. In M. L. Upcraft (Ed.), *The freshmen year experience* (pp. 82–94). Jossey-Bass.

Phillips, M. E. & Graeff, T. R. (2014). Using an in-class simulation in the first accounting class: Moving from surface to deep learning. *Journal of Education for Business*, 89, 241–247.

Rourke, L. & Kanuka, H. (2009). Learning in communities of inquiry: A review of the literature. *The Journal of Distance Education*, 23(1), 19–48.

Shea, P., Vickers, J. & Hayes, S. (2010). Online instructional effort measured through the lens of teaching presence in the community of inquiry framework: A re-examination of measures and approaches. *International Review of Research in Open and Distance Learning*, 11(3), 127–154.

Stewart, M. K. (2017). Communities of inquiry: A heuristic for designing and assessing interactive learning activities in technology-mediated FYC. *Computers and Composition*, 45, 67–84.

Stewart, M. K. (2021). Social presence in online writing instruction: Distinguishing between presence, comfort, attitudes, and learning. *Computers and Composition*, 62, 1–16.

Swan, K., Garrison, D. R. & Richardson, J. C. (2009). A constructivist approach to online learning: The community of inquiry framework. In C. R. Payne, (Ed.), *Information technology and constructivism in higher education: Progressive learning frameworks* (pp. 43–57). IGI Global.

Taylor, J. M., Dunn, M. & Winn, S. K. (2015). Innovative orientation leads to improved success in online courses. *Online Learning*, 19, 112–120.

Wang, J. & Wang, H. (2012). Place existing online business communication classes into the international context: Social presence from potential learners' perspectives. *Journal of Technical Writing and Communication*, 42(4), 431–451.

Watts, J. (2017). Beyond flexibility and convenience: Using the community of inquiry framework to assess the value of online graduate education in technical and professional communication. *Journal of Business and Technical Communication*, 31(4), 481–519.

Watts, J. (2019). Assessing an online student orientation: Impacts on retention, satisfaction, and student learning. *Technical Communication Quarterly*, 28(3), 254–270.

Wozniak, H., Pizzica, J. & Mahoney, M. J. (2012). Design-based research principles for student orientation to online study: Capturing the lessons learnt. *Australasian Journal of Educational Technology, 28*, 896–911.

Zimmerman, B. J. (2008). Investigating self-regulation and motivation: Historical background, methodological developments, and future prospects. *American Educational Research Journal, 45*(1), 166–183.

Appendix A: Week 1

Discussion Prompt: View the video introducing the community of inquiry theory and its application to online teaching and learning. Then read through the blog post, "Five-Step Strategy for Student Success with Online Learning," which identifies behaviors you should carry out to help you become a high-performing online learner.

Take a moment to post your response to the following prompts: (a) Tell us how frequently you have enrolled in online courses and what your experiences with online learning have been. (b) Briefly discuss how the CoI concept introduced in the video aligns with the five-step strategy proposed in the blog post. (c) Name and define one "strategy" (it doesn't necessarily need to be one mentioned in the blog post) that you think could be used to cultivate cognitive, social, or teaching presence in this class.

Response Paper: Read through the attached Lambert and Fischer (2013) PDF, which uses the community of inquiry (CoI) theory to frame its study. Respond in writing to the following 3-part prompt: (a) Think about the reading strategies you've read about this week in the "How to read an article" PDF; then describe the strategies you used to read the Lambert article. Comment on any challenges that you faced understanding the content of the article. (b) What do you believe were the most important findings communicated in the Lambert article? (c) Analyze how you believe one or more of these findings relate to you as a student in this online course.

- Garrison, D. R. (2016). *E-learning in the 21st century: A community of inquiry framework for research and practice*. Routledge. (optional reading)
- Morrison, D. (2015). Five-step strategy for student success in online learning. *Online Learning Insights: A Place for Learning about Online Education*. https://onlinelearninginsights.wordpress.com/2012/09/28/five-step-strategy-for-student-success-with-online-learning/.
- Lambert, J. L. & Fisher, J. L. (2013). Community of inquiry framework: Establishing community in an online course. *Journal of Interactive Online Learning, 12*, 1–16.
- Purugganan, M. & Hewitt, J. (2004). *How to read a scientific article*. Rice University. https://www.owlnet.rice.edu/~cainproj/courses/HowToRead-SciArticle.pdf (optional reading)

Appendix B: Week 8

CoI Reflection and Plan Prompt: During Week 1 of this class, we spent time reading about and discussing the Community of Inquiry (CoI) model analyzing how to "learn how to learn" online using the facets of teaching presence, social presence, and cognitive presence. *Teaching presence* is achieved by properly designing and organizing the course, facilitating discourse, providing direct instruction, and offering feedback about student work. *Social presence* is defined by the premise that interacting and engaging with other students and the instructor helps to foster cognitive presence and deep learning. *Cognitive presence* is characterized by students tackling a complex problem, often by researching, reflecting on it, and applying it in meaningful ways.

Write a 750- to 1,500-word CoI Reflection and Plan explaining how you have experienced social, teaching, and cognitive presences thus far in the course. Reflect on how you have cultivated cognitive and social presence and the ways you have leveraged the teaching presence offered to you. Conclude your draft with a set of recommendations about how you, your peers, and your instructor can improve the social, teaching, and cognitive presence of this course.

Reflection and Plan Discussion Board: Feel free to use the CoI Reflection and Plan document that you submitted to your instructor as a starting point for posting to this discussion board. Respond using complete sentences to the following questions: How did I perceive social, teaching, and cognitive presence exhibited in this class so far? What improvements do I see necessary for our community to achieve deeper social, teaching, and cognitive presence? What specifically do I need to do to help my community achieve this and what do I ask of my peers and instructor?

Peacock, S. & Cowan, J. (2019). Promoting sense of belonging in online communities of inquiry in accredited courses. *Online Learning Journal*, 23(2), 67–81.

Appendix C: Week 15

Final Response Draft: Please respond as thoroughly as possible to the prompt, and draw examples from your experiences as a student. Your Response should total between 750–1,500 words in length and should be drafted into complete sentences and well-developed paragraphs.

During Week 1 of this class, we spent time reading about and discussing the Community of Inquiry (CoI) model analyzing how to "learn how to learn" online using the facets of teaching presence, social presence, and cognitive presence. *Teaching presence* is achieved by properly designing and organizing the course, facilitating discourse, providing direct instruction, and offering feedback about student work. *Social presence* is defined by the premise that interacting and engaging with other students and the instructor helps to foster cognitive presence and deep learning. *Cognitive presence* is characterized by students tackling a complex problem, often by researching, reflecting on it, and applying it in meaningful ways.

Analyze the ways you have "learned how to learn online" throughout your time this semester. Use the CoI concepts of teaching presence, social presence, and cognitive presence to frame and/or inform your analysis.

Fairways and Greens!

Golf drills are excellent ways of working on parts of your game in a way that can improve your skills and prepare you for a specific course. For example, if you are going to play a course that has thick rough, it makes sense to practice hitting a lot of shots out of thick grass. Or a course that has a lot of bunkers—time to work on your sand game! Drills, while somewhat repetitive and tedious, are crucial to revising different parts of your game so you have the confidence to hit certain shots you might not otherwise practice. If your home course doesn't have thick rough or a lot of bunkers, you might not be used to playing those shots. So, drills can help get you in shape!

What we like about this chapter is how Lynn Reid conceptualizes a readiness program for students to prepare them for taking online writing classes. Using sample exercises, Reid provides a solid framework for helping students prepare for taking an online class. These mini "drills" are good practice for students as the semester takes on more complex topics and spaces.

Chapter 18. Literacy Loads, Readiness, and Accessibility: Addressing Students' Perceptions of OWI through Pre-Course Modules

Lynn Reid
FAIRLEIGH DICKINSON UNIVERSITY

Abstract: Despite considerable scholarship in online writing instruction (OWI) about literacy load, students are often unprepared for the extensive literacy demands in online courses. When students are invited to consider their "readiness" for online learning, it is often through self-assessments that inquire about skills in areas such as time management, motivation, self-efficacy, and access to digital resources. Students who score well on these types of readiness assessments may begin a course with an inaccurate perception of how to be successful, and students may find themselves in a situation that is not accessible to their needs as learners. This chapter proposes a series of pre-course modules that allow students to experience the different types of learning and literacy demands they might encounter in an online writing course (OWC). The results of these modules can help students to select a modality of learning that best meets their needs.

Keywords: online writing instruction, e-learning readiness, literacy load, writing program administration, access

In *Reading to Learn and Writing to Teach: Literacy Strategies for Online Writing Instruction*, Beth Hewett (2015) presents something of a profile of what she identifies as the "new" nontraditional student, one who comes to online learning with a range of prior experience with technology, much of which may not be terribly helpful as they attempt to meet the literacy demands of their online writing course. While the complex of factors that can impact online learning was certainly brought to the forefront during the COVID-19 pandemic, there has long been a correlation between students who are drawn to online learning and those for whom caretaking, employment, or other responsibilities are paramount, leaving them with unpredictable schedules or limited opportunities to pursue postsecondary education (Griffin & Minter, 2013; Hachey et al., 2022). With that, however, is also an increased likelihood that students who are burdened by personal challenges that strain economic and cognitive resources may struggle with the independent learning that is often required in asynchronous online writing courses.

For these reasons, *access* is important in online writing instruction research and is a critical part of the PARS framework. In composition studies, access is frequently discussed in the context of disability (Konrad, 2021) and/or access to technology (Ruecker, 2022), but Jessie Borgman and Casey McArdle (2019) also recognize that the term *access* extends beyond both compliance with the Americans with Disabilities Act (ADA) and availability of digital resources:

> Creating . . . truly accessible online courses means considering schedules, holidays, technical support for you if your computer goes down, or the LMS goes down, and a myriad of other underlying support systems that many universities fail to realize the importance of when offering online courses. (pp. 36–37)

In this view, creating an accessible course means considering the ways in which online coursework may intersect with students' lived experiences, other responsibilities, and existing resources (Giordano & Phillips, 2021).

Of course, students follow many paths to college composition, and any number of things might impact their academic performance, including prior experiences with trauma, mental health, socioeconomic factors, family responsibility, illness, disability, and learning a new language, to name a few, so it can be challenging to determine whether a student is struggling with an academic skill or simply a life circumstance at any point along the way. When considering the needs of students who are facing the types of scenarios listed above, the concept of access in regard to an online writing course (OWC) can be fraught. On one hand, the availability of OWCs absolutely provides access to college-level coursework that might not otherwise be available for a student with a complicated personal situation, including things such as military deployment, relocation to care for a family member, or an on-call work schedule. The flip side of this, however, is the unfortunate reality that students whose attention is divided between several demanding tasks often struggle to keep up with coursework. These students may not have had the same opportunities as their classmates with more socioeconomic privilege and stability to develop the academic skills that will ensure their success at the college level (Giordano & Phillips, 2021).

Below, I argue that providing pre-course exercises can create opportunities to make the literacy load in OWCs more transparent to a range of institutional stakeholders, including academic advisors, instructors who may plan to teach an OWC course, and tutors, all of whom play a role in fostering student success. Moreover, data gleaned from pre-course modules can shift agency from writing program administrators (who often determine whether or not it is appropriate to offer asynchronous versions of particular writing courses for distinct populations of students) to students, who will be better equipped to select OWCs based on their understanding of how learning takes place in an online environment.

Learning from Personal Experience

In my own experience teaching asynchronous online writing courses, I have observed that students who are drawn—or sometimes are directed by advisors—to enroll in OWCs are often enrolled in programs that are identified for what my institution terms "academically at-risk" populations. I have taught asynchronous OWCs designed for a range of students, including those who began in developmental writing courses and needed to "catch up" with the rest of their cohort over the summer; those students in a short-lived associate's degree program, many of whom had never imagined attending a four-year university until their senior year of high school; and those students who began in a bilingual program and were continuing on an ESL track as they simultaneously enrolled in the second of our two gen-ed comp courses. Additionally, my asynchronous summer courses are popular among students in a conditional admissions program who are trying to make up credits after enrollment in developmental courses. With that, any time I have taught an asynchronous writing course, regardless of the term, the number of students who are retaking the course has been disproportionately high compared to other courses. While all of these students opted for or needed online asynchronous sections of writing, nearly all represented a growing trend of students taking distance courses while participating in face-to-face courses simultaneously (Allen & Seaman, 2018), and who may therefore have more experience with in-person learning. In short, at least at my institution, asynchronous courses are often most attractive to students who may be deeply emotionally invested in doing well but who are also inexperienced with academic and digital literacies as well as online learning.

What does all of this mean for a writing program administrator (WPA)? For starters, WPAs are often tasked with deciding whether or not a writing course *should* be offered in an asynchronous modality. Thus, a WPA may be asked to weigh the potential benefits of an asynchronous course in terms of access and accessibility with their knowledge of how students generally respond to the literacy load of in-person classes in order to determine the courses in which students are most likely to succeed without real-time interactions with their instructor. Of course, issues pertaining to access and accessibility have been widely studied by OWI practitioners, and just about every online writing instructor is familiar with concerns related to students' access to technology, which can vary widely depending on students' socioeconomic circumstances (Hewett, 2015). However, the term *access* also invokes the need for online courses to adhere to universal design principles so that students can have equitable opportunities to engage with course materials, regardless of disability status (Coombs, 2010). Sushil Oswal (2015) additionally highlights the extent to which the technologies in OWCs can serve as barriers to access for students who may rely on assistive technologies in order to complete their coursework. As the work by these scholars indicates, determining who should have the option to enroll in an asynchronous online course is complex.

Yet, while there may be legitimate reasons to recommend against an asynchronous course for a particular population of students, it is important for WPAs to note that placing limitations on students' ability to utilize technology in their learning "is ultimately a political choice, even if the motive behind such a move appears benign" (Jonaitis, 2012, p. 39). In the case of OWI, the decision about whether and to whom they should be offered can have a significant impact on students' ability to complete their degree requirements. While WPAs may of course be motivated to reduce high attrition rates in online writing courses, particularly for students who are already deemed by the institution to be "academically at-risk," decisions about whether and to whom OWCs should be offered should be evidence-based, and simply examining retention and failure rates in these scenarios can obscure the learning needs of students and factors that may inhibit their success.

Theory and Practice
Conceptualizing Readiness for OWI

One topic that stands out in the existing scholarship about student preparation for online learning is the notion of "readiness." Readiness for online or distance education is often evaluated in terms of areas such as motivation, technological ability and self-efficacy, self-direction, and effective strategies for communicating online (Hung et al., 2010, p. 1080). These factors are generally measured through online readiness assessments, which are frequently among the first things that students encounter as they search a college website for fully online course offerings (Reid, 2022).

Penn State's Online Readiness Questionnaire serves as one example of an online readiness survey that has been widely adopted by other postsecondary institutions across the U.S. This survey asks students if they agree, somewhat agree, or disagree with statements such as "I am good at setting goals and deadlines for myself," "I am willing to send an email to or have discussions with people I might never see," "I plan my work in advance so that I can turn in my assignments on time," and "I have a printer" (see https://pennstate.qualtrics.com/jfe/form/SV_7QCNUPsyH9fo12B for the full survey). In a similar vein, Lisa Melonçon and Heidi Skurat Harris (2015) also suggest that success in OWI is more likely for students who are "self-motivated, goal-oriented, and good at time management" (p. 419). However, because most readiness assessments do not account for the pedagogies and learning needs of particular disciplines, WPAs who are interested in addressing student expectations in an online writing course must instead find strategies to assess the additional components of "readiness" that may be relevant for OWCs in particular.

To address student expectations, Tess Evans (2019) suggests that instructors email students to explain the course expectations (including technology access, requirements for presence in the course, team projects and interactions with peers, and due dates and requirements for major assignments) and attach a syllabus so that students can gain a better understanding of the literacy load for their OWC. While I fully agree that all of what Evans suggests are critical steps toward managing students' expectations of an online course, in that approach, the possibility for students to overestimate their ability to successfully complete assignments and demonstrate mastery of course concepts remains significant; indeed, students may be several weeks into a course before they realize that the instructors' expectations are not what they had anticipated.

The OWI Literacy Load and Student Success

Perhaps the most important element for WPAs to consider in regard to students' preparation for OWCs is the "literacy load," which June Griffin and Deborah Minter (2013) define as "the quantity of text to be read or written" (p. 153), and which I would argue extends to what students may be expected to *do* with the material that they read and write. For students who struggle academically, the literacy demands of OWCs have the potential to create a situation that, despite everyone's best intentions, can become wholly inaccessible (Griffin & Minter, 2013; Sibo, 2021). In my own experience teaching asynchronous online writing courses, students' expectations that an OWC will be easier, less time-consuming, and less scheduled than a face-to-face writing course often remain several weeks into the course, despite my attempts to note the requirements on the syllabus and provide consistent reminders that an OWC requires *more* independent work time to account for both the instructional time that they would spend on an in-person course and the time that is necessary for "homework."

This observation is further supported by the 2011 national survey on OWI, which found that 75 percent of respondents reported that "keeping up with the class" was the most significant challenge they faced in an asynchronous OWC (CCCC OWI Committee, 2011). Students' expectations for OWI are influenced by a number of factors, including potentially misleading advertising for fully online programs and the literacy demands—and related time commitment—associated with online learning (Hewett, 2015). Interestingly, despite these realities, the recently published *CCCC 2021 State of the Art in OWI Report* indicates that roughly half of the respondents to the most recent national survey noted that they prepare students for OWCs with information about workload and expected time commitments (CCCC OWI Standing Group, 2021). Given this fact, it is of little surprise that students may not accurately anticipate what the expectations for an online writing course will actually be. As Borgman and McArdle (2019) have noted, "the gap between online and in-person retention and achievement can be discouraging [to both faculty and students]" (p. 42). Despite this observation, to my knowledge, there is little scholarship that explicitly addresses student preparation for learning in OWCs (Melonçon & Harris, 2015) with regard to material that is developed with students as the intended audience.

This gap is surprising, given the attention that has been paid to the challenges that "literacy load" can pose in OWCs (Silbo, 2021). In one study, Griffin and Minter (2013) found that the reading load of OWCs was 2.75 times greater than that of face-to-face courses. This high reading load could begin to account for Di Xu and Shanna Jaggers' (2013) finding that retention and persistence in online English courses in particular is low (as cited in Hewett, 2015; see also Minter, 2015). Of course, the literacy load in OWCs should be complicated beyond a consideration of how much reading is required to also account for the *type* of reading that students must undertake in order to successfully complete an online writing course, which includes both instructional materials and the materials about which students will be writing (Hewett, 2015). The common expectation that students in college composition courses will engage in critical thinking and textual analysis further adds to the already heavy literacy load of OWCs with the requirement that students read instructional text to then make "a challenging cognitive leap from reading to action," particularly with respect to revising their own drafts (Hewett, 2015, p. 60).

This creates something of a perfect storm. We know that online courses may attract students whose time is constrained and who may, therefore, be disproportionately likely to struggle academically, and we know that the literacy load for OWCs is high and that managing that load is far more complicated than simply expecting that students set aside enough time to read all of the words associated with the course. We also know that students' perceptions are influenced by the ways in which online courses are advertised, which often emphasize flexibility and ease of learning. These conflicting priorities leave WPAs with the challenge of balancing students' needs for accessible course delivery with the very real challenges that online learning can pose for struggling learners.

WPA Work and Student-Facing Resources

In their original discussion of the PARS model, Borgman and McArdle (2019) note that administrators need to consider how to "prepare [their] online instructors for the student demographic they'll face" (p. 77). Here, I extend that discussion to include some thoughts on preparing *students* for what they will likely face in an online writing course, which is often far more complex than what an online readiness assessment that measures their motivation, self-efficacy, and technology skills will reveal. To provide students with a more nuanced understanding of what an online writing course might entail, I propose a series of pre-course modules that will enable a clearer communication to students about what types of literacy and learning activities they might expect in an online writing course. These modules can serve the important functions of allowing students—rather than a WPA—to determine whether a fully online course is a good fit for their learning needs and, if data is captured, revealing patterns in students' responses to online course material that can influence online pedagogy in a writing program. This is especially important to consider in light of our discipline's ongoing conversations about the struggles that students face as they transition from high school to college-level writing and discover that the strategies that served them well in high school may no longer be adequate (Fanetti et al., 2010).

Self-Assessing Readiness with Sample Course Content

Beth Hewett (2015) underscores the importance of effective orientation to online learning as a tool to support students' decision-making regarding OWI: "For example, when students have had adequate and timely orientation, they can make better decisions about whether their family situations, work schedules, and learning preferences will work for them in OWI" (p. 78). Those students who find an OWC to be a particularly burdensome experience often also comment that they would have made a different choice about the modality of the course had they really understood beforehand what it would entail. One strategy for achieving this goal is to provide sample modules that are easily accessible to students through the writing program's website.

This can be challenging for a WPA, given that in the absence of total standardization of content and structure across all sections, each instructor will create a unique pathway for students to work through the learning objectives of the course. This means that any resources developed with a programmatic perspective in mind must focus on introducing students to the ways that reading and writing will function in their OWCs to facilitate both instruction and students' own development as critical readers and writers. The tips for introducing students to the demands of OWCs by providing introductory material and clearly outlining expectations that are provided by Evans (2019) and Scott Warnock and Diana Gasiewski (2018) are critical to promote student success. However, my experience also suggests that students—particularly inexperienced students—may not be able to effectively use those materials in order to truly understand the kinds of thinking, reading, and writing the course demands. Instead, they learn these lessons after several weeks of working through the material and, depending on their credit load and institutional policies about issuing refunds for courses in progress, may choose to remain enrolled in an OWC even after realizing that it might not be the best fit for their learning needs. Thus, providing students with opportunities to practice learning in the format that an OWC might require has the potential to foster a more inclusive environment by helping to align students' expectations with the learning needs that a course demands. For some students, early practice modules might help them to better prepare for the time commitment that an OWC might require. For others, such modules may also allow students to determine that an OWC might not be the best choice for them *before* they have invested significant time, energy, and money into starting a course.

Designing Pre-Course Modules

Here I offer some examples of possible pre-course modules that have the potential to illustrate to students the types of work that is expected in an OWC. These modules are based on my own teaching, as well as on my observations of what other instructors have assigned when I've worked with students in a community college writing center.

Exercise 1

Following Directions

Open a blank Word document. Go to the Purdue OWL MLA Guide at this link: https://owl.purdue.edu/owl/research_and_citation/mla_style/mla_formatting_and_style_guide/mla_formatting_and_style_guide.html

Click on the tab for "General Format" and follow the directions for formatting the first page of a document for Prof. Noname's ENG 1122 course.

Once you are finished, check your document alongside the annotated example available here.

Rationale: Sample Exercise 1 provides one example of a task that can be made available to students prior to enrollment in an OWC to gauge their ability to follow written directions. The initial two steps of following directions and finding important information will help students to see how well they can navigate the types of instructions that they are likely to encounter in an OWC. Following the directions on the Purdue OWL website requires that the student read carefully to find the necessary information on an otherwise crowded website and to apply that information to complete a concrete task. (And while directing students to simply find and duplicate models on a website is, perhaps, not a strong pedagogical move, it is something that I have found students are often expected to do in both F2F and online courses, so it is nonetheless an accurate representation of a potential learning scenario.)

Navigating the syllabus is a bit more complex, as here the student will have to sift through a great deal of material in order to locate the information that is needed. For students who are inexperienced readers, identifying the relationship between different details in a long document (such as a syllabus) can pose a challenge that would be uncovered during the activity.

Exercise 2

Locating Important Information

Open the sample syllabus provided here:

What assignments are due on September 23rd? How much do these assignments count for the overall course grade? Enter your information here and click "submit" when you are finished.

Rationale: The goal of Sample Exercise 2 is for students to assess their level of comfort with locating specific information within one of the course resources. In my own courses, I typically forgo a traditional "syllabus quiz" with questions similar to the ones found here and instead follow Shelley Rodrigo's (2020) advice to assign the reading of important course documents on a shared Google Doc, requiring students to leave questions or comments on the document to indicate their understanding. While this is initially helpful, it is not necessarily a practice that all OWC instructors may adopt. Generally, however, instructors are expected to prepare a syllabus that includes a schedule of assignments and grade distribution. Particularly because some learning management systems can make it difficult for students to see how the material for the course that is located under, say, the "Assignments" tab is conceptually or practically related to the broader course requirements that are outlined on the syllabus, training students to not only read the syllabus but also to *use* the syllabus is an important preparatory step.

Exercise 3

Learning from Multimedia Content

Review the video linked below, which outlines some important steps for completing a rhetorical analysis. Once you have finished watching the video, attempt your own brief rhetorical analysis of the photograph provided below. What is the purpose of the photo? Who is the audience? How does the image use rhetorical appeals to convey its point?

Rationale: Although Hewett (2015) argues that OWCs are primarily text-based courses, instructors are increasingly using multiple modalities to provide instructional content to students (see Costa's [2020] *99 Tips for Creating Simple and Sustainable Educational Videos* for one example). Although students frequently request more audio/visual content, in my own courses and in conversations with colleagues, I have observed that instructors often find that students ignore this instructional content and skip directly to assignments that carry a clear point value. In my courses, I experimented with presenting the majority of content in the form of captioned video lessons and was frustrated to find that, when I checked the analytics on my YouTube page, very few students had even bothered to click the links. What's more, in individual conferences with students about their work, I found that even among those who did watch the material, almost none were able to explain it back to me in a way that revealed any depth of understanding. The latter group of students found this to be particularly frustrating, as they felt sincerely that they had completed the assignment by watching each video through to the end. Yet, it was clear to me that they were not retaining much of the information they watched.

These student experiences are indicative of some of the major disconnects between students and their instructors in OWCs. Students often perceive assignments that carry points differently than they do assignments that contain ungraded instructional content and may fail to recognize their intended connection. Likewise, students who view all of the required instructional material may lack the study skills and metacognitive strategies to distinguish *watching* a video from *learning* the material. Some of this frustration could have potentially been mitigated if students had understood the expectations for *learning* from multimedia content better, as Sample Exercise 3 illustrates. The act of completing a practice exercise and receiving immediate results can help students to recognize some of the different behaviors that actively learning might demand, as well as the relationship between instructional material and assignments that "count" in the gradebook.

Exercise 4

Sample Exercise 4: Working with/from Model Texts

Another common component in composition courses is working with mentor texts that illustrate strengths and areas for potential growth in a sample of writing.

Sample paragraph from Amy Tan's "Mother Tongue"

Defining a Topic Sentence

A strong topic sentence does the following:

Sums up YOUR point in the paragraph: What will you prove with these details?

Uses keywords/phrases to unify the paragraph

Helps the reader to predict what is coming next by inviting questions that the paragraph will answer

Topic Sentences in "Mother Tongue"

Read the example topic sentences below. What questions do they invite for you as the reader? What do you expect the paragraph to PROVE based on the topic sentence?

Example 1

Topic Sentence: Recently, I was made keenly aware of the different Englishes I do use.

Keywords: different Englishes

Predicting What Comes Next: What are the different Englishes that you use? How were you made aware of them?

Here is the full paragraph from Tan's essay. The words in bold indicate some of the details in the paragraph that show WHAT the different Englishes are that Tan uses and HOW she became aware of the difference.

Recently, I was made keenly aware of the different Englishes I do use. I was giving a talk to a large group of people, the same talk I had already given to half a dozen other groups. The nature of the talk was about my writing, my life, and my book, The Joy Luck Club. The talk was going along well enough, until I remembered one major difference that made the whole talk sound wrong. **My mother was in the room. And it was perhaps the first time she had heard me give a lengthy speech, using the kind of English I have never used with her. I was saying things like, "The intersection of memory upon imagination" and "There is an aspect of my fiction that relates to thus-and-thus"—a speech filled with carefully wrought grammatical phrases, burdened, it suddenly seemed to me, with nominalized forms, past perfect tenses, conditional phrases, all the forms of standard English that I had learned in school and through books,** the forms of English I did not use at home with my mother.

Example 2: Try one to practice!

Identify the topic sentence.

Identify any keywords in the topic sentence.

Identify any questions that arise from the topic sentence that help you to predict what comes next.

Mitali often speaks for her older brother and their mother in public when Armen has a tantrum, and passerby think that their mother is unable to discipline her kids. Most children have bad days and throw themselves on the floor to scream and cry when they don't get what they want at a store. For Armen, though, it's different. Because he is unable to speak, this is the only way that he can communicate his feelings to his mom. When this happens and people begin to stare, Mitali will simply look at them and say, "My brother is special, and he needs privacy to show his feelings." This encourages strangers to walk away while also letting them know that Armen acts this way for a reason and that it isn't his mother's fault.

Try it on your own!

Write your own paragraph with a topic sentence. Explain one reason why your favorite restaurant is your favorite. When you are finished, answer the same three questions:

Identify the topic sentence.

Identify any keywords in the topic sentence.

Identify any questions that arise from the topic sentence that help you to predict what comes next.

Rationale: Sample Exercise 4 requires students to learn a concept, study an example of the concept, and then create their own version based on the model. This type of exercise reflects the sorts of cognitive leaps that Joanne Giordano and Cassandra Phillips (2021) indicate may be particularly challenging for academically underprepared students. Certainly, each of the above concerns are common in *all* composition courses. Even in face-to-face settings, some students will ask for clarification about directions for a task without looking at the assignment; some will skip reading that they don't deem to be important; and some will listen intently to a lesson without capturing its primary purpose. In OWCs, however, these problems are compounded in settings that often carry much higher stakes, and the very resources that instructors may use to clarify any misunderstanding (such as written feedback on student work) only serve to further increase the literacy load for the course, again posing a challenge for students who may not be prepared to navigate the volume of written text required for success in the course.

Conclusions and Takeaways

As Borgman and McArdle (2019) note, "the best way to encourage student success is to mitigate confusion" (p. 45). Although this statement was initially intended to describe efforts to make course material accessible, it can also apply to the ways that a WPA may attempt to ensure that students are prepared for the demands of OWI. As noted above, under the guise of providing access for students who may otherwise struggle to fit a college course into their daily lives, OWCs can quickly become inaccessible to the most academically at-risk students, many of whom will anticipate online learning as a way to alleviate a burden rather than add to one. To ensure that OWCs function as a pathway toward accessing higher education and not as a roadblock, it is essential that student-facing resources which illustrate some of the literacy demands of a course be available to students prior to their enrollment so that they can think strategically about how to best meet their own learning needs.

WPAs are in uniquely powerful positions to make large-scale changes based on the information that student-facing modules might reveal about the ways in which students interact with the types of material that are common in OWCs. In departments with standard syllabi, information about how effectively students locate critical information can shape the redesign of these documents. In situations where linking to external sites for instructional material poses a challenge for students, a WPA may be able to argue for the resources needed to develop a programmatic website with material that is designed to meet learners where they are. In cases where either a video or a model text may be insufficient for student learning, WPAs can lead curricular committees dedicated to creating more robust resources that could combine modalities of instruction. Most importantly, however, with the results of pre-course modules for OWI, WPAs can be equipped to more specifically communicate the challenges of OWI to the range of institutional stakeholders who may have a hand in determining the viability of such courses and which students may best benefit from them.

Such an effort shifts the focus from the topics that are often the emphasis in discussions about accessibility and readiness in OWCs. Things such as captioning videos, streamlining the organization of materials, and simplifying directions are often at the forefront of discussion about accessible course design and user experience in OWI. Further, in terms of student readiness, much of the field's existing knowledge is derived from the research in online readiness broadly, which centers on areas such as time management, self-efficacy, motivation, and access to technology. While these are certainly essential components to help ensure student success, more emphasis on how students *learn* in OWI has the potential to help students consider whether or not an OWC is truly providing an accessible experience for them. At minimum, students will need to be able to adapt to the literacy expectations in the following areas:

- Following directions
- Locating and synthesizing important information
- Learning from instructional materials in multiple modalities
- Using a mentor text to guide writing

Rather than providing a broad readiness assessment for students to complete to measure their preparation for online learning, sample exercises that illustrate the way that learning takes place in an OWC can go much further towards ensuring that students who may already struggle with literacy skills or high literacy loads are provided with a low-stakes opportunity to test the waters before determining the course modality that best suits their needs without a WPA having to make the choice for them. What's more, the data from pre-course modules can provide valuable information to a WPA about the online instructional strategies that are/are not effective for learners who, for a variety of reasons, may struggle with the cognitive demands of online writing instruction, thereby opening possibilities for new approaches that could benefit learners who may most *need* the flexibility of an online course.

References

Allen, J. & Seaman, I.E. (2018). Grade increase: Tracking distance education in the United States. *Babson Survey Research Group*. https://eric.ed.gov/?id=ED580852.

Banks, A. J. (2006). *Race, rhetoric, and technology: Searching for higher ground*. Lawrence Erlbaum.

Borgman, J. & McArdle, C. (2019). *Personal, accessible, responsive, strategic: Resources and strategies for online writing instructors*. The WAC Clearinghouse; University Press of Colorado. https://doi.org/10.37514/PRA-B.2019.0322.

CCCC OWI Standing Group. (2021). *The 2021 state of the art of OWI report*. Conference on College Composition and Communication. https://sites.google.com/view/owistandinggroup/state-of-the-art-of-owi-2021.

Conference on College Composition and Communication Committee for Best Practices in Online Writing Instruction. (2011). *Report of the state of the art of OWI*. https://www.owicommunity.org/owi--distance-education-resources.html.

Coombs, N. (2010). *Making online teaching accessible: Inclusive course design for students with disabilities*. Jossey-Bass.

Costa, K. (2020). *99 tips for creating simple and sustainable educational videos: A guide for online teachers and flipped classes*. Stylus.

Downs, D. (2013). What is first-year composition? In R. Malenczyk (Ed.), *A rhetoric for writing program administrators* (pp. 50–63). Parlor Press.

Evans, T. (2019). Managing the OWC user experience by managing student expectations. *Online Literacy Open Resource Effective Practices Journal*. https://gsole.org/olor/ep/2019.05.15.

Fanetti, S., Bushrow, K. M. & DeWeese, D. L. (2010). Closing the gap between high school writing instruction and college writing expectations. *The English Journal*, 99(4), 77–83.

Giordano, J. B. & Phillips, C. (2021). Designing an open-access online writing program: Negotiating tensions between disciplinary ideals and institutional realities. In H. Harris and K. Cole (Eds.), *Transformations: Change work across writing programs, pedagogies, and practices* (pp. 240–258). Utah State University Press.

Griffin, J. & Minter, D. (2013). The rise of the online writing classroom: Reflecting on the material conditions of college composition teaching. *College Composition and Communication*, 65(1), 140–161.

Hachey, A. C., Conway, K. M., Wladis, C. & Karim, S. (2022). Post-secondary online learning in the U.S.: An integrative review of the literature on undergraduate student characteristics. *Journal of Computing in Higher Education: Research & Integration of Instructional Technology*, 34(3), 708–768. https://doi.org/10.1007/s12528-022-09319-0.

Hewett, B. (2015). *Reading to learn and writing to teach: Literacy strategies for online writing instruction*. Bedford/St. Martin's.

Hung, M.-L., Chou, C. & Chen, C.-H. (2010). Learner readiness for online learning: scale development and student perceptions. *Computers & Education*, 55(3), 1080–1090. https://doi.org/10.1016/j.compedu.2010.05.004.

Jonaitis, L. Troubling discourse: Basic writing and computer-mediated technologies. *Journal of Basic Writing*, 31(1), 36–58. https://www.jstor.org/stable/43741085.

Konrad, A. (2021). Access fatigue: The rhetorical work of disability in everyday life. *College English*, Volume 83(3), 179–199. https://library.ncte.org/journals/CE/issues/v83-3/31093

Melonçon, L. & Harris, H. (2015). Preparing students for OWI. In B. L. Hewett & K. E. DePew (Eds.), *Foundational practices of online writing instruction* (pp. 417–444). The WAC Clearinghouse; Parlor Press. https://doi.org/10.37514/PER-B.2015.0650.2.13.

Minter, D. (2015). Administrative decisions for OWI. In B. L. Hewett & K. E. DePew (Eds.), *Foundational practices of online writing instruction* (pp. 217–231). The WAC Clearinghouse; Parlor Press. https://doi.org/10.37514/PER-B.2015.0650.2.06.

Oswal, S. K. (2015). Physical and learning disabilities in OWI. In B. L. Hewett & K. E. DePew (Eds.), *Foundational practices of online writing instruction* (pp. 259–295). The WAC Clearinghouse; Parlor Press. https://doi.org/10.37514/PER-B.2015.0650.2.08.

Reid, L. (2022). Re-assessing "readiness" in OWI: Toward a trauma-informed approach to supporting students in online writing courses. *Computers and Composition*, 66. https://doi.org/10.1016/j.compcom.2022.102738.

Rodrigo, S. & Mitchum, C. (2020). Assign reading major assignment prompts. Teaching Tidbits. https://bit.ly/032320TOTs.

Ruecker, T. (2022). Digital divides in access and use in literacy instruction in rural high schools. *Computers and Composition*, 64, 1–15.

Selfe, C. L. & Selfe, R. J. J. (1994). The politics of the interface: Power and its exercise in electronic contact zones. *College Composition and Communication*, 45(4), 480–504.

Sibo, A. (2021). The literacy load is too damn high!: A PARS approach to cohort-based discussion. In J. Borgman & C. McArdle (Eds.), *PARS in practice: More resources and strategies for online writing instructors* (pp. 71–81). The WAC Clearinghouse; University Press of Colorado. https://doi.org/10.37514/PRA-B.2021.1145.2.04.

Xu, D. & Jaggers, S. (2013). The impact of online learning on students' course outcomes: Evidence from a large community and technical college system. *Economics of Education Review*, 37, 46–57. https://doi.org/10.1016/j.econedurev.2013.08.001.

Warnock, S. & Gasiewski, D. (2018). *Writing together: Ten weeks teaching and studenting in an online writing course*. National Council of Teachers of English.

Reflect and Enjoy Your Round!

Golf is a sport anyone can play. Whether you're just starting out or you're a professional, anyone can pick up a club and play. While golf has not traditionally been an inclusive sport, it's moving in that direction, and now we see people from all over the world playing golf. All ages, races, genders, etc. can now participate in the game of golf as a hobby or with a more ambitious goal in mind (like becoming a pro golfer). Inclusivity is very important, especially in leadership and online writing instruction (OWI). What we like about Joanne Baird Giordano and Cassandra Phillips' chapter is that they continue this conversation of inclusivity with a specific focus on community colleges, where there tends to be less access to many things, specifically technological things like computers and internet.

We really like how Giordano and Phillips' chapter utilizes a reverse design process that supports creating inclusive online learning spaces that support students from community colleges who have experienced educational inequities at previous institutions. We also like how the connection to the PARS approach allows the authors to build open-access online courses in a way that engages students and includes them in the learning process, rather than creating a space that excludes.

Chapter 19. Inclusive, Equitable, and Responsive Strategies for Redesigning Open-Access Online Literacy Courses

Joanne Baird Giordano
SALT LAKE COMMUNITY COLLEGE

Cassandra Phillips
UNIVERSITY OF WISCONSIN MILWAUKEE AT WAUKESHA

Abstract: This chapter is for instructors, disciplinary course developers, and course leads who are working on improving processes and practices for developing online literacy courses for students who are inexperienced with both online learning and academic literacy. We describe a backward design process for developing equitable and inclusive writing and reading courses that support learners from diverse educational backgrounds at two-year colleges and other open-access institutions. We define equitable and inclusive course design, and we describe considerations for developing online literacy courses and adapting PARS to courses in programs without admission standards. We then outline a six-step backward design process for creating open-access online model courses that build in scaffolded and inclusive learning support with accompanying reflective questions to help online faculty adapt the process to their own teaching contexts.

Keywords: access, equity, inclusion, course design process, literacy development

In our work as two-year college online course developers and program coordinators at multiple institutions, we have long been tasked with developing online courses for students with greatly varying cultural and linguistic backgrounds, educational experiences, and literacy needs. Together, we designed and coordinated a statewide, open-access online writing program. While we now teach at different two-year institutions, we continue our work in developing, teaching, and mentoring instructors in online literacy programs. We frequently teach students who would be inadmissible at four-year institutions and whose only option for college is taking courses through an open-access online program. For community colleges, *open-access* means that all adult learners regardless of their educational and literacy backgrounds can participate in higher education. In this chapter, we hope to contribute to disciplinary conversations about online program design principles with a focus on creating equitable learning opportunities for students who have traditionally been excluded from higher education outside of open-access institutions.

Equitable and inclusive course design supports learning and literacy development for all students enrolled in an online writing course regardless of their linguistic, educational, and cultural backgrounds or their prior experiences with online learning. In open-access online courses, students experience inequities when the design of a course, the assignments, and the teaching practices create barriers to course completion, online learning, and their postsecondary literacy development. Courses can also be inequitable when they are designed for students who meet selective admissions standards but not for students who are taking the course. We define *equitable online course design* as an approach to developing, assessing, and redesigning courses using strategies that account for the inequities and barriers that some students previously faced before college and often continue to experience in higher education. Erin L. Castro (2015) explains that "equity in higher education is the idea that students from historically and contemporarily marginalized and minoritized communities have access to what they need in order to be successful" (p. 6). Equitable course design aligns the structure, assignments, activities, teaching practices, and resources of a course with the learning needs of students from the communities that an online course serves. Similarly, we define *inclusive online course design* as strategically building support into courses to help students complete the course, develop as college readers and writers, do their best learning, and participate fully within an online community that values their diverse cultural, linguistic, and social identities. Equitable course design also takes into consideration the working conditions and workloads of instructors who teach in a program.

Equitable and inclusive course design strategies are essential for any online program with diverse student learning needs, but they are especially crucial at community colleges and open-access institutions. Administrators, course developers, and faculty in open-access contexts need online course design strategies that account for students who aren't in other higher education spaces because admission standards don't permit them to enroll, they can't attend in-person courses, or they can't afford four-year tuition and the cost of living away from home. Professionals in online two-year college English programs also need to expand their definitions of program administration beyond writing courses to include other types of open-access literacy education, which (depending on the institution) might include developmental writing, reading, integrated reading and writing, corequisite support, and English for speakers of other languages courses.

This chapter describes a framework for designing online literacy courses to support community college learners who have experienced inequities in their prior educational experiences and who need effective, inclusive, and culturally responsive (Chávez & Longerbeam, 2016) online courses to help them transition to college learning. We use the term *literacy courses* because many two-year college programs include integrated reading and writing, developmental education, corequisite support, and other types of courses that go beyond a traditional degree-credit writing program. This chapter explains how to apply backward design principles (Wiggins & McTighe, 2005) to open-access online literacy programs. Our goal is to provide disciplinary course developers, lead instructors, and faculty with strategies for designing equitable online literacy courses that align with Borgman and McArdle's PARS framework. Equitable course design is essential for creating online educational opportunities for students who need intensive learning support to successfully complete online courses and develop as college readers and writers.

Theory and Practice

Online Literacy Courses at Two-Year Colleges

Open-access, two-year college writing programs arguably serve the broadest range of students with the most diverse learning needs in higher education. Community colleges enroll students from diverse educational, linguistic, and cultural backgrounds. These students often experience educational equity gaps as they transition to college learning. Almost half of students in the United States take courses at community colleges as they work toward a degree (Community College Research Center, n.d.). Even before the COVID-19 pandemic, approximately two million community college students took distance education courses each year, with 37 percent taking at least some online coursework and 15 percent taking only distance education courses (Community College Research Center, n.d.). Studies from the Community College Research Center suggest that success rates are lower for community college students who enroll in online courses, especially developmental English (Jaggars & Xu, 2011, 2016). Because online courses are text-heavy and reading-intensive, they are especially challenging for inexperienced college readers (Martirosyan et al., 2021).

Despite the large and growing numbers of community college students taking online courses, writing studies as a field offers significantly more resources for designing online courses at four-year institutions compared to community colleges. Beth L. Hewett (2015) describes the development of the 2013 CCCC OWI principles as

> a story that admits of uncertainty and a need for *A Position Statement of Principles and Example Effective Practices for OWI* to be organic; changing with research, scholarship, and experience; and one to which the practitioners in the field can contribute as well as from which they can benefit. (p. 37)

The field needs to add to the story that Hewett describes with more research about practices that support online learning for students who can't be admitted to most institutions. For example, online practitioners who teach and design courses at community colleges typically rely more heavily on empirical data related to student success outcomes and retention and less on theories about how online teaching works in other contexts.

Online teaching is a normal part of workload for a large percentage of two-year college English faculty. In a Two-Year College English Association (TYCA) survey, 59 percent of respondents reported that they previously taught asynchronous online courses before the COVID-19 pandemic, and 45 percent taught online synchronous courses before the pandemic (Tinoco et al., 2022). A pre-pandemic TYCA survey suggests that online teaching is a preferred instructional modality for helping some two-year college English instructors manage a teaching-intensive workload that is typically five or more courses (or 30 credits) each semester; however, other respondents reported that they avoid online teaching because of workload issues (Giordano & Wegner, 2020). Because online teaching at an open-access institution is labor-intensive work that requires professional expertise, the TYCA "White Paper on Two-Year College Faculty Workload" recommends providing adjunct instructors with course development shells to reduce workload while also providing professional training for online teaching and compensation for faculty who develop online courses (Giordano et al., 2022, p. 298). Equitable online course design work for open-access literacy programs requires a complex and challenging balance between the intensive high needs of students and the teaching-intensive and often underpaid workloads for faculty.

Adapting the PARS Model for Open-Access Courses

In programs without admissions standards, students need online courses that are strategically designed to support successful course completion. Writing courses are almost universally required for receiving a college degree in the United States, and every open-access online program enrolls students who have limited (or even no) experience with academic reading and writing, college success strategies, and the knowledge required for independently navigating online learning. While all online literacy courses benefit from course design that reflects the PARS framework (personal, accessible, responsive, and strategic), the stakes for applying the basic principles of PARS are higher for course developers and faculty at community colleges and other open-access institutions.

Because of equity issues for both instructors and students, we argue that open-access institutions need to provide instructors with carefully designed standardized model courses (sometimes called development shells, pre-designed courses, or template courses) in a learning management system (LMS) that uses inclusive disciplinary teaching strategies and provides a curricular program structure that supports transfer between courses. These models provide instructors with a completely developed course that they can then adapt and personalize over time as they respond to student needs. Online community college instructors typically work off the tenure track with high teaching loads and often for more than one institution (Suh et al., 2021). Their compensation rarely accounts for labor-intensive work required for designing multiple effective online courses that support equitable learning for students (Giordano et al., 2022). Instructors also need a shared understanding of the curriculum in relation to the local literacy needs of students. An additional benefit of using model courses is that many students take more than one online course, and consistency across courses lets students focus on literacy development and transitions to more complex reading, writing, and research (instead of navigating how the class works).

Students benefit when PARS principles are purposefully embedded into the design of a course and across an entire program to support learning and literacy development for online students with diverse needs. Table 19.1 gives an overview of concepts for adapting the PARS approach to open-access online courses.

Table 19.1. The PARS Approach for Open-Access Online Courses

Personal	Students' diverse literacy needs require individualized learning support. Many students at open-admissions institutions can't transition to online learning without a personalized approach to course design and interaction with an instructor.
Accessible	Model courses need to account for accessibility for students who are inexperienced with online learning, including consistent structure in modules, multiple ways of learning, clear assignment instructions, support for technology, appropriate reading level in course materials, and access to institutional support resources.
Responsive	Incorporating repeated and systematically responsive instruction into a model course is an essential component of open-access literacy course design, especially in courses for students who are inexperienced with both academic literacy and online learning. Courses need to build in opportunities for instructors to respond to student learning needs in varied ways across a course and an entire program.
Strategic	Open-access course design needs to strategically respond to vastly diverse student literacy needs across multiple courses, create an equitable and inclusive learning environment, and support student transitions between courses.

Creating a Course Design Plan

The starting point for redesigning an equitable online literacy program is creating a plan to guide systematic, cohesive changes (or the development of new courses). This can include mapping out the entire program as well as planning for individual courses. Backward design (i.e., backward planning or mapping) is a process for creating courses around learning goals or outcomes to help students apply learning from one situation to a new context (Wiggins & McTighe, 2005). The term *backward* describes a course design process that starts with the student learning goals for the end of a course or program. Developers or faculty work backward through the course or program from the end to the beginning, creating assignments and activities that help students achieve learning goals. Grant Wiggins and Jay McTighe (2005) outline three stages of the backward design process:

- Identify desired results. (What learning goals will students work toward achieving?)
- Determine acceptable evidence for assessing student learning. (What assignments and activities will help students achieve and demonstrate the goals of the course and help instructors assess their learning?)
- Plan learning experiences and instruction. (What activities will help students work toward achieving course goals and complete major assignments?)

Backward design has become a standard practice for online course development, but it's especially important for literacy courses at open-access institutions. Inexperienced college readers, writers, and online learners need a structured approach to literacy instruction that helps them gradually develop increasingly more complex skills and strategies that will help them become successful college students, transfer between courses, and complete writing requirements for attaining a degree. However, backward design can reproduce inequities when the process is used to maintain unachievable standards, weed students out of higher ed, or reinforce teaching practices that are misaligned with open-access education. For this reason, online literacy programs benefit from an equity-focused (Chardin & Nowak, 2021), entire program backward design approach that takes students from the first day of a developmental (or ESL) course through to the last writing course required for an associate's degree or transfer within a state system. Administrators and participating faculty can create a program-level plan for redesigning courses to support inclusive and equitable online learning opportunities for students even when individual courses will be created or revised separately over time.

Any effective backward design process that combines inclusive pedagogy with disciplinary practices can support equitable learning opportunities for all students. However, a systematic, program-level approach to course design is especially crucial for students who are inexperienced with academic literacy and/or online learning. For open-access online literacy programs, course design is problematic when individual courses are developed in isolation from other courses without consideration for the learning that students need to do in their initial writing and reading course to prepare them for subsequent courses and online learning in other disciplines. Because community college students bring varied experiences with language and literacy to online courses, program administrators and participating faculty need to plan for ways to reduce educational inequities and provide consistent learning support for students who would otherwise have difficulty transitioning into and between courses. The following steps and planning questions describe a backward design process for (re)designing an online literacy program to close equity gaps between courses.

Step 1: Identify and evaluate program-level learning outcomes (or goals).

The first step in a program-level backward redesign process is to examine existing program-level student learning outcomes—or to create new ones if they don't exist. Typically, this part of the process includes collaboration with everyone who teaches in an online program. Programs that don't already have learning outcomes that focus on online and digital literacies (National Council of Teachers of English, 2019) can develop them to create a structure for supporting students' transitions to online learning (for example, goals for reading digital texts or engaging in virtual discussions). Program faculty might also collaboratively identify course outcomes that create barriers to student course completion in their teaching context and then make adjustments to outcomes to make them more equitable. The questions in Table 19.2 can help you assess which program-level learning outcomes might be added, removed, or modified to support students' development as college readers and writers in your online teaching environment.

Table 19.2 Questions for Developing Program-Level Outcomes

- Which literacy courses are required for students to attain a degree in your state system? What are the learning goals of those courses?
- What are the most challenging barriers that students face in completing the writing program? Where do those challenges occur in the writing program sequence?
- What are the most important reading, writing, and research strategies that students need to achieve by the end of the writing program to help them be successful college students?
- What literacy skills and strategies help inexperienced students successfully complete reading-intensive and writing-intensive courses at your institution, receive a degree, and transfer to another institution?

The questions in Table 19.3 provide a starting point for discussing how student learning goals for each course fit within the outcomes for an overall online program.

Table 19.3. Questions for Planning Course Learning Outcomes for a Program

- What challenges do students experience in completing writing program requirements? What barriers make it challenging for some students to successfully transition between courses in your program, especially for online students?
- What needs to happen in first-year writing so that students can successfully transition to sophomore courses if they are required by your institution or by transfer institutions?
- What needs to happen in developmental writing, reading, integrated reading and writing, and/or ESL courses to help students successfully transition to first-year writing?

Step 2: Assess, create, and/or revise learning outcomes for each course, starting with the last and ending with the first.

One effective way to get a big picture view of student learning across an entire program is to create a single document that maps out outcomes for each course in the order that students take their coursework online. However, the process for developing the outcomes themselves begins with the final required course (or set of courses if students have more than one choice to fulfill degree requirements). First, identify the literacy skills and strategies students need to develop in the final course to achieve the overall goals of the program. Next, work backward through the learning goals of each course to the first course in the online program. Prioritize essential learning goals that students need to achieve to successfully move between courses and become successful college readers and writers in a virtual environment instead of focusing on small module or lesson-level objectives. For online courses, it's important to think through the order in which students work on learning outcomes in each course to facilitate the process of designing and updating standardized courses. Finally, after mapping out each course, examine the entire sequence of learning outcomes across the program to make sure that they are aligned and provide students with a carefully structured plan for moving from the first day of the first course to the final week of the last course. Table 19.4 has questions to guide the process of developing equitable course-level learning outcomes.

Table 19.4. Revising or Creating Equitable Course Learning Outcomes

- How are students placed into the course, and how do your placement processes shape the community of learners who take the course? How might you account for the individualized and diverse literacy needs of students who are placed into the course, self-select it, or move into it from earlier courses?
- What learning gaps (if any) make it difficult for students to successfully complete the course after taking previous courses in the writing program sequence? How might you address these gaps through revised or new learning outcomes?
- What learning outcomes for online learning, technology, and digital literacy are important for helping students successfully complete this course and prepare to take the next online or hybrid course?
- Does the course have learning objectives that reinforce inequities for students based on their educational or linguistic backgrounds? How might you change those outcomes and/or build in support for achieving them to provide individualized support for struggling students?
- Are the outcomes for the course realistic and attainable for students in your teaching context? What adjustments do you need to make to your program to create course goals that students can reasonably achieve with the time and resources available to them in your program?

Step 3: Create a backward design writing project plan for the entire online program.

A program-level assignment design process creates a basic overview of major projects for each course, which focuses activities on helping students transition between courses. For open-access online literacy education, it's important that the assignments students complete in earlier courses prepare them for learning in subsequent courses. Table 19.5 shows an example of a writing project design plan that supports students' literacy development across a program by introducing literacy skills and strategies that students will build on in later courses.

Table 19.5. Designing Writing Projects Across an Online Program

Focus	Developmental	First-Year Writing	Sophomore Writing
Personal Literacy Practices	Essay exploring prior experiences with reading and writing	Essay analyzing students' own literacy practices in relation to their cultural backgrounds	Essay that responds to texts about literacy, using examples from personal literacy practices
Textual Analysis	Essay analyzing evidence that an author uses to support an argument	Essay analyzing the rhetorical strategies of a website	Essay analyzing several texts from a field of study to draw conclusions about disciplinary writing conventions
Source-Based Writing	Project based on a self-selected issue from course texts	Project based on independent research	Project exploring research and writing practices for a field of study
Self-Assessment	Essay self-assessing learning from the course	Essay analyzing examples from a portfolio to self-assess literacy development	Essay self-assessing literacy development, using examples from both inside and outside the course

Step 4: Create a program-level plan for online learning activities.

A program approach to developing and structuring learning activities supports students who start in basic courses as they transition to more challenging courses and allows them to focus on literacy development rather than requiring them to navigate a completely different course structure. Consider the types of online learning activities that students need to do across the program to successfully complete each major project while also developing as college readers and writers. One effective way to support inexperienced students in online courses is to design modules (or units) and activities so that they have the same structure in

Inclusive, Equitable, and Responsive Strategies   293

every course. For example, an online writing program might include a module structure described in Table 19.6 for all courses.

Table 19.6. Learning Activity Plan Example

Module Section	Purpose
Module introduction	Overview, instructor video, suggested schedule, learning to-do list, etc.
Learning pages	One or more pages focusing on reading and writing strategy topics for the module with definitions, how-tos, videos, and links to resources
Reading assignment	Introduction to readings, links or page numbers for the assignment, and comprehension or analysis questions
Reading discussion	Discussion about texts focusing on reading and writing strategies introduced in the module and reinforcing learning from previous modules (and often helping students analyze sources for a writing project)
Writing workshop	Informal discussion for sharing ideas and receiving feedback on the current project or formal peer review
Review	A page that helps students bring together learning from the module, connect the module to their writing projects, and prepare for the next module

A program plan like this one for online learning activities provides students with a familiar structure as they engage in increasingly more complex literacy tasks over time. The questions in Table 19.7 can also help you use a PARS approach in designing a program-level learning activity plan.

Table 19.7. Questions for Creating an Online Learning Activity Plan

Personal	What types of learning activities across the program will create a personalized experience for students and provide them with inclusive opportunities for learning?
Accessible	What types of activities will reduce barriers to course completion for online students? What is an equitable way to structure learning across the program to make courses accessible?
Responsive	What types of learning activities help build structured opportunities for responsive feedback and frequent instructor interaction into each course? When does responsive interaction need to happen to support student learning?
Strategic	What are the most important considerations for strategically developing learning activities across the program to reduce equity gaps for students and increase student success?

Step 5: Plan for sequenced instruction and learning support within each course.

The most labor-intensive part of an online course redesign process is developing instructional content and learning activities for each course. This includes creating learning opportunities to move students through each writing project; guide them in developing college-level literacy strategies; provide them with individualized, responsive support; and help them achieve the goals of the course. However, this work can take place in stages over several semesters, or different teams of faculty can work on separate online courses using the work developed in the program-level course design process.

In an online literacy course, one of the most important strategies for creating an inclusive and equitable open-access learning environment is to carefully sequence and scaffold instruction and activities with a focus on students who might otherwise struggle to complete each course. The practices described in Table 19.8 can help developers and faculty create courses that support learning for inexperienced online learners.

Table 19.8. Sequencing and Scaffolding Instruction

Strategy	Course Design Activities
Sequence activities strategically.	Order activities to guide students from basic reading, writing, research, and online learning skills to complex and challenging activities.
Build in support for online learning.	Provide low-stakes activities that help students practice using the LMS and digital tools that they will use later in a course for graded assignments.
Break projects into manageable steps.	Break projects into manageable learning tasks to model effective writing processes and help students complete each stage of an assignment with feedback and support from the instructor and the class.
Include recursive instruction.	Loop back to previous literacy skills to give students time to develop strategies for college reading and writing. Include links to pages from previous modules that discuss strategies that students need to use for subsequent, more challenging activities.
End with literacy skills from the next course.	Build in time at the end of the course to help students practice the reading and writing strategies that they will use in the next writing course.
Anticipate the needs of inexperienced readers.	Start with the assumption that some students will struggle with online reading. Write activity and assignment instructions using clear, transparent language at a reading level that is lower than course reading assignments.
Provide multiple methods for learning.	Create multiple ways for students to learn about college reading and writing strategies at an individual level through supplemental resources, along with opportunities for receiving support through discussions and writing workshops.

After designing individual learning activities, it's important to examine the overall course structure to determine whether each component supports learning and literacy development for online students in your local context. The questions in Table 19.9 can help you use an equitable and inclusive approach to embedding learning support into a course.

Table 19.9. Questions for Developing Learning Support

Personal	What activities early in the course can help students develop a sense of belonging in an online learning community? What varied activities throughout the course provide inclusive opportunities for student engagement?
Accessible	What are the most challenging points in the course that create barriers to course completion? What types of activities, instructional support, and resources reduce barriers for the student communities that the course serves?
Responsive	At what points in the course do struggling students most need opportunities for individualized instruction and instructor feedback through discussion activities, virtual workshops, and conferences?
Strategic	How do individual components of the course work together to support student learning and help struggling online learners develop as college readers and writers? What changes need to happen to create consistent, equitable opportunities for students to receive learning support?

Step 6: Assess course revisions for student success and equity over time.
Develop a written plan for assessing the effectiveness of changes to each course, and involve all online program instructors with an opportunity to provide feedback on course changes. Systematic assessment using multiple measures of data helps with ongoing planning for subsequent revisions to the program. A course redesign assessment plan might include some of the following activities: examining institutional data about online success outcomes (disaggregated by student communities), reviewing course LMS data about engagement and assignment completion, and assessing students' end-of-semester assignments to determine their progress toward achieving course goals. Inclusive assessment activities also include feedback from instructors through discussions in a meeting, a survey, written reflections, or focus groups. Courses might also provide a learning activity that asks students to assess their experiences in the course and share recommendations for potential changes. The questions in Table 19.10 can guide you through the process of assessing the inclusivity of student-centered course revisions.

Table 19.10. Reflective Questions for Assessing Redesign Work

Personal	How do course revisions provide students from diverse backgrounds with opportunities for learning that address their individual literacy needs? What further changes might increase success for struggling students?
Accessible	To what extent do revisions reduce barriers to course completion, learning, and literacy development? How might future revisions address ongoing barriers that make online learning difficult for some students?
Responsive	How do the course revisions provide structured opportunities for students to receive instructor support and feedback? What adjustments might help instructors provide responsive support?
Strategic	What does your assessment process show about future changes to make to the program and course to increase equitable learning opportunities for students?

Conclusion and Takeaways

The redesign process outlined in this chapter can be used in any online writing program to support students' literacy development. One takeaway from our program design work is that equitable online course design processes are aligned with the locally situated learning needs of students based on the mission of a program and the communities that it serves. A program-level plan for online teaching helps students who need intensive learning support thrive in online environments throughout a sequence of multiple courses. Another takeaway is that embedding equity and inclusion into model courses provides a foundation that guides instructors through creating online conditions for learning that support literacy development for all students regardless of their educational backgrounds. And finally, the design process that we describe creates a structure across a program that can reduce workload and free up time for instructors to focus on the needs of their students. They can then work to adapt a model course to fit their own teaching needs over time.

References

Borgman, J. & McArdle, C. (2019). *Personal, accessible, responsive, strategic: Resources and strategies for online writing instructors*. The WAC Clearinghouse; University Press of Colorado. https://doi.org/10.37514/PRA-B.2019.0322.

Castro, E. L. (2015). Addressing the conceptual challenges of equity work: A blueprint for getting started. In E. L. Castro (Ed.), *Understanding equity in community college practice* (pp. 5–12). Jossey-Bass.

Chardin, C. & Nowak, K. (2021). *Equity by design: Delivering on the power and promise of UDL*. Corwin Press.

Chávez, A. F. & Longerbeam, S. D. (2016). *Teaching across cultural strengths: A guide to balancing integrated and individualized cultural frameworks in college teaching.* Stylus.

Community College Research Center. (n.d.). *Community college FAQs.* https://ccrc.tc.columbia.edu/community-college-faqs.html.

Giordano, J. B. & Wegner, M. (2020). *TYCA working paper #3: Workload management strategies for teaching English at two-year colleges.* Two-Year College English Association. https://ncte.org/wp-content/uploads/2020/11/TYCA_Working_Paper_3.pdf.

Hewett, B. L. (2015). Grounding principles of OWI. In B. L. Hewitt & K. E. DePew (Eds.), *Foundational practices of online writing instruction* (pp. 33–92). The WAC Clearinghouse; Parlor Press. https://doi.org/10.37514/PER-B.2015.0650.2.01.

Jaggars, S. S. & Xu, D. (2010). Online learning in the Virginia community college system.

Jaggars, S. S. & Xu, D. (2016). How do online course design features influence student performance? *Computers & Education, 95,* 270–284. https://doi.org/10.1016/j.compedu.2016.01.014.

Martirosyan, N. M., Saxon, D. P. & Skidmore, S. T. (2021). Online developmental education instruction: Challenges and instructional practices according to the practitioners. *Journal of College Academic Support Programs, 3*(4), 12–23.

National Council of Teachers of English (2019). *Definition of literacy in a digital age.* https://ncte.org/statement/nctes-definition-literacy-digital-age/.

Suh, E., Giordano, J. B., Griffiths, B., Hassel, H. & Klausman, J. (2021). The profession of teaching English in the two-year college: Findings from the 2019 TYCA workload survey. *Teaching English in the Two-Year College, 48*(3), 332–349.

Tinoco, L., Suh, E., Giordano, J. B. & Hassel, H. (2022). *The COVID-19 pandemic and workload: Results from a national TYCA survey.* Two-Year College English Association. https://ncte.org/wp-content/uploads/2022/03/COVID-19-Pandemic-Workload-Results-from-a-National-TYCA-Survey.pdf.

Two-Year College Association (TYCA) (2022). White paper on two-year college faculty workload. *Teaching English in the Two-Year College, 49*(4), 292–307.

Wiggins, G. & McTighe, J. (2005). *Understanding by design.* Association for Supervision and Curriculum Development.

Nice work, the round is complete!

Golf courses are, by design, meant to be difficult to navigate as you hit a ball. While it can be difficult for your shots to find fairways and greens, they are not supposed to be difficult to navigate when it comes to walking or riding the course! Golf courses can be somewhere in the middle of nowhere, on a single island or the side of a cliff, spread out stretching miles and miles of land, or they can be squished in between housing developments, shopping centers, and restaurants.

Navigating complex institutional processes for faculty can be difficult, even when it is your job. Remember when you were a grad student and you were trying to learn how to navigate a curriculum you were attempting to learn and potentially a new curriculum you were attempting to teach? It was/is not easy!

We really like how in this chapter Heidi Skurat Harris and Rhonda Thomas ground their structure of interaction and support of grad students via PARS. It provides a guide for administrators to help navigate students through complex pathways constructed by the institution in a way that supports rather than confuses.

Chapter 20. Wayfinding in Distance Learning: Finding Our Way Through Times of Stress in Online Writing Graduate Programs

Heidi Skurat Harris and Rhonda Thomas
UNIVERSITY OF ARKANSAS AT LITTLE ROCK

Abstract: When designing online writing (OW) programs and web-based instructional environments, we need to ensure we design for human ways of behaving. By being personal and strategic in how they engage students in the program, online writing program administrators can help graduate students wayfind and change course when necessary, and assist them in constructing mental maps of their learning process in both courses and programs.

Keywords: wayfinding, user-centered design, human-centered design, cognition, graduate students

In *Personal, Accessible, Responsive, Strategic: Resources and Strategies for Online Writing Instructors* (hereafter referred to as *The PARS Approach*), authors Jessie Borgman and Casey McArdle (2019) introduced their model of online writing instruction (OWI), that is, a "*version* of teaching" (p. vii). Along with colleagues George Jensen and Karen Kuralt, we contributed to Borgman and McArdle's follow-up to *The PARS Approach*: the 2021 edited collection *PARS in Practice: More Resources and Strategies for Online Writing Instructors* (hereafter referred to as *PARS in Practice*). To help teachers and administrators "forge strong personal connections with and among their online students," Thomas et al. (2021) shared research collected from students and alumni of their three fully online programs at the University of Arkansas at Little Rock (UALR): the BA and MA in Professional and Technical Writing and the Online Writing Instruction Graduate Certificate program (p. 185; see Borgman & McArdle, 2019, p. 18).

We build on our 2021 *PARS in Practice* contribution by mapping ways that online writing program administrators (OWPAs),[1] writing instructors, and course designers can build personal connections with learners to personalize the learner's experience. Our user-centric design draws from all components of *The PARS Approach* but focuses primarily on the need to make all-important

---

1. Hereafter, when we refer to the OWPA, this reference extends to advisors, course designers, and writing instructors (both current and new faculty, writing teachers, or teachers of writing-intensive classes).

personal (*P*) connections with learners, and offers a strategy (*S*) for operationalizing this process.

As an associate professor and graduate coordinator in the Department of Rhetoric and Writing at UALR, Heidi has advised and mentored hundreds of students and designed and delivered 20 different online writing courses. As such, Heidi is not only an expert WPA/OWPA but also an expert at designing user-centered web-based writing programs and courses. Drawing from her ongoing user-centered design (UCD) research and practical experience, Heidi provides a way forward to designing writing programs and web-based courses that reflect an understanding of "what users need" by incorporating "interfaces, products, and experiences that meet those needs" (Greer & Skurat Harris, 2018, p. 14).

One of the many students Heidi advised and mentored for nearly five years was Rhonda—a fully online student of OWI at UALR. After completing UALR's MA in Professional and Technical Writing and Online Writing Instruction Graduate Certificate (OWIGC), Rhonda completed the Master of Science in Education-Digital Age Learning and Educational Technology program at Johns Hopkins University. After successfully completing writing-intense web-based courses for well over a decade, Rhonda offers insights on human-centered design. As an end-user of web-based environments, Rhonda's insights are important because, as Peter Morville (2009) observes, user experience (UX) designers often "maintain *empathy for the user* as a matter of faith" for the simple reason that they rarely get to "see the personal impact of their work" (p. 15).

That "personal impact" is achieved through direct instruction and through program administration: It should be seen and felt in instructional materials, assignment descriptions, and communications between faculty, students, and administrators. This is because, in addition to taking in higher volumes of reading and writing, online learners spend substantial time finding their way through our information-built writing environments and deciphering our instructional messaging.[2] If our web-based environment is poorly designed, we risk our learners becoming disoriented—that is, they become *lost*. The implication of their becoming lost is that they switch off. When learners switch off, learning potential is arrested. In this chapter, we offer practical techniques OWPAs can apply to their OWI programs and courses that work to keep web-based learners switched on and oriented—techniques that promote the continuous forging of personal connections and that provide the user feedback needed to continuously improve our web-based educational offerings.

The practical techniques we offer in this chapter are presented through the lens of Rhonda's recent examination of a particular human behavior: *wayfinding*.

---

2. Mayer and Alexander [Use full names. Missing from reference list](2017) define an instructional message as "a communication intended to promote learning ... words are verbal representations, such as printed text (delivered on a page or screen) or spoken text (delivered face-to-face or via speakers)" (p. 483).

Reginald Golledge (1999) explains, "Wayfinding is the process of determining and following a path or route between an origin and a destination. It is a purposive, directed, and motivated activity" (p. 6). Thomas (2022) proposes that unimpeded wayfinding is critical to student success in web-based learning. To drive home how important she believes it is, she compares wayfinding to breathing:

> If breathing is what allows us to *be alive*, wayfinding is what allows us to *stay alive*—by permitting us to *benefit from* our spatial environment . . . by driving our physical locomotion through it. Just as we would lose the ability to live if we suddenly found we could no longer breathe, we would lose the ability to stay alive if we lost the ability to wayfind. (p. 10)

Rhonda suggests that the same cognitive processes used to make decisions on how we will move through three-dimensional environments extend to environments that exist only in the mind—such as web-based instructional environments—and that learning and knowledge transfer are embodied in the natural operations of wayfinding. When we design web-based instructional environments that impede wayfinding, we risk learners becoming lost in our multimodal web of instructional information; at the very least, we will cause learners unnecessary anxiety.

Theory and Practice

As many of us know, the brain struggles to process information and learn when it is under stress. The Student Experience in the Research University (SERU) Consortium survey, which investigated the state of student mental health during the COVID-19 pandemic, reveals that students who did not adapt well to remote instruction were 1.5 times more likely to develop generalized anxiety disorder, and emphasizes that, for "graduate and professional students," this number doubled from 2019 to 2020 (Chirikov et al., 2020, p. 1). Of the 15,346 graduate and professional students surveyed from nine public research universities, "32% . . . screened positive for major depressive disorder, while 39% of undergraduate and graduate and professional students screened positive for generalized anxiety disorder" (Chirikov et al., 2020, p. 1).

Losing Our Way: How Did We Get Here?

The fact remains that all graduate students—even the two-thirds who did not develop an anxiety or depressive disorder—must still find their way through, what is for them, the uncharted territory of graduate programs. Most schools or universities provide an orientation in the form of an information dump at the beginning of the student's enrollment. This practice highlights a program design flaw: University and college systems are designed to provide information, not directions. Moreover, even well-written instructions can be full of references to strange-sounding acronyms, personnel titles, and unfamiliar campus locations with illogical names, such as *bursar*. Indeed, before their first day of college, many students are unlikely to have ever encountered a *bursar* out in the wilds of their everyday lived experiences. Directing learners to Records and Registration does little to help them find their way, particularly when they are already feeling the stress induced by being in unfamiliar terrain.

The online graduate student not only deals with all the same issues as the student attending face-to-face classes, but she might live in California and attend a program in Arkansas, where she may not even step on campus until graduation. For distance learners, the university's chosen web-based course management system (CMS) is the closest they will ever come to sitting in a classroom amongst peers. Most of their encounters with others will take place within the CMS. These learners will not be able to simply swing by their professor's office to get a quick answer to a question, grab a coffee with a fellow student, or run over to financial aid to check on the status of an application. Indeed, their entire academic experience is guided by their mental representations of the web-based instructional environments we design for them—environments that exist only in their minds. As such, our learners are at the receiving end of every design decision we make, at both the program level and the course design level.

Lost in Cognitive Space

As highlighted above, a web-based instructional environment exists in the mind. This means that how we design these environments and how we present instructional information in them has a direct bearing on how the environment is constructed and represented in the mind of the learner. In other words, the instructional environment takes on a particular shape, or form, in the mind of the learner as a result of both the learner's prior experience and the information and modalities we select to design the space (Morville, 2009). As Heidi Skurat Harris and Michael Greer (2016) observe, "Technology—including large-scale commercial course management systems—is never neutral. Any digital platform designs and shapes spatial and temporal relations among users" (p. 47). Why does this matter? When learners cannot make sense of our web-based instructional environment, they become lost. When learners become lost, they switch off. When learners switch off, learning stops.

The Implications of Being Lost

"Lost is a state of mind" (Thomas, 2022, pg. 22). Disorientation occurs as a result of how we *feel* about where we are, not about where we *actually* are. When we don't recognize where we are, we feel confused, which induces the unpleasant emotions of fear, panic, and anxiety. Learners feel lost in poorly designed web-based instructional spaces because these spaces hinder their ability to construct, from our multimodal instructional information, an environmental image—a logical "neural structure and the representation of a particular environment" (O'Keefe & Nadel, 1978, p. 7). If learners are unable to "visualize" our environment, then they cannot cognitively map it to their particular versions of reality, which is necessary for them to find their way through it. In his landmark work, *The Image of the City*, Kevin Lynch (1960) explains that the "strategic link" between becoming lost and not becoming lost is our ability to build this environmental image, which is a

> generalized mental picture of the exterior physical world that is held by an individual. This image is the product both of immediate sensation and of the memory of past experience, and it is used to interpret information and to guide action. The need to recognize and pattern our surroundings is so crucial, and has such long roots in the past, that this image has wide practical and emotional importance to the individual. (p. 4)

The web-based instructional environments we design may be located in the digital distance, but they are still part of our physical world. Moreover, to our human minds, the experiences we have in these spaces are "very real" (Rosenfeld et al., 2015, p. 17). Indeed, these *environments of the mind*, like three-dimensional space, have a sort of psychogeography that impacts "the emotions and behavior of individuals" (Tate, n.d.).

Finding Our Way in the Distance

Well-designed online writing (OW) programs and web-based instructional environments are designed with the wayfinding *human* learner in mind. Recall that wayfinding is the cognitive process in operation—primarily in novel situations—as humans make decisions on the path they will follow to get to some destination (Golledge, 1999). To help you better grasp this cognitive process, it might be helpful to break it down into discrete actions. As described by Lynch and Horton (2016), wayfinding—as a decision-making process—includes four cognitive *actions*:

- Orientation
- Route decisions
- Mental mapping
- Closure

When learners arrive in a web-based instructional environment, they must orient themselves. They need to make sense of the space in order to cognitively situate *themselves* within it. In other words, they must be able to determine, based on prior experience, where they are *now* by building a generalized mental picture of the environment. Establishing where they are now relies on learners being able to interpret directing cues strategically embedded in instructional information—cues purposefully designed to promote learners looking back to prior experience to make decisions on how they will proceed through the space.

Based on the success of orientation, learners next make decisions on the route, or path, they will follow through the instructional space. To make these decisions, learners rely on prior experience and directing cues in the learning environment. Learners must also, however, incorporate instructional information into their decisions. This might include information gleaned from course introductions; syllabi and schedules; text-based, video, or audio lectures; and assignments.

After making route decisions, learners select from available directing cues, integrate this information with instructional information, and mentally map the path they will follow through the instructional space. The adult brain relies heavily on prediction to make meaning and construct particular versions of reality. In this way, learners make the space their own, connecting what they "see" before them in novel space to their prior experience in order to predict what comes next.

Finally, closure is a cognitive action whereby the learner checks their cognitive location (alternatively, this final step might be thought of as a checkpoint). Closure also requires that the learner look back to ensure they are advancing forward in the right direction.

Promoting Wayfinding at the Program Level Through Advising and Mentoring

Helping learners find their way begins with advising—before they even place a proverbial foot into our instructional environments. We continue to help them find their way through mentoring experiences. Helping learners find their way during advising and mentoring requires speaking to learners in *a language* that advances cognitive mapmaking and, therefore, wayfinding. To put it another way, communicating with learners in a way that helps them construct and revise their own stories confined within the ever-shifting, ever-moving walls of bureaucratic systems. Fortunately, we all speak this language. It is the language of storytelling. As Thomas (2022) observes, "storytelling, mapmaking, and wayfinding are in our DNA" (p. 56). The human mind seems designed to communicate in this way. We tell stories to convey information and apply what we learn from stories to find our way through novel situations.

To tell a story requires application of the *personal* (P) element of *The PARS Approach* during advising. Here, we think it important to digress for a moment and ask what we mean by *personal* and to whom it applies—to the OWPA or to the learner. As Borgman and McArdle (2019) observe, "Teaching writing has always been personal for faculty and learning to write has always been personal for students" (p. 10). As such, the *P* element applies to both the work of the OWPA and to the student of writing.

The OWPA as Advisor/Mentor

Before the *P* element can be applied to the learner, it must first be applied to the OWPA. To cultivate relationships and build personal connections with learners begins with the OWPA having a knowable "identity and presence" (Borgman & McArdle, 2019, p. 7; Thomas et al., 2021, p. 197). This begins at the program level, outside the web-based instructional environment. Through a series of planned OWPA-learner touchpoints, OWPAs can build and establish themselves as knowable by being the first to share something personal about themselves. For example, OWPAs can share a story about how they struggled with rhetorical theory and what steps they took to overcome those challenges. They might share that the title of the course "Writing Software Documentation" sounds intimidating to them, too, but that it is an excellent course that students should take. The story of the OWPA's journey can provide a model of what to do (and what not to do) in the student's learning process.

The Learner

Advising and mentoring online graduate students who live both near and far involves more than helping them select classes, acquire internships and assistantships, or complete graduate theses. It also requires helping learners position their life contexts within the program. First-generation college students, in particular, may not have the kind of prior experience that transfers to the world of academia, and even at the graduate level will need help navigating this novel experience—one that requires a great deal of self-direction and intrinsic motivation. Prior to beginning their first course in the program, some learners may not have made a clear path through their educational journey that relates to their life contexts and to their career or personal goals. Therefore, in addition to striving to be knowable by their learners, OWPAs should have authentic conversations with learners and encourage them to tell their stories, to become knowable themselves. Having already shared something of themselves establishes that OWPAs are willing to take the same risks they are asking of learners when querying them for the kind of information required to personalize their experiences. As such, *P* is applied to learners to draw out from them this critical information.

 A good example of measures we can take to help learners continue to position their life contexts within our programs, and that also works to ensure we do not obstruct learners' paths through their educational journeys, is in how we advise individuals looking for a change in direction, but who are likely not clear about what that change might look like, or how what they have done in the past and what they are doing now transfers to novel academic experiences. In both the MA in Professional and Technical Writing program and the OWIGC at UALR, the OWPA not only deliberately works to provide professionalization experiences to learners through coursework, but they also strive to help learners articulate their goals so that learners can continue to mentally map the program and upcoming courses to their life contexts. Take, for example, the graduate student who enters the MA program to follow the editing and publishing concentration, only to find that they love their nonfiction classes and want to change to that concentration mid-degree. The OWPA needs to work with the student so that they understand the concentration as well as the course and other changes that might come about when changing concentrations—for example, the opportunities for internship, publishing, and even job opportunities.

Advising as an Iterative Process

Building personal connections with learners cannot be established with a series of random, disconnected interactions. Moreover, making and building personal connections with learners is not a singular event: The OWPAs' attempts to personally connect—like our OW course design—must be repeated. In other words, it is an iterative process. Each *instance* of connection-building should be seen as part of a process designed into the program and its OW courses to build personal connections, improve the individual learner's experience, and improve the program.

One final note: We should clarify what personal does not mean. As we highlight in our *PARS in Practice* chapter, "being personal in online classes isn't simply having a good personality" (Thomas et al., 2021, p. 187). While we each may have distinct characteristics, mannerisms, and other qualities, personality is not what we are concerned about when applying the PARS *P* element to what we do. In fact, a 15-year study strongly suggests that "despite some popular beliefs to the contrary, personality played little or no role in successful teaching" (Bain, 2004, p. 136). The study identified

an elaborate pattern of beliefs, attitudes, conceptions, and perceptions behind the way outstanding teachers treated the people who took their classes. The patterns alone couldn't transform otherwise ineffective teaching, but the most effective instructors as a group always came closer to following them than did even their slightly less effective colleagues . . . the best teachers we studied displayed not power but an investment in the students. Their practices stem from a concern with learning that is strongly felt and powerfully communicated. (Bain, 2004, pp. 136–137)

Research conducted by Rebecca Glazier and Heidi Skurat Harris (2021a, 2021b) reinforces these findings and demonstrates that student retention is significantly linked to efforts instructors make to establish rapport, or personal connections, initiated and enforced by instructors who demonstrate their care and concern for students by communicating with them clearly and often (see also Glazier, 2021).

Promoting Wayfinding in the OW Environment

Human-centered design (HCD), as a philosophy, is to design with the user's experience in mind. This suggests that to design OW instructional environments with our wayfinding learners in mind means we must have "a deep understanding of users, what they need, what they value, their abilities, and also their limitations" (Usability.gov, n.d.). To apply HCD means that OW course design is iterative (just like advising and mentoring), relying heavily on ongoing user feedback "throughout the design and development process" (Usability.gov, n.d.). In discussing the need for this feedback in UCD, Greer and Harris (2018) explain,

The overarching goal of user experience research is to discover what users need, and to design interfaces, products, and experiences that meet those needs. . . . Most user experience professionals today view themselves as user advocates and perceive their role in terms of working to persuade product development teams to build around users and their human needs and experiences rather than the needs of abstractly defined system specifications. (p. 14)

As a product, a web-based instructional environment must be designed to promote personal connection-building between instructor and learner and solicit the feedback needed to personalize the learning experience for individual learners. We need to continuously improve the OW space and ensure that it does not impede learners finding their way. This requires a front-end *strategy—The PARS Approach S* element with the learner's experience at its center (Borgman & McArdle, 2019, p 71): a "systematic program . . . to assess [our] efforts and to make appropriate changes" (Bain, 2004, p. 19).

Building an Environmental Image of the OW Space

Whether or not we are aware, when we design an OW space, our goal should be to design an environment that is perceptible to users. Recall that in HCD, what we design should revolve around human "needs, capabilities . . . and ways of behaving" (Norman, 1988/2013, p. 8). With that in mind, let us consider for a moment the multimodal web of instructional information our human learners are expected to engage with in a typical web-based course. During a single course offering, learners might be asked to map their way across several platforms (e.g., Blackboard, Google Drive, Google Sites). On each platform, our wayfinding learners interact with embedded course schedules and syllabi in either Google Docs, Word, or Adobe Acrobat PDF formats. They encounter course introductions and assignment instructions as on-screen texts, videos, or audio, and embedded readings or third-party web-based readings. Learners are expected to engage with embedded or linked PowerPoint, Prezi, or Google Slides presentations; mix with mashups; and interact with peers via CMS discussions or via third-party apps such as FlipGrid or other social learning platforms. As if this is not enough, learners may be purposely sent away from the CMS and out into the wilds of the World Wide Web—for example, to conduct research. From this multimodal web of instructional information, our wayfinding learners are expected to build a generalized mental picture of our *instructional space* and map it for meaning (Thomas, 2022).

As OWPAs, it may seem a cakewalk to bounce from platform to platform and from app to app. To novice learners, however, our instructional information may come across as a confused mixture of disparate information. If this is the case, learners will be unable to build a generalized mental picture. Wayfinding humans must be able to cognitively *see* our environment before they can situate themselves within it. Our human learners must first learn *the* map of what is our instructional space before learning can begin.

Operationalizing the building of personal connection and the design of personalized learner experiences may seem counterintuitive. In advising and course design, however, our strategies must scale to multiple learners across multiple courses. This scalability requires strategic planning. In the next section, we offer implementable, scalable techniques that work to keep web-based learners cognitively switched on.

Conclusion and Takeaways

Keeping Web-Based Learners on Track at the Program Design Level

Heidi regularly advises between 40 and 60 graduate students every term in addition to recruiting new students, supporting applicants, coordinating the graduate committee, and teaching her graduate classes (not to mention research, committee work, and writing time). This advising load is exhausting. But having a systematic approach helps organize some of the chaos and develops healthy habits of mind for OWPAs. On a set schedule, she downloads active student rosters and keeps spreadsheets of key information—such as student ID numbers—that will be used regularly. In addition to entering advising notes in Ellucian Degree Works—the academic advising and degree audit tool—Heidi sends out listserv or group emails for multiple students who have the same question.

Heidi applies the entire PARS approach to sum up what OWPAs can do at the program level to help learners find their way:

Personal

Make contact with your students at least twice a semester, one of which should be a dedicated advising time where you talk not only about classes but about their concerns, changes in their lives, modifications in their degree path, or their experience in the program.

Regularly update and scan graduate student lists to identify students who have been silent or to just send out a "Hey, I'm thinking about you. Let me know if I can help you with anything" email.

Listen more than you talk. Encourage students to share by holding space for their concerns.

Accessible

Offer multiple ways for the student to contact you so that they can benefit from connecting in the way they feel most comfortable. All grad students in our program, whether at a distance or on campus, can select their method of advising each semester: in-person, phone call, Zoom conference, or email.

Keep a listserv (or other email or social media group) of graduate students that you update regularly, and use it at least once or twice a week to make announcements, post jobs, recruit for internships, and provide reminders or information that they will need to navigate the semester.

Responsive

Write out notes from advising calls or videoconferences and distribute them through email or post them in an advising system such as Degree Works. The notes should reflect what was discussed, why the student needs to proceed along a particular path, *how* the student can proceed, and specific directives that instruct them on their next steps in the process.

Encourage students to check these notes when they face a problem or can't remember a step in a process.

Offer occasional recorded videoconferences (individual conferences or small group conferences) so that students can attend or access them later when they have the time and mental energy to process the information.

Strategic

Lay out multiple options in advising sessions, and keep a degree plan of what students should or could take for at least the next two terms in their degree. These plans help students feel grounded in their journey, but allow for flexibility in what might come next on their journey.

Check in during each advising session to discuss not only what classes to take for the following term, but also to prepare students for their final project work—which might include choosing committee members or preparing for final examinations.

Connect the program outcomes to student goals beyond the program. Communicate these outcomes to students with examples of alumni who transferred skills developed during the program to work or writing and publishing opportunities.

If your degree program or graduate certificate doesn't allow for the type of flexibility some of these suggestions require, or you find yourself spending more time trying to figure out how to make your current program work for the learner rather than working with the learner in the program, consider revising the program based on feedback you collect from previous students and alumni. Our department, for example, regularly seeks feedback from current students and alumni about their experiences in the program via surveys, focus groups, and one-on-one meetings. We have collected data from 2017–2021 on student needs in regard to class planning, final project options, preferred modalities, and the application of their classwork to their "real world" situations.

As a result of this information, we spent a year reviewing and restructuring our program to make it more intuitive for students; for example, we removed a portfolio option that served our program well a decade earlier but has since grown confusing. Our primary goal was to streamline the process for students, make possible paths through the degree program clearer, and allow for more flexibility in program options (for example, making it easy to switch between nonfiction, editing and publishing, or technical writing concentrations). Finally, we embedded common experiences during the program through two required core courses at the end of the program where learners reflect on their journey in a capstone project preparation class and then work with a committee to complete a thesis, a professional portfolio, or a digital project. These new, expanded options for student final projects allow a closer connection between student coursework and the final project, rather than a student choosing to complete the 36-hour "thesis track" or the 42-hour "portfolio track."

Keeping Learners on Track at the OW Course Design Level

How can we keep learners switched on and on track in an environment that can easily be experienced as a wall of words? One way is through the strategic use of visualization aids in our instructional information, that is, pictures and graphics. Mayer and Alexander (2017) define instructional visualization as "a visual-spatial representation intended to promote learning" (p. 483). It is well known that, when applied purposefully, "people learn better from words and pictures than from words alone" (p. 483). As a simple example, Figure 20.1 is a visual-spatial representation of Rhonda's journey through UALR's OWIGC.[3] It illustrates, on a smaller scale, how pictures and graphics can aid learners in mentally mapping a larger academic program that spans several semesters—and that for many learners will be a novel experience.

---

3. The OWIGC is an 18-hour program that also requires one elective in Rhetoric and Writing, not represented in this graphic. Students can complete the OWIGC 1) as a concentration in the MA in Professional and Technical Writing; 2) as a stand-alone, nine-month program (nine hours per term); or 3) one course at a time (finish in roughly two years). Source: https://ualr.edu/rhetoric/graduate/owi/. Figure 20.1 [See previous comment about figure numbers.] was designed using a free PowerPoint template, downloadable from https://templates.office.com. Themes can be quickly edited and then saved in a number of formats, including JPEG and PDF.

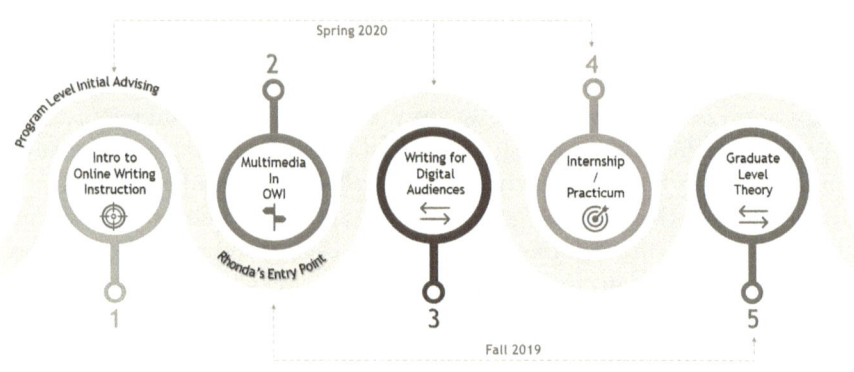

Figure 20.1. Graphical representation of Rhonda's journey through the OWIGC Program.

Rhonda suggests using visual-spatial representations similar to that shown in Figure 20.1 whenever and wherever appropriate in your course design. This specific example could also be used as an aid during advising and as a roadmap at the beginning of each course in the program, to help learners reorient themselves to where they are, for example, on their OWIGC journey. Such visual aids may seem elementary, but they can illuminate aspects of a learner's journey through a program that might otherwise be overlooked. Notice, for example, that Rhonda entered the OWIGC program in Fall 2019, during a semester the *Intro to Online Writing Instruction* course was not on offer. This reminds us that movement through a program such as the OWIGC is never linear and that learners benefit from strategically designed advising.

Our preference for visualizing information goes hand-in-hand with our need to map for meaning, to wayfind and to integrate stories into our particular versions of reality. As Thomas (2022) observes, web-based instruction environments "lend themselves well to storytelling and mapmaking" (p. 56). Just as we can use the language of storytelling at the program level to keep learners switched on, we can also use storytelling at the OW course design level. For learners to find their way, they need instructional narratives that, to them, are real and personal:

Make it *real*: Find opportunities to help learners connect the dots to past, present, and future learning; that is, share how the current course connects to the overall program and how it connects to other courses in the program. Help learners connect coursework to what they have done in the past, what they are doing now, and what they would like to do in the future. For learners hoping to change their professional direction, for example, these connections become the cognitive stepping stones that lead to a desired change.

Make it *personal*: Find opportunities to help learners *own* what they are doing in a course. Convey the real-life situations and experiences of others; for example, share how others have applied what is being taught in a course. Doing so can help students begin to establish for themselves how a course and the overall program might be applied to their particular life contexts.

Author Reflections

Heidi's favorite quote is from James Berlin (1982): "To teach writing is to argue for a version of reality, and the best way of knowing and communicating it" (p. 766). As OWPAs, our primary responsibility is to understand the reality of our students' lives, to appreciate where they are on their educational and life journey, and to place the stones in the river to help them get across to the next adventure.

Simply put, when we lose our way as OWPAs, we lose our learners. But the fact remains that all of us at one time have found ourselves lost on our professional and educational journeys, and there is much in life that we have no control over. In recent years, many have suffered actual loss—loved ones, jobs, homes, and financial and emotional security. Faculty thrust for the first time into emergency remote teaching in March 2020 (due to the COVID-19 pandemic) were suddenly lost in a place that once felt familiar—the World Wide Web—as they suddenly taught in a CMS for which some had little to no training or preparation. This change of venue caused many to feel like strangers in a foreign place and left them understandably shaken in their confidence as instructors. Students dropped out of college under increased pressure brought on by the pandemic and cultural and economic upheavals—foregoing education to just exist. For many learners, including adult learners and those entering graduate programs, just staying the course proved almost impossible.

We do, fortunately, have some control. We have control over how we plan and carry out advising and mentoring, over how we design web-based OW spaces, and over how we work to continuously improve learners' educational experiences. We can work within our means on the parts of reality we can shape, the paths we can set, and the support we can give to our learners as they map their way through an ever more difficult higher education landscape.

Rhonda's favorite quote is from Peter Turchi (2004): "To ask for a map is to say, 'Tell me a story'" (p. 11). To map environments that exist only in their minds, learners must be able to integrate their stories with the objectives of a structured learning experience; that is, they must be able to transfer prior experience to our instructional environment in order to find their way and anchor themselves to the novel situation.

The more we invest in learners through our endeavors to personally connect and understand their needs, the more human-centered our program and course designs become, and the more rewarding the experiences had by learners. Think of the efforts we make to connect as ongoing UX research. We do this through a series of planned OWPA touchpoints that occur both outside the instructional environment and inside the instructional environment.

To design with wayfinding *human* learners in mind, we must endeavor to not obstruct their ability to gain a generalized mental picture of our OW programs and web-based OW environments. When our learners become lost at either the program level or within an OW course, it impedes their learning and causes them undue stress. To ensure we are doing what we can to help learners find their way, we should design with the learner's need to wayfind in mind. When we construct a program and environmental image that is perceptible to learners and that stimulates the operations of wayfinding behavior, we increase the likelihood of learners remaining cognitively switched on.

References

Bain, K. (2004). *What the best college teachers do*. Harvard University Press.

Berlin, J. A. (1982). Contemporary composition: The major pedagogical theories. *College English, 44*(8), 765–777. https://doi.org/10.2307/377329.

Borgman, J. & McArdle, C. (2019). *Personal, accessible, responsive, strategic: Resources and strategies for online writing instructors*. The WAC Clearinghouse; University Press of Colorado. https://doi.org/10.37514/PRA-B.2019.0322.

Borgman, J. & McArdle, C. (Eds.). (2021). *PARS in practice: More resources and strategies for online writing instructors*. The WAC Clearinghouse; University Press of Colorado. https://doi.org/10.37514/PRA-B.2021.1145.

Chirikov, I., Soria, K. M., Horgos, B. & Jones-White, D. (2020). *Undergraduate and graduate students' mental health during the COVID-19 pandemic*. UC Berkeley: Center for Studies in Higher Education. https://escholarship.org/uc/item/80k5d5hw.

Glazier, R. (2021). *Connecting in the online classroom: Building rapport between teachers and students*. Johns Hopkins University.

Glazier, R. & Harris, H. S. (2021a). How teaching with rapport can improve online student success and retention: Data from empirical studies. *Quarterly Review of Distance Education, 21*(4), 1–17.

Glazier, R. & Skurat Harris, H. (2021a). Instructor presence and student satisfaction across modalities: Survey data on preferences in online and on-campus courses. *International Review of Research in Open and Distributed Learning, 22*(3), 77–98.

Golledge, R. G. (Ed.). (1999). *Wayfinding behavior: Cognitive mapping and other spatial processes*. Johns Hopkins University Press.

Greer, M. & Skurat Harris, H. (2018). User-centered design as a foundation for effective online writing instruction. *Computers and Composition, 49*, 14–24.

Harris, H. S. & Greer, M. (2016). Over, under, or through: Design strategies to supplement the LMS and enhance interaction in online writing courses. *Communication Design Quarterly, 4*(4), 46–54.

Lynch, K. (1960). *The image of the city*. The MIT Press.

Lynch, P. & Horton, S. (2016). Navigation and wayfinding. *Web style guide*. https://webstyleguide.com/wsg3/4-interface-design/2-navigation.html.

Mayer, R. E. (2017). Instruction based on visualizations. In R. E. Mayer & P. A. Alexander (Eds.), *Handbook of research on learning and instruction* (2nd ed., pp. 483–501). Routledge.

Mayer, R. E. & Alexander, P. A. (2017). Introduction to research on learning. In R. E. Mayer & P. A. Alexander (Eds.), *Handbook of research on learning and instruction,* 2nd ed. (pp. 3–7). New York: Routledge.

McLeod, S. H. (2007). *Writing program administration.* Parlor Press; The WAC Clearinghouse. https://wac.colostate.edu/books/referenceguides/mcleod-wpa/.

Morville, P. (2009). *Ambient findability: What we find changes who we become.* O'Reilly.

Mulcahy, E. R. (2022, March). Developing a philosophy of advising graduate students. *Academic Advising Today, 45*(1). https://nacada.ksu.edu/Resources/Academic-Advising-Today/View-Articles/Developing-a-Philosophy-of-Advising-Graduate-Students.aspx.

Norman, D. (2013). *The design of everyday things.* Basic Books. (Original work published 1988)

O'Keefe, J. & Nadel, L. (1978). *The hippocampus as a cognitive map.* Clarendon Press; Oxford University Press.

Rosenfeld, L., Morville, P. & Arango, J. (2015). *Information architecture: For the web and beyond* (4th ed.). O'Reilly.

Tate. (n.d.). *Psychogeography: Psychogeography describes the effect of a geographical location on the emotions and behaviour of individuals.* https://www.tate.org.uk/art/art-terms/p/psychogeography.

Thomas, R. (2022). *Mapping for meaning in a multimodal web: Advancing learning using web-based instruction that stimulates wayfinding behavior* (Publication No. 29061338) [Master's thesis, University of Arkansas at Little Rock]. ProQuest Dissertations & Theses.

Thomas, R., Kuralt, K., Skurat Harris, H. & Jensen, G. (2021). Create, support, and facilitate personal online writing courses in online writing programs. In J. Borgman & C. McArdle (Eds.), *PARS in practice: More resources and strategies for online writing instructors* (pp. 185–207). The WAC Clearinghouse; University Press of Colorado. https://doi.org/10.37514/PRA-B.2021.1145.2.11.

Turchi, P. (2004). *Maps of the imagination: The writer as cartographer.* Trinity University Press.

Usability.gov. (n.d.). *User experience basics.* https://www.usability.gov/what-and-why/user-experience.html.

Afterword. Before, During, and (Hopefully) After COVID

Steven Krause
Eastern Michigan University

When Jessie Borgman and Casey McArdle invited me to write the afterword for this collection of essays, I was flattered, I immediately agreed, and then I put it on the back burner as I continued my other work. But then as the deadline for this afterword approached, I realized I wasn't exactly sure what I had agreed to do. So, the first thing I did was to return to the previous books in the PARS series to see what my predecessors had done in their afterwords.

Bill Hart-Davidson wrote the afterword for *Personal, Accessible, Responsive, Strategic: Resources and Strategies for Online Writing Instructors*. This was, of course, the book Jessie and Casey co-wrote that began the series. I read the book when it was first published in 2019, and even though I had been teaching at least some of my courses online for years and had spent a great deal of time researching and writing about online courses generally and Massive Open Online Courses in particular, the book was useful in my own teaching. The PARS approach shed a different light on the courses I had been teaching online, and it both inspired new ideas and provided a vocabulary to some of what I had already been doing in my online courses. I recommended the book to many.

Like the book as a whole, Bill's afterword was friendly, casual, and encouraging. Also like the book as a whole, the primary audience Bill seems to have had in mind were writing teachers who perhaps had considered teaching online before (or who perhaps found themselves in a situation where they had no choice but to teach online) but who needed both a pedagogical apparatus and also a bit of a pep talk. "In online learning environments we simply must practice an approach like PARS in order to make up (for) our own inability to be improvisational, to shift things on the fly, as instructors may be accustomed to doing in face-to-face classrooms" (Borgman & McArdle, 2019, p. 95), and Bill's afterword is an invitation to taking that approach. Online spaces can be just as transformative for learners and teachers as face-to-face ones, but it does take "a deliberate effort on the part of those who teach to help realize this potential. That is what this book," Bill tells us, "will help you do" (Borgman & McArdle, 2019, p. 97).

PARS in Practice: More Resources and Strategies for Online Writing Instructors, the follow-up collection of essays from contributors inspired by the PARS approach to online teaching, was published just two years later and its approach is quite different. If *Personal, Accessible, Responsive, Strategic* was an effort to persuade those new to teaching online to give the approach a try, the over two dozen contributors to *PARS in Practice* demonstrated how the approach worked for them, and they wrote for an audience already engaged in teaching writing online at the college level. The depth and breadth of the readings in that collection reflected the work that many of us had been doing for years. Before the COVID-19 pandemic, most estimates suggested well over a third of college students across all types of institutions took at least one online course as a part of their studies, and of course many students were enrolled in programs that are offered entirely online. So, if Jessie and Casey's first co-authored book was an effort to welcome would-be instructors to the "PARS party," their first edited collection introduced readers to the many practitioners who have been at that party for quite some time.

Once again, the afterword—this time by Kirk St.Amant—suited the context and voice of the book perfectly. In his afterword titled "Re-Mapping the Global Context for Online Education," St.Amant wrote that billions of people worldwide now have online access and that "over the last two decades, hardware and software have evolved to the point that online interactions are a regular part of the daily lives of many individuals" (p. 356), both in traditional schooling and in lifelong learning opportunities.

PARS in Practice was first published electronically in early January 2021. The pace of academic publishing being what it is, I assume most of the chapters and St.Amant's afterword were all but complete and being prepared for press somewhere around late spring/early summer 2020, just when the reality of the COVID-19 pandemic and its lockdowns were beginning in the United States. Certainly, many of the chapters in *PARS in Practice* and St.Amant's afterword discuss the pandemic's impact on online teaching, but I must say I found this passage somewhat surprising when I reread it as I was writing this essay in early fall 2022:

> In online educational settings, written communiques like emails and text messages are central to providing regular updates and notifications. Similarly, the online venues where individuals

> share ideas and debate concepts—discussion boards, chat rooms, and online forums—also rely heavily on written messages for exchanges. Even in situations where the mechanism for interactions seems visual in nature (e.g., a graphic user interface), the use of such media often requires corresponding written texts explaining how to operate a technology in order to access educational content and participate in related exchanges. Essentially, interactions usually done orally in face-to-face classrooms must be re-cast in textual form to create parallel exchanges in online spaces. (p. 357)

I agreed then and I agree now with St.Amant's point: moving a class from the face-to-face classroom to online delivery requires significant adjustments to the differences, affordances, and limitations of the format, and most of that work means "re-casting" both content and interaction from synchronous activities and live oral communication to asynchronous activities and textual and other pre-recorded communication. I think it's fair to say that St.Amant's observation was not only the conventional wisdom and practice of all (or nearly all) of the dozens of scholars contributing to *PARS in Practice*; it was the conventional wisdom and practice in distance education at most institutions that offered courses and degree programs online before the COVID pandemic.

And then along came Zoom! For much to my surprise (and I suspect much to the surprise of many of the contributors to *PARS in Practice* and also this collection, *PARS in Charge*), a majority of faculty new to online teaching during the COVID pandemic decided to forgo much of the previously assumed best practices. Instead, a majority of faculty new to online teaching decided on their own (and most faculty did indeed have choices about how they wanted to teach during the pandemic) to teach their courses synchronously and with the use of video-conferencing software. For those of us who had been teaching online asynchronously for years and largely with courses "re-cast in textual form," this approach to online teaching didn't make a lot of sense. As Bill Hart-Davidson put it to me when we were chatting early in the COVID pandemic (possibly while on a golf course, actually), teaching online during a Zoom session is sort of like teaching a face-to-face class on a moving bus: You could do that, but why?

Personally, I found the choice of so many faculty to teach with Zoom baffling, which is why I began my current research project about college faculty experiences with teaching online during COVID. This work began as a survey I distributed via social media between December 2020 and June 2021; I collected responses from 104 college-level instructors (mostly in writing studies). I then invited respondents to the survey to participate in a more detailed follow-up interview, and between January 2022 and June 2022, I conducted about 35 interviews exploring in more detail my interviewees' choices and experiences teaching online during the pandemic. I presented summaries of this research at the March

2022 Conference for College Composition and Communication meeting in an "on demand" session titled "When 'You' Cannot be 'Here:' What Shifting Teaching Online Teaches Us about Access, Diversity, Inclusion, and Opportunity," and at the May 2022 Computers and Writing Conference at an "on demand" session titled "Online Teaching and 'The New Normal:' A survey of Faculty in the Midst of an Unprecedented 'Natural Experiment.'" I also published a much more detailed webtext for a December 2022 special issue of *Computers and Composition Online* focused on online teaching, titled "The Role of Previous Online Teaching Experience During the Covid Pandemic: An Exploratory Study of Faculty Perceptions and Approaches." My current work of analyzing the 270,000–300,000 words of transcribed conversations with faculty about their experiences continues, and I suspect I will be conducting follow-up interviews in 2023 and 2024. But for now, I will mention three observations as they relate to both the PARS approach generally and to this collection, *PARS in Charge,* in particular.

First, I think the main values of the PARS approach are in the balance of a pragmatic focus on literally how to "do" online teaching and a pedagogical philosophy about how teaching online must be engaging and tailored to the format, and not merely face-to-face teaching "poured" into an online course shell via a video-conferencing software. Rather, online teaching must be adaptive, and it must be, well, personal, accessible, responsive, and strategic, requiring teachers to adjust the delivery of the course to their students and the situation. In *PARS in Charge*, we see that same mix of pragmatism and ideals extended to the role of the writing program administrator (WPA), and how WPAs adjusted to become online writing program administrators (OWPAs)—especially for those who were charged with coordinating a successful shift from "emergency remote teaching" to more routine online writing instruction (OWI).

The research and interviews I've done to date suggest that for many of the instructors who taught online for the first time during COVID and who taught synchronously with Zoom, revising their courses for the asynchronous online format either seemed like too much work or it never even occurred to them as something that would need to be done. If these instructors had been exposed to the practices and pedagogies exemplified by PARS prior to COVID, I am certain many would have taken a different approach. That seems especially clear to me in several different essays in *PARS in Charge* that tell stories about how these authors in their roles as OWPAs made systematic and programmatic efforts to prepare faculty to teach online, both before and during the pandemic.

Second, the PARS approach is flexible enough to accommodate the new technologies and approaches to OWI that have come from instructors and program administrators who did not have experience teaching online prior to COVID. The clearest example of this for me is actually the use of synchronous video-conferencing software, because while Zoom didn't play much of a role in online writing courses prior to COVID, it's clearly part of the standard practice now. That's reflected in numerous essays in *PARS in Charge* as well. Video-conferencing software is a key tool OWPAs are using for facilitating hybrid classes, for hosting organizational meetings and training sessions with program instructors, and for continuing informal meetings and to facilitate "safe space" discussions. Many of those activities have once again resumed happening face to face, but even amongst those of us who grew "fatigued" with video conferencing during COVID, Zoom still has its advantages after the pandemic, especially for facilitating those Friday afternoon program meetings.

Third, the many stories I heard from the faculty I interviewed about their experiences teaching during COVID and the many stories here in *PARS in Charge* illustrate how different writing programs (not to mention different institutions) function in ways that are simultaneously similar and strikingly different. At the risk of overworking the golf metaphor of PARS, it reminds me of how courses are also always very much the same and very much different. Golf courses all have 18 holes (setting aside the so-called executive nine-hole courses); they all have a similar mix of par 3/par 4/par 5 holes; those holes all have recognizably similar tees, greens, fairways, sand traps, and so forth; and the rules for playing different courses are all the same. The other trappings of a golf course tend to be similar as well: golf carts; groundskeepers; the "pro shop" where players pay for their rounds and perhaps also buy some tees, balls, or even clubs; and the so-called "19th hole" bar area with beverages, snacks (the ubiquitous golf course hot dog), and sometimes more elaborate offerings.

And yet every golf course is unique, and the level of difficulty of courses varies tremendously. Some courses are for "members only" (not where I play!), some are private but open to the public, and some are a part of municipal or county park systems. Some courses are horrifically expensive and fancy, though many (certainly the courses I play regularly) are not. And most courses have at least one odd feature that requires a certain amount of "previous experience" to navigate. For example, the course I play most often (which is not difficult, privately owned but open to the public, inexpensive, and with a wide variety of beverages but a narrow selection of hot dogs and snacks) includes a hole where players must hit their tee shots off of a wooden-planked and AstroTurf-covered platform, a surface that is just dissimilar enough from a regular grass tee to frustrate golfers new to the course.

PARS in Charge is a fine example of these simultaneous similarities and differences between writing programs, OWPAs, and the premises of writing instruction and program administration. As I read these essays, I see a lot of similarities, at least in broad terms. The writers in all of these essays speak about a "personal" approach for welcoming individual perspectives to teaching within program guidelines. They all discuss how to be "accessible" to both instructors and students through support materials like pre-designed course shells and an awareness of acknowledging different approaches to writing instruction that can meet similar goals, and the needs to maximize "responsiveness" by communicating with instructors and adapting to their needs. Perhaps the most common denominator for all OWPAs at all types of institutions is the need to be "strategic," especially in terms of mentoring and supporting faculty and also by incorporating an awareness of other guiding principles and assessment protocols present at an institution, such as "Quality Matters" or other large strategic initiatives on campus.

And yet, each of the chapters and the stories from OWPAs in *PARS in Charge* is different. Some of these contributors are describing OWI initiatives and programs established long before the COVID pandemic, and others describe their experiences leading programs through emergency remote teaching and beyond. The definitions of "online" range from all courses in a program offered entirely online (and typically asynchronously), to a mix of modes, including hybrid courses. By "writing," many of the contributors here mean the first-year writing experience, though others mean a different selection of writing courses, including general education writing courses beyond the typical first-year composition class, technical writing programs, courses in the major or in the graduate program, and so forth. Many of these stories recount the experience of facilitating training and support for the instructors teaching in their programs, and all the small and large differences are there—how the process actually worked, who the instructors were and what sort of support and training they need, what the institutional restraints and requirements were, and so forth. These similarities and differences are what kept me going as a reader, finding parts of the stories I identify with and also noting the ways in which, for better or worse, my experiences are different.

Let me close by perhaps priming the pump for another PARS volume in the post-COVID era. I believe we are in the midst of a clear and rapid paradigm shift regarding distance education and online instruction across the board—certainly in higher education, but also in online instruction at the elementary and secondary levels, and online learning opportunities beyond higher education. COVID forced nearly everyone in higher education to move their courses online, and the majority of students and instructors did this against their will. The reality of the global pandemic—particularly during the 2020–21 school year—meant that if students and faculty wanted to continue to be engaged in higher education, it was going to have a significant remote-learning component. Now, many of the faculty I interviewed as part of my survey research (not to mention many of my colleagues at my university and around the country) who were new to online teaching found the experience inspiring and liberating, and they are anxious to teach online in the future and in more "normal times." Obviously, some faculty felt completely the opposite, though I will say most of my interviewees were at a minimum open to the idea of teaching online again. In part, I assume that is part of a self-selection bias since I doubt someone who was adamantly against online teaching in the future would have bothered to have taken my survey in the first place, let alone agreed to participate in an interview. And while this isn't a part of my research, my sense from my own teaching is that students are in a similar position.

At my university, a public regional institution where around 25 percent of the courses were online before the pandemic, the president and provost want to return us to a "pre-COVID" balance of online and face-to-face offerings. This seems to be a national trend, and one that is even more acute at traditionally residential colleges and flagship universities. Administrators have claimed students and their parents have complained and demanded a return to face-to-face instruction. That is perhaps true, though it also seems unlikely that administrators would receive a lot of emails or notes from students or their parents expressing happiness about online courses. My own sense from talking with my online students before, during, and now (hopefully) after COVID is that the demand for face-to-face versus online courses is mixed. Of course, students who were forced to take online courses against their will and who had bad experiences want to return to the face-to-face classroom, but I also encountered many students who took online courses for the first time during COVID and were pleasantly surprised with the results.

My own admittedly cynical and jaded view is that university administrators have to find ways of getting students to physically come back to campuses in order to spend money on things like dorms, meal plans, student center purchases, campus parking, sporting events, expensive-to-build-and-operate recreation facilities, and so forth. The reality is I don't think anyone yet knows what the balance of online versus face-to-face offerings should be after COVID, and it's likely to take most universities a few years to figure that out. But I think it is quite obvious that online teaching and the need to support and facilitate OWI is going to continue, which means that *PARS in Charge* and the other books in the PARS series are going to have a place on the shelf of any ongoing or would-be OWPA.

References

Borgman, J. & McArdle, C. (2019). *Personal, accessible, responsive, strategic: Resources and strategies for online writing instructors.* The WAC Clearinghouse; University Press of Colorado. https://doi.org/10.37514/PRA-B.2019.0322.

Borgman, J. & McArdle, C. (Eds.). (2021). *PARS in practice: More resources and strategies for online writing instructors.* The WAC Clearinghouse; University Press of Colorado. https://doi.org/10.37514/PRA-B.2021.1145.

Contributors

About the Editors

Jessie Borgman, Ph.D. and Casey McArdle, Ph.D. have been online writing instructors and course designers for over a decade. They both began teaching online with no experience at for-profit schools. They have since worked to grow their careers together and individually in the fields of rhetoric and writing studies, technical communication, and user experience (UX). Together, Borgman and McArdle co-created The Online Writing Instruction Community resources website in 2015. In 2019, they co-authored *Personal, Accessible, Responsive, Strategic: Resources and Strategies for Online Writing Instructors*, which was the winner of the 2020 *Computers and Composition* Distinguished Book Award. In 2021 they co-edited *PARS in Practice: More Resources and Strategies for Online Writing Instructors*. They have presented for multiple institutions across the country and been featured speakers by organizations, such as the Conference on College Composition and Communication (CCCCs), Bedford/St. Martin's, and the Council of Writing Program Administrators. They were featured in an interview for the National Council of Teachers of English *Council Chronicle* in 2020. They served as mentors for the CCCCs Emergent Researcher award winner for the 2021 year.

Jessie Borgman, Ph.D. is an online writing instructor in the Writers' Studio at Arizona State University and has taught both face-to-face and online since 2009. She has published several articles and book chapters and has presented at conferences such as the Conference on College Composition and Communications, Computers and Writing, and Two-Year College English Association. She has served on the CCCC OWI Standing Group in multiple capacities and currently serves as the chair. As the CCCC OWI Standing Group chair, she co-led a national survey on online writing instruction and collaborated with the research group to write *The 2021 State of the Art of OWI Report*. Her research interests include online writing instruction, instructional design, content strategy, user experience, two-year colleges, and writing program administration.

Casey McArdle is the associate chair for undergraduate studies in the Department of Writing, Rhetoric, and American Cultures at Michigan State University, where he directs the Experience Architecture and Professional and Public Writing programs. He is an advocate for usability, accessibility, and sustainability in and out of the classroom and has been involved with OWI for many years via publications, presentations, and research teams that focus on distance education and learning experience design.

About the Authors

Abram Anders is Director of Communication Innovation and an Associate Professor of English at Iowa State University. His research interests include academic innovation, creative collaboration, innovation and entrepreneurship, and leadership communication.

Jeanine Elise Aune is Director of the ISUComm Advanced Communication (AdvComm) program and a Professor at Iowa State University (ISU). She received her Ph.D. from the University of Wisconsin-Madison. Two multi-section courses she directs recently earned Quality Matters certification, the first multi-section courses to receive such certification at ISU. She is the co-author of *Business Communication* 13e with Jo Mackiewicz and *Technical Writing for Engineers & Scientists* 4e with Leslie Potter. She has received several awards for teaching and for her work with ISU's learning communities.

Joseph Bartolotta is Associate Professor of Writing Studies and Rhetoric at Hofstra University. He holds a Ph.D. in Rhetoric & Scientific and Technical Communication from the University of Minnesota. Prior to joining Hofstra, Dr. Bartolotta was a Lecturer and Visiting Assistant Professor at the University of New Mexico, where he co-founded the Laboratory for Usability, Communication, and Information Design (LUCID) and directed the professional writing internship program. His work appears in journals like *Technical Communication Quarterly* and *Communication Design Quarterly*. Professor Bartolotta is a member of the Society for American Baseball Research, plays chess in his spare time, has defeated Ganon across multiple consoles, and plays as Luigi in MarioKart.

Tiffany Bourelle is Associate Professor at the University of New Mexico, where she runs an online writing program called eComposition (eComp). She also teaches a practicum for graduate students that emphasizes best practices for teaching composition in the digital era, which blends multimodal composition with online pedagogies. Her work has been published in *Computers and Composition*, *Kairos*, *Technical Communication Quarterly*, and *Communication Design Quarterly*. She is the co-author of *Teaching Writing in the Twenty-First*

Century and *Administering Writing Programs in the Twenty-First Century* (with Beth Hewett and Scott Warnock).

Miranda L. Egger is Senior Instructor and Assistant Director of Composition at the University of Colorado Denver. She's taught for more than 20 years, but only recently (after raising two sons) finished her Ph.D. in Rhetoric, Writing, and Discourse Studies at Old Dominion University. Her dissertation examined "Reading with Social, Digital Annotation: Encouraging Engaged Critical Reading in a Challenging Age," a project that focused on student-centered research around digital discursive tools, specifically employed in asynchronous first-year composition (FYC) courses. Her research interests also include literacy studies (particularly theories of reading and writing connections); situating rhetorical reading in theories of rhetorical circulation; networked, digital technologies of communication; the role of discourse in democratic deliberation; writing program administration (WPA) scholarship; and pedagogies that address online education, particularly in response to the needs of at-risk undergraduate students.

Lourdes Fernandez is a former assistant professor and assistant director for composition at George Mason University. Her research interests include hybrid course design and pedagogy, program administration, workplace communication, and rhetorics of sexual assault. Her work has been published in *Journal of Response to Writing, Programmatic Perspectives, Technical Communication Quarterly, Rhetoric Review, Academic Labor: Research and Artistry*, and *Reflections: A Journal of Community-Engaged Writing and Rhetoric*. She currently works as an employment and education researcher in private industry.

Kerry Folan is Assistant Professor at George Mason University, where she teaches composition, literature, and creative writing. Her research interests include hybrid course design, critical language awareness, and the teaching of creative nonfiction as literature, for which she received a GMU curriculum development grant in 2021. She has been nominated by students for GMU's General Teaching Excellence and Online Teaching Excellence Awards.

Katharine Fulton is the Online Learning Coordinator and Associate Teaching Professor in the Department of English at Iowa State University. She received her MA in English Literature from Iowa State University in 2009 and a Micro-Masters in Instructional Design and Technology from University of Maryland University College in 2018. Katie is a Quality Matters-certified peer reviewer and has supported the development and Quality Matters certification of three courses at ISU.

Joanne Baird Giordano is Associate Professor of English, Linguistics, and Writing Studies at Salt Lake Community College. She previously coordinated the developmental reading, writing, and ESL program for the University of Wisconsin System's two-year colleges. Her online literacy education work focuses on designing courses and mentoring instructors in open-access writing programs. She is the course developer and co-facilitator for an online equitable and inclusive teaching practices faculty development program for community college educators. Her research and writing on two-year college writers and teaching has appeared in *College English, CCC, Teaching English in the Two-Year College, WPA Journal, Pedagogy,* the *Journal of Writing Assessment, Open Words,* the *Community College Journal of Research and Practice,* and edited collections. She serves as Associate Chair (and incoming Chair) of the Two-Year College English Association.

Ariel M. Goldenthal is Assistant Professor of Composition at George Mason University. Her research interests include community-engaged courses and hybrid first-year composition, which she has taught since the university pilot of the course in Fall 2017. Her recent presentations at the Conference on College Composition and Communication and EDUCAUSE share findings on hybrid course design and implementation. Her work has been published in *The Journal of Response to Writing* and *WPA: Writing Program Administration.*

Rachael Groner is Professor of Instruction in English and the Director of the First Year Writing Program at Temple University. She teaches graduate and undergraduate courses in composition, contemporary literature and trauma studies. She has been in writing program administration for 12 years and is committed to advocating for equitable policies and increased opportunities for non-tenure track faculty.

Heidi Skurat Harris is Associate Professor and the Graduate Coordinator for the Department of Writing and Rhetoric at the University of Arkansas at Little Rock. She has worked with online students and programs since 2006, and has published articles on online professional development, online writing program administration, and online student advising and support. She teaches courses in creative nonfiction, technical writing, and online writing instruction.

John Holland is Lecturer in the Composition Program at San Francisco State University. He brings a multidisciplinary perspective to the teaching of undergraduate writing, having earned a Master of Arts in Psychology from Humboldt State University, a Master of Science in Curriculum & Instruction from the University of Oregon, and a Master of Arts in English (with a specialty in teaching multilingual students) from San Francisco State University. This multidimensional background forms the foundation of his evidence-based pedagogical practices.

Andrew Hollinger is Coordinator of First-Year Writing at the University of Texas Rio Grande Valley, which earned the 2020–2021 CCCC Writing Program Certificate of Excellence. His work focuses on first-year writing and curriculum, WPA work and definitions, as well as materiality, publics and circulation, and genre. In addition to his teaching, scholarship, and published work, he is interested in maker rhetorics and is a practicing bookbinder, linocut artist, and illusionist.

Tania Islam was the Graduate Composition Assistant of the First-Year Writing Program at Temple University for the 2020–21 academic year, from where she received her Ph.D. in English in 2022. Her research and teaching interests, though varied, have influenced her approach towards teaching rhetoric and composition and first-year writing extensively. She is currently Assistant Professor in the School of Liberal Arts and Design Studies at Vidyashilp University, India.

Steven D. Krause is the author of *More Than A Moment: Contextualizing the Past, Present, and Future of MOOCs*, the co-editor of *Invasion of the MOOCs: The Promises and Perils of Massive Open Online Courses*, and the author of *The Process of Research Writing*, a research writing textbook. He is a professor at Eastern Michigan University in Ypsilanti and he teaches both online and face to face courses, mostly about the connections between writing and technology.

Anne C. Kretsinger-Harries is the Communication Studies Online Program Director at the University of Kansas. Previously, she was the Director of Public Speaking at Iowa State University from 2017–2022. She received her Ph.D. in Communication Arts & Sciences from Pennsylvania State University. Her research examines rhetoric and pedagogy and has appeared in venues such as *Rhetoric & Public Affairs* and *Communication Teacher*.

Bethany Mannon is Assistant Professor of English at Appalachian State University, where she directs the Rhetoric and Composition Program. Her research focuses on religious and feminist rhetoric, writing program administration, and personal narrative. Bethany's work has appeared in journals including *Rhetoric Society Quarterly*, *Enculturation*, and *Writing Center Journal*. She completed her Ph.D. at Penn State University in 2015.

Leslie Robertson Mateer is Assistant Teaching Professor in the Department of English at Penn State University, where she has taught both face-to-face and online courses at University Park for over 20 years, specializing in business and technical communication. She also serves as the Assistant Director of the Digital English Studio, where she works as an instructional designer, editor, and manager of the Penn State English Department online course portfolio.

Jessica Matthews is Associate Director of Composition for George Mason University. From 2019 to 2021, she served as the faculty fellow for the George Mason Stearns Center for Teaching and Learning, where she provides professional development for online course design and pedagogy. Her recent presentations at EDUCAUSE, the annual meeting of the American Educational Research Association, and the Conference on College Composition and Communication focus on how students and faculty evaluate the quality of learning in online writing courses.

Tiffany N. Mitchell is Senior Lecturer and the Classroom Technologies and Website Coordinator for the English Department at the University of Tennessee at Chattanooga (UTC). She teaches first-year writing and professional writing courses and co-teaches courses on adolescent literature and intersectional oppressions. She's taught online and hybrid courses since 2012, and has also taught courses for both the ESL Program and Honors College at UTC. As a long-time non-tenure-track (NTT) lecturer and one of the earliest adopters of online/hybrid writing at UTC, she's passionate about NTT issues and mentoring her colleagues who may be new to UTC and/or new to online and hybrid instruction. She co-authored a professional writing textbook titled *The Write Path: Communicating Your Way to Professional Success*, and her scholarly work has been published in the *Journal of Library & Information Services in Distance Learning*.

Catrina Mitchum is Adjunct Associate Professor at the University of Maryland Global Campus and a former online writing program administrator at the University of Arizona. She has been teaching online since 2009, and online only since 2010. Her research interests are in retention and online course design and delivery of online writing classes. She has scholarly work published in *Currents in Teaching and Learning, Composition Forum*, and *The Journal of Teaching and Learning with Technology*, among other journals and edited collections. She was awarded, with other scholars, the CCCC Research Initiative Grant in 2018 and a Digital Learning Tech Seed Grant in 2021. She has been awarded the Professional and Technical Writing Teaching Award and the Collaborative Teaching Award in the Writing Program. She teaches first-year writing courses as well as upper-level undergraduate courses in professional and technical writing, entirely online.

Cassandra Phillips is Professor of English at the University of Wisconsin Milwaukee at Waukesha, where she also serves as the First-Year Writing and Developmental English Coordinator. Her research focuses on writing program development and pedagogies for access institutions and has appeared in *TETYC, WPA, Pedagogy, Peitho*, and edited collections. She is the co-author of *Materiality and Writing Studies: Aligning Labor, Scholarship and Teaching*, which was published in 2022 in the NCTE Studies in Writing and Rhetoric series.

Lynn Reid is Assistant Professor of Rhetoric and Composition and Director of Basic Writing at Fairleigh Dickinson University. She holds a Ph.D. in Composition and TESOL from Indiana University of Pennsylvania, where she was awarded the Patrick Hartwell Memorial Award for Promising Research in Composition. Her work has appeared in *WPA Journal, Journal of Basic Writing, TESOL Encyclopedia*, and several edited collections. Dr. Reid has served as the co-chair of the Council on Basic Writing, a CCCC standing group, and is Associate Editor for the *Basic Writing* e-Journal.

Dylan Retzinger is a college-track professor at New Mexico State University and a special projects assistant to the Writing Program as online pedagogy consultant and online course designer. His research explores identity politics in online writing instruction.

Rochelle (Shelley) Rodrigo is Senior Director of the Writing Program; Associate Professor in the Rhetoric, Composition, and the Teaching of English (RCTE); and Associate Writing Specialist (Continuing Status) in the Department of English at the University of Arizona. Prior to her position as the Sr. Director at UArizona, she served as the Associate Director of Online Writing, hired to design and develop UArizona's online writing program. She researches how "newer" technologies better facilitate communicative interactions, specifically teaching and learning. She has been teaching and researching online writing instruction for more than 20 years.

Stuart A. Selber is Professor of English and Director of Digital Education in the English department at Penn State, where he directs the Penn State Digital English Studio. His latest book is *Institutional Literacies: Engaging Academic IT*

Contexts for Writing and Communication (University of Chicago Press), which won the 2022 Distinguished Book Award from *Computers and Composition*.

Kellie Sharp-Hoskins is Associate Professor and Writing Program Administrator at New Mexico State University, where she also teaches courses in critical rhetorics and writing studies. Her research centers the complex relations among language and bodies that materialize in pedagogical and public spaces; it has appeared in *Rhetoric Review, Enculturation, Peitho*, and a number of edited collections, including one she co-edited: *Kenneth Burke + The Posthuman*.

Jennifer Stewart is Assistant Professor of English and Director of Composition at University of Tennessee at Chattanooga. She teaches graduate and undergraduate courses in teaching college writing, workplace literacies and project management, and the rhetoric of popular culture heroines. She has taught online and hybrid FYC and rhetoric and professional writing courses since 2009. Much of her scholarship comes from the work in her program or in her classroom; recent research projects are situated in incorporating diversity-themed common readers and multimodal composition into writing programs and using institutional ethnographic methods to investigate standard writing program practices. She is also greatly invested in non-tenure-track faculty and graduate student advocacy, professional development, and mentoring.

Jennifer Seibel Trainor is the author of several articles on the teaching of writing. Her articles have appeared in *CCC, Research in the Teaching of English*, and *College English*. She is the co-director of San Francisco State's First-Year Writing Program, where she works with teachers to develop critical and social justice approaches to literacy development. She teaches undergraduate writing and graduate courses on literacy, critical pedagogy, and composition pedagogy.

Rhonda Thomas is a graduate of the BA and MA programs in Professional and Technical Writing and the Graduate Certificate in Online Writing Instruction from the University of Arkansas at Little Rock. She is currently completing a Master of Science in Education—Digital Age Learning and Educational Technology at Johns Hopkins University. Her research interests include adult education, digital-age learning, online writing instruction, and human wayfinding behavior as it relates to how learners find their way in web-based learning environments. www.rhonthom.com

Daniel Tripp is Associate Director of Digital Education and the Digital English Studio for the Department of English at The Pennsylvania State University. He has taught online courses for over 20 years at a variety of institutions. At Penn State, he teaches online writing classes, trains other instructors to teach online, and designs and manages the English department's online courses, including those offered through the Penn State World Campus.

Mariya Tseptsura is Director of the Online Writing Program at the University of Arizona's English department, where, among other responsibilities, she manages and studies the program's pre-designed courses (PDCs). She has been teaching online since 2015, and her research interests encompass OWI, writing program administration, and multilingual and second language writing. Her work has appeared in *College Composition and Communication* and *Research in Online Literacy Education*.

Amy Walton is Assistant Director of ISUComm Foundation Courses and an Associate Teaching Professor at Iowa State University. She received her MA in Teaching English to Speakers of Other Languages from Iowa State. Her interests include communication pedagogy, computer-assisted language learning, and teacher training. Before joining the faculty at Iowa State, Amy taught high school English, French, and computer science.

Julie Watts is Professor of English and Chair of the English, Philosophy, and Communication Studies Department at the University of Wisconsin-Stout. She was Founding Director of the online MS Technical and Professional Communication program and directed it for 12 years. She teaches courses in composition, document design, and theory and research in technical and professional communication. Her research interests focus on program assessment as well as the communicative dynamics and culture of the online learning community and what instructors can do to facilitate student learning.

Casey White is Assistant Director of the ISUComm Advanced Communication program and an Assistant Teaching Professor at Iowa State University. He received his Ph.D. in Rhetoric and Professional Communication from Iowa State University in 2014 and then stayed to teach and help administer the AdvComm program. Casey is involved in the design and development of three multi-section online writing courses covering business and technical communication.

Courtney Adams Wooten is Associate Chair, Composition at George Mason University. She is a co-editor of *WPAs in Transition* and *The Things We Carry: Strategies for Recognizing and Negotiating Emotional Labor in Writing Program Administration*, and her work has been published in *College English*, *Composition Studies*, *WPA*, *Academic Labor: Research and Artistry*, and *Harlot* as well as in several edited collections. She has been nominated for GMU's Online Teaching Excellence Award.

Anthony Yarbrough is an MFA student in Fiction at the University of New Mexico, where he teaches composition and creative writing. He studies pedagogies for the digital classroom, multiliteracies, instructional design, and multimodal writing strategies. His creative work explores memory, sexuality, violence, introspection, and creating equity in a predatory world. Recently, he was recognized with the University of New Mexico's Hillerman/McGarrity Scholarship for creative work that shows exceptional promise.

Marisa Yerace is a Ph.D. student in Rhetoric and Composition at Purdue University, with previous work appearing in *Computers and Composition Online* and *Rhetoric Review*. Her dissertation study focuses on how writing program administrators supported their faculty and students in the early COVID-19 pandemic, and updates can be found at https://myerace.com/diss.

www.ingramcontent.com/pod-product-compliance
Lightning Source LLC
Chambersburg PA
CBHW060549080526
44585CB00013B/503